AWS®
Certified Solutions Architect Official
Study Guide - Associate Exam

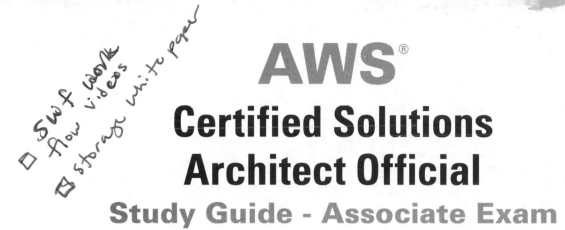

AWS®
Certified Solutions
Architect Official
Study Guide - Associate Exam

Joe Baron, Hisham Baz, Tim Bixler, Biff Gaut,

Kevin E. Kelly, Sean Senior, John Stamper

SYBEX®
A Wiley Brand

Senior Acquisitions Editor: Kenyon Brown
Project Editor: Gary Schwartz
Production Editor: Dassi Zeidel
Copy Editor: Kezia Endsley
Editorial Manager: Mary Beth Wakefield
Production Manager: Kathleen Wisor
Executive Editor: Jim Minatel
Book Designers: Judy Fung and Bill Gibson
Proofreader: Nancy Carrasco
Indexer: Johnna vanHoose Dinse
Project Coordinator, Cover: Brent Savage
Cover Designer: Wiley
Cover Image: ©Getty Images, Inc./Jeremy Woodhouse

For the original AWS instructor, Mike Culver, who taught us how to teach, lead, and inspire with tenacity and kindness.

Acknowledgments

The authors would like to thank a few people who helped us develop and write this *AWS Certified Solutions Architect Official Study Guide: Associate Exam*.

First, thanks to all our families who put up with us spending weekends and evenings creating content, writing questions, and reviewing each other's chapters. Their patience and support made this book possible.

Niamh O'Byrne, AWS Certification Manager, who introduced all of the authors and many more solutions architects at AWS to certification testing and got this book started by challenging some of us to extend our reach and help more cloud practitioners get certified.

Nathan Bower and Victoria Steidel, amazing technical writers at AWS who reviewed and edited all the content and every question and gently made us better writers and communicators. They were tireless in reviewing and helping us hone and focus our content.

Patrick Shumate, a fellow AWS solutions architect who contributed test questions right when we needed the help to get us over the finish line.

We could not have written this book without the help of our friends at Wiley. Kenyon Brown, Senior Acquisitions Editor, corralled us and focused us on the end goal. Additionally, we were guided by Gary Schwartz, Project Editor; Kezia Endsley, Copyeditor; and Dassi Zeidel, Production Editor who took output from different authors and turned it into a cohesive and complete finished product.

Lastly, we want to thank all the solutions architects at AWS who participated in certification blueprint development, question writing, and review sessions, and the development of a world-class certification program for cloud practitioners that is setting the standard for our industry.

About the Authors

Joe Baron, Principal Solutions Architect for AWS, is currently working with customers in the Southeastern United States. Joe joined AWS in 2009 as one of the first solutions architects, and in the years since he has helped customers of all sizes, from small startups to some of the largest enterprises in the world, to architect their infrastructures and migrate their applications to the cloud. He was also an early contributor to the AWS Associate and Professional Certified Solutions Architect programs. Joe holds a BS degree in engineering physics from Cornell University and is proud to be an "expert generalist." Prior to joining AWS, Joe had 25 years of experience in technology, with roles in data center automation, virtualization, life sciences, high-performance computing, 3D visualization, hardware and software development, and Independent Software Vendor (ISV) program management. He is also a dedicated husband to Carol and father of two children, Matt and Jessie. When not helping customers migrate all the things to the cloud, Joe is an amateur classical pianist and collector of traditional woodworking tools. He lives in the Raleigh, NC area.

Hisham Baz is a passionate software engineer and systems architect with expertise building distributed applications and high-performance, mission-critical systems. Since 2013, Hisham has been a solutions architect with AWS working with customers like Pinterest, Airbnb, and General Electric to build resilient architectures in the cloud with a focus on big data and analytics. Prior to Amazon, Hisham founded two early-stage startups, modernized the communications network connecting critical transportation infrastructure, and improved cellular networks with large-scale data analytics. Hisham is based in San Francisco, CA and lives with his wife, Suki. They can often be found hiking the redwoods.

Tim Bixler, Commercial Americas Southeast Area Solutions Architecture Leader for AWS, leads teams of solutions architects who provide AWS technical enablement, evangelism, and knowledge transfer to customers like Capital One, The Coca-Cola Company, AOL, Koch Industries, Cox Automotive, NASCAR, Emdeon, and Neustar. Tim has over 20 years of experience in improving systems and operational performance, productivity, and customer satisfaction for private and public global corporations as well as government agencies. He is also a public speaker for Amazon and enjoys helping customers adopt innovative solutions on AWS. But if you ask his 7-year-old son TJ what he does, he might say that daddy is a builder and a fixer. When not otherwise tasked, you can find him burrowed in his lab building robots driven by microcontrollers or at the local BrickFair admiring the creations that he has no time to build.

Biff Gaut started writing programs for a living on CP/M on the Osborne 1. Since those early days, he obtained a BS in engineering from Virginia Tech while writing C code on MS-DOS, married his wife, Holly, while writing his first GUI apps, and raised two children while transitioning from COM objects in C++ to web apps in .NET. Along the way, he led development teams from 1 to 50 members for companies including NASDAQ, Thomson Reuters, Verizon, Microsoft, FINRA, and Marriott. He has collaborated on two books and spoken at countless conferences, including Windows World and the Microsoft PDC. Biff is currently a solutions architect at AWS, helping customers across the country realize the benefits of the cloud by deploying secure, available, efficient workloads on AWS. And yes, that's his real name.

Kevin E. Kelly, Solutions Architecture Manager and early contributor to the AWS Solutions Architecture Certification exams, has been at AWS for over seven years helping companies architect their infrastructures and migrate their applications to the cloud. Kevin has a BS in computer science from Mercer University and a Master of Information Systems in business from the University of Montana. Before joining Amazon, Kevin was an Air Force officer, a programmer—including embedded programming—and a technical presales leader. Kevin has been the chairman of the Worldwide Web Consortium (W3C) Compound Document Format Working Group and led that open-standards working group in developing the Web Interactive Compound Document (WICD) profile for mobile and desktop devices. He has also served as the W3C Advisory Council Representative for Health Level 7 (HL7). Kevin lives in Virginia with his wife, Laurie, and their two daughters, Caroline and Amelia. Kevin is an amateur violin and mandolin player and a zymurgist.

Sean Senior is a solutions architect at AWS. Sean is a builder at heart and thrives in a fast-paced environment with continuous challenges. Sean has a BS in computer information and sciences from the University of Maryland University College. Sean is a devoted husband and father of a beautiful girl. He is a U.S. Navy veteran, avid sports fan, and gym rat. He loathes talking about himself in the third person, but can be persuaded to do so for a good reason.

John Stamper, Principal Solutions Architect at AWS, is a co-inventor for multiple AWS patents and is particularly fond of distributed systems at scale. John holds a BS in mathematics from James Madison University (94) and an MS in Information Systems from George Mason University (04). In addition to building systems on the cloud and helping customers reimagine their businesses, John is a dedicated husband and father of three children. He is a CrossFit athlete, youth sports coach, and vocal supporter of the arts.

Contents at a Glance

Contents

Table of Exercises

Foreword

This *AWS Certified Solutions Architect Official Study Guide: Associate Exam* has been written to help you prepare for the AWS Certified Solutions Architect – Associate exam. This certification is becoming an increasingly important credential that every information technology professional and cloud practitioner who plans, designs, and builds application architectures for deployment on AWS should obtain. Passing the AWS Certified Solutions Architect – Associate exam demonstrates to your colleagues, employers, and the industry at large that you know how to build and deploy AWS solutions that are highly available, secure, performant, and cost effective.

This study guide was written by AWS solutions architects who wrote and reviewed exam questions for the AWS Certified Solutions Architect exams. Although nothing replaces hands-on experience building and deploying a variety of cloud applications and controls on AWS, this study guide, and the questions and exercises in each chapter, provide you with coverage of the basic AWS Cloud services combined with architectural recommendations and best practices that will help prepare you for the exam. Combining this study guide with production application deployment experience and taking the practice exams online will prepare you well and allow you to take the exam with confidence. Adding the AWS Certified Solutions Architect—Associate certification to your credentials will establish you as an industry-recognized solutions architect for the AWS platform!

—Kevin E. Kelly
Americas Solutions Architecture Lead
AWS Certified Solutions Architect – Associate
AWS Certified Solutions Architect – Professional
Herndon, VA

Introduction

Studying for any certification exam can seem daunting. This *AWS Certified Solutions Architect Official Study Guide: Associate Exam* was designed and developed with relevant topics, questions, and exercises to enable a cloud practitioner to focus their precious study time and effort on the germane set of topics targeted at the right level of abstraction so they can confidently take the AWS Certified Solutions Architect – Associate exam.

This study guide presents a set of topics needed to round out a cloud practitioner's hands-on experiences with AWS by covering the basic AWS Cloud services and concepts within the scope of the AWS Certified Solutions Architect – Associate exam. This study guide begins with an introduction to AWS, which is then followed by chapters on specific AWS Cloud services. In addition to the services chapters, the topics of security, risk and compliance, and architecture best practices are covered, providing the reader with a solid base for understanding how to build and deploy applications on the AWS platform. Furthermore, the AWS architectural best practices and principles are reinforced in every chapter and reflected in the self-study questions and examples to highlight the development and deployment of applications for AWS that are secure, highly available, performant, and cost effective. Each chapter includes specific information on the service or topic covered, followed by an Exam Essentials section that contains key information needed in your exam preparation. The Exam Essentials section is followed by an Exercise section with exercises designed to help reinforce the topic of the chapter with hands-on learning. Next, each chapter contains sample questions to get you accustomed to answering questions about AWS Cloud services and architecture topics. The book also contains a self-assessment exam with 25 questions, two practice exams, with 50 questions each to help you gauge your readiness to take the exam, and flashcards to help you learn and retain key facts needed to prepare for the exam.

If you are looking for a targeted book written by solutions architects who wrote, reviewed, and developed the AWS Certified Solutions Architect – Associate exam, then this is the book for you.

What Does This Book Cover?

This book covers topics you need to know to prepare for the Amazon Web Services (AWS) Certified Solutions Architect – Associate exam:

Chapter 1: Introduction to AWS   This chapter provides an introduction to the AWS Cloud computing platform. It discusses the advantages of cloud computing and the fundamentals of AWS. It provides an overview of the AWS Cloud services that are fundamentally important for the exam.

Chapter 2: Amazon Simple Storage Service (Amazon S3) and Amazon Glacier Storage   This chapter provides you with a basic understanding of the core object storage services available on AWS: Amazon Simple Storage Service (Amazon S3) and Amazon Glacier. These services are used to store objects on AWS.

Chapter 3: Amazon Elastic Compute Cloud (Amazon EC2) and Amazon Elastic Block Store (Amazon EBS)   In this chapter, you will learn how Amazon Elastic Compute Cloud (Amazon EC2) and Amazon Elastic Block Store (Amazon EBS) provide the basic elements of compute and block-level storage to run your workloads on AWS.

Chapter 4: Amazon Virtual Private Cloud (Amazon VPC)   This chapter describes Amazon Virtual Private Cloud (Amazon VPC), which is a custom-defined virtual network within AWS. You will learn how to design secure architectures using Amazon VPC to provision your own logically isolated section of AWS.

Chapter 5: Elastic Load Balancing, Amazon CloudWatch, and Auto Scaling   In this chapter, you will learn how Elastic Load Balancing, Amazon CloudWatch, and Auto Scaling work independently and together to help you efficiently and cost-effectively deploy highly available and optimized workloads on AWS.

Chapter 6: AWS Identity and Access Management (IAM)   This chapter covers AWS Identity and Access Management (IAM), which is used to secure transactions with the AWS resources in your AWS account.

Chapter 7: Databases and AWS   This chapter covers essential database concepts and introduces three of AWS managed database services: Amazon Relational Database Service (Amazon RDS), Amazon DynamoDB, and Amazon Redshift. These managed services simplify the setup and operation of relational databases, NoSQL databases, and data warehouses.

Chapter 8: SQS, SWF, and SNS   This chapter focuses on application services in AWS, specifically Amazon Simple Queue Service (Amazon SQS), Amazon Simple Workflow Service (SWF), and Amazon Simple Notification Service (Amazon SNS). It also covers architectural guidance on using these services and the use of Amazon SNS in mobile applications.

Chapter 9: Domain Name System (DNS) and Amazon Route 53   In this chapter, you will learn about Domain Name System (DNS) and the Amazon Route 53 service, which is designed to help users find your website or application over the Internet.

Chapter 10: Amazon ElastiCache   This chapter focuses on building high-performance applications using in-memory caching technologies and Amazon ElastiCache.

Chapter 11: Additional Key Services   Additional services not covered in other chapters are covered in this chapter. Topics include Amazon CloudFront, AWS Storage Gateway, AWS Directory Service, AWS Key Management Service (KMS), AWS CloudHSM, AWS CloudTrail, Amazon Kinesis, Amazon Elastic Map Reduce (Amazon EMR), AWS Data Pipeline, AWS Import/Export, AWS OpsWorks, AWS CloudFormation, AWS Elastic Beanstalk, AWS Trusted Advisor, and AWS Config.

Chapter 12: Security on AWS   This chapter covers the relevant security topics that are within scope for the AWS Certified Solutions Architect – Associate exam.

Chapter 13: AWS Risk and Compliance   This chapter covers topics associated with risk and compliance, risk mitigation, and the shared responsibility model of using AWS.

Chapter 14: Architecture Best Practices The final chapter covers the AWS-recommended design principles and best practices for architecting systems and applications for the Cloud.

Interactive Online Learning Environment and Test Bank

The authors have worked hard to provide some really great tools to help you with your certification process. The interactive online learning environment that accompanies the *AWS Certified Solutions Architect Official Study Guide: Associate Exam* provides a test bank with study tools to help you prepare for the certification exam—and increase your chances of passing it the first time! The test bank includes the following:

Sample Tests All the questions in this book are provided, including the assessment test at the end of this Introduction and the chapter tests that include the review questions at the end of each chapter. In addition, there are two practice exams with 50 questions each. Use these questions to test your knowledge of the study guide material. The online test bank runs on multiple devices.

Flashcards The online text banks include 100 flashcards specifically written to hit you hard, so don't get discouraged if you don't ace your way through them at first. They're there to ensure that you're really ready for the exam. And no worries—armed with the review questions, practice exams, and flashcards, you'll be more than prepared when exam day comes. Questions are provided in digital flashcard format (a question followed by a single correct answer). You can use the flashcards to reinforce your learning and provide last-minute test prep before the exam.

Glossary A glossary of key terms from this book is available as a fully searchable PDF.

Go to http://www.wiley.com/go/sybextestprep to register and gain access to this interactive online learning environment and test bank with study tools.

Exam Objectives

The AWS Certified Solutions Architect—Associate exam is intended for people who have experience in designing distributed applications and systems on the AWS platform. Here are some of the key exam topics that you should understand for this exam:

- Designing and deploying scalable, highly available, and fault-tolerant systems on AWS
- Migrating existing on-premises applications to AWS

- Ingress and egress of data to and from AWS
- Selecting the appropriate AWS service based on data, compute, database, or security requirements
- Identifying appropriate use of AWS architectural best practices
- Estimating AWS costs and identifying cost control mechanisms

In general, candidates should have the following:

- One or more years of hands-on experience designing highly available, cost efficient, secure, fault tolerant, and scalable distributed systems on AWS
- In-depth knowledge of at least one high-level programming language
- Ability to identify and define requirements for an AWS-based application
- Experience with deploying hybrid systems with on-premises and AWS components
- Capability to provide best practices for building secure and reliable applications on the AWS platform

The exam covers four different domains, with each domain broken down into objectives and subobjectives.

Objective Map

The following table lists each domain and its weighting in the exam, along with the chapters in the book where that domain's objectives and subobjectives are covered.

Domain	Percentage of Exam	Chapter
1 Domain 1.0: Designing highly available, cost-efficient, fault-tolerant, scalable systems	60%	
1.1 Identify and recognize cloud architecture considerations, such as fundamental components and effective designs.		1, 2, 3, 4, 5, 7, 8, 9, 10, 11, 14
Content may include the following:		
How to design cloud services		1, 2, 3, 4, 8, 9, 11, 14
Planning and design		1, 2, 3, 4, 7, 8, 9, 10, 11, 14
Monitoring and logging		2, 3, 8, 9, 11
Familiarity with:		
Best practices for AWS architecture		1, 2, 4, 7, 8, 9, 10, 14
Developing to client specifications, including pricing/cost (e.g., on Demand vs. Reserved vs. Spot; RTO and RPO DR Design)		2, 7, 9
Architectural trade-off decisions (e.g., high availability vs. cost, Amazon Relational Database Service (RDS) vs. installing your own database on Amazon Elastic Compute Cloud (EC2))		2, 4, 7, 8, 9, 10
Hybrid IT architectures (e.g., Direct Connect, Storage Gateway, VPC, Directory Services)		1, 2, 4, 14
Elasticity and scalability (e.g., Auto Scaling, SQS, ELB, CloudFront)		1, 2, 5, 7, 8, 9, 10, 14

Domain	Percentage of Exam	Chapter
2 Domain 2.0: Implementation/Deployment	10%	
2.1 Identify the appropriate techniques and methods using Amazon EC2, Amazon S3, AWS Elastic Beanstalk, AWS CloudFormation, AWS OpsWorks, Amazon Virtual Private Cloud (VPC), and AWS Identity and Access Management (IAM) to code and implement a cloud solution.		1, 2, 3, 4, 5, 6, 8, 11, 13
Content may include the following:		
Configure an Amazon Machine Image (AMI).		2, 3, 11
Operate and extend service management in a hybrid IT architecture.		1, 4
Configure services to support compliance requirements in the cloud.		2, 3, 4, 11, 13
Launch instances across the AWS global infrastructure.		1, 2, 3, 5, 8, 11
Configure IAM policies and best practices.		2, 6
3 Domain 3.0: Data Security	20%	
3.1 Recognize and implement secure practices for optimum cloud deployment and maintenance.		2, 4, 10, 12, 13
Content may include the following:		
AWS shared responsibility model		12, 13
AWS platform compliance		11, 12, 13
AWS security attributes (customer workloads down to physical layer)		4, 11, 12, 13
AWS administration and security services		7, 10, 11, 12
AWS Identity and Access Management (IAM)		6, 12
Amazon Virtual Private Cloud (VPC)		4, 12

Domain	Percentage of Exam	Chapter
AWS CloudTrail		11, 12
Ingress vs. egress filtering, and which AWS services and features fit		11, 12
"Core" Amazon EC2 and S3 security feature sets		2, 4, 12
Incorporating common conventional security products (Firewall, VPN)		4, 12
Design patterns		7, 13
DDoS mitigation		12
Encryption solutions (e.g., key services)		2, 11, 12
Complex access controls (building sophisticated security groups, ACLs, etc.)		2, 12
Amazon CloudWatch for the security architect		5
Trusted Advisor		11
CloudWatch Logs		5
3.2 Recognize critical disaster recovery techniques and their implementation.		3, 7, 9, 10
Content may include the following:		
Disaster recovery		3
Recovery time objective		7
Recovery point objective		7
Amazon Elastic Block Store		3
AWS Import/Export		11
AWS Storage Gateway		11
Amazon Route53		9

Domain	Percentage of Exam	Chapter
Validation of data recovery method		3
4 Domain 4.0: Troubleshooting	10%	
Content may include the following:		
General troubleshooting information and questions		5, 8

Assessment Test

1. Under a single AWS account, you have set up an Auto Scaling group with a maximum capacity of 50 Amazon Elastic Compute Cloud (Amazon EC2) instances in us-west-2. When you scale out, however, it only increases to 20 Amazon EC2 instances. What is the likely cause?

   A. Auto Scaling has a hard limit of 20 Amazon EC2 instances.

   B. If not specified, the Auto Scaling group maximum capacity defaults to 20 Amazon EC2 instances.

   C. The Auto Scaling group desired capacity is set to 20, so Auto Scaling stopped at 20 Amazon EC2 instances.

   D. You have exceeded the default Amazon EC2 instance limit of 20 per region.

2. Elastic Load Balancing allows you to distribute traffic across which of the following?

   A. Only within a single Availability Zone

   B. Multiple Availability Zones within a region

   C. Multiple Availability Zones within and between regions

   D. Multiple Availability Zones within and between regions and on-premises virtualized instances running OpenStack

3. Amazon CloudWatch offers which types of monitoring plans? (Choose 2 answers)

   A. Basic

   B. Detailed

   C. Diagnostic

   D. Precognitive

   E. Retroactive

4. An Amazon Elastic Compute Cloud (Amazon EC2) instance in an Amazon Virtual Private Cloud (Amazon VPC) subnet can send and receive traffic from the Internet when which of the following conditions are met? (Choose 3 answers)

   A. Network Access Control Lists (ACLs) and security group rules disallow all traffic except relevant Internet traffic.

   B. Network ACLs and security group rules allow relevant Internet traffic.

   C. Attach an Internet Gateway (IGW) to the Amazon VPC and create a subnet route table to send all non-local traffic to that IGW.

   D. Attach a Virtual Private Gateway (VPG) to the Amazon VPC and create subnet routes to send all non-local traffic to that VPG.

   E. The Amazon EC2 instance has a public IP address or Elastic IP (EIP) address.

   F. The Amazon EC2 instance does not need a public IP or Elastic IP when using Amazon VPC.

5. If you launch five Amazon Elastic Compute Cloud (Amazon EC2) instances in an Amazon Virtual Private Cloud (Amazon VPC) without specifying a security group, the instances will be launched into a default security group that provides which of the following? (Choose 3 answers)

   A. The five Amazon EC2 instances can communicate with each other.

   B. The five Amazon EC2 instances cannot communicate with each other.

   C. All inbound traffic will be allowed to the five Amazon EC2 instances.

   D. No inbound traffic will be allowed to the five Amazon EC2 instances.

   E. All outbound traffic will be allowed from the five Amazon EC2 instances.

   F. No outbound traffic will be allowed from the five Amazon EC2 instances.

6. Your company wants to host its secure web application in AWS. The internal security policies consider any connections to or from the web server as insecure and require application data protection. What approaches should you use to protect data in transit for the application? (Choose 2 answers)

   A. Use BitLocker to encrypt data.

   B. Use HTTPS with server certificate authentication.

   C. Use an AWS Identity and Access Management (IAM) role.

   D. Use Secure Sockets Layer (SSL)/Transport Layer Security (TLS) for database connection.

   E. Use XML for data transfer from client to server.

7. You have an application that will run on an Amazon Elastic Compute Cloud (Amazon EC2) instance. The application will make requests to Amazon Simple Storage Service (Amazon S3) and Amazon DynamoDB. Using best practices, what type of AWS Identity and Access Management (IAM) identity should you create for your application to access the identified services?

   A. IAM role

   B. IAM user

   C. IAM group

   D. IAM directory

8. When a request is made to an AWS Cloud service, the request is evaluated to decide whether it should be allowed or denied. The evaluation logic follows which of the following rules? (Choose 3 answers)

   A. An explicit allow overrides any denies.

   B. By default, all requests are denied.

   C. An explicit allow overrides the default.

   D. An explicit deny overrides any allows.

   E. By default, all requests are allowed.

9. What is the data processing engine behind Amazon Elastic MapReduce (Amazon EMR)?

   A. Apache Hadoop

   B. Apache Hive

   C. Apache Pig

   D. Apache HBase

10. What type of AWS Elastic Beanstalk environment tier provisions resources to support a web application that handles background processing tasks?

   A. Web server environment tier

   B. Worker environment tier

   C. Database environment tier

   D. Batch environment tier

11. What Amazon Relational Database Service (Amazon RDS) feature provides the high availability for your database?

   A. Regular maintenance windows

   B. Security groups

   C. Automated backups

   D. Multi-AZ deployment

12. What administrative tasks are handled by AWS for Amazon Relational Database Service (Amazon RDS) databases? (Choose 3 answers)

   A. Regular backups of the database

   B. Deploying virtual infrastructure

   C. Deploying the schema (for example, tables and stored procedures)

   D. Patching the operating system and database software

   E. Setting up non-admin database accounts and privileges

13. Which of the following use cases is well suited for Amazon Redshift?

   A. A 500TB data warehouse used for market analytics

   B. A NoSQL, unstructured database workload

   C. A high traffic, e-commerce web application

   D. An in-memory cache

14. Which of the following statements about Amazon DynamoDB secondary indexes is true?

   A. There can be many per table, and they can be created at any time.

   B. There can only be one per table, and it must be created when the table is created.

   C. There can be many per table, and they can be created at any time.

   D. There can only be one per table, and it must be created when the table is created.

15. What is the primary use case of Amazon Kinesis Firehose?

    A. Ingest huge streams of data and allow custom processing of data in flight.

    B. Ingest huge streams of data and store it to Amazon Simple Storage Service (Amazon S3), Amazon Redshift, or Amazon Elasticsearch Service.

    C. Generate a huge stream of data from an Amazon S3 bucket.

    D. Generate a huge stream of data from Amazon DynamoDB.

16. Your company has 17TB of financial trading records that need to be stored for seven years by law. Experience has shown that any record more than a year old is unlikely to be accessed. Which of the following storage plans meets these needs in the most cost-efficient manner?

    A. Store the data on Amazon Elastic Block Store (Amazon EBS) volume attached to t2.large instances.

    B. Store the data on Amazon Simple Storage Service (Amazon S3) with lifecycle policies that change the storage class to Amazon Glacier after one year, and delete the object after seven years.

    C. Store the data in Amazon DynamoDB, and delete data older than seven years.

    D. Store the data in an Amazon Glacier Vault Lock.

17. What must you do to create a record of who accessed your Amazon Simple Storage Service (Amazon S3) data and from where?

    A. Enable Amazon CloudWatch logs.

    B. Enable versioning on the bucket.

    C. Enable website hosting on the bucket.

    D. Enable server access logs on the bucket.

    E. Create an AWS Identity and Access Management (IAM) bucket policy.

18. Amazon Simple Storage Service (Amazon S3) is an eventually consistent storage system. For what kinds of operations is it possible to get stale data as a result of eventual consistency?

    A. GET after PUT of a new object

    B. GET or LIST after a DELETE

    C. GET after overwrite PUT (PUT to an existing key)

    D. DELETE after GET of new object

19. How is data stored in Amazon Simple Storage Service (Amazon S3) for high durability?

    A. Data is automatically replicated to other regions.

    B. Data is automatically replicated to different Availability Zones within a region.

    C. Data is replicated only if versioning is enabled on the bucket.

    D. Data is automatically backed up on tape and restored if needed.

20. Your company needs to provide streaming access to videos to authenticated users around the world. What is a good way to accomplish this?

    A. Use Amazon Simple Storage Service (Amazon S3) buckets in each region with website hosting enabled.

    B. Store the videos on Amazon Elastic Block Store (Amazon EBS) volumes.

    C. Enable Amazon CloudFront with geolocation and signed URLs.

    D. Run a fleet of Amazon Elastic Compute Cloud (Amazon EC2) instances to host the videos.

21. Which of the following are true about the AWS shared responsibility model? (Choose 3 answers)

    A. AWS is responsible for all infrastructure components (that is, AWS Cloud services) that support customer deployments.

    B. The customer is responsible for the components from the guest operating system upward (including updates, security patches, and antivirus software).

    C. The customer may rely on AWS to manage the security of their workloads deployed on AWS.

    D. While AWS manages security of the cloud, security in the cloud is the responsibility of the customer.

    E. The customer must audit the AWS data centers personally to confirm the compliance of AWS systems and services.

22. Which process in an Amazon Simple Workflow Service (Amazon SWF) workflow implements a task?

    A. Decider

    B. Activity worker

    C. Workflow starter

    D. Business rule

23. Which of the following is true if you stop an Amazon Elastic Compute Cloud (Amazon EC2) instance with an Elastic IP address in an Amazon Virtual Private Cloud (Amazon VPC)?

    A. The instance is disassociated from its Elastic IP address and must be re-attached when the instance is restarted.

    B. The instance remains associated with its Elastic IP address.

    C. The Elastic IP address is released from your account.

    D. The instance is disassociated from the Elastic IP address temporarily while you restart the instance.

24. Which Amazon Elastic Compute Cloud (Amazon EC2) pricing model allows you to pay a set hourly price for compute, giving you full control over when the instance launches and terminates?

A. Spot instances

B. Reserved instance

C. On Demand instances

D. Dedicated instances

25. Under what circumstances will Amazon Elastic Compute Cloud (Amazon EC2) instance store data not be preserved?

A. The associated security groups are changed.

B. The instance is stopped or rebooted.

C. The instance is rebooted or terminated.

D. The instance is stopped or terminated.

E. None of the above

Answers to Assessment Test

1. D. Auto Scaling may cause you to reach limits of other services, such as the default number of Amazon EC2 instances you can currently launch within a region, which is 20.

2. B. The Elastic Load Balancing service allows you to distribute traffic across a group of Amazon Elastic Compute Cloud (Amazon EC2) instances in one or more Availability Zones within a region.

3. A and B. Amazon CloudWatch has two plans: basic and detailed. There are no diagnostic, precognitive, or retroactive monitoring plans for Amazon CloudWatch.

4. B, C, and E. You must do the following to create a public subnet with Internet access:

    Attach an IGW to your Amazon VPC.

    Create a subnet route table rule to send all non-local traffic (for example, 0.0.0.0/0) to the IGW.

    Configure your network ACLs and security group rules to allow relevant traffic to flow to and from your instance.

    You must do the following to enable an Amazon EC2 instance to send and receive traffic from the Internet:

    Assign a public IP address or EIP address.

5. A, D, and E. If a security group is not specified at launch, then an Amazon EC2 instance will be launched into the default security group for the Amazon VPC. The default security group allows communication between all resources within the security group, allows all outbound traffic, and denies all other traffic.

6. B and D. To protect data in transit from the clients to the web application, HTTPS with server certificate authentication should be used. To protect data in transit from the web application to the database, SSL/TLS for database connection should be used.

7. A. Don't create an IAM user (or an IAM group) and pass the user's credentials to the application or embed the credentials in the application. Instead, create an IAM role that you attach to the Amazon EC2 instance to give applications running on the instance temporary security credentials. The credentials have the permissions specified in the policies attached to the role. A directory is not an identity object in IAM.

8. B, C, and D. When a request is made, the AWS service decides whether a given request should be allowed or denied. The evaluation logic follows these rules:

    1) By default, all requests are denied (in general, requests made using the account credentials for resources in the account are always allowed).

    2) An explicit allow overrides this default.

    3) An explicit deny overrides any allows.

9. A. Amazon EMR uses Apache Hadoop as its distributed data processing engine. Hadoop is an open source, Java software framework that supports data-intensive distributed applications running on large clusters of commodity hardware. Hive, Pig, and HBase are packages that run on top of Hadoop.

10. B. An environment tier whose web application runs background jobs is known as a worker tier. An environment tier whose web application processes web requests is known as a web server tier. Database and batch are not valid environment tiers.

11. D. Multi-AZ deployment uses synchronous replication to a different Availability Zone so that operations can continue on the replica if the master database stops responding for any reason. Automated backups provide disaster recovery, not high availability. Security groups, while important, have no effect on availability. Maintenance windows are actually times when the database may not be available.

12. A, B, and D. Amazon RDS will launch Amazon Elastic Compute Cloud (Amazon EC2) instances, install the database software, handle all patching, and perform regular backups. Anything within the database software (schema, user accounts, and so on) is the responsibility of the customer.

13. A. Amazon Redshift is a petabyte-scale data warehouse. It is not well suited for unstructured NoSQL data or highly dynamic transactional data. It is in no way a cache.

14. D. There can be one secondary index per table, and it must be created when the table is created.

15. B. The Amazon Kinesis family of services provides functionality to ingest large streams of data. Amazon Kinesis Firehose is specifically designed to ingest a stream and save it to any of the three storage services listed in Response B.

16. B. Amazon S3 and Amazon Glacier are the most cost-effective storage services. After a year, when the objects are unlikely to be accessed, you can save costs by transferring the objects to Amazon Glacier where the retrieval time is three to five hours.

17. D. Server access logs provide a record of any access to an object in Amazon S3.

18. C. Amazon S3 provides read-after-write consistency for PUTs to new objects (new key), but eventual consistency for GETs and DELETEs of existing objects (existing key). Response C changes the existing object so that a subsequent GET may fetch the previous and inconsistent object.

19. B. AWS will never transfer data between regions unless directed to by you. Durability in Amazon S3 is achieved by replicating your data geographically to different Availability Zones regardless of the versioning configuration. AWS doesn't use tapes.

20. C. Amazon CloudFront provides the best user experience by delivering the data from a geographically advantageous edge location. Signed URLs allow you to control access to authenticated users.

21. A, B, and D. In the AWS shared responsibility model, customers retain control of what security they choose to implement to protect their own content, platform, applications, systems, and networks, no differently than they would for applications in an on-site data center.

22. B. An activity worker is a process or thread that performs the activity tasks that are part of your workflow. Each activity worker polls Amazon SWF for new tasks that are appropriate for that activity worker to perform; certain tasks can be performed only by certain activity workers. After receiving a task, the activity worker processes the task to completion and then reports to Amazon SWF that the task was completed and provides the result. The activity task represents one of the tasks that you identified in your application.

23. B. In an Amazon VPC, an instance's Elastic IP address remains associated with an instance when the instance is stopped.

24. C. You pay a set hourly price for an On Demand instance from when you launch it until you explicitly stop or terminate it. Spot instances can be terminated when the spot price goes above your bid price. Reserved instances involve paying for an instance over a one- or three-year term. Dedicated instances run on hardware dedicated to your account and are not a pricing model.

25. D. The data in an instance store persists only during the lifetime of its associated instance. If an instance is stopped or terminated, then the instance store does not persist. Rebooting an instance does not shut down the instance; if an instance reboots (intentionally or unintentionally), data on the instance store persists. Security groups have nothing to do with the lifetime of an instance and have no effect here.

AWS®
Certified Solutions Architect Official
Study Guide - Associate Exam

Introduction to AWS

THE AWS CERTIFIED SOLUTIONS ARCHITECT ASSOCIATE EXAM OBJECTIVES COVERED IN THIS CHAPTER MAY INCLUDE, BUT ARE NOT LIMITED TO, THE FOLLOWING:

Domain 1.0: Designing highly available, cost-efficient, fault-tolerant, scalable systems

✓ **1.1 Identify and recognize cloud architecture considerations, such as fundamental components and effective designs.**

Content may include the following:

- How to design cloud services

- Planning and design

- Familiarity with:

  - Best practices for AWS architecture

  - Hybrid IT architectures (e.g., AWS Direct Connect, AWS Storage Gateway, Amazon Virtual Private Cloud [Amazon VPC], AWS Directory Service)

  - Elasticity and scalability (e.g., Auto Scaling, Amazon Simple Queue Service [Amazon SQS], Elastic Load Balancing, Amazon CloudFront)

Domain 2.0: Implementation/Deployment

✓ **2.1 Identify the appropriate techniques and methods using Amazon Elastic Compute Cloud (Amazon EC2), Amazon Simple Storage Service (Amazon S3), AWS Elastic Beanstalk, AWS CloudFormation, AWS OpsWorks, Amazon VPC, and AWS Identity and Access Management (IAM) to code and implement a cloud solution.**

Content may include the following:

- Operate and extend service management in a hybrid IT architecture.

- Configure services to support compliance requirements in the cloud.

- Launch instances across the AWS global infrastructure.

In 2006, Amazon Web Services, Inc. (AWS) began offering IT infrastructure services to businesses in the form of web services, now commonly known as *cloud computing*. One of the key benefits of cloud computing is the opportunity to replace up-front capital infrastructure expenses with low variable costs that scale with your business. With the cloud, businesses no longer need to plan for and procure servers and other IT infrastructure weeks or months in advance. Instead, they can instantly spin up hundreds or thousands of servers in minutes and deliver results faster.

Today, AWS provides a highly reliable, scalable, and low-cost infrastructure platform in the cloud that powers hundreds of thousands of businesses in more than 190 countries around the world.

This chapter provides an introduction to the AWS Cloud computing platform. It discusses the advantages of cloud computing and the fundamentals of AWS. It provides an overview of the AWS Cloud services that are fundamentally important for the exam.

What Is Cloud Computing?

Cloud computing is the on-demand delivery of IT resources and applications via the Internet with pay-as-you-go pricing. Whether you run applications that share photos to millions of mobile users or deliver services that support the critical operations of your business, the cloud provides rapid access to flexible and low-cost IT resources. With cloud computing, you don't need to make large up-front investments in hardware and spend a lot of time managing that hardware. Instead, you can provision exactly the right type and size of computing resources you need to power your newest bright idea or operate your IT department. With cloud computing, you can access as many resources as you need, almost instantly, and only pay for what you use.

In its simplest form, cloud computing provides an easy way to access servers, storage, databases, and a broad set of application services over the Internet. Cloud computing providers such as AWS own and maintain the network-connected hardware required for these application services, while you provision and use what you need for your workloads.

Advantages of Cloud Computing

Cloud computing introduces a revolutionary shift in how technology is obtained, used, and managed, and in how organizations budget and pay for technology services. With the ability to reconfigure the computing environment quickly to adapt to changing business requirements, organizations can optimize spending. Capacity can be automatically scaled up or down to meet fluctuating usage patterns. Services can be temporarily taken offline or shut down permanently as business demands dictate. In addition, with pay-per-use billing, AWS Cloud services become an operational expense instead of a capital expense.

While each organization experiences a unique journey to the cloud with numerous benefits, six advantages become apparent time and time again, as illustrated in Figure 1.1.

FIGURE 1.1   Six advantages of cloud computing

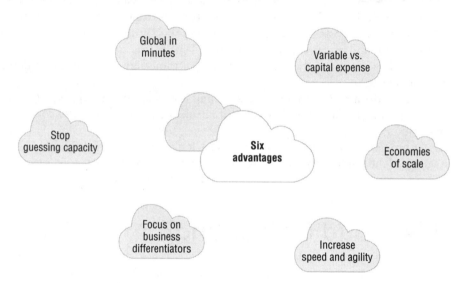

Variable vs. Capital Expense

Let's begin with the ability to *trade capital expense for variable operational expense.* Instead of having to invest heavily in data centers and servers before knowing how you're going to use them, you can pay only when you consume computing resources and pay only for how much you consume.

Economies of Scale

Another advantage of cloud computing is that *organizations benefit from massive economies of scale.* By using cloud computing, you can achieve a lower variable cost than you would get on your own. Because usage from hundreds of thousands of customers is aggregated in the cloud, providers such as AWS can achieve higher economies of scale, which translates into lower prices.

Stop Guessing Capacity

When you make a capacity decision prior to deploying an application, you often end up either sitting on expensive idle resources or dealing with limited capacity. With cloud computing, organizations can *stop guessing about capacity requirements* for the infrastructure necessary to meet their business needs. They can access as much or as little as they need and scale up or down as required with only a few minutes' notice.

Increase Speed and Agility

In a cloud computing environment, new IT resources are one click away, which allows organizations to reduce the time it takes to make those resources available to developers from weeks to just minutes. This results in a dramatic *increase in speed and agility* for the organization, because the cost and time it takes to experiment and develop is significantly lower.

Focus on Business Differentiators

Cloud computing allows organizations to focus on their business priorities, instead of on the heavy lifting of racking, stacking, and powering servers. By embracing this paradigm shift, organizations can *stop spending money on running and maintaining data centers*. This allows organizations to focus on projects that differentiate their businesses, such as analyzing petabytes of data, delivering video content, building great mobile applications, or even exploring Mars.

Go Global in Minutes

Another advantage of cloud computing is the ability to *go global in minutes*. Organizations can easily deploy their applications to multiple locations around the world with just a few clicks. This allows organizations to provide redundancy across the globe and to deliver lower latency and better experiences to their customers at minimal cost. Going global used to be something only the largest enterprises could afford to do, but cloud computing democratizes this ability, making it possible for any organization.

While specific questions on these advantages of cloud computing are unlikely to be on the exam, having exposure to these benefits can help rationalize the appropriate answers.

Cloud Computing Deployment Models

The two primary cloud computing deployment models that the exam focuses on are "all-in" cloud-based deployments and hybrid deployments. It is important to understand how each strategy applies to architectural options and decisions.

An *all-in cloud-based application* is fully deployed in the cloud, with all components of the application running in the cloud. Applications in the cloud have either been created in the cloud or have been migrated from an existing infrastructure to take advantage of the benefits of cloud computing. Cloud-based applications can be built on low-level infrastructure pieces or can use higher-level services that provide abstraction from the management, architecting, and scaling requirements of core infrastructure.

A *hybrid deployment* is a common approach taken by many enterprises that connects infrastructure and applications between cloud-based resources and existing resources, typically in an existing data center. The most common method of hybrid deployment is between the cloud and existing on-premises infrastructure to extend and grow an organization's infrastructure while connecting cloud resources to internal systems. Choosing between an existing investment in infrastructure and moving to the cloud does not need to be a binary decision. Leveraging dedicated connectivity, identity federation, and integrated tools allows organizations to run hybrid applications across on-premises and cloud services.

AWS Fundamentals

At its core, AWS provides on-demand delivery of IT resources via the Internet on a secure cloud services platform, offering compute power, storage, databases, content delivery, and other functionality to help businesses scale and grow. Using AWS resources instead of your own is like purchasing electricity from a power company instead of running your own generator, and it provides the key advantages of cloud computing: Capacity exactly matches your need, you pay only for what you use, economies of scale result in lower costs, and the service is provided by a vendor experienced in running large-scale networks.

AWS global infrastructure and AWS approach to security and compliance are key foundational concepts to understand as you prepare for the exam.

Global Infrastructure

AWS serves over one million active customers in more than 190 countries, and it continues to expand its global infrastructure steadily to help organizations achieve lower latency and higher throughput for their business needs.

AWS provides a highly available technology infrastructure platform with multiple locations worldwide. These locations are composed of regions and Availability Zones. Each *region* is a separate geographic area. Each region has multiple, isolated locations known as *Availability Zones*. AWS enables the placement of resources and data in multiple locations. Resources aren't replicated across regions unless organizations choose to do so.

Each region is completely independent and is designed to be completely isolated from the other regions. This achieves the greatest possible fault tolerance and stability. Each Availability Zone is also isolated, but the Availability Zones in a region are connected through low-latency links. Availability Zones are physically separated within a typical metropolitan region and are located in lower-risk flood plains (specific flood zone categorization varies by region). In addition to using a discrete uninterruptable power supply (UPS) and on-site backup generators, they are each fed via different grids from independent utilities (when available) to reduce single points of failure further. Availability Zones are all redundantly connected to multiple tier-1 transit providers. By placing resources in separate Availability Zones, you can protect your website or application from a service disruption impacting a single location.

You can achieve high availability by deploying your application across multiple Availability Zones. Redundant instances for each tier (for example, web, application, and database) of an application should be placed in distinct Availability Zones, thereby creating a multisite solution. At a minimum, the goal is to have an independent copy of each application stack in two or more Availability Zones.

Security and Compliance

Whether on-premises or on AWS, information security is of paramount importance to organizations running critical workloads. Security is a core functional requirement that protects mission-critical information from accidental or deliberate theft, leakage, integrity compromise, and deletion. Helping to protect the confidentiality, integrity, and availability of systems and data is of the utmost importance to AWS, as is maintaining your trust and confidence.

This section is intended to provide a very brief introduction to AWS approach to security and compliance. Chapter 12, "Security on AWS," and Chapter 13, "AWS Risk and Compliance," will address these topics in greater detail, including the importance of each on the exam.

Security

Cloud security at AWS is the number one priority. All AWS customers benefit from data center and network architectures built to satisfy the requirements of the most security-sensitive organizations. AWS and its partners offer hundreds of tools and features to help organizations meet their security objectives for visibility, auditability, controllability, and agility. This means that organizations can have the security they need, but without the capital outlay and with much lower operational overhead than in an on-premises environment.

Organizations leveraging AWS inherit all the best practices of AWS policies, architecture, and operational processes built to satisfy the requirements of the most security-sensitive customers. The AWS infrastructure has been designed to provide the highest availability while putting strong safeguards in place regarding customer privacy and segregation. When deploying systems on the AWS Cloud computing platform, AWS helps by sharing the security responsibilities with the organization. AWS manages the underlying infrastructure, and the organization can secure anything it deploys on AWS. This affords each organization the flexibility and agility they need in security controls.

This infrastructure is built and managed not only according to security best practices and standards, but also with the unique needs of the cloud in mind. AWS uses redundant and layered controls, continuous validation and testing, and a substantial amount of automation to ensure that the underlying infrastructure is monitored and protected 24/7. AWS ensures that these controls are consistently applied in every new data center or service.

Compliance

When customers move their production workloads to the AWS Cloud, both parties become responsible for managing the IT environment. Customers are responsible for setting up their environment in a secure and controlled manner. Customers also need to maintain adequate governance over their entire IT control environment. By tying together governance-focused, audit-friendly service features with applicable compliance or audit standards, AWS enables customers to build on traditional compliance programs. This helps organizations establish and operate in an AWS security control environment.

Organizations retain complete control and ownership over the region in which their data is physically located, allowing them to meet regional compliance and data residency requirements.

The IT infrastructure that AWS provides to organizations is designed and managed in alignment with security best practices and a variety of IT security standards. The following is a partial list of the many certifications and standards with which AWS complies:

- Service Organization Controls (SOC) 1/International Standard on Assurance Engagements (ISAE) 3402, SOC 2, and SOC 3

- Federal Information Security Management Act (FISMA), Department of Defense Information Assurance Certification and Accreditation Process (DIACAP), and Federal Risk and Authorization Management Program (FedRAMP)

- Payment Card Industry Data Security Standard (PCI DSS) Level 1

- International Organization for Standardization (ISO) 9001, ISO 27001, and ISO 27018

AWS provides a wide range of information regarding its IT control environment to help organizations achieve regulatory commitments in the form of reports, certifications, accreditations, and other third-party attestations.

AWS Cloud Computing Platform

AWS provides many cloud services that you can combine to meet business or organizational needs (see Figure 1.2). While being knowledgeable about all the platform services will allow you to be a well-rounded solutions architect, understanding the services and fundamental concepts outlined in this book will help prepare you for the AWS Certified Solutions Architect – Associate exam.

This section introduces the major AWS Cloud services by category. Subsequent chapters provide a deeper view of the services pertinent to the exam.

FIGURE 1.2   AWS Cloud computing platform

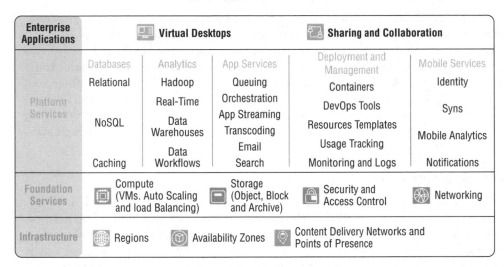

Accessing the Platform

To access AWS Cloud services, you can use the AWS Management Console, the AWS Command Line Interface (CLI), or the AWS Software Development Kits (SDKs).

The *AWS Management Console* is a web application for managing AWS Cloud services. The console provides an intuitive user interface for performing many tasks. Each service has its own console, which can be accessed from the AWS Management Console. The console also provides information about the account and billing.

The *AWS Command Line Interface (CLI)* is a unified tool used to manage AWS Cloud services. With just one tool to download and configure, you can control multiple services from the command line and automate them through scripts.

The *AWS Software Development Kits (SDKs)* provide an application programming interface (API) that interacts with the web services that fundamentally make up the AWS platform. The SDKs provide support for many different programming languages and platforms to allow you to work with your preferred language. While you can certainly make HTTP calls directly to the web service endpoints, using the SDKs can take the complexity out of coding by providing programmatic access for many of the services.

Compute and Networking Services

AWS provides a variety of compute and networking services to deliver core functionality for businesses to develop and run their workloads. These compute and networking services can be leveraged with the storage, database, and application services to provide a complete solution for computing, query processing, and storage across a wide range of applications. This section offers a high-level description of the core computing and networking services.

Amazon Elastic Compute Cloud (Amazon EC2)

Amazon Elastic Compute Cloud (Amazon EC2) is a web service that provides resizable compute capacity in the cloud. It allows organizations to obtain and configure virtual servers in Amazon's data centers and to harness those resources to build and host software systems. Organizations can select from a variety of operating systems and resource configurations (memory, CPU, storage, and so on) that are optimal for the application profile of each workload. Amazon EC2 presents a true virtual computing environment, allowing organizations to launch compute resources with a variety of operating systems, load them with custom applications, and manage network access permissions while maintaining complete control.

AWS Lambda

AWS Lambda is a zero-administration compute platform for back-end web developers that runs your code for you on the AWS Cloud and provides you with a fine-grained pricing structure. AWS Lambda runs your back-end code on its own AWS compute fleet of Amazon EC2 instances across multiple Availability Zones in a region, which provides the high availability, security, performance, and scalability of the AWS infrastructure.

Auto Scaling

Auto Scaling allows organizations to scale Amazon EC2 capacity up or down automatically according to conditions defined for the particular workload (see Figure 1.3). Not only can it be used to help maintain application availability and ensure that the desired number of Amazon EC2 instances are running, but it also allows resources to scale in and out to match the demands of dynamic workloads. Instead of provisioning for peak load, organizations can optimize costs and use only the capacity that is actually needed.

FIGURE 1.3   Auto scaling capacity

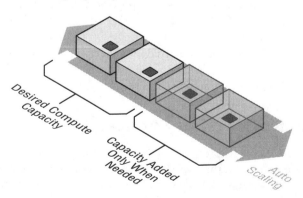

Auto Scaling is well suited both to applications that have stable demand patterns and to applications that experience hourly, daily, or weekly variability in usage.

Elastic Load Balancing

Elastic Load Balancing automatically distributes incoming application traffic across multiple Amazon EC2 instances in the cloud. It enables organizations to achieve greater levels of fault tolerance in their applications, seamlessly providing the required amount of load balancing capacity needed to distribute application traffic.

AWS Elastic Beanstalk

AWS Elastic Beanstalk is the fastest and simplest way to get a web application up and running on AWS. Developers can simply upload their application code, and the service automatically handles all the details, such as resource provisioning, load balancing, Auto Scaling, and monitoring. It provides support for a variety of platforms, including PHP, Java, Python, Ruby, Node.js, .NET, and Go. With AWS Elastic Beanstalk, organizations retain full control over the AWS resources powering the application and can access the underlying resources at any time.

Amazon Virtual Private Cloud (Amazon VPC)

Amazon Virtual Private Cloud (Amazon VPC) lets organizations provision a logically isolated section of the AWS Cloud where they can launch AWS resources in a virtual network that they define. Organizations have complete control over the virtual environment, including selection of the IP address range, creation of subnets, and configuration of route tables and network gateways. In addition, organizations can extend their corporate data center networks to AWS by using hardware or software *virtual private network (VPN)* connections or dedicated circuits by using AWS Direct Connect.

AWS Direct Connect

AWS Direct Connect allows organizations to establish a dedicated network connection from their data center to AWS. Using AWS Direct Connect, organizations can establish private connectivity between AWS and their data center, office, or colocation environment, which in many cases can reduce network costs, increase bandwidth throughput, and provide a more consistent network experience than Internet-based VPN connections.

Amazon Route 53

Amazon Route 53 is a highly available and scalable Domain Name System (DNS) web service. It is designed to give developers and businesses an extremely reliable and cost-effective way to route end users to Internet applications by translating human readable names, such as www.example.com, into the numeric IP addresses, such as 192.0.2.1, that computers use to connect to each other. Amazon Route 53 also serves as domain registrar, allowing you to purchase and manage domains directly from AWS.

Storage and Content Delivery

AWS provides a variety of services to meet your storage needs, such as Amazon Simple Storage Service, Amazon CloudFront, and Amazon Elastic Block Store. This section provides an overview of the storage and content delivery services.

Amazon Simple Storage Service (Amazon S3)

Amazon Simple Storage Service (Amazon S3) provides developers and IT teams with highly durable and scalable object storage that handles virtually unlimited amounts of data and large numbers of concurrent users. Organizations can store any number of objects of any type, such as HTML pages, source code files, image files, and encrypted data, and access them using HTTP-based protocols. Amazon S3 provides cost-effective object storage for a wide variety of use cases, including backup and recovery, nearline archive, big data analytics, disaster recovery, cloud applications, and content distribution.

Amazon Glacier

Amazon Glacier is a secure, durable, and extremely low-cost storage service for data archiving and long-term backup. Organizations can reliably store large or small amounts of data for a very low cost per gigabyte per month. To keep costs low for customers, Amazon Glacier is optimized for infrequently accessed data where a retrieval time of several hours is suitable. Amazon S3 integrates closely with Amazon Glacier to allow organizations to choose the right storage tier for their workloads.

Amazon Elastic Block Store (Amazon EBS)

Amazon Elastic Block Store (Amazon EBS) provides persistent block-level storage volumes for use with Amazon EC2 instances. Each Amazon EBS volume is automatically replicated within its Availability Zone to protect organizations from component failure, offering high availability and durability. By delivering consistent and low-latency performance, Amazon EBS provides the disk storage needed to run a wide variety of workloads.

AWS Storage Gateway

AWS Storage Gateway is a service connecting an on-premises software appliance with cloud-based storage to provide seamless and secure integration between an organization's on-premises IT environment and the AWS storage infrastructure. The service supports industry-standard storage protocols that work with existing applications. It provides low-latency performance by maintaining a cache of frequently accessed data on-premises while securely storing all of your data encrypted in Amazon S3 or Amazon Glacier.

Amazon CloudFront

Amazon CloudFront is a content delivery web service. It integrates with other AWS Cloud services to give developers and businesses an easy way to distribute content to users across the world with low latency, high data transfer speeds, and no minimum usage commitments. Amazon CloudFront can be used to deliver your entire website, including dynamic, static, streaming, and interactive content, using a global network of edge locations. Requests for content are automatically routed to the nearest edge location, so content is delivered with the best possible performance to end users around the globe.

Database Services

AWS provides fully managed relational and NoSQL database services, and in-memory caching as a service and a petabyte-scale data warehouse solution. This section provides an overview of the products that the database services comprise.

Amazon Relational Database Service (Amazon RDS)

Amazon Relational Database Service (Amazon RDS) provides a fully managed relational database with support for many popular open source and commercial database engines. It's a cost-efficient service that allows organizations to launch secure, highly available, fault-tolerant, production-ready databases in minutes. Because Amazon RDS manages time-consuming administration tasks, including backups, software patching, monitoring, scaling, and replication, organizational resources can focus on revenue-generating applications and business instead of mundane operational tasks.

Amazon DynamoDB

Amazon DynamoDB is a fast and flexible NoSQL database service for all applications that need consistent, single-digit millisecond latency at any scale. It is a fully managed database and supports both document and key/value data models. Its flexible data model and reliable performance make it a great fit for mobile, web, gaming, ad-tech, Internet of Things, and many other applications.

Amazon Redshift

Amazon Redshift is a fast, fully managed, petabyte-scale data warehouse service that makes it simple and cost effective to analyze structured data. Amazon Redshift provides a standard SQL interface that lets organizations use existing business intelligence tools. By leveraging columnar storage technology that improves I/O efficiency and parallelizing queries across multiple nodes, Amazon Redshift is able to deliver fast query performance. The Amazon Redshift architecture allows organizations to automate most of the common administrative tasks associated with provisioning, configuring, and monitoring a cloud data warehouse.

Amazon ElastiCache

Amazon ElastiCache is a web service that simplifies deployment, operation, and scaling of an in-memory cache in the cloud. The service improves the performance of web applications by allowing organizations to retrieve information from fast, managed, in-memory caches, instead of relying entirely on slower, disk-based databases. As of this writing, Amazon ElastiCache supports Memcached and Redis cache engines.

Management Tools

AWS provides a variety of tools that help organizations manage your AWS resources. This section provides an overview of the management tools that AWS provides to organizations.

Amazon CloudWatch

Amazon CloudWatch is a monitoring service for AWS Cloud resources and the applications running on AWS. It allows organizations to collect and track metrics, collect and monitor log files, and set alarms. By leveraging Amazon CloudWatch, organizations can gain system-wide visibility into resource utilization, application performance, and operational health. By using these insights, organizations can react, as necessary, to keep applications running smoothly.

AWS CloudFormation

AWS CloudFormation gives developers and systems administrators an effective way to create and manage a collection of related AWS resources, provisioning and updating them in an orderly and predictable fashion. AWS CloudFormation defines a JSON-based templating language that can be used to describe all the AWS resources that are necessary for a workload. Templates can be submitted to AWS CloudFormation and the service will take care of provisioning and configuring those resources in appropriate order (see Figure 1.4).

FIGURE 1.4   AWS CloudFormation workflow summary

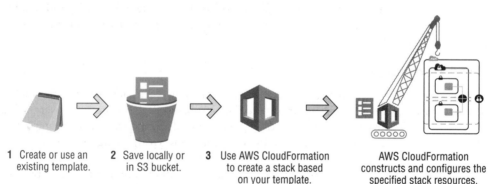

1 Create or use an existing template.   **2** Save locally or in S3 bucket.   **3** Use AWS CloudFormation to create a stack based on your template.   AWS CloudFormation constructs and configures the specified stack resources.

AWS CloudTrail

AWS CloudTrail is a web service that records AWS API calls for an account and delivers log files for audit and review. The recorded information includes the identity of the API caller, the time of the API call, the source IP address of the API caller, the request parameters, and the response elements returned by the service.

AWS Config

AWS Config is a fully managed service that provides organizations with an AWS resource inventory, configuration history, and configuration change notifications to enable security and governance. With AWS Config, organizations can discover existing AWS resources, export an inventory of their AWS resources with all configuration details, and determine how a resource was configured at any point in time. These capabilities enable compliance auditing, security analysis, resource change tracking, and troubleshooting.

Security and Identity

AWS provides security and identity services that help organizations secure their data and systems on the cloud. The following section explores these services at a high level.

AWS Identity and Access Management (IAM)

AWS Identity and Access Management (IAM) enables organizations to securely control access to AWS Cloud services and resources for their users. Using IAM, organizations can create and manage AWS users and groups and use permissions to allow and deny their access to AWS resources.

AWS Key Management Service (KMS)

AWS Key Management Service (KMS) is a managed service that makes it easy for organizations to create and control the encryption keys used to encrypt their data and uses Hardware Security Modules (HSMs) to protect the security of your keys. AWS KMS is integrated with several other AWS Cloud services to help protect data stored with these services.

AWS Directory Service

AWS Directory Service allows organizations to set up and run Microsoft Active Directory on the AWS Cloud or connect their AWS resources with an existing on-premises Microsoft Active Directory. Organizations can use it to manage users and groups, provide single sign-on to applications and services, create and apply Group Policies, domain join Amazon EC2 instances, and simplify the deployment and management of cloud-based Linux and Microsoft Windows workloads.

AWS Certificate Manager

AWS Certificate Manager is a service that lets organizations easily provision, manage, and deploy Secure Sockets Layer/Transport Layer Security (SSL/TLS) certificates for use with AWS Cloud services. It removes the time-consuming manual process of purchasing, uploading, and renewing SSL/TLS certificates. With AWS Certificate Manager, organizations can quickly request a certificate, deploy it on AWS resources such as Elastic Load Balancing or Amazon CloudFront distributions, and let AWS Certificate Manager handle certificate renewals.

AWS Web Application Firewall (WAF)

AWS Web Application Firewall (WAF) helps protect web applications from common attacks and exploits that could affect application availability, compromise security, or consume excessive resources. AWS WAF gives organizations control over which traffic to allow or block to their web applications by defining customizable web security rules.

Application Services

AWS provides a variety of managed services to use with applications. The following section explores the application services at a high level.

Amazon API Gateway

Amazon API Gateway is a fully managed service that makes it easy for developers to create, publish, maintain, monitor, and secure APIs at any scale. Organizations can create an API that acts as a "front door" for applications to access data, business logic, or functionality from back-end services, such as workloads running on Amazon EC2, code running on AWS Lambda, or any web application. Amazon API Gateway handles all the tasks involved in accepting and processing up to hundreds of thousands of concurrent API calls, including traffic management, authorization and access control, monitoring, and API version management.

Amazon Elastic Transcoder

Amazon Elastic Transcoder is media transcoding in the cloud. It is designed to be a highly scalable and cost-effective way for developers and businesses to convert (or transcode) media files from their source formats into versions that will play back on devices like smartphones, tablets, and PCs.

Amazon Simple Notification Service (Amazon SNS)

Amazon Simple Notification Service (Amazon SNS) is a web service that coordinates and manages the delivery or sending of messages to recipients. In Amazon SNS, there are two types of clients—publishers and subscribers—also referred to as producers and consumers. Publishers communicate asynchronously with subscribers by producing and sending a message to a topic, which is a logical access point and communication channel. Subscribers consume or receive the message or notification over one of the supported protocols when they are subscribed to the topic.

Amazon Simple Email Service (Amazon SES)

Amazon Simple Email Service (Amazon SES) is a cost-effective email service that organizations can use to send transactional email, marketing messages, or any other type of content to their customers. Amazon SES can also be used to receive messages and deliver them to an Amazon S3 bucket, call custom code via an AWS Lambda function, or publish notifications to Amazon SNS.

Amazon Simple Workflow Service (Amazon SWF)

Amazon Simple Workflow Service (Amazon SWF) helps developers build, run, and scale background jobs that have parallel or sequential steps. Amazon SWF can be thought of as a fully managed state tracker and task coordinator on the cloud. In common architectural patterns, if your application's steps take more than 500 milliseconds to complete, it is vitally important to track the state of processing and to provide the ability to recover or retry if a task fails. Amazon SWF helps organizations achieve this reliability.

Amazon Simple Queue Service (Amazon SQS)

Amazon Simple Queue Service (Amazon SQS) is a fast, reliable, scalable, fully managed message queuing service. Amazon SQS makes it simple and cost effective to decouple the components of a cloud application. With Amazon SQS, organizations can transmit any volume of data, at any level of throughput, without losing messages or requiring other services to be always available.

Summary

The term "cloud computing" refers to the on-demand delivery of IT resources via the Internet with pay-as-you-go pricing. Instead of buying, owning, and maintaining data centers and servers, organizations can acquire technology such as compute power, storage, databases, and other services on an as-needed basis. With cloud computing, AWS manages and maintains the technology infrastructure in a secure environment and businesses access these resources via the Internet to develop and run their applications. Capacity can grow or shrink instantly and businesses pay only for what they use.

Cloud computing introduces a revolutionary shift in how technology is obtained, used, and managed, and how organizations budget and pay for technology services. While each organization experiences a unique journey to the cloud with numerous benefits, six advantages become apparent time and time again. Understanding these advantages allows architects to shape solutions that deliver continuous benefits to organizations.

AWS provides a highly available technology infrastructure platform with multiple locations worldwide. These locations are composed of regions and Availability Zones. This enables organizations to place resources and data in multiple locations around the globe. Helping to protect the confidentiality, integrity, and availability of systems and data is of the utmost importance to AWS, as is maintaining the trust and confidence of organizations around the world.

AWS offers a broad set of global compute, storage, database, analytics, application, and deployment services that help organizations move faster, lower IT costs, and scale applications. Having a broad understanding of these services allows solutions architects to design effective distributed applications and systems on the AWS platform.

Exam Essentials

Understand the global infrastructure.   AWS provides a highly available technology infrastructure platform with multiple locations worldwide. These locations are composed of regions and Availability Zones. Each region is located in a separate geographic area and has multiple, isolated locations known as Availability Zones.

Understand regions.   An AWS region is a physical geographic location that consists of a cluster of data centers. AWS regions enable the placement of resources and data in multiple locations around the globe. Each region is completely independent and is designed to be completely isolated from the other regions. This achieves the greatest possible fault tolerance and stability. Resources aren't replicated across regions unless organizations choose to do so.

Understand Availability Zones.   An Availability Zone is one or more data centers within a region that are designed to be isolated from failures in other Availability Zones. Availability Zones provide inexpensive, low-latency network connectivity to other zones in the same region. By placing resources in separate Availability Zones, organizations can protect their website or application from a service disruption impacting a single location.

Understand the hybrid deployment model.   A hybrid deployment model is an architectural pattern providing connectivity for infrastructure and applications between cloud-based resources and existing resources that are not located in the cloud.

Review Questions

1. Which of the following describes a physical location around the world where AWS clusters data centers?

   A. Endpoint

   B. Collection

   C. Fleet

   D. Region

2. Each AWS region is composed of two or more locations that offer organizations the ability to operate production systems that are more highly available, fault tolerant, and scalable than would be possible using a single data center. What are these locations called?

   A. Availability Zones

   B. Replication areas

   C. Geographic districts

   D. Compute centers

3. What is the deployment term for an environment that extends an existing on-premises infrastructure into the cloud to connect cloud resources to internal systems?

   A. All-in deployment

   B. Hybrid deployment

   C. On-premises deployment

   D. Scatter deployment

4. Which AWS Cloud service allows organizations to gain system-wide visibility into resource utilization, application performance, and operational health?

   A. AWS Identity and Access Management (IAM)

   B. Amazon Simple Notification Service (Amazon SNS)

   C. Amazon CloudWatch

   D. AWS CloudFormation

5. Which of the following AWS Cloud services is a fully managed NoSQL database service?

   A. Amazon Simple Queue Service (Amazon SQS)

   B. Amazon DynamoDB

   C. Amazon ElastiCache

   D. Amazon Relational Database Service (Amazon RDS)

6. Your company experiences fluctuations in traffic patterns to their e-commerce website based on flash sales. What service can help your company dynamically match the required compute capacity to the spike in traffic during flash sales?

   A. Auto Scaling

   B. Amazon Glacier

    C.   Amazon Simple Notification Service (Amazon SNS)

    D.   Amazon Virtual Private Cloud (Amazon VPC)

7. Your company provides an online photo sharing service. The development team is looking for ways to deliver image files with the lowest latency to end users so the website content is delivered with the best possible performance. What service can help speed up distribution of these image files to end users around the world?

    A.   Amazon Elastic Compute Cloud (Amazon EC2)

    B.   Amazon Route 53

    C.   AWS Storage Gateway

    D.   Amazon CloudFront

8. Your company runs an Amazon Elastic Compute Cloud (Amazon EC2) instance periodically to perform a batch processing job on a large and growing filesystem. At the end of the batch job, you shut down the Amazon EC2 instance to save money but need to persist the filesystem on the Amazon EC2 instance from the previous batch runs. What AWS Cloud service can you leverage to meet these requirements?

    A.   Amazon Elastic Block Store (Amazon EBS)

    B.   Amazon DynamoDB

    C.   Amazon Glacier

    D.   AWS CloudFormation

9. What AWS Cloud service provides a logically isolated section of the AWS Cloud where organizations can launch AWS resources in a virtual network that they define?

    A.   Amazon Simple Workflow Service (Amazon SWF)

    B.   Amazon Route 53

    C.   Amazon Virtual Private Cloud (Amazon VPC)

    D.   AWS CloudFormation

10. Your company provides a mobile voting application for a popular TV show, and 5 to 25 million viewers all vote in a 15-second timespan. What mechanism can you use to decouple the voting application from your back-end services that tally the votes?

    A.   AWS CloudTrail

    B.   Amazon Simple Queue Service (Amazon SQS)

    C.   Amazon Redshift

    D.   Amazon Simple Notification Service (Amazon SNS)

Chapter 2

Amazon Simple Storage Service (Amazon S3) and Amazon Glacier Storage

---

THE AWS CERTIFIED SOLUTIONS ARCHITECT ASSOCIATE EXAM OBJECTIVES COVERED IN THIS CHAPTER MAY INCLUDE, BUT ARE NOT LIMITED TO, THE FOLLOWING:

Domain 1.0: Designing highly available, cost-efficient, fault-tolerant, scalable systems

✓ **1.1 Identify and recognize cloud architecture considerations, such as fundamental components and effective designs.**

Content may include the following:

- How to design cloud services

- Planning and design

- Monitoring and logging

- Familiarity with:

  - Best practices for AWS architecture

  - Developing to client specifications, including pricing/ cost (e.g., On Demand vs. Reserved vs. Spot; Recovery Time Objective [RTO] and Recovery Point Objective [RPO] disaster recovery design)

  - Architectural trade-off decisions (e.g., high availability vs. cost)

  - Hybrid IT architectures

  - Elasticity and scalability

Domain 2.0: Implementation/Deployment

✓ **2.1   Identify the appropriate techniques and methods using Amazon Simple Storage Service (Amazon S3) to code and implement a cloud solution.**

Content may include the following:

- Configure services to support compliance requirements in the cloud.

- Launch instances across the AWS global infrastructure.

- Configure AWS Identity and Access Management (IAM) policies and best practices.

Domain 3.0: Data Security

✓ **3.1   Recognize and implement secure practices for optimum cloud deployment and maintenance**

Content may include the following:

- Security Architecture with AWS

  - "Core" Amazon S3 security feature sets

  - Encryption solutions (e.g., key services)

  - Complex access controls (building sophisticated security groups, Access Control Lists [ACLs], etc.)

Introduction

This chapter is intended to provide you with a basic understanding of the core object storage services available on AWS: Amazon Simple Storage Service (Amazon S3) and Amazon Glacier.

Amazon S3 provides developers and IT teams with secure, durable, and highly-scalable cloud storage. Amazon S3 is easy-to-use *object storage* with a simple web service interface that you can use to store and retrieve any amount of data from anywhere on the web. Amazon S3 also allows you to pay only for the storage you actually use, which eliminates the capacity planning and capacity constraints associated with traditional storage.

Amazon S3 is one of first services introduced by AWS, and it serves as one of the foundational web services—nearly any application running in AWS uses Amazon S3, either directly or indirectly. Amazon S3 can be used alone or in conjunction with other AWS services, and it offers a very high level of integration with many other AWS cloud services. For example, Amazon S3 serves as the durable target storage for Amazon Kinesis and Amazon Elastic MapReduce (Amazon EMR), it is used as the storage for Amazon Elastic Block Store (Amazon EBS) and Amazon Relational Database Service (Amazon RDS) snapshots, and it is used as a data staging or loading storage mechanism for Amazon Redshift and Amazon DynamoDB, among many other functions. Because Amazon S3 is so flexible, so highly integrated, and so commonly used, it is important to understand this service in detail.

Common use cases for Amazon S3 storage include:

- Backup and archive for on-premises or cloud data
- Content, media, and software storage and distribution
- Big data analytics
- Static website hosting
- Cloud-native mobile and Internet application hosting
- Disaster recovery

To support these use cases and many more, Amazon S3 offers a range of *storage classes* designed for various generic use cases: general purpose, infrequent access, and archive. To help manage data through its lifecycle, Amazon S3 offers configurable lifecycle policies. By using lifecycle policies, you can have your data automatically migrate to the most appropriate storage class, without modifying your application code. In order to control who has access to your data, Amazon S3 provides a rich set of permissions, access controls, and encryption options.

Amazon Glacier is another cloud storage service related to Amazon S3, but optimized for data archiving and long-term backup at extremely low cost. Amazon Glacier is suitable for "cold data," which is data that is rarely accessed and for which a retrieval time of three to five hours is acceptable. Amazon Glacier can be used both as a storage class of Amazon S3 (see Storage Classes and Object Lifecycle Management topics in the Amazon S3 Advanced Features section), and as an independent archival storage service (see the Amazon Glacier section).

Object Storage versus Traditional Block and File Storage

In traditional IT environments, two kinds of storage dominate: *block storage* and *file storage*. Block storage operates at a lower level—the raw storage device level—and manages data as a set of numbered, fixed-size blocks. File storage operates at a higher level—the operating system level—and manages data as a named hierarchy of files and folders. Block and file storage are often accessed over a network in the form of a Storage Area Network (SAN) for block storage, using protocols such as iSCSI or Fibre Channel, or as a Network Attached Storage (NAS) file server or "filer" for file storage, using protocols such as Common Internet File System (CIFS) or Network File System (NFS). Whether directly-attached or network-attached, block or file, this kind of storage is very closely associated with the server and the operating system that is using the storage.

Amazon S3 object storage is something quite different. Amazon S3 is cloud *object storage*. Instead of being closely associated with a server, Amazon S3 storage is independent of a server and is accessed over the Internet. Instead of managing data as blocks or files using SCSI, CIFS, or NFS protocols, data is managed as objects using an Application Program Interface (API) built on standard HTTP verbs.

Each Amazon S3 object contains both data and metadata. Objects reside in containers called *buckets*, and each object is identified by a unique user-specified key (filename). Buckets are a simple flat folder with no file system hierarchy. That is, you can have multiple buckets, but you can't have a sub-bucket within a bucket. Each bucket can hold an unlimited number of objects.

It is easy to think of an Amazon S3 object (or the data portion of an object) as a file, and the key as the filename. However, keep in mind that Amazon S3 is not a traditional file system and differs in significant ways. In Amazon S3, you GET an object or PUT an object, operating on the whole object at once, instead of incrementally updating portions of the object as you would with a file. You can't "mount" a bucket, "open" an object, install an operating system on Amazon S3, or run a database on it.

Instead of a file system, Amazon S3 is highly-durable and highly-scalable object storage that is optimized for reads and is built with an intentionally minimalistic feature set. It provides a simple and robust abstraction for file storage that frees you from many underlying details that you normally do have to deal with in traditional storage. For example, with Amazon S3 you don't have to worry about device or file system storage limits and capacity planning—a single bucket can store an unlimited number of files. You also don't need to worry about data durability or replication across Availability Zones—Amazon S3 objects are automatically replicated on multiple devices in multiple facilities within a region. The same with scalability—if your request rate grows steadily, Amazon S3 automatically partitions buckets to support very high request rates and simultaneous access by many clients.

> If you need traditional block or file storage in addition to Amazon S3 storage, AWS provides options. The Amazon EBS service provides block level storage for Amazon Elastic Compute Cloud (Amazon EC2) instances. Amazon Elastic File System (AWS EFS) provides network-attached shared file storage (NAS storage) using the NFS v4 protocol.

Amazon Simple Storage Service (Amazon S3) Basics

Now that you have an understanding of some of the key differences between traditional block and file storage versus cloud object storage, we can explore the basics of Amazon S3 in more detail.

Buckets

A *bucket* is a container (web folder) for objects (files) stored in Amazon S3. Every Amazon S3 object is contained in a bucket. Buckets form the top-level namespace for Amazon S3, and bucket names are global. This means that your bucket names must be unique across all AWS accounts, much like Domain Name System (DNS) domain names, not just within your own account. Bucket names can contain up to 63 lowercase letters, numbers, hyphens, and periods. You can create and use multiple buckets; you can have up to 100 per account by default.

> It is a best practice to use bucket names that contain your domain name and conform to the rules for DNS names. This ensures that your bucket names are your own, can be used in all regions, and can host static websites.

AWS Regions

Even though the namespace for Amazon S3 buckets is global, each Amazon S3 bucket is created in a specific region that you choose. This lets you control where your data is stored. You can create and use buckets that are located close to a particular set of end users or customers in order to minimize latency, or located in a particular region to satisfy data locality and sovereignty concerns, or located far away from your primary facilities in order to satisfy disaster recovery and compliance needs. You control the location of your data; data in an Amazon S3 bucket is stored in that region unless you explicitly copy it to another bucket located in a different region.

Objects

Objects are the entities or files stored in Amazon S3 buckets. An object can store virtually any kind of data in any format. Objects can range in size from 0 bytes up to 5TB, and a single bucket can store an unlimited number of objects. This means that Amazon S3 can store a virtually unlimited amount of data.

Each object consists of data (the file itself) and *metadata* (data about the file). The data portion of an Amazon S3 object is opaque to Amazon S3. This means that an object's data is treated as simply a stream of bytes—Amazon S3 doesn't know or care what type of data you are storing, and the service doesn't act differently for text data versus binary data.

The metadata associated with an Amazon S3 object is a set of name/value pairs that describe the object. There are two types of metadata: system metadata and user metadata. System metadata is created and used by Amazon S3 itself, and it includes things like the date last modified, object size, MD5 digest, and HTTP Content-Type. User metadata is optional, and it can only be specified at the time an object is created. You can use custom metadata to tag your data with attributes that are meaningful to you.

Keys

Every object stored in an S3 bucket is identified by a unique identifier called a *key*. You can think of the key as a filename. A key can be up to 1024 bytes of Unicode UTF-8 characters, including embedded slashes, backslashes, dots, and dashes.

Keys must be unique within a single bucket, but different buckets can contain objects with the same key. The combination of bucket, key, and optional version ID uniquely identifies an Amazon S3 object.

Object URL

Amazon S3 is storage for the Internet, and every Amazon S3 object can be addressed by a unique URL formed using the web services endpoint, the bucket name, and the object key. For example, with the URL:

```
http://mybucket.s3.amazonaws.com/jack.doc
```

mybucket is the S3 bucket name, and jack.doc is the key or filename. If another object is created, for instance:

```
http://mybucket.s3.amazonaws.com/fee/fi/fo/fum/jack.doc
```

then the bucket name is still mybucket, but now the key or filename is the string fee/fi/fo/fum/jack.doc. A key may contain delimiter characters like slashes or backslashes to help you name and logically organize your Amazon S3 objects, but to Amazon S3 it is simply a long key name in a flat namespace. There is no actual file and folder hierarchy. See the topic "Prefixes and Delimiters" in the "Amazon S3 Advanced Features" section that follows for more information.

For convenience, the Amazon S3 console and the Prefix and Delimiter feature allow you to navigate within an Amazon S3 bucket as if there were a folder hierarchy. However, remember that a bucket is a single flat namespace of keys with no structure.

Amazon S3 Operations

The Amazon S3 API is intentionally simple, with only a handful of common operations. They include:

- Create/delete a bucket
- Write an object
- Read an object
- Delete an object
- List keys in a bucket

REST Interface

The native interface for Amazon S3 is a *REST (Representational State Transfer)* API. With the REST interface, you use standard HTTP or HTTPS requests to create and delete buckets, list keys, and read and write objects. REST maps standard HTTP "verbs" (HTTP methods) to the familiar CRUD (Create, Read, Update, Delete) operations. Create is HTTP PUT (and sometimes POST); read is HTTP GET; delete is HTTP DELETE; and update is HTTP POST (or sometimes PUT).

Always use HTTPS for Amazon S3 API requests to ensure that your requests and data are secure.

In most cases, users do not use the REST interface directly, but instead interact with Amazon S3 using one of the higher-level interfaces available. These include the AWS Software Development Kits (SDKs) (wrapper libraries) for iOS, Android, JavaScript, Java, .NET, Node.js, PHP, Python, Ruby, Go, and C++, the AWS Command Line Interface (CLI), and the AWS Management Console.

Amazon S3 originally supported a SOAP (Simple Object Access Protocol) API in addition to the REST API, but you should use the REST API. The legacy HTTPS endpoint is still available, but new features are not supported.

Durability and Availability

Data *durability* and *availability* are related but slightly different concepts. Durability addresses the question, "Will my data still be there in the future?" Availability addresses the question, "Can I access my data right now?" Amazon S3 is designed to provide both very high durability and very high availability for your data.

Amazon S3 standard storage is designed for 99.999999999% durability and 99.99% availability of objects over a given year. For example, if you store 10,000 objects with Amazon S3, you can on average expect to incur a loss of a single object once every 10,000,000 years. Amazon S3 achieves high durability by automatically storing data redundantly on multiple devices in multiple facilities within a region. It is designed to sustain the concurrent loss of data in two facilities without loss of user data. Amazon S3 provides a highly durable storage infrastructure designed for mission-critical and primary data storage.

If you need to store non-critical or easily reproducible derived data (such as image thumbnails) that doesn't require this high level of durability, you can choose to use Reduced Redundancy Storage (RRS) at a lower cost. RRS offers 99.99% durability with a lower cost of storage than traditional Amazon S3 storage.

> Even though Amazon S3 storage offers very high durability at the infrastructure level, it is still a best practice to protect against user-level accidental deletion or overwriting of data by using additional features such as versioning, cross-region replication, and MFA Delete.

Data Consistency

Amazon S3 is an *eventually consistent* system. Because your data is automatically replicated across multiple servers and locations within a region, changes in your data may take some time to propagate to all locations. As a result, there are some situations where information that you read immediately after an update may return stale data.

For PUTs to new objects, this is not a concern—in this case, Amazon S3 provides read-after-write consistency. However, for PUTs to existing objects (object overwrite to an existing key) and for object DELETEs, Amazon S3 provides *eventual consistency*.

Eventual consistency means that if you PUT new data to an existing key, a subsequent GET might return the old data. Similarly, if you DELETE an object, a subsequent GET for that object might still read the deleted object. In all cases, updates to a single key are atomic— for eventually-consistent reads, you will get the new data or the old data, but never an inconsistent mix of data.

Access Control

Amazon S3 is secure by default; when you create a bucket or object in Amazon S3, only you have access. To allow you to give controlled access to others, Amazon S3 provides both coarse-grained access controls (Amazon S3 Access Control Lists [ACLs]), and fine-grained

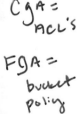

access controls (Amazon S3 bucket policies, AWS Identity and Access Management [IAM] policies, and query-string authentication).

Amazon S3 ACLs allow you to grant certain coarse-grained permissions: READ, WRITE, or FULL-CONTROL at the object or bucket level. ACLs are a legacy access control mechanism, created before IAM existed. ACLs are best used today for a limited set of use cases, such as enabling bucket logging or making a bucket that hosts a static website be world-readable.

Amazon S3 bucket policies are the recommended access control mechanism for Amazon S3 and provide much finer-grained control. Amazon S3 bucket policies are very similar to IAM policies, which were discussed in Chapter 6, "AWS Identity and Access Management (IAM)," but are subtly different in that:

- They are associated with the bucket resource instead of an IAM principal.
- They include an explicit reference to the IAM principal in the policy. This principal can be associated with a different AWS account, so Amazon S3 bucket policies allow you to assign cross-account access to Amazon S3 resources.

Using an Amazon S3 bucket policy, you can specify who can access the bucket, from where (by Classless Inter-Domain Routing [CIDR] block or IP address), and during what time of day.

Finally, IAM policies may be associated directly with IAM principals that grant access to an Amazon S3 bucket, just as it can grant access to any AWS service and resource. Obviously, you can only assign IAM policies to principals in AWS accounts that you control.

Static Website Hosting

A very common use case for Amazon S3 storage is *static website* hosting. Many websites, particularly micro-sites, don't need the services of a full web server. A static website means that all of the pages of the website contain only static content and do not require server-side processing such as PHP, ASP.NET, or JSP. (Note that this does not mean that the website cannot be interactive and dynamic; this can be accomplished with client-side scripts, such as JavaScript embedded in static HTML webpages.) Static websites have many advantages: they are very fast, very scalable, and can be more secure than a typical dynamic website. If you host a static website on Amazon S3, you can also leverage the security, durability, availability, and scalability of Amazon S3.

Because every Amazon S3 object has a URL, it is relatively straightforward to turn a bucket into a website. To host a static website, you simply configure a bucket for website hosting and then upload the content of the static website to the bucket.

To configure an Amazon S3 bucket for static website hosting:

1. Create a bucket with the same name as the desired website hostname.
2. Upload the static files to the bucket.
3. Make all the files public (world readable).
4. Enable static website hosting for the bucket. This includes specifying an Index document and an Error document.

5. The website will now be available at the S3 website URL:

   `<bucket-name>.s3-website-<AWS-region>.amazonaws.com`.

6. Create a friendly DNS name in your own domain for the website using a DNS CNAME, or an Amazon Route 53 alias that resolves to the Amazon S3 website URL.

7. The website will now be available at your website domain name.

Amazon S3 Advanced Features

Beyond the basics, there are some advanced features of Amazon S3 that you should also be familiar with.

Prefixes and Delimiters

While Amazon S3 uses a flat structure in a bucket, it supports the use of *prefix* and *delimiter* parameters when listing key names. This feature lets you organize, browse, and retrieve the objects within a bucket hierarchically. Typically, you would use a slash (/) or backslash (\) as a delimiter and then use key names with embedded delimiters to emulate a file and folder hierarchy within the flat object key namespace of a bucket.

For example, you might want to store a series of server logs by server name (such as server42), but organized by year and month, like so:

```
logs/2016/January/server42.log
logs/2016/February/server42.log
logs/2016/March/server42.log
```

The REST API, wrapper SDKs, AWS CLI, and the Amazon Management Console all support the use of delimiters and prefixes. This feature lets you logically organize new data and easily maintain the hierarchical folder-and-file structure of existing data uploaded or backed up from traditional file systems. Used together with IAM or Amazon S3 bucket policies, prefixes and delimiters also allow you to create the equivalent of departmental "subdirectories" or user "home directories" within a single bucket, restricting or sharing access to these "subdirectories" (defined by prefixes) as needed.

 Use delimiters and object prefixes to hierarchically organize the objects in your Amazon S3 buckets, but always remember that Amazon S3 is not really a file system.

Storage Classes

Amazon S3 offers a range of *storage classes* suitable for various use cases.

Amazon S3 Standard offers high durability, high availability, low latency, and high performance object storage for general purpose use. Because it delivers low first-byte latency and high throughput, Standard is well-suited for short-term or long-term storage of frequently accessed data. For most general purpose use cases, Amazon S3 Standard is the place to start.

Amazon S3 Standard – Infrequent Access (Standard-IA) offers the same durability, low latency, and high throughput as Amazon S3 Standard, but is designed for long-lived, less frequently accessed data. Standard-IA has a lower per GB-month storage cost than Standard, but the price model also includes a minimum object size (128KB), minimum duration (30 days), and per-GB retrieval costs, so it is best suited for infrequently accessed data that is stored for longer than 30 days.

Amazon S3 Reduced Redundancy Storage (RRS) offers slightly lower durability (4 nines) than Standard or Standard-IA at a reduced cost. It is most appropriate for derived data that can be easily reproduced, such as image thumbnails.

Finally, the *Amazon Glacier* storage class offers secure, durable, and extremely low-cost cloud storage for data that does not require real-time access, such as archives and long-term backups. To keep costs low, Amazon Glacier is optimized for infrequently accessed data where a retrieval time of several hours is suitable. To retrieve an Amazon Glacier object, you issue a restore command using one of the Amazon S3 APIs; three to five hours later, the Amazon Glacier object is copied to Amazon S3 RRS. Note that the restore simply creates a copy in Amazon S3 RRS; the original data object remains in Amazon Glacier until explicitly deleted. Also be aware that Amazon Glacier allows you to retrieve up to 5% of the Amazon S3 data stored in Amazon Glacier for free each month; restores beyond the daily restore allowance incur a restore fee. Refer to the Amazon Glacier pricing page on the AWS website for full details.

In addition to acting as a storage tier in Amazon S3, Amazon Glacier is also a standalone storage service with a separate API and some unique characteristics. However, when you use Amazon Glacier as a storage class of Amazon S3, you always interact with the data via the Amazon S3 APIs. Refer to the Amazon Glacier section for more details.

Set a data retrieval policy to limit restores to the free tier or to a maximum GB-per-hour limit to avoid or minimize Amazon Glacier restore fees.

Object Lifecycle Management

Amazon S3 *Object Lifecycle Management* is roughly equivalent to automated *storage tiering* in traditional IT storage infrastructures. In many cases, data has a natural lifecycle, starting out as "hot" (frequently accessed) data, moving to "warm" (less frequently accessed) data as it ages, and ending its life as "cold" (long-term backup or archive) data before eventual deletion.

For example, many business documents are frequently accessed when they are created, then become much less frequently accessed over time. In many cases, however, compliance rules require business documents to be archived and kept accessible for years. Similarly, studies show that file, operating system, and database backups are most frequently accessed in the first few days after they are created, usually to restore after an inadvertent error. After a week or two, these backups remain a critical asset, but they are much less likely to be accessed for a restore. In many cases, compliance rules require that a certain number of backups be kept for several years.

Using Amazon S3 lifecycle configuration rules, you can significantly reduce your storage costs by automatically transitioning data from one storage class to another or even automatically deleting data after a period of time. For example, the lifecycle rules for backup data might be:

- Store backup data initially in Amazon S3 Standard.
- After 30 days, transition to Amazon Standard-IA.
- After 90 days, transition to Amazon Glacier.
- After 3 years, delete.

Lifecycle configurations are attached to the bucket and can apply to all objects in the bucket or only to objects specified by a prefix.

Encryption

It is strongly recommended that all sensitive data stored in Amazon S3 be encrypted, both in flight and at rest.

To encrypt your Amazon S3 data in flight, you can use the Amazon S3 Secure Sockets Layer (SSL) API endpoints. This ensures that all data sent to and from Amazon S3 is encrypted while in transit using the HTTPS protocol.

To encrypt your Amazon S3 data at rest, you can use several variations of *Server-Side Encryption (SSE)*. Amazon S3 encrypts your data at the object level as it writes it to disks in its data centers and decrypts it for you when you access it. All SSE performed by Amazon S3 and AWS Key Management Service (Amazon KMS) uses the 256-bit Advanced Encryption Standard (AES). You can also encrypt your Amazon S3 data at rest using *Client-Side Encryption*, encrypting your data on the client before sending it to Amazon S3.

SSE-S3 (AWS-Managed Keys)

This is a fully integrated "check-box-style" encryption solution where AWS handles the key management and key protection for Amazon S3. Every object is encrypted with a unique key. The actual object key itself is then further encrypted by a separate master key. A new master key is issued at least monthly, with AWS rotating the keys. Encrypted data, encryption keys, and master keys are all stored separately on secure hosts, further enhancing protection.

SSE-KMS (AWS KMS Keys)

This is a fully integrated solution where Amazon handles your key management and protection for Amazon S3, but where you manage the keys. SSE-KMS offers several additional benefits compared to SSE-S3. Using SSE-KMS, there are separate permissions for using the master key, which provide protection against unauthorized access to your objects stored in Amazon S3 and an additional layer of control. AWS KMS also provides auditing, so you can see who used your key to access which object and when they tried to access this object. AWS KMS also allows you to view any failed attempts to access data from users who did not have permission to decrypt the data.

SSE-C (Customer-Provided Keys)

This is used when you want to maintain your own encryption keys but don't want to manage or implement your own client-side encryption library. With SSE-C, AWS will do the encryption/decryption of your objects while you maintain full control of the keys used to encrypt/decrypt the objects in Amazon S3.

Client-Side Encryption

Client-side encryption refers to encrypting data on the client side of your application before sending it to Amazon S3. You have the following two options for using data encryption keys:

- Use an AWS KMS-managed customer master key.

- Use a client-side master key.

When using client-side encryption, you retain end-to-end control of the encryption process, including management of the encryption keys.

> For maximum simplicity and ease of use, use server-side encryption with AWS-managed keys (SSE-S3 or SSE-KMS).

Versioning

Amazon S3 versioning helps protects your data against accidental or malicious deletion by keeping multiple versions of each object in the bucket, identified by a unique version ID. Versioning allows you to preserve, retrieve, and restore every version of every object stored in your Amazon S3 bucket. If a user makes an accidental change or even maliciously deletes an object in your S3 bucket, you can restore the object to its original state simply by referencing the version ID in addition to the bucket and object key. Versioning is turned on at the bucket level. Once enabled, versioning cannot be removed from a bucket; it can only be suspended.

MFA Delete

MFA Delete adds another layer of data protection on top of bucket versioning. MFA Delete requires additional authentication in order to permanently delete an object version or change the versioning state of a bucket. In addition to your normal security credentials, MFA Delete requires an authentication code (a temporary, one-time password) generated by a hardware or virtual Multi-Factor Authentication (MFA) device. Note that MFA Delete can only be enabled by the root account.

Pre-Signed URLs

All Amazon S3 objects by default are private, meaning that only the owner has access. However, the object owner can optionally share objects with others by creating a *pre-signed URL*, using their own security credentials to grant time-limited permission to download the objects. When you create a pre-signed URL for your object, you must provide your security credentials and specify a bucket name, an object key, the HTTP method (GET to download the object), and an expiration date and time. The pre-signed URLs are valid only for the specified duration. This is particularly useful to protect against "content scraping" of web content such as media files stored in Amazon S3.

Multipart Upload

To better support uploading or copying of large objects, Amazon S3 provides the Multipart Upload API. This allows you to upload large objects as a set of parts, which generally gives better network utilization (through parallel transfers), the ability to pause and resume, and the ability to upload objects where the size is initially unknown.

Multipart upload is a three-step process: initiation, uploading the parts, and completion (or abort). Parts can be uploaded independently in arbitrary order, with retransmission if needed. After all of the parts are uploaded, Amazon S3 assembles the parts in order to create an object.

In general, you *should* use multipart upload for objects larger than 100 Mbytes, and you *must* use multipart upload for objects larger than 5GB. When using the low-level APIs, you must break the file to be uploaded into parts and keep track of the parts. When using the high-level APIs and the high-level Amazon S3 commands in the AWS CLI (aws s3 cp, aws s3 mv, and aws s3 sync), multipart upload is automatically performed for large objects.

You can set an object lifecycle policy on a bucket to abort incomplete multipart uploads after a specified number of days. This will minimize the storage costs associated with multipart uploads that were not completed.

Range GETs

It is possible to download (GET) only a portion of an object in both Amazon S3 and Amazon Glacier by using something called a *Range* GET. Using the Range HTTP header in the GET request or equivalent parameters in one of the SDK wrapper libraries, you specify a range of bytes of the object. This can be useful in dealing with large objects when you have poor connectivity or to download only a known portion of a large Amazon Glacier backup.

Cross-Region Replication

Cross-region replication is a feature of Amazon S3 that allows you to asynchronously replicate all new objects in the source bucket in one AWS region to a target bucket in another region. Any metadata and ACLs associated with the object are also part of the replication. After you set up cross-region replication on your source bucket, any changes to the data, metadata, or ACLs on an object trigger a new replication to the destination bucket. To enable cross-region replication, versioning must be turned on for both source and destination buckets, and you must use an IAM policy to give Amazon S3 permission to replicate objects on your behalf.

Cross-region replication is commonly used to reduce the latency required to access objects in Amazon S3 by placing objects closer to a set of users or to meet requirements to store backup data at a certain distance from the original source data.

If turned on in an existing bucket, cross-region replication will only replicate new objects. Existing objects will not be replicated and must be copied to the new bucket via a separate command.

Logging

In order to track requests to your Amazon S3 bucket, you can enable Amazon S3 server access logs. Logging is off by default, but it can easily be enabled. When you enable logging for a bucket (the source bucket), you must choose where the logs will be stored (the target bucket). You can store access logs in the same bucket or in a different bucket. Either way, it is optional (but a best practice) to specify a prefix, such as logs/ or yourbucketname/ logs/, so that you can more easily identify your logs.

Once enabled, logs are delivered on a best-effort basis with a slight delay. Logs include information such as:

- Requestor account and IP address

- Bucket name

- Request time

- Action (GET, PUT, LIST, and so forth)

- Response status or error code

Event Notifications

Amazon S3 *event notifications* can be sent in response to actions taken on objects uploaded or stored in Amazon S3. Event notifications enable you to run workflows, send alerts, or perform other actions in response to changes in your objects stored in Amazon S3. You can use Amazon S3 event notifications to set up triggers to perform actions, such as transcoding media files when they are uploaded, processing data files when they become available, and synchronizing Amazon S3 objects with other data stores.

Amazon S3 event notifications are set up at the bucket level, and you can configure them through the Amazon S3 console, through the REST API, or by using an AWS SDK. Amazon S3 can publish notifications when new objects are created (by a PUT, POST, COPY, or multipart upload completion), when objects are removed (by a DELETE), or when

Amazon S3 detects that an RRS object was lost. You can also set up event notifications based on object name prefixes and suffixes. Notification messages can be sent through either Amazon Simple Notification Service (Amazon SNS) or Amazon Simple Queue Service (Amazon SQS) or delivered directly to AWS Lambda to invoke AWS Lambda functions.

Best Practices, Patterns, and Performance

It is a common pattern to use Amazon S3 storage in hybrid IT environments and applications. For example, data in on-premises file systems, databases, and compliance archives can easily be backed up over the Internet to Amazon S3 or Amazon Glacier, while the primary application or database storage remains on-premises.

Another common pattern is to use Amazon S3 as bulk "blob" storage for data, while keeping an index to that data in another service, such as Amazon DynamoDB or Amazon RDS. This allows quick searches and complex queries on key names without listing keys continually.

Amazon S3 will scale automatically to support very high request rates, automatically re-partitioning your buckets as needed. If you need request rates higher than 100 requests per second, you may want to review the Amazon S3 best practices guidelines in the Developer Guide. To support higher request rates, it is best to ensure some level of random distribution of keys, for example by including a hash as a prefix to key names.

If you are using Amazon S3 in a GET-intensive mode, such as a static website hosting, for best performance you should consider using an Amazon CloudFront distribution as a caching layer in front of your Amazon S3 bucket.

Amazon Glacier

Amazon Glacier is an extremely low-cost storage service that provides durable, secure, and flexible storage for data archiving and online backup. To keep costs low, Amazon Glacier is designed for infrequently accessed data where a retrieval time of three to five hours is acceptable.

Amazon Glacier can store an unlimited amount of virtually any kind of data, in any format. Common use cases for Amazon Glacier include replacement of traditional tape solutions for long-term backup and archive and storage of data required for compliance purposes. In most cases, the data stored in Amazon Glacier consists of large TAR (Tape Archive) or ZIP files.

Like Amazon S3, Amazon Glacier is extremely durable, storing data on multiple devices across multiple facilities in a region. Amazon Glacier is designed for 99.999999999% durability of objects over a given year.

Archives

In Amazon Glacier, data is stored in *archives*. An archive can contain up to 40TB of data, and you can have an unlimited number of archives. Each archive is assigned a unique archive ID at the time of creation. (Unlike an Amazon S3 object key, you cannot specify a user-friendly archive name.) All archives are automatically encrypted, and archives are immutable—after an archive is created, it cannot be modified.

Vaults

Vaults are containers for archives. Each AWS account can have up to 1,000 vaults. You can control access to your vaults and the actions allowed using IAM policies or vault access policies.

Vaults Locks

You can easily deploy and enforce compliance controls for individual Amazon Glacier vaults with a *vault lock* policy. You can specify controls such as Write Once Read Many (WORM) in a vault lock policy and lock the policy from future edits. Once locked, the policy can no longer be changed.

Data Retrieval

You can retrieve up to 5% of your data stored in Amazon Glacier for free each month, calculated on a daily prorated basis. If you retrieve more than 5%, you will incur retrieval fees based on your maximum retrieval rate. To eliminate or minimize those fees, you can set a data retrieval policy on a vault to limit your retrievals to the free tier or to a specified data rate.

Amazon Glacier versus Amazon Simple Storage Service (Amazon S3)

Amazon Glacier is similar to Amazon S3, but it differs in several key aspects. Amazon Glacier supports 40TB archives versus 5TB objects in Amazon S3. Archives in Amazon Glacier are identified by system-generated archive IDs, while Amazon S3 lets you use "friendly" key names. Amazon Glacier archives are automatically encrypted, while encryption at rest is optional in Amazon S3. However, by using Amazon Glacier as an Amazon S3 storage class together with object lifecycle policies, you can use the Amazon S3 interface to get most of the benefits of Amazon Glacier without learning a new interface.

Summary

Amazon S3 is the core object storage service on AWS, allowing you to store an unlimited amount of data with very high durability.

Common Amazon S3 use cases include backup and archive, web content, big data analytics, static website hosting, mobile and cloud-native application hosting, and disaster recovery.

Amazon S3 is integrated with many other AWS cloud services, including AWS IAM, AWS KMS, Amazon EC2, Amazon EBS, Amazon EMR, Amazon DynamoDB, Amazon Redshift, Amazon SQS, AWS Lambda, and Amazon CloudFront.

Object storage differs from traditional block and file storage. Block storage manages data at a device level as addressable blocks, while file storage manages data at the operating system level as files and folders. Object storage manages data as objects that contain both data and metadata, manipulated by an API.

Amazon S3 buckets are containers for objects stored in Amazon S3. Bucket names must be globally unique. Each bucket is created in a specific region, and data does not leave the region unless explicitly copied by the user.

Amazon S3 objects are files stored in buckets. Objects can be up to 5TB and can contain any kind of data. Objects contain both data and metadata and are identified by keys. Each Amazon S3 object can be addressed by a unique URL formed by the web services endpoint, the bucket name, and the object key.

Amazon S3 has a minimalistic API—create/delete a bucket, read/write/delete objects, list keys in a bucket—and uses a REST interface based on standard HTTP verbs—GET, PUT, POST, and DELETE. You can also use SDK wrapper libraries, the AWS CLI, and the AWS Management Console to work with Amazon S3.

Amazon S3 is highly durable and highly available, designed for 11 nines of durability of objects in a given year and four nines of availability.

Amazon S3 is eventually consistent, but offers read-after-write consistency for new object PUTs.

Amazon S3 objects are private by default, accessible only to the owner. Objects can be marked public readable to make them accessible on the web. Controlled access may be provided to others using ACLs and AWS IAM and Amazon S3 bucket policies.

Static websites can be hosted in an Amazon S3 bucket.

Prefixes and delimiters may be used in key names to organize and navigate data hierarchically much like a traditional file system.

Amazon S3 offers several storage classes suited to different use cases: Standard is designed for general-purpose data needing high performance and low latency. Standard-IA is for less frequently accessed data. RRS offers lower redundancy at lower cost for easily reproduced data. Amazon Glacier offers low-cost durable storage for archive and long-term backups that can are rarely accessed and can accept a three- to five-hour retrieval time.

Object lifecycle management policies can be used to automatically move data between storage classes based on time.

Amazon S3 data can be encrypted using server-side or client-side encryption, and encryption keys can be managed with Amazon KMS.

Versioning and MFA Delete can be used to protect against accidental deletion.

Cross-region replication can be used to automatically copy new objects from a source bucket in one region to a target bucket in another region.

Pre-signed URLs grant time-limited permission to download objects and can be used to protect media and other web content from unauthorized "web scraping."

Multipart upload can be used to upload large objects, and Range GETs can be used to download portions of an Amazon S3 object or Amazon Glacier archive.

Server access logs can be enabled on a bucket to track requestor, object, action, and response.

Amazon S3 event notifications can be used to send an Amazon SQS or Amazon SNS message or to trigger an AWS Lambda function when an object is created or deleted.

Amazon Glacier can be used as a standalone service or as a storage class in Amazon S3.

Amazon Glacier stores data in archives, which are contained in vaults. You can have up to 1,000 vaults, and each vault can store an unlimited number of archives.

Amazon Glacier vaults can be locked for compliance purposes.

Exam Essentials

Know what Amazon S3 is and what it is commonly used for.   Amazon S3 is secure, durable, and highly scalable cloud storage that can be used to store an unlimited amount of data in almost any format using a simple web services interface. Common use cases include backup and archive, content storage and distribution, big data analytics, static website hosting, cloud-native application hosting, and disaster recovery.

Understand how object storage differs from block and file storage.   Amazon S3 cloud object storage manages data at the application level as objects using a REST API built on HTTP. Block storage manages data at the operating system level as numbered addressable blocks using protocols such as SCSI or Fibre Channel. File storage manages data as shared files at the operating system level using a protocol such as CIFS or NFS.

Understand the basics of Amazon S3.   Amazon S3 stores data in objects that contain data and metadata. Objects are identified by a user-defined key and are stored in a simple flat folder called a bucket. Interfaces include a native REST interface, SDKs for many languages, an AWS CLI, and the AWS Management Console.

Know how to create a bucket; how to upload, download, and delete objects; how to make objects public; and how to open an object URL.

Understand the durability, availability, and data consistency model of Amazon S3.   Amazon S3 standard storage is designed for 11 nines durability and four nines availability of objects over a year. Other storage classes differ. Amazon S3 is eventually consistent, but offers read-after-write consistency for PUTs to new objects.

Know how to enable static website hosting on Amazon S3.   To create a static website on Amazon S3, you must create a bucket with the website hostname, upload your static content and make it public, enable static website hosting on the bucket, and indicate the index and error page objects.

Know how to protect your data on Amazon S3.   Encrypt data in flight using HTTPS and at rest using SSE or client-side encryption. Enable versioning to keep multiple versions of an object in a bucket. Enable MFA Delete to protect against accidental deletion. Use ACLs Amazon S3 bucket policies and AWS IAM policies for access control. Use pre-signed URLs for time-limited download access. Use cross-region replication to automatically replicate data to another region.

Know the use case for each of the Amazon S3 storage classes.   Standard is for general purpose data that needs high durability, high performance, and low latency access. Standard-IA is for data that is less frequently accessed, but that needs the same performance and availability when accessed. RRS offers lower durability at lower cost for easily replicated data. Amazon Glacier is for storing rarely accessed archival data at lowest cost, when three- to five-hour retrieval time is acceptable.

Know how to use lifecycle configuration rules.   Lifecycle rules can be configured in the AWS Management Console or the APIs. Lifecycle configuration rules define actions to transition objects from one storage class to another based on time.

Know how to use Amazon S3 event notifications.   Event notifications are set at the bucket level and can trigger a message in Amazon SNS or Amazon SQS or an action in AWS Lambda in response to an upload or a delete of an object.

Know the basics of Amazon Glacier as a standalone service.   Data is stored in encrypted archives that can be as large as 40TB. Archives typically contain TAR or ZIP files. Vaults are containers for archives, and vaults can be locked for compliance.

Exercises

For assistance in completing the following exercises, reference the following documentation:

- Getting started with Amazon S3:
  http://docs.aws.amazon.com/AmazonS3/latest/gsg/GetStartedWithS3.html
- Setting up a static website:
  http://docs.aws.amazon.com/AmazonS3/latest/dev/HostingWebsiteOnS3Setup.html
- Using versioning:
  http://docs.aws.amazon.com/AmazonS3/latest/dev/Versioning.html
- Object Lifecycle Management:
  http://docs.aws.amazon.com/AmazonS3/latest/dev/object-lifecycle-mgmt.html

EXERCISE 2.1

Create an Amazon Simple Storage Service (Amazon S3) Bucket

In this exercise, you will create a new Amazon S3 bucket in your selected region. You will use this bucket in the following exercises.

1. Log in to the AWS Management Console.

2. Choose an appropriate region, such as US West (Oregon).

3. Navigate to the Amazon S3 console. Notice that the region indicator now says Global. Remember that Amazon S3 buckets form a global namespace, even though each bucket is created in a specific region.

4. Start the create bucket process.

5. When prompted for Bucket Name, use **mynewbucket**.

6. Choose a region, such as US West (Oregon).

7. Try to create the bucket. You almost surely will get a message that the requested bucket name is not available. Remember that a bucket name must be unique globally.

8. Try again using your surname followed by a hyphen and then today's date in a six-digit format as the bucket name (a bucket name that is not likely to exist already).

You should now have a new Amazon S3 bucket.

EXERCISE 2.2

Upload, Make Public, Rename, and Delete Objects in Your Bucket

In this exercise, you will upload a new object to your bucket. You will then make this object public and view the object in your browser. You will then rename the object and finally delete it from the bucket.

Upload an Object

1. Load your new bucket in the Amazon S3 console.

2. Select Upload, then Add Files.

3. Locate a file on your PC that you are okay with uploading to Amazon S3 and making public to the Internet. (We suggest using a non-personal image file for the purposes of this exercise.)

4. Select a suitable file, then Start Upload. You will see the status of your file in the Transfers section.

5. After your file is uploaded, the status should change to Done.

The file you uploaded is now stored as an Amazon S3 object and should be now listed in the contents of your bucket.

Open the Amazon S3 URL

6. Now open the properties for the object. The properties should include bucket, name, and link.

7. Copy the Amazon S3 URL for the object.

8. Paste the URL in the address bar of a new browser window or tab.

You should get a message with an XML error code `AccessDenied`. Even though the object has a URL, it is private by default, so it cannot be accessed by a web browser.

Make the Object Public

9. Go back to the Amazon S3 Console and select Make Public. (Equivalently, you can change the object's permissions and add grantee Everyone and permissions Open/Download.)

10. Copy the Amazon S3 URL again and try to open it in a browser or tab. Your public image file should now display in the browser or browser tab.

Rename Object

11. In the Amazon S3 console, select Rename.

12. Rename the object, but keep the same file extension.

13. Copy the new Amazon S3 URL and try to open it in a browser or tab. You should see the same image file.

Delete the Object

14. In the Amazon S3 console, select Delete. Select OK when prompted if you want to delete the object.

15. The object has now been deleted.

16. To verify, try to reload the deleted object's Amazon S3 URL.

You should once again get the XML `AccessDenied` error message.

Enable Version Control

In this exercise, you will enable version control on your newly created bucket.

Enable Versioning

1. In the Amazon S3 console, load the properties of your bucket. Don't open the bucket.

2.   Enable versioning in the properties and select OK to verify. Your bucket now has versioning enabled. (Note that versioning can be suspended, but not turned off.)

Create Multiple Versions of an Object

3.   Create a text file named foo.txt on your computer and write the word **blue** in the text file.

4.   Save the text file to a location of your choosing.

5.   Upload the text file to your bucket. This will be version 1.

6.   After you have uploaded the text file to your bucket, open the copy on your local computer and change the word **blue** to **red**. Save the text file with the original filename.

7.   Upload the modified file to your bucket.

8.   Select Show Versions on the uploaded object.

You will now see two different versions of the object with different Version IDs and possibly different sizes. Note that when you select Show Version, the Amazon S3 URL now includes the version ID in the query string after the object name.

EXERCISE 2.4

Delete an Object and Then Restore It

In this exercise, you will delete an object in your Amazon S3 bucket and then restore it.

Delete an Object

1.   Open the bucket containing the text file for which you now have two versions.

2.   Select Hide Versions.

3.   Select Delete, and then select OK to verify.

4.   Your object will now be deleted, and you can no longer see the object.

5.   Select Show Versions.

Both versions of the object now show their version IDs.

Restore an Object

6.   Open your bucket.

7.   Select Show Versions.

8.   Select the oldest version and download the object. Note that the filename is simply foo.txt with no version indicator.

EXERCISE 2.4 *(continued)*

9. Upload foo.txt to the same bucket.

10. Select Hide Versions, and the file foo.txt should re-appear.

To restore a version, you copy the desired version into the same bucket. In the Amazon S3 console, this requires a download then re-upload of the object. Using APIs, SDKs, or AWS CLI, you can copy a version directly without downloading and re-uploading.

EXERCISE 2.5

Lifecycle Management

In this exercise, you will explore the various options for lifecycle management.

1. Select your bucket in the Amazon S3 console.

2. Under Properties, add a Lifecycle Rule.

3. Explore the various options to add lifecycle rules to objects in this bucket. It is recommended that you do not implement any of these options, as you may incur additional costs. After you have finished, click the Cancel button.

Most lifecycle rules require some number of days to expire before the transition takes effect. For example, it takes a minimum of 30 days to transition from Amazon S3 Standard to Amazon S3 Standard-IA. This makes it impractical to create a lifecycle rule and see the actual result in an exercise.

EXERCISE 2.6

Enable Static Hosting on Your Bucket

In this exercise, you will enable static hosting on your newly created bucket.

1. Select your bucket in the Amazon S3 console.

2. In the Properties section, select Enable Website Hosting.

3. For the index document name, enter **index.txt**, and for the error document name, enter **error.txt**.

4. Use a text editor to create two text files and save them as **index.txt** and **error.txt**. In the index.txt file, write the phrase "**Hello World**," and in the error.txt file, write the phrase "**Error Page**." Save both text files and upload them to your bucket.

5. Make the two objects public.

6. Copy the Endpoint: link under Static Website Hosting and paste it in a browser window or tab. You should now see the phrase "Hello World" displayed.

7. In the address bar in your browser, try adding a forward slash followed by a made-up filename (for example, /test.html). You should now see the phrase "Error Page" displayed.

8. To clean up, delete all of the objects in your bucket and then delete the bucket itself.

Review Questions

1. In what ways does Amazon Simple Storage Service (Amazon S3) object storage differ from block and file storage? (Choose 2 answers)

    A. Amazon S3 stores data in fixed size blocks.

    B. Objects are identified by a numbered address.

    C. Objects can be any size.

    D. Objects contain both data and metadata.

    E. Objects are stored in buckets.

2. Which of the following are not appropriates use cases for Amazon Simple Storage Service (Amazon S3)? (Choose 2 answers)

    A. Storing web content

    B. Storing a file system mounted to an Amazon Elastic Compute Cloud (Amazon EC2) instance

    C. Storing backups for a relational database

    D. Primary storage for a database

    E. Storing logs for analytics

3. What are some of the key characteristics of Amazon Simple Storage Service (Amazon S3)? (Choose 3 answers)

    A. All objects have a URL.

    B. Amazon S3 can store unlimited amounts of data.

    C. Objects are world-readable by default.

    D. Amazon S3 uses a REST (Representational State Transfer) Application Program Interface (API).

    E. You must pre-allocate the storage in a bucket.

4. Which features can be used to restrict access to Amazon Simple Storage Service (Amazon S3) data? (Choose 3 answers)

    A. Enable static website hosting on the bucket.

    B. Create a pre-signed URL for an object.

    C. Use an Amazon S3 Access Control List (ACL) on a bucket or object.

    D. Use a lifecycle policy.

    E. Use an Amazon S3 bucket policy.

5. Your application stores critical data in Amazon Simple Storage Service (Amazon S3), which must be protected against inadvertent or intentional deletion. How can this data be protected? (Choose 2 answers)

    A. Use cross-region replication to copy data to another bucket automatically.

    B. Set a vault lock.

    C.   Enable versioning on the bucket.

    D.   Use a lifecycle policy to migrate data to Amazon Glacier.

    E.   Enable MFA Delete on the bucket.

6.   Your company stores documents in Amazon Simple Storage Service (Amazon S3), but it wants to minimize cost. Most documents are used actively for only about a month, then much less frequently. However, all data needs to be available within minutes when requested. How can you meet these requirements?

    A.   Migrate the data to Amazon S3 Reduced Redundancy Storage (RRS) after 30 days.

    B.   Migrate the data to Amazon Glacier after 30 days.

    C.   Migrate the data to Amazon S3 Standard – Infrequent Access (IA) after 30 days.

    D.   Turn on versioning, then migrate the older version to Amazon Glacier.

7.   How is data stored in Amazon Simple Storage Service (Amazon S3) for high durability?

    A.   Data is automatically replicated to other regions.

    B.   Data is automatically replicated within a region.

    C.   Data is replicated only if versioning is enabled on the bucket.

    D.   Data is automatically backed up on tape and restored if needed.

8.   Based on the following Amazon Simple Storage Service (Amazon S3) URL, which one of the following statements is correct?

`https://bucket1.abc.com.s3.amazonaws.com/folderx/myfile.doc`

    A.   The object "myfile.doc" is stored in the folder "folderx" in the bucket "bucket1.abc.com."

    B.   The object "myfile.doc" is stored in the bucket "bucket1.abc.com."

    C.   The object "folderx/myfile.doc" is stored in the bucket "bucket1.abc.com."

    D.   The object "myfile.doc" is stored in the bucket "bucket1."

9.   To have a record of who accessed your Amazon Simple Storage Service (Amazon S3) data and from where, you should do what?

    A.   Enable versioning on the bucket.

    B.   Enable website hosting on the bucket.

    C.   Enable server access logs on the bucket.

    D.   Create an AWS Identity and Access Management (IAM) bucket policy.

    E.   Enable Amazon CloudWatch logs.

10.   What are some reasons to enable cross-region replication on an Amazon Simple Storage Service (Amazon S3) bucket? (Choose 2 answers)

    A.   You want a backup of your data in case of accidental deletion.

    B.   You have a set of users or customers who can access the second bucket with lower latency.

    C.   For compliance reasons, you need to store data in a location at least 300 miles away from the first region.

    D.   Your data needs at least five nines of durability.

11. Your company requires that all data sent to external storage be encrypted before being sent. Which Amazon Simple Storage Service (Amazon S3) encryption solution will meet this requirement?

A. Server-Side Encryption (SSE) with AWS-managed keys (SSE-S3)

B. SSE with customer-provided keys (SSE-C)

C. Client-side encryption with customer-managed keys

D. Server-side encryption with AWS Key Management Service (AWS KMS) keys (SSE-KMS)

12. You have a popular web application that accesses data stored in an Amazon Simple Storage Service (Amazon S3) bucket. You expect the access to be very read-intensive, with expected request rates of up to 500 GETs per second from many clients. How can you increase the performance and scalability of Amazon S3 in this case?

A. Turn on cross-region replication to ensure that data is served from multiple locations.

B. Ensure randomness in the namespace by including a hash prefix to key names.

C. Turn on server access logging.

D. Ensure that key names are sequential to enable pre-fetch.

13. What is needed before you can enable cross-region replication on an Amazon Simple Storage Service (Amazon S3) bucket? (Choose 2 answers)

A. Enable versioning on the bucket.

B. Enable a lifecycle rule to migrate data to the second region.

C. Enable static website hosting.

D. Create an AWS Identity and Access Management (IAM) policy to allow Amazon S3 to replicate objects on your behalf.

14. Your company has 100TB of financial records that need to be stored for seven years by law. Experience has shown that any record more than one-year old is unlikely to be accessed. Which of the following storage plans meets these needs in the most cost efficient manner?

A. Store the data on Amazon Elastic Block Store (Amazon EBS) volumes attached to t2.micro instances.

B. Store the data on Amazon Simple Storage Service (Amazon S3) with lifecycle policies that change the storage class to Amazon Glacier after one year and delete the object after seven years.

C. Store the data in Amazon DynamoDB and run daily script to delete data older than seven years.

D. Store the data in Amazon Elastic MapReduce (Amazon EMR).

15. Amazon Simple Storage Service (S3) bucket policies can restrict access to an Amazon S3 bucket and objects by which of the following? (Choose 3 answers)

A. Company name

B. IP address range

C. AWS account

    D.   Country of origin

    E.   Objects with a specific prefix

16. Amazon Simple Storage Service (Amazon S3) is an eventually consistent storage system. For what kinds of operations is it possible to get stale data as a result of eventual consistency? (Choose 2 answers)

    A.   GET after PUT of a new object

    B.   GET or LIST after a DELETE

    C.   GET after overwrite PUT (PUT to an existing key)

    D.   DELETE after PUT of new object

17. What must be done to host a static website in an Amazon Simple Storage Service (Amazon S3) bucket? (Choose 3 answers)

    A.   Configure the bucket for static hosting and specify an index and error document.

    B.   Create a bucket with the same name as the website.

    C.   Enable File Transfer Protocol (FTP) on the bucket.

    D.   Make the objects in the bucket world-readable.

    E.   Enable HTTP on the bucket.

18. You have valuable media files hosted on AWS and want them to be served only to authenticated users of your web application. You are concerned that your content could be stolen and distributed for free. How can you protect your content?

    A.   Use static web hosting.

    B.   Generate pre-signed URLs for content in the web application.

    C.   Use AWS Identity and Access Management (IAM) policies to restrict access.

    D.   Use logging to track your content.

19. Amazon Glacier is well-suited to data that is which of the following? (Choose 2 answers)

    A.   Is infrequently or rarely accessed

    B.   Must be immediately available when needed

    C.   Is available after a three- to five-hour restore period

    D.   Is frequently erased within 30 days

20. Which statements about Amazon Glacier are true? (Choose 3 answers)

    A.   Amazon Glacier stores data in objects that live in archives.

    B.   Amazon Glacier archives are identified by user-specified key names.

    C.   Amazon Glacier archives take three to five hours to restore.

    D.   Amazon Glacier vaults can be locked.

    E.   Amazon Glacier can be used as a standalone service and as an Amazon S3 storage class.

Amazon Elastic Compute Cloud (Amazon EC2) and Amazon Elastic Block Store (Amazon EBS)

THE AWS CERTIFIED SOLUTIONS ARCHITECT ASSOCIATE EXAM OBJECTIVES COVERED IN THIS CHAPTER MAY INCLUDE, BUT ARE NOT LIMITED TO, THE FOLLOWING:

Domain 1.0: Designing highly available, cost-efficient, fault-tolerant, scalable systems

✓ **1.1 Identify and recognize cloud architecture considerations, such as fundamental components and effective designs.**

Content may include the following:

- How to design cloud services
- Planning and design
- Monitoring and logging

Domain 2.0: Implementation/Deployment

✓ **2.1 Identify the appropriate techniques and methods using Amazon EC2, Amazon Simple Storage Service (Amazon S3), AWS Elastic Beanstalk, AWS CloudFormation, AWS OpsWorks, Amazon Virtual Private Cloud (Amazon VPC), and AWS Identity and Access Management (IAM) to code and implement a cloud solution.**

Content may include the following:

- Configure an Amazon Machine Image (AMI)
- Configure services to support compliance requirements in the cloud
- Launch instances across the AWS global infrastructure

Domain 3.0: Data Security

✓ **3.2 Recognize critical disaster recovery techniques and their implementation.**

Content may include the following:

- Disaster recovery
- Amazon EB

Introduction

In this chapter, you learn how Amazon Elastic Compute Cloud (Amazon EC2) and Amazon Elastic Block Store (Amazon EBS) provide the basic elements of compute and block-level storage to run your workloads on AWS. It focuses on key topics you need to understand for the exam, including:

- How instance types and Amazon Machine Images (AMIs) define the capabilities of instances you launch on the cloud
- How to securely access your instances running on the cloud
- How to protect your instances with virtual firewalls called security groups
- How to have your instances configure themselves for unattended launch
- How to monitor and manage your instances on the cloud
- How to change the capabilities of an existing instance
- The payment options available for the best mix of affordability and flexibility
- How tenancy options and placement groups provide options to optimize compliance and performance
- How instance stores differ from Amazon EBS volumes and when they are effective
- What types of volumes are available through Amazon EBS
- How to protect your data on Amazon EBS

Amazon Elastic Compute Cloud (Amazon EC2)

Amazon EC2 is AWS primary web service that provides resizable compute capacity in the cloud.

Compute Basics

Compute refers to the amount of computational power required to fulfill your workload. If your workload is very small, such as a website that receives few visitors, then your compute needs are very small. A large workload, such as screening ten million compounds against a common cancer target, might require a great deal of compute. The amount of compute you need might change drastically over time.

Amazon EC2 allows you to acquire compute through the launching of virtual servers called *instances*. When you launch an instance, you can make use of the compute as you wish, just as you would with an on-premises server. Because you are paying for the computing power of the instance, you are charged per hour while the instance is running. When you stop the instance, you are no longer charged.

There are two concepts that are key to launching instances on AWS: (1) the amount of virtual hardware dedicated to the instance and (2) the software loaded on the instance. These two dimensions of new instances are controlled, respectively, by the instance type and the AMI.

Instance Types

The instance type defines the virtual hardware supporting an Amazon EC2 instance. There are dozens of instance types available, varying in the following dimensions:

- Virtual CPUs (vCPUs)
- Memory
- Storage (size and type)
- Network performance

Instance types are grouped into families based on the ratio of these values to each other. For instance, the m4 family provides a balance of compute, memory, and network resources, and it is a good choice for many applications. Within each family there are several choices that scale up linearly in size. Figure 3.1 shows the four instance sizes in the m4 family. Note that the ratio of vCPUs to memory is constant as the sizes scale linearly. The hourly price for each size scales linearly as well. For example, an m4.xlarge instance costs twice as much as the m4.large instance.

FIGURE 3.1   Memory and vCPUs for the m4 instance family

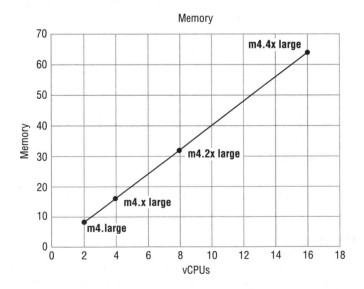

Different instance type families tilt the ratio to accommodate different types of workloads, but they all exhibit this linear scale up behavior within the family. Table 3.1 lists some of the families available.

TABLE 3.1 Sample Instance Type Families

Family	
c4	**Compute optimized**—For workloads requiring significant processing
r3	**Memory optimized**—For memory-intensive workloads
i2	**Storage optimized**—For workloads requiring high amounts of fast SSD storage
g2	**GPU-based instances**—Intended for graphics and general-purpose GPU compute workloads

In response to customer demand and to take advantage of new processor technology, AWS occasionally introduces new instance families. Check the AWS website for the current list.

Another variable to consider when choosing an instance type is network performance. For most instance types, AWS publishes a relative measure of network performance: low, moderate, or high. Some instance types specify a network performance of 10 Gbps. The network performance increases within a family as the instance type grows.

For workloads requiring greater network performance, many instance types support *enhanced networking*. Enhanced networking reduces the impact of virtualization on network performance by enabling a capability called Single Root I/O Virtualization (SR-IOV). This results in more Packets Per Second (PPS), lower latency, and less jitter. At the time of this writing, there are instance types that support enhanced networking in the C3, C4, D2, I2, M4, and R3 families (consult the AWS documentation for a current list). Enabling enhanced networking on an instance involves ensuring the correct drivers are installed and modifying an instance attribute. Enhanced networking is available only for instances launched in an Amazon Virtual Private Cloud (Amazon VPC), which is discussed in Chapter 4, "Amazon Virtual Private Cloud (Amazon VPC)."

Amazon Machine Images (AMIs)

The *Amazon Machine Image (AMI)* defines the initial software that will be on an instance when it is launched. An AMI defines every aspect of the software state at instance launch, including:

- The Operating System (OS) and its configuration
- The initial state of any patches
- Application or system software

All AMIs are based on x86 OSs, either Linux or Windows.

There are four sources of AMIs:

- *Published by AWS*—AWS publishes AMIs with versions of many different OSs, both Linux and Windows. These include multiple distributions of Linux (including Ubuntu, Red Hat, and Amazon's own distribution) and Windows 2008 and Windows 2012. Launching an instance based on one of these AMIs will result in the default OS settings, similar to installing an OS from the standard OS ISO image. As with any OS installation, you should immediately apply all appropriate patches upon launch.

- *The AWS Marketplace*—AWS Marketplace is an online store that helps customers find, buy, and immediately start using the software and services that run on Amazon EC2. Many AWS partners have made their software available in the AWS Marketplace. This provides two benefits: the customer does not need to install the software, and the license agreement is appropriate for the cloud. Instances launched from an AWS Marketplace AMI incur the standard hourly cost of the instance type plus an additional per-hour charge for the additional software (some open-source AWS Marketplace packages have no additional software charge).

- *Generated from Existing Instances*—An AMI can be created from an existing Amazon EC2 instance. This is a very common source of AMIs. Customers launch an instance from a published AMI, and then the instance is configured to meet all the customer's corporate standards for updates, management, security, and so on. An AMI is then generated from the configured instance and used to generate all instances of that OS. In this way, all new instances follow the corporate standard and it is more difficult for individual projects to launch non-conforming instances.

- *Uploaded Virtual Servers*—Using AWS VM Import/Export service, customers can create images from various virtualization formats, including raw, VHD, VMDK, and OVA. The current list of supported OSs (Linux and Windows) can be found in the AWS documentation. It is incumbent on the customers to remain compliant with the licensing terms of their OS vendor.

Securely Using an Instance

Once launched, instances can be managed over the Internet. AWS has several services and features to ensure that this management can be done simply and securely.

Addressing an Instance

There are several ways that an instance may be addressed over the web upon creation:

- *Public Domain Name System (DNS) Name*—When you launch an instance, AWS creates a DNS name that can be used to access the instance. This DNS name is generated automatically and cannot be specified by the customer. The name can be found in the Description tab of the AWS Management Console or via the Command Line Interface (CLI) or Application Programming Interface (API). This DNS name persists only while the instance is running and cannot be transferred to another instance.

- *Public IP*—A launched instance may also have a public IP address assigned. This IP address is assigned from the addresses reserved by AWS and cannot be specified. This IP address is unique on the Internet, persists only while the instance is running, and cannot be transferred to another instance.

- *Elastic IP*—An elastic IP address is an address unique on the Internet that you reserve independently and associate with an Amazon EC2 instance. While similar to a public IP, there are some key differences. This IP address persists until the customer releases it and is not tied to the lifetime or state of an individual instance. Because it can be transferred to a replacement instance in the event of an instance failure, it is a public address that can be shared externally without coupling clients to a particular instance.

Private IP addresses and Elastic Network Interfaces (ENIs) are additional methods of addressing instances that are available in the context of an Amazon VPC. These are discussed in Chapter 4.

Initial Access

Amazon EC2 uses public-key cryptography to encrypt and decrypt login information. Public-key cryptography uses a public key to encrypt a piece of data and an associated private key to decrypt the data. These two keys together are called a *key pair*. Key pairs can be created through the AWS Management Console, CLI, or API, or customers can upload their own key pairs. AWS stores the public key, and the private key is kept by the customer. The private key is essential to acquiring secure access to an instance for the first time.

Store your private keys securely. When Amazon EC2 launches a Linux instance, the public key is stored in the ~/.ssh/authorized_keys file on the instance and an initial user is created. The initial user can vary depending on the OS. For example, the Amazon Linux distribution initial user is ec2-user. Initial access to the instance is obtained by using the ec2-user and the private key to log in via SSH. At this point, you can configure other users and enroll in a directory such as LDAP.

When launching a Windows instance, Amazon EC2 generates a random password for the local administrator account and encrypts the password using the public key. Initial access to the instance is obtained by decrypting the password with the private key, either in the console or through the API. The decrypted password can be used to log in to the instance with the local administrator account via RDP. At this point, you can create other local users and/or connect to an Active Directory domain.

It is a best practice to change the initial local administrator password.

Virtual Firewall Protection

AWS allows you to control traffic in and out of your instances through virtual firewalls called *security groups*. Security groups allow you to control traffic based on port, protocol, and source/destination. Security groups have different capabilities depending on whether they are associated with an Amazon VPC or Amazon EC2-Classic. Table 3.2 compares these different capabilities (Amazon VPC is discussed in Chapter 4).

TABLE 3.2   Different Security Groups

Type of Security Group	Capabilities
EC2-Classic Security Groups	Control outgoing instance traffic
VPC Security Groups	Control outgoing and incoming instance traffic

Security groups are associated with instances when they are launched. Every instance must have at least one security group but can have more.

A security group is default deny; that is, it does not allow any traffic that is not explicitly allowed by a security group rule. A rule is defined by the three attributes in Table 3.3. When an instance is associated with multiple security groups, the rules are aggregated and all traffic allowed by each of the individual groups is allowed. For example, if security group A allows RDP traffic from 72.58.0.0/16 and security group B allows HTTP and HTTPS traffic from 0.0.0.0/0 and your instance is associated with both groups, then both the RDP and HTTP/S traffic will be allowed in to your instance.

TABLE 3.3   Security Group Rule Attributes

Attribute	Meaning
Port	The port number affected by this rule. For instance, port 80 for HTTP traffic.
Protocol	The communications standard for the traffic affected by this rule.

Attribute	Meaning
Source/Destination	Identifies the other end of the communication, the source for incoming traffic rules, or the destination for outgoing traffic rules. The source/destination can be defined in two ways: *CIDR block*—An x.x.x.x/x style definition that defines a specific range of IP addresses. *Security group*—Includes any instance that is associated with the given security group. This helps prevent coupling security group rules with specific IP addresses.

A security group is a stateful firewall; that is, an outgoing message is remembered so that the response is allowed through the security group without an explicit inbound rule being required.

Security groups are applied at the instance level, as opposed to a traditional on-premises firewall that protects at the perimeter. The effect of this is that instead of having to breach a single perimeter to access all the instances in your security group, an attacker would have to breach the security group repeatedly for each individual instance.

The Lifecycle of Instances

Amazon EC2 has several features and services that facilitate the management of Amazon EC2 instances over their entire lifecycle.

Launching

There are several additional services that are useful when launching new Amazon EC2 instances.

Bootstrapping   A great benefit of the cloud is the ability to script virtual hardware management in a manner that is not possible with on-premises hardware. In order to realize the value of this, there has to be some way to configure instances and install applications programmatically when an instance is launched. The process of providing code to be run on an instance at launch is called *bootstrapping*.

One of the parameters when an instance is launched is a string value called *UserData*. This string is passed to the operating system to be executed as part of the launch process the first time the instance is booted. On Linux instances this can be shell script, and on Windows instances this can be a batch style script or a PowerShell script. The script can perform tasks such as:

- Applying patches and updates to the OS
- Enrolling in a directory service
- Installing application software

- Copying a longer script or program from storage to be run on the instance
- Installing Chef or Puppet and assigning the instance a role so the configuration management software can configure the instance

 UserData is stored with the instance and is not encrypted, so it is important to not include any secrets such as passwords or keys in the UserData.

VM Import/Export   In addition to importing virtual instances as AMIs, VM Import/Export enables you to easily import Virtual Machines (VMs) from your existing environment as an Amazon EC2 instance and export them back to your on-premises environment. You can only export previously imported Amazon EC2 instances. Instances launched within AWS from AMIs cannot be exported.

Instance Metadata   *Instance metadata* is data about your instance that you can use to configure or manage the running instance. This is unique in that it is a mechanism to obtain AWS properties of the instance from within the OS without making a call to the AWS API. An HTTP call to http://169.254.169.254/latest/meta-data/ will return the top node of the instance metadata tree. Instance metadata includes a wide variety of attributes, including:

- The associated security groups
- The instance ID
- The instance type
- The AMI used to launch the instance

   This only begins to scratch the surface of the information available in the metadata. Consult the AWS documentation for a full list.

Managing Instances

When the number of instances in your account starts to climb, it can become difficult to keep track of them. Tags can help you manage not just your Amazon EC2 instances, but also many of your AWS Cloud services. Tags are key/value pairs you can associate with your instance or other service. Tags can be used to identify attributes of an instance like project, environment (dev, test, and so on), billable department, and so forth. You can apply up to 10 tags per instance. Table 3.4 shows some tag suggestions.

TABLE 3.4   Sample Tags

Key	Value
Project	TimeEntry
Environment	Production
BillingCode	4004

Monitoring Instances

AWS offers a service called Amazon CloudWatch that provides monitoring and alerting for Amazon EC2 instances, and also other AWS infrastructure. Amazon CloudWatch is discussed in detail in Chapter 5, "Elastic Load Balancing, Amazon CloudWatch, and Auto Scaling."

Modifying an Instance

There are several aspects of an instance that can be modified after launch.

Instance Type   The ability to change the instance type of an instance contributes greatly to the agility of running workloads in the cloud. Instead of committing to a certain hardware configuration months before a workload is launched, the workload can be launched using a best estimate for the instance type. If the compute needs prove to be higher or lower than expected, the instances can be changed to a different size more appropriate to the workload.

Instances can be resized using the AWS Management Console, CLI, or API. To resize an instance, set the state to Stopped. Choose the "Change Instance Type" function in the tool of your choice (the instance type is listed as an Instance Setting in the console and an Instance Attribute in the CLI) and select the desired instance type. Restart the instance and the process is complete.

Security Groups   If an instance is running in an Amazon VPC (discussed in Chapter 4), you can change which security groups are associated with an instance while the instance is running. For instances outside of an Amazon VPC (called EC2-Classic), the association of the security groups cannot be changed after launch.

Termination Protection

When an Amazon EC2 instance is no longer needed, the state can be set to Terminated and the instance will be shut down and removed from the AWS infrastructure. In order to prevent termination via the AWS Management Console, CLI, or API, *termination protection* can be enabled for an instance. While enabled, calls to terminate the instance will fail until termination protection is disabled. This helps to prevent accidental termination through human error.

Note that this just protects from termination calls from the AWS Management Console, CLI, or API. It does not prevent termination triggered by an OS shutdown command, termination from an Auto Scaling group (discussed in Chapter 5), or termination of a Spot Instance due to Spot price changes (discussed in the next section).

Options

There are several additional options available in Amazon EC2 to improve cost optimization, security, and performance that are important to know for the exam.

Pricing Options

You are charged for Amazon EC2 instances for each hour that they are in a running state, but the amount you are charged per hour can vary based on three pricing options: On-Demand Instances, Reserved Instances, and Spot Instances.

On-Demand Instances   The price per hour for each instance type published on the AWS website represents the price for *On-Demand Instances*. This is the most flexible pricing option, as it requires no up-front commitment, and the customer has control over when the instance is launched and when it is terminated. It is the least cost effective of the three pricing options per compute hour, but its flexibility allows customers to save by provisioning a variable level of compute for unpredictable workloads.

Reserved Instances   The *Reserved Instance* pricing option enables customers to make capacity reservations for predictable workloads. By using Reserved Instances for these workloads, customers can save up to 75 percent over the on-demand hourly rate. When purchasing a reservation, the customer specifies the instance type and Availability Zone for that Reserved Instance and achieves a lower effective hourly price for that instance for the duration of the reservation. An additional benefit is that capacity in the AWS data centers is reserved for that customer. There are two factors that determine the cost of the reservation: the term commitment and the payment option.

The *term commitment* is the duration of the reservation and can be either one or three years. The longer the commitment, the bigger the discount.

There are three different payment options for Reserved Instances:

- *All Upfront*—Pay for the entire reservation up front. There is no monthly charge for the customer during the term.

- *Partial Upfront*—Pay a portion of the reservation charge up front and the rest in monthly installments for the duration of the term.

- *No Upfront*—Pay the entire reservation charge in monthly installments for the duration of the term.

The amount of the discount is greater the more the customer pays up front.

For example, let's look at the effect of an all upfront, three-year reservation on the effective hourly cost of an m4.2xlarge instance. The cost of running one instance continuously for three years (or 26,280 hours) at both pricing options is shown in Table 3.5.

TABLE 3.5   Reserved Instance Pricing Example

Pricing Option	Effective Hourly Cost	Total Three-Year Cost
On-Demand	$0.479/hour	$0.479/hour* 26280 hours = $12588.12
Three-Year All Upfront Reservation	$4694/26280 hours = $0.1786/hour	$4694
Savings		63%

This example uses the published prices at the time of this writing. AWS has lowered prices many times to date, so check the AWS website for current pricing information.

When your computing needs change, you can modify your Reserved Instances and continue to benefit from your capacity reservation. Modification does not change the remaining term of your Reserved Instances; their end dates remain the same. There is no fee, and you do not receive any new bills or invoices. Modification is separate from purchasing and does not affect how you use, purchase, or sell Reserved Instances. You can modify your whole reservation, or just a subset, in one or more of the following ways:

- Switch Availability Zones within the same region.
- Change between EC2-VPC and EC2-Classic.
- Change the instance type within the same instance family (Linux instances only).

Spot Instances   For workloads that are not time critical and are tolerant of interruption, *Spot Instances* offer the greatest discount. With Spot Instances, customers specify the price they are willing to pay for a certain instance type. When the customer's bid price is above the current Spot price, the customer will receive the requested instance(s). These instances will operate like all other Amazon EC2 instances, and the customer will only pay the Spot price for the hours that instance(s) run. The instances will run until:

- The customer terminates them.
- The Spot price goes above the customer's bid price.
- There is not enough unused capacity to meet the demand for Spot Instances.

If Amazon EC2 needs to terminate a Spot Instance, the instance will receive a termination notice providing a two-minute warning prior to Amazon EC2 terminating the instance.

Because of the possibility of interruption, Spot Instances should only be used for workloads tolerant of interruption. This could include analytics, financial modeling, big data, media encoding, scientific computing, and testing.

Architectures with Different Pricing Models   For the exam, it's important to know how to take advantage of the different pricing models to create a cost-efficient architecture. Such an architecture may include different pricing models within the same workload. For instance, a website that averages 5,000 visits a day, but ramps up to 20,000 visits a day during periodic peaks, may purchase two Reserved Instances to handle the average traffic, but depend on On-Demand Instances to fulfill compute needs during the peak times. Figure 3.2 shows such an architecture.

FIGURE 3.2   A workload using a mix of On-Demand and Reserved Instances

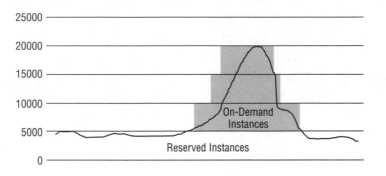

Tenancy Options

There are several *tenancy* options for Amazon EC2 instances that can help customers achieve security and compliance goals.

Shared Tenancy   Shared tenancy is the default tenancy model for all Amazon EC2 instances, regardless of instance type, pricing model, and so forth. Shared tenancy means that a single host machine may house instances from different customers. As AWS does not use overprovisioning and fully isolates instances from other instances on the same host, this is a secure tenancy model.

Dedicated Instances   Dedicated Instances run on hardware that's dedicated to a single customer. As a customer runs more Dedicated Instances, more underlying hardware may be dedicated to their account. Other instances in the account (those not designated as dedicated) will run on shared tenancy and will be isolated at the hardware level from the Dedicated Instances in the account.

Dedicated Host   An Amazon EC2 Dedicated Host is a physical server with Amazon EC2 instance capacity fully dedicated to a single customer's use. Dedicated Hosts can help you address licensing requirements and reduce costs by allowing you to use your existing server-bound software licenses. The customer has complete control over which specific host runs an instance at launch. This differs from Dedicated Instances in that a Dedicated Instance can launch on any hardware that has been dedicated to the account.

Placement Groups

A *placement group* is a logical grouping of instances within a single Availability Zone. Placement groups enable applications to participate in a low-latency, 10 Gbps network. Placement groups are recommended for applications that benefit from low network latency, high network throughput, or both. Remember that this represents network connectivity between instances. To fully use this network performance for your placement group, choose an instance type that supports enhanced networking and 10 Gbps network performance.

Instance Stores

An *instance store* (sometimes referred to as *ephemeral storage*) provides temporary block-level storage for your instance. This storage is located on disks that are physically attached to the host computer. An instance store is ideal for temporary storage of information that changes frequently, such as buffers, caches, scratch data, and other temporary content, or for data that is replicated across a fleet of instances, such as a load-balanced pool of web servers.

The size and type of instance stores available with an Amazon EC2 instance depend on the instance type. At this writing, storage available with various instance types ranges from no instance stores up to 24 2 TB instance stores. The instance type also determines the type of hardware for the instance store volumes. While some provide Hard Disk Drive (HDD) instance stores, other instance types use Solid State Drives (SSDs) to deliver very high random I/O performance.

Instance stores are included in the cost of an Amazon EC2 instance, so they are a very cost-effective solution for appropriate workloads. The key aspect of instance stores is that they are temporary. Data in the instance store is lost when:

- The underlying disk drive fails.
- The instance stops (the data will persist if an instance reboots).
- The instance terminates.

Therefore, do not rely on instance stores for valuable, long-term data. Instead, build a degree of redundancy via RAID or use a file system that supports redundancy and fault tolerance such as Hadoop's HDFS. Back up the data to more durable data storage solutions such as Amazon Simple Storage Service (Amazon S3) or Amazon EBS often enough to meet recovery point objectives.

Amazon Elastic Block Store (Amazon EBS)

While instance stores are an economical way to fulfill appropriate workloads, their limited persistence makes them ill-suited for many other workloads. For workloads requiring more durable block storage, Amazon provides Amazon EBS.

Elastic Block Store Basics

Amazon EBS provides persistent block-level storage volumes for use with Amazon EC2 instances. Each Amazon EBS volume is automatically replicated within its Availability Zone to protect you from component failure, offering high availability and durability. Amazon EBS volumes are available in a variety of types that differ in performance characteristics and price. Multiple Amazon EBS volumes can be attached to a single Amazon EC2 instance, although a volume can only be attached to a single instance at a time.

Types of Amazon EBS Volumes

Amazon EBS volumes are available in several different types. Types vary in areas such as underlying hardware, performance, and cost. It is important to know the properties of the different types so you can specify the most cost-efficient type that meets a workload's performance demands on the exam.

Magnetic Volumes

Magnetic volumes have the lowest performance characteristics of all Amazon EBS volume types. As such, they cost the lowest per gigabyte. They are an excellent, cost-effective solution for appropriate workloads.

A magnetic Amazon EBS volume can range in size from 1 GB to 1 TB and will average 100 *IOPS*, but has the ability to burst to hundreds of IOPS. They are best suited for:

- Workloads where data is accessed infrequently

- Sequential reads

- Situations where low-cost storage is a requirement

Magnetic volumes are billed based on the amount of data space provisioned, regardless of how much data you actually store on the volume.

General-Purpose SSD

General-purpose SSD volumes offer cost-effective storage that is ideal for a broad range of workloads. They deliver strong performance at a moderate price point that is suitable for a wide range of workloads.

A general-purpose SSD volume can range in size from 1 GB to 16 TB and provides a baseline performance of three IOPS per gigabyte provisioned, capping at 10,000 IOPS. For instance, if you provision a 1 TB volume, you can expect a baseline performance of 3,000 IOPS. A 5 TB volume will not provide a 15,000 IOPS baseline, as it would hit the cap at 10,000 IOPS.

General-purpose SSD volumes under 1 TB also feature the ability to burst to up to 3,000 IOPS for extended periods of time. For instance, if you have a 500 GB volume you can expect a baseline of 1,500 IOPS. Whenever you are not using these IOPS, they are accumulated as I/O credits. When your volume then has heavy traffic, it will use the I/O credits at a rate of up to 3,000 IOPS until they are depleted. At that point, your performance reverts to 1,500 IOPS. At 1 TB, the baseline performance of the volume is already at 3,000 IOPS, so bursting behavior does not apply.

General-purpose SSD volumes are billed based on the amount of data space provisioned, regardless of how much data you actually store on the volume. They are suited for a wide range of workloads where the very highest disk performance is not critical, such as:

- System boot volumes

- Small- to medium-sized databases

- Development and test environments

Provisioned IOPS SSD

Provisioned IOPS SSD volumes are designed to meet the needs of I/O-intensive workloads, particularly database workloads that are sensitive to storage performance and consistency in random access I/O throughput. While they are the most expensive Amazon EBS volume type per gigabyte, they provide the highest performance of any Amazon EBS volume type in a predictable manner.

A Provisioned IOPS SSD volume can range in size from 4 GB to 16 TB. When you provision a Provisioned IOPS SSD volume, you specify not just the size, but also the desired number of IOPS, up to the lower of the maximum of 30 times the number of GB of the volume, or 20,000 IOPS. You can stripe multiple volumes together in a RAID 0 configuration for larger size and greater performance. Amazon EBS delivers within 10 percent of the provisioned IOPS performance 99.9 percent of the time over a given year.

Pricing is based on the size of the volume and the amount of IOPS reserved. The cost per gigabyte is slightly more than that of general-purpose SSD volumes and is applied based on the size of the volume, not the amount of the volume used to store data. An additional monthly fee is applied based on the number of IOPS provisioned, whether they are consumed or not.

Provisioned IOPS SSD volumes provide predictable, high performance and are well suited for:

- Critical business applications that require sustained IOPS performance
- Large database workloads

Table 3.6 compares these Amazon EBS volume types.

TABLE 3.6   EBS Volume Type Comparison

Characteristic	General-Purpose SSD	Provisioned IOPS SSD	Magnetic
Use cases	<ul><li>System boot volumes</li><li>Virtual desktops</li><li>Small-to-medium sized databases</li><li>Development and test environments</li></ul>	<ul><li>Critical business applications that require sustained IOPS performance or more than 10,000 IOPS or 160MB of throughput per volume</li><li>Large database workloads</li></ul>	<ul><li>Cold workloads where data is infrequently accessed</li><li>Scenarios where the lowest storage cost is important</li></ul>
Volume size	1 GiB–16TiB	4 GiB–16TiB	1 GiB–1TiB
Maximum throughput	160MB	320MB	40–90MB

TABLE 3.6   EBS Volume Type Comparison *(continued)*

Characteristic	General-Purpose SSD	Provisioned IOPS SSD	Magnetic
IOPS performance	Baseline performance of 3 IOPS/GiB (up to 10,000 IOPS) with the ability to burst to 3,000 IOPS for volumes under 1,000 GiB	Consistently performs at provisioned level, up to 20,000 IOPS maximum	Averages 100 IOPS, with the ability to burst to hundreds of IOPS

At the time of this writing, AWS released two new HDD volume types: Throughput-Optimized HDD and Cold HDD. Over time, it is expected that these new types will eclipse the current magnetic volume type, fulfilling the needs of any workload requiring HDD performance.

Throughput-Optimized HDD volumes are low-cost HDD volumes designed for frequent-access, throughput-intensive workloads such as big data, data warehouses, and log processing. Volumes can be up to 16 TB with a maximum IOPS of 500 and maximum throughput of 500 MB/s. These volumes are significantly less expensive than general-purpose SSD volumes.

Cold HDD volumes are designed for less frequently accessed workloads, such as colder data requiring fewer scans per day. Volumes can be up to 16 TB with a maximum IOPS of 250 and maximum throughput of 250 MB/s. These volumes are significantly less expensive than Throughput-Optimized HDD volumes.

Amazon EBS-Optimized Instances

When using any volume type other than magnetic and Amazon EBS I/O is of consequence, it is important to use Amazon EBS-optimized instances to ensure that the Amazon EC2 instance is prepared to take advantage of the I/O of the Amazon EBS volume. An Amazon EBS-optimized instance uses an optimized configuration stack and provides additional, dedicated capacity for Amazon EBS I/O. This optimization provides the best performance for your Amazon EBS volumes by minimizing contention between Amazon EBS I/O and other traffic from your instance. When you select Amazon EBS-optimized for an instance, you pay an additional hourly charge for that instance. Check the AWS documentation to confirm which instance types are available as Amazon EBS-optimized instance.

Protecting Data

Over the lifecycle of an Amazon EBS volume, there are several practices and services that you should know about when taking the exam.

Backup/Recovery (Snapshots)

You can back up the data on your Amazon EBS volumes, regardless of volume type, by taking point-in-time snapshots. Snapshots are incremental backups, which means that only the blocks on the device that have changed since your most recent snapshot are saved.

Taking Snapshots   You can take snapshots in many ways:

- Through the AWS Management Console
- Through the CLI
- Through the API
- By setting up a schedule of regular snapshots

Data for the snapshot is stored using Amazon S3 technology. The action of taking a snapshot is free. You pay only the storage costs for the snapshot data.

When you request a snapshot, the point-in-time snapshot is created immediately and the volume may continue to be used, but the snapshot may remain in pending status until all the modified blocks have been transferred to Amazon S3.

It's important to know that while snapshots are stored using Amazon S3 technology, they are stored in AWS-controlled storage and not in your account's Amazon S3 buckets. This means you cannot manipulate them like other Amazon S3 objects. Rather, you must use the Amazon EBS snapshot features to manage them. Snapshots are constrained to the region in which they are created, meaning you can use them to create new volumes only in the same region. If you need to restore a snapshot in a different region, you can copy a snapshot to another region.

Creating a Volume from a Snapshot   To use a snapshot, you create a new Amazon EBS volume from the snapshot. When you do this, the volume is created immediately but the data is loaded lazily. This means that the volume can be accessed upon creation, and if the data being requested has not yet been restored, it will be restored upon first request. Because of this, it is a best practice to initialize a volume created from a snapshot by accessing all the blocks in the volume.

Snapshots can also be used to increase the size of an Amazon EBS volume. To increase the size of an Amazon EBS volume, take a snapshot of the volume, then create a new volume of the desired size from the snapshot. Replace the original volume with the new volume.

Recovering Volumes

Because Amazon EBS volumes persist beyond the lifetime of an instance, it is possible to recover data if an instance fails. If an Amazon EBS-backed instance fails and there is data on the boot drive, it is relatively straightforward to detach the volume from the instance. Unless the DeleteOnTermination flag for the volume has been set to false, the volume should be detached before the instance is terminated. The volume can then be attached as a data volume to another instance and the data read and recovered.

Encryption Options

Many workloads have requirements that data be encrypted at rest, either because of compliance regulations or internal corporate standards. Amazon EBS offers native encryption on all volume types.

When you launch an encrypted Amazon EBS volume, Amazon uses the *AWS Key Management Service (KMS)* to handle key management. A new master key will be created unless you select a master key that you created separately in the service. Your data and associated keys are encrypted using the industry-standard AES-256 algorithm. The encryption occurs on the servers that host Amazon EC2 instances, so the data is actually encrypted in transit between the host and the storage media and also on the media. (Consult the AWS documentation for a list of instance types that support Amazon EBS encryption.) Encryption is transparent, so all data access is the same as unencrypted volumes, and you can expect the same IOPS performance on encrypted volumes as you would with unencrypted volumes, with a minimal effect on latency. Snapshots that are taken from encrypted volumes are automatically encrypted, as are volumes that are created from encrypted snapshots.

Summary

Compute is the amount of computational power required to fulfill your workload. Amazon EC2 is the primary service for providing compute to customers.

The instance type defines the virtual hardware supporting the instance. Available instance types vary in vCPUs, memory, storage, and network performance to address nearly any workload.

An AMI defines the initial software state of the instance, both OS and applications. There are four sources of AMIs: AWS published generic OSs, partner-published AMIs in the AWS Marketplace with software packages preinstalled, customer-generated AMIs from existing Amazon EC2 instances, and uploaded AMIs from virtual servers.

Instances can be addressed by public DNS name, public IP address, or elastic IP address. To access a newly launched Linux instance, use the private half of the key pair to connect to the instance via SSH. To access a newly created Windows instance, use the private half of the key pair to decrypt the randomly initialized local administrator password.

Network traffic in and out of an instance can be controlled by a virtual firewall called a security group. A security group allows rules that block traffic based on direction, port, protocol, and source/destination address.

Bootstrapping allows you to run a script to initialize your instance with OS configurations and applications. This feature allows instances to configure themselves upon launch. Once an instance is launched, you can change its instance type or, for Amazon VPC instances, the security groups with which it is associated.

The three pricing options for instances are On-Demand, Reserved Instance, and Spot. On-Demand has the highest per hour cost, requiring no up-front commitment and giving you complete control over the lifetime of the instance. Reserved Instances require a commitment and provide a reduced overall cost over the lifetime of the reservation. Spot Instances are idle compute capacity that AWS makes available based on bid prices from customers. The savings on the per-hour cost can be significant, but instances can be shut down when the bid price exceeds the customer's current bid.

Instance stores are block storage included with the hourly cost of the instance. The amount and type of storage available varies with the instance type. Instance stores terminate when the associated instance is stopped, so they should only be used for temporary data or in architectures providing redundancy such as Hadoop's HDFS.

Amazon EBS provides durable block storage in several types. Magnetic has the lowest cost per gigabyte and delivers modest performance. General-purpose SSD is cost-effective storage that can provide up to 10,000 IOPS. Provisioned IOPS SSD has the highest cost per gigabyte and is well suited for I/O-intensive workloads sensitive to storage performance. Snapshots are incremental backups of Amazon EBS volumes stored in Amazon S3. Amazon EBS volumes can be encrypted.

Exam Essentials

Know the basics of launching an Amazon EC2 instance.   To launch an instance, you must specify an AMI, which defines the software on the instance at launch, and an instance type, which defines the virtual hardware supporting the instance (memory, vCPUs, and so on).

Know what architectures are suited for what Amazon EC2 pricing options.   Spot Instances are best suited for workloads that can accommodate interruption. Reserved Instances are best for consistent, long-term compute needs. On-Demand Instances provide flexible compute to respond to scaling needs.

Know how to combine multiple pricing options that result in cost optimization and scalability.   On-Demand Instances can be used to scale up a web application running on Reserved Instances in response to a temporary traffic spike. For a workload with several Reserved Instances reading from a queue, it's possible to use Spot Instances to alleviate heavy traffic in a cost-effective way. These are just two of countless examples where a workload may use different pricing options.

Know the benefits of enhanced networking.   Enhanced networking enables you to get significantly higher PPS performance, lower network jitter, and lower latencies.

Know the capabilities of VM Import/Export.   VM Import/Export allows you to import existing VMs to AWS as Amazon EC2 instances or AMIs. Amazon EC2 instances that were imported through VM Import/Export can also be exported back to a virtual environment.

Know the methods for accessing an instance over the internet.   You can access an Amazon EC2 instance over the web via public IP address, elastic IP address, or public DNS name.

There are additional ways to access an instance within an Amazon VPC, including private IP addresses and ENIs.

Know the lifetime of an instance store.   Data on an instance store is lost when the instance is stopped or terminated. Instance store data survives an OS reboot.

Know the properties of the Amazon EC2 pricing options.   On-Demand Instances require no up-front commitment, can be launched any time, and are billed by the hour. Reserved Instances require an up-front commitment and vary in cost depending on whether they are paid all up front, partially up front, or not up front. Spot Instances are launched when your bid price exceeds the current spot price. Spot Instances will run until the spot price exceeds your bid price, in which case the instance will get a two-minute warning and terminate.

Know what determines network performance.   Every instance type is rated for low, moderate, high, or 10 Gbps network performance, with larger instance types generally having higher ratings. Additionally, some instance types offer enhanced networking, which provides additional improvement in network performance.

Know what instance metadata is and how it's obtained.   Metadata is information about an Amazon EC2 instance, such as instance ID, instance type, and security groups, that is available from within the instance. It can be obtained through an HTTP call to a specific IP address.

Know how security groups protect instances.   Security groups are virtual firewalls controlling traffic in and out of your Amazon EC2 instances. They are deny by default, and you can allow traffic by adding rules specifying traffic direction, port, protocol, and destination address (via Classless Inter-Domain Routing [CIDR] block). They are applied at the instance level, meaning that traffic between instances in the same security group must adhere to the rules of that security group. They are stateful, meaning that an outgoing rule will allow the response without a correlating incoming rule.

Know how to interpret the effect of security groups.   When an instance is a member of multiple security groups, the effect is a union of all the rules in all the groups.

Know the different Amazon EBS volume types, their characteristics, and their appropriate workloads.   Magnetic volumes provide an average performance of 100 IOPS and can be provisioned up to 1 TB. They are good for cold and infrequently accessed data. General-purpose SSD volumes provide three IOPS/GB up to 10,000 IOPS, with smaller volumes able to burst 3,000 IOPS. They can be provisioned up to 16 TB and are appropriate for dev/test environments, small databases, and so forth. Provisioned IOPS SSD can provide up to 20,000 consistent IOPS for volumes up to 16 TB. They are the best choice for workloads such as large databases executing many transactions.

Know how to encrypt an Amazon EBS volume.   Any volume type can be encrypted at launch. Encryption is based on AWS KMS and is transparent to applications on the attached instances.

Understand the concept and process of snapshots.   Snapshots provide a point-in-time backup of an Amazon EBS volume and are stored in Amazon S3. Subsequent snapshots are incremental—they only store deltas. When you request a snapshot, the point-in-time snapshot is created immediately and the volume may continue to be used, but the snapshot may remain in pending status until all the modified blocks have been transferred to Amazon S3. Snapshots may be copied between regions.

Know how Amazon EBS-optimized instances affect Amazon EBS performance. In addition to the IOPS that control the performance in and out of the Amazon EBS volume, use Amazon EBS-optimized instances to ensure additional, dedicated capacity for Amazon EBS I/O.

Exercises

For assistance in completing these exercises, refer to these user guides:

- *Amazon EC2 (Linux)*—http://docs.aws.amazon.com/AWSEC2/latest/UserGuide/concepts.html

- *Amazon EC2 (Windows)*—http://docs.aws.amazon.com/AWSEC2/latest/WindowsGuide/concepts.html

- *Amazon EBS*—http://docs.aws.amazon.com/AWSEC2/latest/UserGuide/AmazonEBS.html

---

EXERCISE 3.1

Launch and Connect to a Linux Instance

In this exercise, you will launch a new Linux instance, log in with SSH, and install any security updates.

1. Launch an instance in the Amazon EC2 console.

2. Choose the Amazon Linux AMI.

3. Choose the t2.medium instance type.

4. Launch the instance in either the default VPC or EC2-Classic.

5. Assign the instance a public IP address.

6. Add a tag to the instance of Key: Name, Value: **Exercise 3.1**.

7. Create a new security group called **Cert Book**.

8. Add a rule to Cert Book allowing SSH access from the IP address of your workstation (www.WhatsMyIP.org is a good way to determine your IP address).

9. Launch the instance.

10. When prompted for a key pair, choose a key pair you already have or create a new one and download the private portion.

    Amazon generates a keyname.pem file, and you will need a keyname.ppk file to connect to the instance via SSH. Puttygen.exe is one utility that will create a .ppk file from a .pem file.

11. SSH into the instance using the public IP address, the user name ec2-user, and the keyname.ppk file.

12. From the command-line prompt, run sudo yum update-security -y.

13. Close the SSH window and terminate the instance.

EXERCISE 3.2

Launch a Windows Instance with Bootstrapping

In this exercise, you will launch a Windows instance and specify a very simple bootstrap script. You will then confirm that the bootstrap script was executed on the instance.

1. Launch an instance in the Amazon EC2 console.

2. Choose the Microsoft Windows Server 2012 Base AMI.

3. Choose the t2.medium instance type.

4. Launch the instance in either the default VPC or EC2-Classic.

5. Assign the instance a public IP address.

6. In the Advanced Details section, enter the following text as UserData:

```
<script>
md c:\temp
</script>
```

7. Add a tag to the instance of Key: Name, Value: **Exercise 3.2**.

8. Use the Cert Book security group from Exercise 3.1.

9. Launch the instance.

10. Use the key pair from Exercise 3.1.

11. On the Connect Instance UI, decrypt the administrator password and then download the RDP file to attempt to connect to the instance. Your attempt should fail because the Cert Book security group does not allow RDP access.

12. Open the Cert Book security group and add a rule that allows RDP access from your IP address.

13. Attempt to access the instance via RDP again.

14. Once the RDP session is connected, open Windows Explorer and confirm that the c:\temp folder has been created.

15. End the RDP session and terminate the instance.

EXERCISE 3.3

Confirm That Instance Stores Are Lost When an Instance Is Stopped

In this exercise, you will observe that the data on an Amazon EC2 instance store is lost when the instance is stopped.

1. Launch an instance in the Amazon Management Console.

2. Choose the Microsoft Windows Server 2012 Base AMI.

3. Choose the m3.medium instance type.

4. Launch the instance in either the default VPC or EC2-Classic.

5. Assign the instance a public IP address.

6. Add a tag to the instance of Key: Name, Value: **Exercise 3.3**.

7. Use the Cert Book security group as updated in Exercise 3.2.

8. Launch the instance.

9. Use the key pair from Exercise 3.1.

10. Decrypt the administrator password login to the instance via RDP.

11. Once the RDP session is connected, open Windows Explorer.

12. Create a new folder named **z:\temp**.

13. Log out of the RDP session.

14. In the console, set the state of the instance to Stopped.

15. Once the instance is stopped, start it again.

16. Log back into the instance using RDP.

17. Open Windows Explorer and confirm that the z:\temp folder is gone.

18. End the RDP session and terminate the instance.

Launch a Spot Instance

In this exercise, you will create a Spot Instance.

1. In the Amazon EC2 console, go to the Spot Request page.

2. Look at the pricing history for m3.medium, especially the recent price.

3. Make a note of the most recent price and Availability Zone.

4. Launch an instance in the Amazon EC2 console.

5. Choose the Amazon Linux AMI.

6. Choose the t2.medium instance type.

7. On the Configure Instance page, request a Spot Instance.

8. Launch the instance in either the Default VPC or EC2-Classic. (Note the Default VPC will define the Availability Zone for the instance.)

9. Assign the instance a public IP address.

10. Request a Spot Instance and enter a bid a few cents above the recorded Spot price.

11. Finish launching the instance.

12. Go back to the Spot Request page.

    Watch your request. If your bid was high enough, you should see it change to Active and an instance ID appear.

13. Find the instance on the instances page of the Amazon EC2 console.

    Note the Lifecycle field in the Description that says Spot.

14. Once the instance is running, terminate it.

Access Metadata

In this exercise, you will access the instance metadata from the OS.

1. Launch an instance in the Amazon EC2 console.

2. Choose the Amazon Linux AMI.

3. Choose the t2.medium instance type.

4. Launch the instance in either the default VPC or EC2-Classic.

5. Assign the instance a public IP address.

6. Add a tag to the instance of Key: Name, Value: **Exercise 3.5**.

7. Use the Cert Book security group.

8. Launch the instance.

9. Use the key pair from Exercise 3.1.

10. Connect the instance via SSH using the public IP address, the user name `ec2-user`, and the `keyname.ppk` file.

11. At the Linux command prompt, retrieve a list of the available metadata by typing:

`curl http://169.254.169.254/latest/meta-data/`

12. To see a value, add the name to the end of the URL. For example, to see the security groups, type:

`curl http://169.254.169.254/latest/meta-data/security-groups`

13. Try other values as well. Names that end with a / indicate a longer list of sub-values.

14. Close the SSH window and terminate the instance.

EXERCISE 3.6

Create an Amazon EBS Volume and Show That It Remains After the Instance Is Terminated

In this exercise, you will see how an Amazon EBS volume persists beyond the life of an instance.

1. Launch an instance in the Amazon EC2 console.

2. Choose the Amazon Linux AMI.

3. Choose the t2.medium instance type.

4. Launch the instance in either the default VPC or EC2-Classic.

5. Assign the instance a public IP address.

6. Add a second Amazon EBS volume of size 50 GB. Note that the Root Volume is set to Delete on Termination.

7. Add a tag to the instance of Key: Name, Value: **Exercise 3.6**.

8. Use the Cert Book security group from earlier exercises.

9. Launch the instance.

10. Find the two Amazon EBS volumes on the Amazon EBS console. Name them both **Exercise 3.6**.

11. Terminate the instance.

Notice that the boot drive is destroyed, but the additional Amazon EBS volume remains and now says Available. Do not delete the Available volume.

EXERCISE 3.7

Take a Snapshot and Restore

This exercise guides you through taking a snapshot and restoring it in three different ways.

1. Find the volume you created in Exercise 3.6 in the Amazon EBS console.

2. Take a snapshot of that volume. Name the snapshot **Exercise 3.7**.

3. On the snapshot console, wait for the snapshot to be completed. (As the volume was empty, this should be very quick.)

4. On the snapshot page in the AWS Management Console, choose the new snapshot and select Create Volume.

5. Create the volume with all the defaults.

6. Locate the snapshot again and again choose Create Volume, setting the size of the new volume to 100 GB (taking a snapshot and restoring the snapshot to a new, larger volume is how you address the problem of increasing the size of an existing volume). Locate the snapshot again and choose Copy. Copy the snapshot to another region. Make the description **Exercise 3.7**.

7. Go to the other region and wait for the snapshot to become available.

8. Create a volume from the snapshot in the new region. This is how you share an Amazon EBS volume between regions; that is, by taking a snapshot and copying the snapshot.

9. Delete all four volumes.

EXERCISE 3.8

Launch an Encrypted Volume

In this exercise, you will launch an Amazon EC2 instance with an encrypted Amazon EBS volume and store some data on it to confirm that the encryption is transparent to the instance itself.

1. Launch an instance in the Amazon EC2 console.

2. Choose the Microsoft Windows Server 2012 Base AMI.

3. Choose the m3.medium instance type.

4. Launch the instance in either the default VPC or EC2-Classic.

5. Assign the instance a public IP address.

6. On the storage page, add a 50 GB encrypted Amazon EBS volume.

7. Add a tag to the instance of Key: Name, Value: **Exercise 3.8**.

8. Use the Cert Book security group as updated in Exercise 3.2.

9. Launch the instance.

10. Choose the key pair from Exercise 3.1.

11. Decrypt the administrator password and log in to the instance using RDP.

12. Once the RDP session is connected, open Notepad.

13. Type some random information into Notepad, save it at d:\testfile.txt, and then close Notepad.

14. Find d:\testfile.txt in Windows Explorer and open it with Notepad. Confirm that the data is not encrypted in Notepad.

15. Log out.

16. Terminate the instance.

EXERCISE 3.9

Detach a Boot Drive and Reattach to Another Instance

In this exercise, you will practice removing an Amazon EBS volume from a stopped drive and attaching to another instance to recover the data.

1. Launch an instance in the Amazon EC2 console.

2. Choose the Microsoft Windows Server 2012 Base AMI.

3. Choose the t2.medium instance type.

4. Launch the instance in either the default VPC or EC2-Classic.

5. Assign the instance a public IP address.

6. Add a tag to the instance of Key: Name, Value: **Exercise 3.9 Source**.

7. Use the Cert Book security group from earlier exercises.

8. Launch the instance with the key pair from Exercise 3.1.

9. Launch a second instance in the Amazon EC2 Console.

10. Choose the Microsoft Windows Server 2012 Base AMI.

11. Choose the t2.medium instance type.

12. Launch the instance in either the default VPC or EC2-Classic.

13. Assign the instance a public IP address.

14. Add a tag to the instance of Key: Name, Value: **Exercise 3.9 Destination**.

EXERCISE 3.9 *(continued)*

15. Use the Cert Book security group from earlier exercises.

16. Launch the instance with the key pair you used in Exercise 3.1.

17. Once both instances are running, stop the first instance (Source). Make a note of the instance ID.

18. Go to the Amazon EBS page in the Amazon EC2 console and find the volume attached to the Source instance via the instance ID. Detach the instance.

19. When the volume becomes Available, attach the instance to the second instance (Destination).

20. Log in to the Destination instance via RDP using the administrator account.

21. Open a command window (cmd.exe).

22. At the command prompt, type the following commands:

```
C:\Users\Administrator >diskpart
DISKPART>select disk 1
DISKPART>online disk
DISKPART>exit
C:\Users\Administrator>dir e:
```

The volume removed from the stopped source drive can now be read as the E: drive on the destination instance, so its data can be retrieved.

23. Terminate all the instances and ensure the volumes are deleted in the process.

Review Questions

1. Your web application needs four instances to support steady traffic nearly all of the time. On the last day of each month, the traffic triples. What is a cost-effective way to handle this traffic pattern?

    A. Run 12 Reserved Instances all of the time.

    B. Run four On-Demand Instances constantly, then add eight more On-Demand Instances on the last day of each month.

    C. Run four Reserved Instances constantly, then add eight On-Demand Instances on the last day of each month.

    D. Run four On-Demand Instances constantly, then add eight Reserved Instances on the last day of each month.

2. Your order-processing application processes orders extracted from a queue with two Reserved Instances processing 10 orders/minute. If an order fails during processing, then it is returned to the queue without penalty. Due to a weekend sale, the queues have several hundred orders backed up. While the backup is not catastrophic, you would like to drain it so that customers get their confirmation emails faster. What is a cost-effective way to drain the queue for orders?

    A. Create more queues.

    B. Deploy additional Spot Instances to assist in processing the orders.

    C. Deploy additional Reserved Instances to assist in processing the orders.

    D. Deploy additional On-Demand Instances to assist in processing the orders.

3. Which of the following must be specified when launching a new Amazon Elastic Compute Cloud (Amazon EC2) Windows instance? (Choose 2 answers)

    A. The Amazon EC2 instance ID

    B. Password for the administrator account

    C. Amazon EC2 instance type

    D. Amazon Machine Image (AMI)

4. You have purchased an m3.xlarge Linux Reserved instance in us-east-1a. In which ways can you modify this reservation? (Choose 2 answers)

    A. Change it into two m3.large instances.

    B. Change it to a Windows instance.

    C. Move it to us-east-1b.

    D. Change it to an m4.xlarge.

5. Your instance is associated with two security groups. The first allows Remote Desktop Protocol (RDP) access over port 3389 from Classless Inter-Domain Routing (CIDR) block 72.14.0.0/16. The second allows HTTP access over port 80 from CIDR block 0.0.0.0/0. What traffic can reach your instance?

    A. RDP and HTTP access from CIDR block 0.0.0.0/0

    B. No traffic is allowed.

   C. RDP and HTTP traffic from 72.14.0.0/16

   D. RDP traffic over port 3389 from 72.14.0.0/16 and HTTP traffic over port 80 from 0.0.00/0

6. Which of the following are features of enhanced networking? (Choose 3 answers)

   A. More Packets Per Second (PPS)

   B. Lower latency

   C. Multiple network interfaces

   D. Border Gateway Protocol (BGP) routing

   E. Less jitter

7. You are creating a High-Performance Computing (HPC) cluster and need very low latency and high bandwidth between instances. What combination of the following will allow this? (Choose 3 answers)

   A. Use an instance type with 10 Gbps network performance.

   B. Put the instances in a placement group.

   C. Use Dedicated Instances.

   D. Enable enhanced networking on the instances.

   E. Use Reserved Instances.

8. Which Amazon Elastic Compute Cloud (Amazon EC2) feature ensures that your instances will not share a physical host with instances from any other AWS customer?

   A. Amazon Virtual Private Cloud (VPC)

   B. Placement groups

   C. Dedicated Instances

   D. Reserved Instances

9. Which of the following are true of instance stores? (Choose 2 answers)

   A. Automatic backups

   B. Data is lost when the instance stops.

   C. Very high IOPS

   D. Charge is based on the total amount of storage provisioned.

10. Which of the following are features of Amazon Elastic Block Store (Amazon EBS)? (Choose 2 answers)

   A. Data stored on Amazon EBS is automatically replicated within an Availability Zone.

   B. Amazon EBS data is automatically backed up to tape.

   C. Amazon EBS volumes can be encrypted transparently to workloads on the attached instance.

   D. Data on an Amazon EBS volume is lost when the attached instance is stopped.

11. You need to take a snapshot of an Amazon Elastic Block Store (Amazon EBS) volume. How long will the volume be unavailable?

    A.   It depends on the provisioned size of the volume.

    B.   The volume will be available immediately.

    C.   It depends on the amount of data stored on the volume.

    D.   It depends on whether the attached instance is an Amazon EBS-optimized instance.

12. You are restoring an Amazon Elastic Block Store (Amazon EBS) volume from a snapshot. How long will it be before the data is available?

    A.   It depends on the provisioned size of the volume.

    B.   The data will be available immediately.

    C.   It depends on the amount of data stored on the volume.

    D.   It depends on whether the attached instance is an Amazon EBS-optimized instance.

13. You have a workload that requires 15,000 consistent IOPS for data that must be durable. What combination of the following steps do you need? (Choose 2 answers)

    A.   Use an Amazon Elastic Block Store (Amazon EBS)-optimized instance.

    B.   Use an instance store.

    C.   Use a Provisioned IOPS SSD volume.

    D.   Use a magnetic volume.

14. Which of the following can be accomplished through bootstrapping?

    A.   Install the most current security updates.

    B.   Install the current version of the application.

    C.   Configure Operating System (OS) services.

    D.   All of the above.

15. How can you connect to a new Linux instance using SSH?

    A.   Decrypt the root password.

    B.   Using a certificate

    C.   Using the private half of the instance's key pair

    D.   Using Multi-Factor Authentication (MFA)

16. VM Import/Export can import existing virtual machines as: (Choose 2 answers)

    A.   Amazon Elastic Block Store (Amazon EBS) volumes

    B.   Amazon Elastic Compute Cloud (Amazon EC2) instances

    C.   Amazon Machine Images (AMIs)

    D.   Security groups

17. Which of the following can be used to address an Amazon Elastic Compute Cloud (Amazon EC2) instance over the web? (Choose 2 answers)

   A. Windows machine name

   B. Public DNS name

   C. Amazon EC2 instance ID

   D. Elastic IP address

18. Using the correctly decrypted Administrator password and RDP, you cannot log in to a Windows instance you just launched. Which of the following is a possible reason?

   A. There is no security group rule that allows RDP access over port 3389 from your IP address.

   B. The instance is a Reserved Instance.

   C. The instance is not using enhanced networking.

   D. The instance is not an Amazon EBS-optimized instance.

19. You have a workload that requires 1 TB of durable block storage at 1,500 IOPS during normal use. Every night there is an Extract, Transform, Load (ETL) task that requires 3,000 IOPS for 15 minutes. What is the most appropriate volume type for this workload?

   A. Use a Provisioned IOPS SSD volume at 3,000 IOPS.

   B. Use an instance store.

   C. Use a general-purpose SSD volume.

   D. Use a magnetic volume.

20. How are you billed for elastic IP addresses?

   A. Hourly when they are associated with an instance

   B. Hourly when they are not associated with an instance

   C. Based on the data that flows through them

   D. Based on the instance type to which they are attached

Chapter
4

Amazon Virtual Private Cloud (Amazon VPC)

Domain 1.0: Designing highly available, cost-efficient, fault-tolerant, scalable systems

✓ **1.1 Identify and recognize cloud architecture considerations, such as fundamental components and effective designs.**

Content may include the following:

- How to design cloud services

- Planning and design

- Familiarity with:

  - Best practices for AWS architecture

  - Architectural trade-off decisions (for example, high availability vs. cost, Amazon Relational Database Service [RDS] vs. installing your own database on Amazon Elastic Compute Cloud—EC2)

  - Hybrid IT architectures (for example, Direct Connect, Storage Gateway, VPC, Directory Services)

Domain 2.0: Implementation/Deployment

✓ **2.1 Identify the appropriate techniques and methods using Amazon EC2, Amazon S3, AWS Elastic Beanstalk, AWS CloudFormation, AWS OpsWorks, Amazon Virtual Private Cloud (VPC), and AWS Identity and Access Management (IAM) to code and implement a cloud solution.**

Content may include the following:

- Operate and extend service management in a hybrid IT architecture
- Configure services to support compliance requirements in the cloud

Domain 3.0: Data Security

✓ **3.1 Recognize and implement secure practices for optimum cloud deployment and maintenance.**

Content may include the following:

- AWS security attributes (customer workloads down to the physical layer)
- Amazon Virtual Private Cloud (VPC)
- Ingress vs. egress filtering, and which AWS services and features fit
- "Core" Amazon EC2 and S3 security feature sets
- Incorporating common conventional security products (Firewall and VPNs)
- Complex access controls (building sophisticated security groups, ACLs, and so on)

Introduction

The *Amazon Virtual Private Cloud (Amazon VPC)* is a custom-defined virtual network within the AWS Cloud. You can provision your own logically isolated section of AWS, similar to designing and implementing a separate independent network that would operate in an on-premises data center. This chapter explores the core components of Amazon VPC and, in the exercises, you learn how to build your own Amazon VPC in the cloud. A strong understanding of Amazon VPC topology and troubleshooting is required to pass the exam, and we highly recommend that you complete the exercises in this chapter.

Amazon Virtual Private Cloud (Amazon VPC)

Amazon VPC is the networking layer for Amazon Elastic Compute Cloud (Amazon EC2), and it allows you to build your own virtual network within AWS. You control various aspects of your Amazon VPC, including selecting your own IP address range; creating your own *subnets*; and configuring your own route tables, network gateways, and security settings. Within a region, you can create multiple Amazon VPCs, and each Amazon VPC is logically isolated even if it shares its IP address space.

When you create an Amazon VPC, you must specify the IPv4 address range by choosing a *Classless Inter-Domain Routing (CIDR)* block, such as 10.0.0.0/16. The address range of the Amazon VPC cannot be changed after the Amazon VPC is created. An Amazon VPC address range may be as large as /16 (65,536 available addresses) or as small as /28 (16 available addresses) and should not overlap any other network with which they are to be connected.

The Amazon VPC service was released after the Amazon EC2 service; because of this, there are two different networking platforms available within AWS: EC2-Classic and EC2-VPC. Amazon EC2 originally launched with a single, flat network shared with other AWS customers called EC2-Classic. As such, AWS accounts created prior to the arrival of the

Amazon VPC service can launch instances into the EC2-Classic network and EC2-VPC. AWS accounts created after December 2013 only support launching instances using EC2-VPC. AWS accounts that support EC2-VPC will have a default VPC created in each region with a default subnet created in each Availability Zone. The assigned CIDR block of the VPC will be 172.31.0.0/16.

Figure 4.1 illustrates an Amazon VPC with an address space of 10.0.0.0/16, two subnets with different address ranges (10.0.0.0/24 and 10.0.1.0/24) placed in different Availability Zones, and a route table with the local route specified.

FIGURE 4.1 VPC, subnets, and a route table

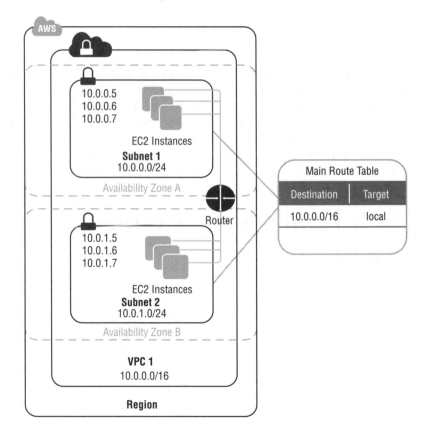

An Amazon VPC consists of the following components:

- Subnets
- Route tables
- Dynamic Host Configuration Protocol (DHCP) option sets
- Security groups
- Network Access Control Lists (ACLs)

An Amazon VPC has the following optional components:

- Internet Gateways (IGWs)
- Elastic IP (EIP) addresses
- Elastic Network Interfaces (ENIs)
- Endpoints
- Peering
- Network Address Translation (NATs) instances and NAT gateways
- Virtual Private Gateway (VPG), Customer Gateways (CGWs), and Virtual Private Networks (VPNs)

Subnets

A *subnet* is a segment of an Amazon VPC's IP address range where you can launch Amazon EC2 instances, Amazon Relational Database Service (Amazon RDS) databases, and other AWS resources. CIDR blocks define subnets (for example, 10.0.1.0/24 and 192.168.0.0/24). The smallest subnet that you can create is a /28 (16 IP addresses). AWS reserves the first four IP addresses and the last IP address of every subnet for internal networking purposes. For example, a subnet defined as a /28 has 16 available IP addresses; subtract the 5 IPs needed by AWS to yield 11 IP addresses for your use within the subnet.

After creating an Amazon VPC, you can add one or more subnets in each Availability Zone. Subnets reside within one Availability Zone and cannot span zones. This is an important point that can come up in the exam, so remember that one subnet equals one Availability Zone. You can, however, have multiple subnets in one Availability Zone.

Subnets can be classified as public, private, or VPN-only. A public subnet is one in which the associated route table (discussed later) directs the subnet's traffic to the Amazon VPC's IGW (also discussed later). A private subnet is one in which the associated route table does not direct the subnet's traffic to the Amazon VPC's IGW. A VPN-only subnet is one in which the associated route table directs the subnet's traffic to the Amazon VPC's VPG (discussed later) and does not have a route to the IGW. Regardless of the type of subnet, the internal IP address range of the subnet is always private (that is, non-routable on the Internet).

Default Amazon VPCs contain one public subnet in every Availability Zone within the region, with a netmask of /20.

Route Tables

A *route table* is a logical construct within an Amazon VPC that contains a set of rules (called routes) that are applied to the subnet and used to determine where network traffic is directed. A route table's routes are what permit Amazon EC2 instances within different subnets within an Amazon VPC to communicate with each other. You can modify route tables and add your own custom routes. You can also use route tables to specify which subnets are public (by directing Internet traffic to the IGW) and which subnets are private (by not having a route that directs traffic to the IGW).

Each route table contains a default route called the local route, which enables communication within the Amazon VPC, and this route cannot be modified or removed. Additional routes can be added to direct traffic to exit the Amazon VPC via the IGW (discussed later), the VPG (discussed later), or the NAT instance (discussed later). In the exercises at the end of this chapter, you can practice how this is accomplished.

You should remember the following points about route tables:

- Your VPC has an implicit router.

- Your VPC automatically comes with a main route table that you can modify.

- You can create additional custom route tables for your VPC.

- Each subnet must be associated with a route table, which controls the routing for the subnet. If you don't explicitly associate a subnet with a particular route table, the subnet uses the main route table.

- You can replace the main route table with a custom table that you've created so that each new subnet is automatically associated with it.

- Each route in a table specifies a destination CIDR and a target; for example, traffic destined for 172.16.0.0/12 is targeted for the VPG. AWS uses the most specific route that matches the traffic to determine how to route the traffic.

Internet Gateways

An *Internet Gateway (IGW)* is a horizontally scaled, redundant, and highly available Amazon VPC component that allows communication between instances in your Amazon VPC and the Internet. An IGW provides a target in your Amazon VPC route tables for Internet-routable traffic, and it performs network address translation for instances that have been assigned public IP addresses.

Amazon EC2 instances within an Amazon VPC are only aware of their private IP addresses. When traffic is sent from the instance to the Internet, the IGW translates the reply address to the instance's public IP address (or EIP address, covered later) and maintains the one-to-one map of the instance private IP address and public IP address. When an instance receives traffic from the Internet, the IGW translates the destination address (public IP address) to the instance's private IP address and forwards the traffic to the Amazon VPC.

You must do the following to create a public subnet with Internet access:

- Attach an IGW to your Amazon VPC.

- Create a subnet route table rule to send all non-local traffic (0.0.0.0/0) to the IGW.

- Configure your network ACLs and security group rules to allow relevant traffic to flow to and from your instance.

You must do the following to enable an Amazon EC2 instance to send and receive traffic from the Internet:

- Assign a public IP address or EIP address.

You can scope the route to all destinations not explicitly known to the route table (0.0.0.0/0), or you can scope the route to a narrower range of IP addresses, such as the public IP addresses of your company's public endpoints outside of AWS or the EIP addresses of other Amazon EC2 instances outside your Amazon VPC.

Figure 4.2 illustrates an Amazon VPC with an address space of 10.0.0.0/16, one subnet with an address range of 10.0.0.0/24, a route table, an attached IGW, and a single Amazon EC2 instance with a private IP address and an EIP address. The route table contains two routes: the local route that permits inter-VPC communication and a route that sends all non-local traffic to the IGW (igw-id). Note that the Amazon EC2 instance has a public IP address (EIP = 198.51.100.2); this instance can be accessed from the Internet, and traffic may originate and return to this instance.

FIGURE 4.2 VPC, subnet, route table, and an Internet gateway

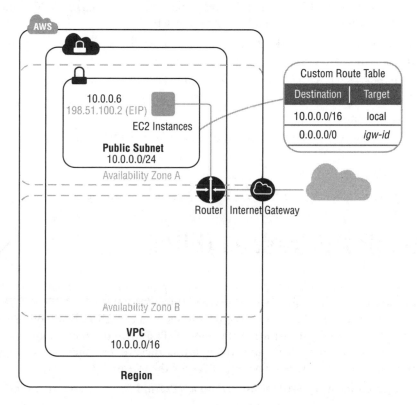

Dynamic Host Configuration Protocol (DHCP) Option Sets

Dynamic Host Configuration Protocol (DHCP) provides a standard for passing configuration information to hosts on a TCP/IP network. The options field of a DHCP message contains the configuration parameters. Some of those parameters are the domain name, domain name server, and the netbios-node-type.

AWS automatically creates and associates a DHCP option set for your Amazon VPC upon creation and sets two options: domain-name-servers (defaulted to AmazonProvidedDNS) and domain-name (defaulted to the domain name for your region). AmazonProvidedDNS is an Amazon Domain Name System (DNS) server, and this option enables DNS for instances that need to communicate over the Amazon VPC's IGW.

The DHCP option sets element of an Amazon VPC allows you to direct Amazon EC2 host name assignments to your own resources. To assign your own domain name to your instances, create a custom DHCP option set and assign it to your Amazon VPC. You can configure the following values within a DHCP option set:

- *domain-name-servers*—The IP addresses of up to four domain name servers, separated by commas. The default is AmazonProvidedDNS.

- *domain-name*—Specify the desired domain name here (for example, mycompany.com).

- *ntp-servers*—The IP addresses of up to four Network Time Protocol (NTP) servers, separated by commas

- *netbios-name-servers*—The IP addresses of up to four NetBIOS name servers, separated by commas

- *netbios-node-type*—Set this value to 2.

Every Amazon VPC must have only one DHCP option set assigned to it.

Elastic IP Addresses (EIPs)

AWS maintains a pool of public IP addresses in each region and makes them available for you to associate to resources within your Amazon VPCs. An *Elastic IP Addresses (EIP)* is a static, public IP address in the pool for the region that you can allocate to your account (pull from the pool) and release (return to the pool). EIPs allow you to maintain a set of IP addresses that remain fixed while the underlying infrastructure may change over time. Here are the important points to understand about EIPs for the exam:

- You must first allocate an EIP for use within a VPC and then assign it to an instance.

- EIPs are specific to a region (that is, an EIP in one region cannot be assigned to an instance within an Amazon VPC in a different region).

- There is a one-to-one relationship between network interfaces and EIPs.

- You can move EIPs from one instance to another, either in the same Amazon VPC or a different Amazon VPC within the same region.

- EIPs remain associated with your AWS account until you explicitly release them.

- There are charges for EIPs allocated to your account, even when they are not associated with a resource.

Elastic Network Interfaces (ENIs)

An *Elastic Network Interface (ENI)* is a virtual network interface that you can attach to an instance in an Amazon VPC. ENIs are only available within an Amazon VPC, and they are associated with a subnet upon creation. They can have one public IP address and multiple private IP addresses. If there are multiple private IP addresses, one of them is primary. Assigning a second network interface to an instance via an ENI allows it to be dual-homed (have network presence in different subnets). An ENI created independently of a particular instance persists regardless of the lifetime of any instance to which it is attached; if an underlying instance fails, the IP address may be preserved by attaching the ENI to a replacement instance.

ENIs allow you to create a management network, use network and security appliances in your Amazon VPC, create dual-homed instances with workloads/roles on distinct subnets, or create a low-budget, high-availability solution.

Endpoints

An Amazon VPC *endpoint* enables you to create a private connection between your Amazon VPC and another AWS service without requiring access over the Internet or through a NAT instance, VPN connection, or AWS Direct Connect. You can create multiple endpoints for a single service, and you can use different route tables to enforce different access policies from different subnets to the same service.

Amazon VPC endpoints currently support communication with Amazon Simple Storage Service (Amazon S3), and other services are expected to be added in the future.

You must do the following to create an Amazon VPC endpoint:

- Specify the Amazon VPC.

- Specify the service. A service is identified by a prefix list of the form `com.amazonaws.<region>.<service>`.

- Specify the policy. You can allow full access or create a custom policy. This policy can be changed at any time.

- Specify the route tables. A route will be added to each specified route table, which will state the service as the destination and the endpoint as the target.

Table 4.1 is an example route table that has an existing route that directs all Internet traffic (0.0.0.0/0) to an IGW. Any traffic from the subnet that is destined for another AWS service (for example, Amazon S3 or Amazon DynamoDB) will be sent to the IGW in order to reach that service.

TABLE 4.1   Route Table with an IGW Routing Rule

Destination	Target
10.0.0.0/16	Local
0.0.0.0/0	igw-1a2b3c4d

Table 4.2 is an example route table that has existing routes directing all Internet traffic to an IGW and all Amazon S3 traffic to the Amazon VPC endpoint.

TABLE 4.2   Route Table with an IGW Routing Rule and VPC Endpoint Rule

Destination	Target
10.0.0.0/16	Local
0.0.0.0/0	igw-1a2b3c4d
pl-1a2b3c4d	vpce-11bb22cc

The route table depicted in Table 4.2 will direct any traffic from the subnet that's destined for Amazon S3 in the same region to the endpoint. All other Internet traffic goes to your IGW, including traffic that's destined for other services and for Amazon S3 in other regions.

Peering

An Amazon VPC *peering* connection is a networking connection between two Amazon VPCs that enables instances in either Amazon VPC to communicate with each other as if they are within the same network. You can create an Amazon VPC peering connection between your own Amazon VPCs or with an Amazon VPC in another AWS account within a single region. A peering connection is neither a gateway nor an Amazon VPN connection and does not introduce a single point of failure for communication.

Peering connections are created through a request/accept protocol. The owner of the requesting Amazon VPC sends a request to peer to the owner of the peer Amazon VPC. If the peer Amazon VPC is within the same account, it is identified by its VPC ID. If the peer VPC is within a different account, it is identified by Account ID and VPC ID. The owner of the peer Amazon VPC has one week to accept or reject the request to peer with the requesting Amazon VPC before the peering request expires.

An Amazon VPC may have multiple peering connections, and peering is a one-to-one relationship between Amazon VPCs, meaning two Amazon VPCs cannot have two peering agreements between them. Also, peering connections do not support transitive routing. Figure 4.3 depicts transitive routing.

FIGURE 4.3   VPC peering connections do not support transitive routing

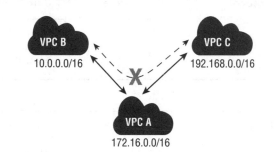

In Figure 4.3, VPC A has two peering connections with two different VPCs: VPC B and VPC C. Therefore, VPC A can communicate directly with VPCs B and C. Because peering connections do not support transitive routing, VPC A cannot be a transit point for traffic between VPCs B and C. In order for VPCs B and C to communicate with each other, a peering connection must be explicitly created between them.

Here are the important points to understand about peering for the exam:

- You cannot create a peering connection between Amazon VPCs that have matching or overlapping CIDR blocks.

- You cannot create a peering connection between Amazon VPCs in different regions.

- Amazon VPC peering connections do not support transitive routing.

- You cannot have more than one peering connection between the same two Amazon VPCs at the same time.

Security Groups

A *security group* is a virtual stateful firewall that controls inbound and outbound network traffic to AWS resources and Amazon EC2 instances. All Amazon EC2 instances must be launched into a security group. If a security group is not specified at launch, then the instance will be launched into the default security group for the Amazon VPC. The default security group allows communication between all resources within the security group, allows all outbound traffic, and denies all other traffic. You may change the rules for the default security group, but you may not delete the default security group. Table 4.3 describes the settings of the default security group.

TABLE 4.3   Security Group Rules

Inbound

Source	Protocol	Port Range	Comments
sg-xxxxxxxx	All	All	Allow inbound traffic from instances within the same security group.

Outbound

Destination	Protocol	Port Range	Comments
0.0.0.0/0	All	All	Allow all outbound traffic.

For each security group, you add rules that control the inbound traffic to instances and a separate set of rules that control the outbound traffic. For example, Table 4.4 describes a security group for web servers.

TABLE 4.4   Security Group Rules for a Web Server

Inbound

Source	Protocol	Port Range	Comments
0.0.0.0/0	TCP	80	Allow inbound traffic from the Internet to port 80.
Your network's public IP address range	TCP	22	Allow Secure Shell (SSH) traffic from your company network.
Your network's public IP address range	TCP	3389	Allow Remote Desktop Protocol (RDP) traffic from your company network.

Outbound			
Destination	**Protocol**	**Port Range**	**Comments**
The ID of the security group for your MySQL database servers	TCP	3306	Allow outbound MySQL access to instances in the specified security group.
The ID of the security group for your Microsoft SQL Server database servers	TCP	1433	Allow outbound Microsoft SQL Server access to instances in the specified security group.

Here are the important points to understand about security groups for the exam:

- You can create up to 500 security groups for each Amazon VPC.
- You can add up to 50 inbound and 50 outbound rules to each security group. If you need to apply more than 100 rules to an instance, you can associate up to five security groups with each network interface.
- You can specify allow rules, but not deny rules. This is an important difference between security groups and ACLs.
- You can specify separate rules for inbound and outbound traffic.
- By default, no inbound traffic is allowed until you add inbound rules to the security group.
- By default, new security groups have an outbound rule that allows all outbound traffic. You can remove the rule and add outbound rules that allow specific outbound traffic only.
- Security groups are stateful. This means that responses to allowed inbound traffic are allowed to flow outbound regardless of outbound rules and vice versa. This is an important difference between security groups and network ACLs.
- Instances associated with the same security group can't talk to each other unless you add rules allowing it (with the exception being the default security group).
- You can change the security groups with which an instance is associated after launch, and the changes will take effect immediately.

Network Access Control Lists (ACLs)

A network *access control list (ACL)* is another layer of security that acts as a stateless firewall on a subnet level. A network ACL is a numbered list of rules that AWS evaluates in order, starting with the lowest numbered rule, to determine whether traffic is allowed in or out of any subnet associated with the network ACL. Amazon VPCs are created with a modifiable default network ACL associated with every subnet that allows all inbound and outbound traffic. When you create a custom network ACL, its initial configuration will deny all inbound and outbound traffic until you create rules that allow otherwise. You may set up network ACLs with rules similar to your security groups in order to add a layer of security to your Amazon VPC, or you may choose to use the default network ACL that does not filter traffic traversing the subnet boundary. Overall, every subnet must be associated with a network ACL.

Table 4.5 explains the differences between a security group and a network ACL. You should remember the following differences between security groups and network ACLs for the exam.

TABLE 4.5   Comparison of Security Groups and Network ACLs

Security Group	Network ACL
Operates at the instance level (first layer of defense)	Operates at the subnet level (second layer of defense)
Supports allow rules only	Supports allow rules and deny rules
Stateful: Return traffic is automatically allowed, regardless of any rules	Stateless: Return traffic must be explicitly allowed by rules.
AWS evaluates all rules before deciding whether to allow traffic	AWS processes rules in number order when deciding whether to allow traffic.
Applied selectively to individual instances	Automatically applied to all instances in the associated subnets; this is a backup layer of defense, so you don't have to rely on someone specifying the security group.

Network Address Translation (NAT) Instances and NAT Gateways

By default, any instance that you launch into a private subnet in an Amazon VPC is not able to communicate with the Internet through the IGW. This is problematic if the instances within private subnets need direct access to the Internet from the Amazon VPC in order to apply security updates, download patches, or update application software. AWS provides NAT instances and NAT gateways to allow instances deployed in private subnets to gain Internet access. For common use cases, we recommend that you use a NAT gateway instead of a NAT instance. The NAT gateway provides better availability and higher bandwidth, and requires less administrative effort than NAT instances.

NAT Instance

A *network address translation (NAT) instance* is an Amazon Linux Amazon Machine Image (AMI) that is designed to accept traffic from instances within a private subnet, translate the source IP address to the public IP address of the NAT instance, and forward the traffic to the IGW. In addition, the NAT instance maintains the state of the forwarded traffic in order to return response traffic from the Internet to the proper instance in the private subnet. These instances have the string amzn-ami-vpc-nat in their names, which is searchable in the Amazon EC2 console.

To allow instances within a private subnet to access Internet resources through the IGW via a NAT instance, you must do the following:

- Create a security group for the NAT with outbound rules that specify the needed Internet resources by port, protocol, and IP address.

- Launch an Amazon Linux NAT AMI as an instance in a public subnet and associate it with the NAT security group.

- Disable the Source/Destination Check attribute of the NAT.

- Configure the route table associated with a private subnet to direct Internet-bound traffic to the NAT instance (for example, i-1a2b3c4d).

- Allocate an EIP and associate it with the NAT instance.

This configuration allows instances in private subnets to send outbound Internet communication, but it prevents the instances from receiving inbound traffic initiated by someone on the Internet.

NAT Gateway

A *NAT gateway* is an Amazon managed resource that is designed to operate just like a NAT instance, but it is simpler to manage and highly available within an Availability Zone.

To allow instances within a private subnet to access Internet resources through the IGW via a NAT gateway, you must do the following:

- Configure the route table associated with the private subnet to direct Internet-bound traffic to the NAT gateway (for example, nat-1a2b3c4d).

- Allocate an EIP and associate it with the NAT gateway.

Like a NAT instance, this managed service allows outbound Internet communication and prevents the instances from receiving inbound traffic initiated by someone on the Internet.

To create an Availability Zone-independent architecture, create a NAT gateway in each Availability Zone and configure your routing to ensure that resources use the NAT gateway in the same Availability Zone.

The exercises will demonstrate how a NAT gateway works.

Virtual Private Gateways (VPGs), Customer Gateways (CGWs), and Virtual Private Networks (VPNs)

You can connect an existing data center to Amazon VPC using either hardware or software VPN connections, which will make Amazon VPC an extension of the data center. Amazon VPC offers two ways to connect a corporate network to a VPC: VPG and CGW.

A *virtual private gateway (VPG)* is the *virtual private network (VPN)* concentrator on the AWS side of the VPN connection between the two networks. A *customer gateway (CGW)* represents a physical device or a software application on the customer's side of the VPN connection. After these two elements of an Amazon VPC have been created, the last step is to create a VPN tunnel. The VPN tunnel is established after traffic is generated from the customer's side of the VPN connection. Figure 4.4 illustrates a single VPN connection between a corporate network and an Amazon VPC.

FIGURE 4.4   VPC with VPN connection to a customer network

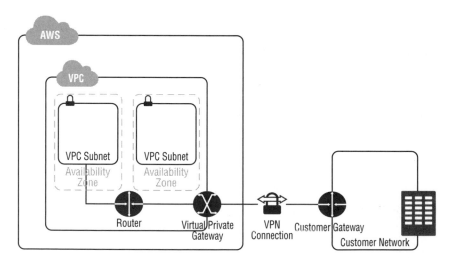

You must specify the type of routing that you plan to use when you create a VPN connection. If the CGW supports Border Gateway Protocol (BGP), then configure the VPN connection for dynamic routing. Otherwise, configure the connections for static routing. If you will be using static routing, you must enter the routes for your network that should be communicated to the VPG. Routes will be propagated to the Amazon VPC to allow your resources to route network traffic back to the corporate network through the VGW and across the VPN tunnel.

Amazon VPC also supports multiple CGWs, each having a VPN connection to a single VPG (many-to-one design). In order to support this topology, the CGW IP addresses must be unique within the region.

Amazon VPC will provide the information needed by the network administrator to configure the CGW and establish the VPN connection with the VPG. The VPN connection consists of two Internet Protocol Security (IPSec) tunnels for higher availability to the Amazon VPC.

Following are the important points to understand about VPGs, CGWs, and VPNs for the exam:

- The VPG is the AWS end of the VPN tunnel.
- The CGW is a hardware or software application on the customer's side of the VPN tunnel.
- You must initiate the VPN tunnel from the CGW to the VPG.
- VPGs support both dynamic routing with BGP and static routing.
- The VPN connection consists of two tunnels for higher availability to the VPC.

Summary

In this chapter, you learned that Amazon VPC is the networking layer for Amazon EC2, and it allows you to create your own private virtual network within the cloud. You can provision your own logically isolated section of AWS similar to designing and implementing a separate independent network that you'd operate in a physical data center.

A VPC consists of the following components:

- Subnets
- Route tables
- DHCP option sets
- Security groups
- Network ACLs

A VPC has the following optional components:

- IGWs
- EIP addresses
- Endpoints

- Peering
- NAT instance and NAT gateway
- VPG, CGW, and VPN

Subnets can be public, private, or VPN-only. A public subnet is one in which the associated route table directs the subnet's traffic to the Amazon VPC's IGW. A private subnet is one in which the associated route table does not direct the subnet's traffic to the Amazon VPC's IGW. A VPN-only subnet is one in which the associated route table directs the subnet's traffic to the Amazon VPC's VPG and does not have a route to the IGW. Regardless of the type of subnet, the internal IP address range of the subnet is always private (non-routable on the Internet).

A route table is a logical construct within an Amazon VPC that contains a set of rules (called routes) that are applied to the subnet and used to determine where network traffic is directed. A route table's routes are what permit Amazon EC2 instances within different subnets within an Amazon VPC to communicate with each other. You can modify route tables and add your own custom routes. You can also use route tables to specify which subnets are public (by directing Internet traffic to the IGW) and which subnets are private (by not having a route that directs traffic to the IGW). An IGW is a horizontally scaled, redundant, and highly available Amazon VPC component that allows communication between instances in your Amazon VPC and the Internet. IGWs are fully redundant and have no bandwidth constraints. An IGW provides a target in your Amazon VPC route tables for Internet-routable traffic, and it performs network address translation for instances that have been assigned public IP addresses.

The DHCP option sets element of an Amazon VPC allows you to direct Amazon EC2 host name assignment to your own resources. In order for you to assign your own domain name to your instances, you create a custom DHCP option set and assign it to your Amazon VPC.

An EIP address is a static, public IP address in the pool for the region that you can allocate to your account (pull from the pool) and release (return to the pool). EIPs allow you to maintain a set of IP addresses that remain fixed while the underlying infrastructure may change over time.

An Amazon VPC endpoint enables you to create a private connection between your Amazon VPC and another AWS service without requiring access over the Internet or through a NAT instance, VPN connection, or AWS Direct Connect. You can create multiple endpoints for a single service, and you can use different route tables to enforce different access policies from different subnets to the same service.

An Amazon VPC peering connection is a networking connection between two Amazon VPCs that enables instances in either Amazon VPC to communicate with each other as if they were within the same network. You can create an Amazon VPC peering connection between your own Amazon VPCs or with an Amazon VPC in another AWS account within a single region. A peering connection is neither a gateway nor a VPN connection and does not introduce a single point of failure for communication.

A security group is a virtual stateful firewall that controls inbound and outbound traffic to Amazon EC2 instances. When you first launch an Amazon EC2 instance into an Amazon VPC, you must specify the security group with which it will be associated. AWS provides a default security group for your use, which has rules that allow all instances associated with the security group to communicate with each other and allow all outbound traffic.

You may change the rules for the default security group, but you may not delete the default security group.

A network ACL is another layer of security that acts as a stateless firewall on a subnet level. Amazon VPCs are created with a modifiable default network ACL associated with every subnet that allows all inbound and outbound traffic. If you want to create a custom network ACL, its initial configuration will deny all inbound and outbound traffic until you create a rule that states otherwise.

A NAT instance is a customer-managed instance that is designed to accept traffic from instances within a private subnet, translate the source IP address to the public IP address of the NAT instance, and forward the traffic to the IGW. In addition, the NAT instance maintains the state of the forwarded traffic in order to return response traffic from the Internet to the proper instance in the private subnet.

A NAT gateway is an AWS-managed service that is designed to accept traffic from instances within a private subnet, translate the source IP address to the public IP address of the NAT gateway, and forward the traffic to the IGW. In addition, the NAT gateway maintains the state of the forwarded traffic in order to return response traffic from the Internet to the proper instance in the private subnet.

A VPG is the VPN concentrator on the AWS side of the VPN connection between the two networks. A CGW is a physical device or a software application on the customer's side of the VPN connection. After these two elements of an Amazon VPC have been created, the last step is to create a VPN tunnel. The VPN tunnel is established after traffic is generated from the customer's side of the VPN connection.

Exam Essentials

Understand what a VPC is and its core and optional components.   An Amazon VPC is a logically isolated network in the AWS Cloud. An Amazon VPC is made up of the following core elements: subnets (public, private, and VPN-only), route tables, DHCP option sets, security groups, and network ACLs. Optional elements include an IGW, EIP addresses, endpoints, peering connections, NAT instances, VPGs, CGWs, and VPN connections.

Understand the purpose of a subnet.   A subnet is a segment of an Amazon VPC's IP address range where you can place groups of isolated resources. Subnets are defined by CIDR blocks—for example, 10.0.1.0/24 and 10.0.2.0/24—and are contained within an Availability Zone.

Identify the difference between a public subnet, a private subnet, and a VPN-Only subnet.   If a subnet's traffic is routed to an IGW, the subnet is known as a public subnet. If a subnet doesn't have a route to the IGW, the subnet is known as a private subnet. If a subnet doesn't have a route to the IGW, but has its traffic routed to a VPG, the subnet is known as a VPN-only subnet.

Understand the purpose of a route table.   A route table is a set of rules (called routes) that are used to determine where network traffic is directed. A route table allows Amazon

EC2 instances within different subnets to communicate with each other (within the same Amazon VPC). The Amazon VPC router also enables subnets, IGWs, and VPGs to communicate with each other.

Understand the purpose of an IGW.   An IGW is a horizontally scaled, redundant, and highly available Amazon VPC component that allows communication between instances in your Amazon VPC and the Internet. IGWs are fully redundant and have no bandwidth constraints. An IGW provides a target in your Amazon VPC route tables for Internet-routable traffic and performs network address translation for instances that have been assigned public IP addresses.

Understand what DHCP option sets provide to an Amazon VPC.   The DHCP option sets element of an Amazon VPC allows you to direct Amazon EC2 host name assignment to your own resources. You can specify the domain name for instances within an Amazon VPC and identify the IP addresses of custom DNS servers, NTP servers, and NetBIOS servers.

Know the difference between an Amazon VPC public IP address and an EIP address. A public IP address is an AWS-owned IP that can be automatically assigned to instances launched within a subnet. An EIP address is an AWS-owned public IP address that you allocate to your account and assign to instances or network interfaces on demand.

Understand what endpoints provide to an Amazon VPC.   An Amazon VPC endpoint enables you to create a private connection between your Amazon VPC and another AWS service without requiring access over the Internet or through a NAT instance, a VPN connection, or AWS Direct Connect. Endpoints support services within the region only.

Understand Amazon VPC peering.   An Amazon VPC peering connection is a networking connection between two Amazon VPCs that enables instances in either Amazon VPC to communicate with each other as if they are within the same network. Peering connections are created through a request/accept protocol. Transitive peering is not supported, and peering is only available between Amazon VPCs within the same region.

Know the difference between a security group and a network ACL.   A security group applies at the instance level. You can have multiple instances in multiple subnets that are members of the same security groups. Security groups are stateful, which means that return traffic is automatically allowed, regardless of any outbound rules. A network ACL is applied on a subnet level, and traffic is stateless. You need to allow both inbound and outbound traffic on the network ACL in order for Amazon EC2 instances in a subnet to be able to communicate over a particular protocol.

Understand what a NAT provides to an Amazon VPC.   A NAT instance or NAT gateway enables instances in a private subnet to initiate outbound traffic to the Internet. This allows outbound Internet communication to download patches and updates, for example, but prevents the instances from receiving inbound traffic initiated by someone on the Internet.

Understand the components needed to establish a VPN connection from a network to an Amazon VPC.   A VPG is the VPN concentrator on the AWS side of the VPN connection between the two networks. A CGW represents a physical device or a software application on the customer's side of the VPN connection. The VPN connection must be initiated from the CGW side, and the connection consists of two IPSec tunnels.

Exercises

The best way to become familiar with Amazon VPC is to build your own custom Amazon VPC and then deploy Amazon EC2 instances into it, which is what you'll be doing in this section. You should repeat these exercises until you can create and decommission Amazon VPCs with confidence.

For assistance completing these exercises, refer to the Amazon VPC User Guide located at http://aws.amazon.com/documentation/vpc/.

EXERCISE 4.1

Create a Custom Amazon VPC

1. Sign in to the AWS Management Console as an administrator or power user.

2. Select the Amazon VPC icon to launch the Amazon VPC Dashboard.

3. Create an Amazon VPC with a CIDR block equal to 192.168.0.0/16, a name tag of **My First VPC**, and default tenancy.

You have created your first custom VPC.

EXERCISE 4.2

Create Two Subnets for Your Custom Amazon VPC

1. Create a subnet with a CIDR block equal to 192.168.1.0/24 and a name tag of **My First Public Subnet**. Create the subnet in the Amazon VPC from Exercise 4.1, and specify an Availability Zone for the subnet (for example, US-East-1a).

2. Create a subnet with a CIDR block equal to 192.168.2.0/24 and a name tag of **My First Private Subnet**. Create the subnet in the Amazon VPC from Exercise 4.1, and specify a different Availability Zone for the subnet than previously specified (for example, US-East-1b).

You have now created two new subnets, each in its own Availability Zone. It's important to remember that one subnet equals one Availability Zone. You cannot stretch a subnet across multiple Availability Zones.

EXERCISE 4.3

Connect Your Custom Amazon VPC to the Internet and Establish Routing

For assistance with this exercise, refer to the Amazon EC2 key pair documentation at:

http://docs.aws.amazon.com/AWSEC2/latest/UserGuide/ec2-key-pairs.html

---

EXERCISE 4.3 *(continued)*

For additional assistance with this exercise, refer to the NAT instances documentation at:

http://docs.aws.amazon.com/AmazonVPC/latest/UserGuide/VPC_NAT_Instance
.html#NATInstance

1. Create an Amazon EC2 key pair in the same region as your custom Amazon VPC.

2. Create an IGW with a name tag of **My First IGW** and attach it to your custom Amazon VPC.

3. Add a route to the main route table for your custom Amazon VPC that directs Internet traffic (0.0.0.0/0) to the IGW.

4. Create a NAT gateway, place it in the public subnet of your custom Amazon VPC, and assign it an EIP.

5. Create a new route table with a name tag of **My First Private Route Table** and place it within your custom Amazon VPC. Add a route to it that directs Internet traffic (0.0.0.0/0) to the NAT gateway and associate it with the private subnet.

You have now created a connection to the Internet for resources within your Amazon VPC. You established routing rules that direct Internet traffic to the IGW regardless of the originating subnet.

EXERCISE 4.4

Launch an Amazon EC2 Instance and Test the Connection to the Internet

1. Launch a t2.micro Amazon Linux AMI as an Amazon EC2 instance into the public subnet of your custom Amazon VPC, give it a name tag of **My First Public Instance**, and select the newly-created key pair for secure access to the instance.

2. Securely access the Amazon EC2 instance in the public subnet via SSH with the newly-created key pair.

3. Execute an update to the operating system instance libraries by executing the following command:

   # sudo yum update -y

4. You should see output showing the instance downloading software from the Internet and installing it.

You have now provisioned an Amazon EC2 instance in a public subnet. You can apply patches to the Amazon EC2 instance in the public subnet, and you have demonstrated connectivity to the Internet.

Review Questions

1. What is the minimum size subnet that you can have in an Amazon VPC?

   A. /24

   B. /26

   C. /28

   D. /30

2. You are a solutions architect working for a large travel company that is migrating its existing server estate to AWS. You have recommended that they use a custom Amazon VPC, and they have agreed to proceed. They will need a public subnet for their web servers and a private subnet in which to place their databases. They also require that the web servers and database servers be highly available and that there be a minimum of two web servers and two database servers each. How many subnets should you have to maintain high availability?

   A. 2

   B. 3

   C. 4

   D. 1

3. Which of the following is an optional security control that can be applied at the subnet layer of a VPC?

   A. Network ACL

   B. Security Group

   C. Firewall

   D. Web application firewall

4. What is the maximum size IP address range that you can have in an Amazon VPC?

   A. /16

   B. /24

   C. /28

   D. /30

5. You create a new subnet and then add a route to your route table that routes traffic out from that subnet to the Internet using an IGW. What type of subnet have you created?

   A. An internal subnet

   B. A private subnet

   C. An external subnet

   D. A public subnet

6. What happens when you create a new Amazon VPC?

   A. A main route table is created by default.

   B. Three subnets are created by default—one for each Availability Zone.

   C. Three subnets are created by default in one Availability Zone.

   D. An IGW is created by default.

7. You create a new VPC in US-East-1 and provision three subnets inside this Amazon VPC. Which of the following statements is true?

   A. By default, these subnets will not be able to communicate with each other; you will need to create routes.

   B. All subnets are public by default.

   C. All subnets will be able to communicate with each other by default.

   D. Each subnet will have identical CIDR blocks.

8. How many IGWs can you attach to an Amazon VPC at any one time?

   A. 1

   B. 2

   C. 3

   D. 4

9. What aspect of an Amazon VPC is stateful?

   A. Network ACLs

   B. Security groups

   C. Amazon DynamoDB

   D. Amazon S3

10. You have created a custom Amazon VPC with both private and public subnets. You have created a NAT instance and deployed this instance to a public subnet. You have attached an EIP address and added your NAT to the route table. Unfortunately, instances in your private subnet still cannot access the Internet. What may be the cause of this?

    A. Your NAT is in a public subnet, but it needs to be in a private subnet.

    B. Your NAT should be behind an Elastic Load Balancer.

    C. You should disable source/destination checks on the NAT.

    D. Your NAT has been deployed on a Windows instance, but your other instances are Linux. You should redeploy the NAT onto a Linux instance.

11. Which of the following will occur when an Amazon Elastic Block Store (Amazon EBS)-backed Amazon EC2 instance in an Amazon VPC with an associated EIP is stopped and started? (Choose 2 answers)

    A. The EIP will be dissociated from the instance.

    B. All data on instance store devices will be lost.

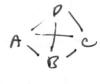

C. All data on Amazon EBS devices will be lost.

D. The ENI is detached.

E. The underlying host for the instance is changed.

12. How many VPC Peering connections are required for four VPCs located within the same AWS region to be able to send traffic to each of the others?

A. 3

B. 4

C. 5

D. 6

13. Which of the following AWS resources would you use in order for an EC2-VPC instance to resolve DNS names outside of AWS?

A. A VPC peering connection

B. A DHCP option set

C. A routing rule

D. An IGW

14. Which of the following is the Amazon side of an Amazon VPN connection?

A. An EIP

B. A CGW

C. An IGW

D. A VPG

15. What is the default limit for the number of Amazon VPCs that a customer may have in a region?

A. 5

B. 6

C. 7

D. There is no default maximum number of VPCs within a region.

16. You are responsible for your company's AWS resources, and you notice a significant amount of traffic from an IP address in a foreign country in which your company does not have customers. Further investigation of the traffic indicates the source of the traffic is scanning for open ports on your EC2-VPC instances. Which one of the following resources can deny the traffic from reaching the instances?

A. Security group

B. Network ACL

C. NAT instance

D. An Amazon VPC endpoint

17. Which of the following is the security protocol supported by Amazon VPC?

    A. SSH

    B. Advanced Encryption Standard (AES)

    C. Point-to-Point Tunneling Protocol (PPTP)

    D. IPsec

18. Which of the following Amazon VPC resources would you use in order for EC2-VPC instances to send traffic directly to Amazon S3?

    A. Amazon S3 gateway

    B. IGW

    C. CGW

    D. VPC endpoint

19. What properties of an Amazon VPC must be specified at the time of creation? (Choose 2 answers)

    A. The CIDR block representing the IP address range

    B. One or more subnets for the Amazon VPC

    C. The region for the Amazon VPC

    D. Amazon VPC Peering relationships

20. Which Amazon VPC feature allows you to create a dual-homed instance?

    A. EIP address

    B. ENI

    C. Security groups

    D. CGW

Chapter 5

Elastic Load Balancing, Amazon CloudWatch, and Auto Scaling

THE AWS CERTIFIED SOLUTIONS ARCHITECT EXAM TOPICS COVERED IN THIS CHAPTER MAY INCLUDE, BUT ARE NOT LIMITED TO, THE FOLLOWING:

Domain 1.0: Designing highly available, cost-effective, fault-tolerant, scalable systems

✓ 1.1 Identify and recognize cloud architecture considerations, such as fundamental components and effective designs.

  ▪ Elasticity and scalability

Domain 2.0: Implementation/Deployment

✓ 2.1 Identify the appropriate techniques and methods using Amazon Elastic Compute Cloud (Amazon EC2), Amazon Simple Storage Service (Amazon S3), AWS Elastic Beanstalk, AWS CloudFormation, AWS OpsWorks, Amazon Virtual Private Cloud (Amazon VPC), and AWS Identity and Access Management (IAM) to code and implement a cloud solution.

Content may include the following:

  ▪ Launch instances across the AWS global infrastructure

Domain 3.0: Data Security

✓ 3.1 Recognize and implement secure practices for optimum cloud deployment and maintenance.

  ▪ CloudWatch Logs

Domain 4.0: Troubleshooting

Content may include the following:

  ▪ General troubleshooting information and questions

Introduction

In this chapter, you will learn how Elastic Load Balancing, Amazon CloudWatch, and Auto Scaling work both independently and together to help you efficiently and cost-effectively deploy highly available and optimized workloads on AWS.

Elastic Load Balancing is a highly available service that distributes traffic across Amazon Elastic Compute Cloud (Amazon EC2) instances and includes options that provide flexibility and control of incoming requests to Amazon EC2 instances.

Amazon CloudWatch is a service that monitors AWS Cloud resources and applications running on AWS. It collects and tracks metrics, collects and monitors log files, and sets alarms. Amazon CloudWatch has a basic level of monitoring for no cost and a more detailed level of monitoring for an additional cost.

Auto Scaling is a service that allows you to maintain the availability of your applications by scaling Amazon EC2 capacity up or down in accordance with conditions you set.

This chapter covers all three services separately, but it also highlights how they can work together to build more robust and highly available architectures on AWS.

Elastic Load Balancing

An advantage of having access to a large number of servers in the cloud, such as Amazon EC2 instances on AWS, is the ability to provide a more consistent experience for the end user. One way to ensure consistency is to balance the request load across more than one server. A load balancer is a mechanism that automatically distributes traffic across multiple Amazon EC2 instances. You can either manage your own virtual load balancers on Amazon EC2 instances or leverage an AWS Cloud service called Elastic Load Balancing, which provides a managed load balancer for you.

The Elastic Load Balancing service allows you to distribute traffic across a group of Amazon EC2 instances in one or more *Availability Zones*, enabling you to achieve high availability in your applications. Elastic Load Balancing supports routing and load balancing of Hypertext Transfer Protocol (HTTP), Hypertext Transfer Protocol Secure (HTTPS),

Transmission Control Protocol (TCP), and *Secure Sockets Layer (SSL)* traffic to Amazon EC2 instances. Elastic Load Balancing provides a stable, single *Canonical Name record (CNAME)* entry point for *Domain Name System (DNS)* configuration and supports both Internet-facing and internal application-facing load balancers. Elastic Load Balancing supports health checks for Amazon EC2 instances to ensure traffic is not routed to unhealthy or failing instances. Also, Elastic Load Balancing can automatically scale based on collected metrics.

There are several advantages of using Elastic Load Balancing. Because Elastic Load Balancing is a managed service, it scales in and out automatically to meet the demands of increased application traffic and is highly available within a region itself as a service. Elastic Load Balancing helps you achieve high availability for your applications by distributing traffic across healthy instances in multiple Availability Zones. Additionally, Elastic Load Balancing seamlessly integrates with the Auto Scaling service to automatically scale the Amazon EC2 instances behind the load balancer. Finally, Elastic Load Balancing is secure, working with Amazon Virtual Private Cloud (Amazon VPC) to route traffic internally between application tiers, allowing you to expose only Internet-facing public IP addresses. Elastic Load Balancing also supports integrated certificate management and SSL termination.

> Elastic Load Balancing is a highly available service itself and can be used to help build highly available architectures.

Types of Load Balancers

Elastic Load Balancing provides several types of load balancers for handling different kinds of connections including Internet-facing, internal, and load balancers that support encrypted connections.

Internet-Facing Load Balancers

An *Internet-facing load balancer* is, as the name implies, a load balancer that takes requests from clients over the Internet and distributes them to Amazon EC2 instances that are registered with the load balancer.

When you configure a load balancer, it receives a public DNS name that clients can use to send requests to your application. The DNS servers resolve the DNS name to your load balancer's public IP address, which can be visible to client applications.

> An AWS recommended best practice is always to reference a load balancer by its DNS name, instead of by the IP address of the load balancer, in order to provide a single, stable entry point.

Because Elastic Load Balancing scales in and out to meet traffic demand, it is not recommended to bind an application to an IP address that may no longer be part of a load balancer's pool of resources.

Elastic Load Balancing in Amazon VPC supports IPv4 addresses only. Elastic Load Balancing in EC2-Classic supports both IPv4 and IPv6 addresses.

Internal Load Balancers

In a multi-tier application, it is often useful to load balance between the tiers of the application. For example, an Internet-facing load balancer might receive and balance external traffic to the presentation or web tier whose Amazon EC2 instances then send its requests to a load balancer sitting in front of the application tier. You can use *internal load balancers* to route traffic to your Amazon EC2 instances in VPCs with private subnets.

HTTPS Load Balancers

You can create a load balancer that uses the SSL/Transport Layer Security (TLS) protocol for encrypted connections (also known as *SSL offload*). This feature enables traffic encryption between your load balancer and the clients that initiate HTTPS sessions, and for connections between your load balancer and your back-end instances. Elastic Load Balancing provides security policies that have predefined SSL negotiation configurations to use to negotiate connections between clients and the load balancer. In order to use SSL, you must install an SSL certificate on the load balancer that it uses to terminate the connection and then decrypt requests from clients before sending requests to the back-end Amazon EC2 instances. You can optionally choose to enable authentication on your back-end instances.

Elastic Load Balancing does not support *Server Name Indication (SNI)* on your load balancer. This means that if you want to host multiple websites on a fleet of Amazon EC2 instances behind Elastic Load Balancing with a single SSL certificate, you will need to add a *Subject Alternative Name (SAN)* for each website to the certificate to avoid site users seeing a warning message when the site is accessed.

Listeners

Every load balancer must have one or more *listeners* configured. A listener is a process that checks for connection requests—for example, a CNAME configured to the A record name of the load balancer. Every listener is configured with a protocol and a port (client to load balancer) for a front-end connection and a protocol and a port for the back-end (load balancer to Amazon EC2 instance) connection. Elastic Load Balancing supports the following protocols:

- HTTP
- HTTPS
- TCP
- SSL

Elastic Load Balancing supports protocols operating at two different *Open System Interconnection (OSI)* layers. In the OSI model, Layer 4 is the transport layer that describes the TCP connection between the client and your back-end instance through the load balancer. Layer 4 is the lowest level that is configurable for your load balancer. Layer 7 is the application layer that describes the use of HTTP and HTTPS connections from clients to the load balancer and from the load balancer to your back-end instance.

The SSL protocol is primarily used to encrypt confidential data over insecure networks such as the Internet. The SSL protocol establishes a secure connection between a client and the back-end server and ensures that all the data passed between your client and your server is private.

Configuring Elastic Load Balancing

Elastic Load Balancing allows you to configure many aspects of the load balancer, including *idle connection timeout, cross-zone load balancing, connection draining, proxy protocol, sticky sessions,* and *health checks.* Configuration settings can be modified using either the AWS Management Console or a Command Line Interface (CLI). Some of the options are described next.

Idle Connection Timeout

For each request that a client makes through a load balancer, the load balancer maintains two connections. One connection is with the client and the other connection is to the back-end instance. For each connection, the load balancer manages an idle timeout that is triggered when no data is sent over the connection for a specified time period. After the idle time-out period has elapsed, if no data has been sent or received, the load balancer closes the connection.

By default, Elastic Load Balancing sets the idle timeout to 60 seconds for both connections. If an HTTP request doesn't complete within the idle timeout period, the load balancer closes the connection, even if data is still being transferred. You can change the idle timeout setting for the connections to ensure that lengthy operations, such as file uploads, have time to complete.

If you use HTTP and HTTPS listeners, we recommend that you enable the *keep-alive* option for your Amazon EC2 instances. You can enable keep-alive in your web server settings or in the kernel settings for your Amazon EC2 instances. Keep-alive, when enabled, allows the load balancer to reuse connections to your back-end instance, which reduces CPU utilization.

> **TIP**
> To ensure that the load balancer is responsible for closing the connections to your back-end instance, make sure that the value you set for the keep-alive time is greater than the idle timeout setting on your load balancer.

Cross-Zone Load Balancing

To ensure that request traffic is routed evenly across all back-end instances for your load balancer, regardless of the Availability Zone in which they are located, you should enable cross-zone load balancing on your load balancer. Cross-zone load balancing reduces the need to maintain equivalent numbers of back-end instances in each Availability Zone and improves your application's ability to handle the loss of one or more back-end instances. However, it is still recommended that you maintain approximately equivalent numbers of instances in each Availability Zone for higher fault tolerance.

For environments where clients cache DNS lookups, incoming requests might favor one of the Availability Zones. Using cross-zone load balancing, this imbalance in the request load is spread across all available back-end instances in the region, reducing the impact of misconfigured clients.

Connection Draining

You should enable *connection draining* to ensure that the load balancer stops sending requests to instances that are deregistering or unhealthy, while keeping the existing connections open. This enables the load balancer to complete in-flight requests made to these instances.

When you enable connection draining, you can specify a maximum time for the load balancer to keep connections alive before reporting the instance as deregistered. The maximum timeout value can be set between 1 and 3,600 seconds (the default is 300 seconds). When the maximum time limit is reached, the load balancer forcibly closes connections to the deregistering instance.

Proxy Protocol

When you use TCP or SSL for both front-end and back-end connections, your load balancer forwards requests to the back-end instances without modifying the request headers. If you enable *Proxy Protocol*, a human-readable header is added to the request header with connection information such as the source IP address, destination IP address, and port numbers. The header is then sent to the back-end instance as part of the request.

Before using Proxy Protocol, verify that your load balancer is not behind a proxy server with Proxy Protocol enabled. If Proxy Protocol is enabled on both the proxy server and the load balancer, the load balancer adds another header to the request, which already has a header from the proxy server. Depending on how your back-end instance is configured, this duplication might result in errors.

Sticky Sessions

By default, a load balancer routes each request independently to the registered instance with the smallest load. However, you can use the *sticky session* feature (also known as *session affinity*), which enables the load balancer to bind a user's session to a specific instance. This ensures that all requests from the user during the session are sent to the same instance.

The key to managing sticky sessions is to determine how long your load balancer should consistently route the user's request to the same instance. If your application has its own session cookie, you can configure Elastic Load Balancing so that the session cookie follows the duration specified by the application's session cookie. If your application does not have its own session cookie, you can configure Elastic Load Balancing to create a session cookie by specifying your own stickiness duration. Elastic Load Balancing creates a cookie named AWSELB that is used to map the session to the instance.

Health Checks

Elastic Load Balancing supports health checks to test the status of the Amazon EC2 instances behind an Elastic Load Balancing load balancer. The status of the instances that are healthy at the time of the health check is InService. The status of any instances that are unhealthy at the time of the health check is OutOfService. The load balancer performs health checks on all registered instances to determine whether the instance is in a healthy state or an unhealthy state. A health check is a ping, a connection attempt, or a page that is checked periodically. You can set the time interval between health checks and also the amount of time to wait to respond in case the health check page includes a computational aspect. Finally, you can set a threshold for the number of consecutive health check failures before an instance is marked as unhealthy.

Updates Behind an Elastic Load Balancing Load Balancer

Long-running applications will eventually need to be maintained and updated with a newer version of the application. When using Amazon EC2 instances running behind an Elastic Load Balancing load balancer, you may deregister these long-running Amazon EC2 instances associated with a load balancer manually and then register newly launched Amazon EC2 instances that you have started with the new updates installed.

Amazon CloudWatch

Amazon CloudWatch is a service that you can use to monitor your AWS resources and your applications in real time. With Amazon CloudWatch, you can collect and track metrics, create alarms that send notifications, and make changes to the resources being monitored based on rules you define.

For example, you might choose to monitor CPU utilization to decide when to add or remove Amazon EC2 instances in an application tier. Or, if a particular application-specific metric that is not visible to AWS is the best indicator for assessing your scaling needs, you can perform a PUT request to push that metric into Amazon CloudWatch. You can then use this custom metric to manage capacity.

You can specify parameters for a metric over a time period and configure alarms and automated actions when a threshold is reached. Amazon CloudWatch supports multiple types of actions such as sending a notification to an Amazon Simple Notification Service (Amazon SNS) topic or executing an Auto Scaling policy.

Amazon CloudWatch offers either basic or detailed monitoring for supported AWS products. *Basic monitoring* sends data points to Amazon CloudWatch every five minutes for a limited number of preselected metrics at no charge. *Detailed monitoring* sends data points to Amazon CloudWatch every minute and allows data aggregation for an additional charge. If you want to use detailed monitoring, you must enable it—basic is the default.

Amazon CloudWatch supports monitoring and specific metrics for most AWS Cloud services, including: Auto Scaling, Amazon CloudFront, Amazon CloudSearch, Amazon DynamoDB, Amazon EC2, Amazon EC2 Container Service (Amazon ECS), Amazon ElastiCache, Amazon Elastic Block Store (Amazon EBS), Elastic Load Balancing, Amazon Elastic MapReduce (Amazon EMR), Amazon Elasticsearch Service, Amazon Kinesis Streams, Amazon Kinesis Firehose, AWS Lambda, Amazon Machine Learning, AWS OpsWorks, Amazon Redshift, Amazon Relational Database Service (Amazon RDS), Amazon Route 53, Amazon SNS, Amazon Simple Queue Service (Amazon SQS), Amazon S3, AWS Simple Workflow Service (Amazon SWF), AWS Storage Gateway, AWS WAF, and Amazon WorkSpaces.

Read Alert

You may have an application that leverages Amazon DynamoDB, and you want to know when read requests reach a certain threshold and alert yourself with an email. You can do this by using `ProvisionedReadCapacityUnits` for the Amazon DynamoDB table for which you want to set an alarm. You simply set a threshold value during a number of consecutive periods and then specify email as the notification type. Now, when the threshold is sustained over the number of periods, your specified email will alert you to the read activity.

Amazon CloudWatch metrics can be retrieved by performing a GET request. When you use detailed monitoring, you can also aggregate metrics across a length of time you specify. Amazon CloudWatch does not aggregate data across regions but can aggregate across Availability Zones within a region.

AWS provides a rich set of metrics included with each service, but you can also define custom metrics to monitor resources and events AWS does not have visibility into—for example, Amazon EC2 instance memory consumption and disk metrics that are visible to the operating system of the Amazon EC2 instance but not visible to AWS or application-specific thresholds running on instances that are not known to AWS. Amazon CloudWatch supports an Application Programming Interface (API) that allows programs and scripts to PUT metrics into Amazon CloudWatch as name-value pairs that can then be used to create events and trigger alarms in the same manner as the default Amazon CloudWatch metrics.

Amazon CloudWatch Logs can be used to monitor, store, and access log files from Amazon EC2 instances, AWS CloudTrail, and other sources. You can then retrieve the log data and monitor in real time for events—for example, you can track the number of errors in your application logs and send a notification if an error rate exceeds a threshold. Amazon CloudWatch Logs can also be used to store your logs in Amazon S3 or Amazon Glacier. Logs can be retained indefinitely or according to an aging policy that will delete older logs as no longer needed.

A *CloudWatch Logs agent* is available that provides an automated way to send log data to CloudWatch Logs for Amazon EC2 instances running Amazon Linux or Ubuntu. You can use the Amazon CloudWatch Logs agent installer on an existing Amazon EC2 instance to install and configure the CloudWatch Logs agent. After installation is complete, the agent confirms that it has started and it stays running until you disable it.

Amazon CloudWatch has some limits that you should keep in mind when using the service. Each AWS account is limited to 5,000 alarms per AWS account, and metrics data is retained for two weeks by default (at the time of this writing). If you want to keep the data longer, you will need to move the logs to a persistent store like Amazon S3 or Amazon Glacier. You should familiarize yourself with the limits for Amazon CloudWatch in the Amazon CloudWatch Developer Guide.

Auto Scaling

A distinct advantage of deploying applications to the cloud is the ability to launch and then release servers in response to variable workloads. Provisioning servers on demand and then releasing them when they are no longer needed can provide significant cost savings for workloads that are not steady state. Examples include a website for a specific sporting event, an end-of-month data-input system, a retail shopping site supporting flash sales, a music artist website during the release of new songs, a company website announcing successful earnings, or a nightly processing run to calculate daily activity.

Auto Scaling is a service that allows you to scale your Amazon EC2 capacity automatically by scaling out and scaling in according to criteria that you define. With Auto Scaling, you can ensure that the number of running Amazon EC2 instances increases during demand spikes or peak demand periods to maintain application performance and decreases automatically during demand lulls or troughs to minimize costs.

Embrace the Spike

Many web applications have unplanned load increases based on events outside of your control. For example, your company may get mentioned on a popular blog or television program driving many more people to visit your site than expected. Setting up Auto Scaling in advance will allow you to embrace and survive this kind of fast increase in the number of requests. Auto Scaling will scale up your site to meet the increased demand and then scale down when the event subsides.

Auto Scaling Plans

Auto Scaling has several schemes or plans that you can use to control how you want Auto Scaling to perform.

Maintain Current Instance Levels

You can configure your Auto Scaling group to maintain a minimum or specified number of running instances at all times. To maintain the current instance levels, Auto Scaling performs a periodic health check on running instances within an *Auto Scaling group*. When Auto Scaling finds an unhealthy instance, it terminates that instance and launches a new one.

> Steady state workloads that need a consistent number of Amazon EC2 instances at all times can use Auto Scaling to monitor and keep that specific number of Amazon EC2 instances running.

Manual Scaling

Manual scaling is the most basic way to scale your resources. You only need to specify the change in the maximum, minimum, or desired capacity of your Auto Scaling group. Auto Scaling manages the process of creating or terminating instances to maintain the updated capacity.

> Manual scaling out can be very useful to increase resources for an infrequent event, such as the release of a new game version that will be available for download and require a user registration. For extremely large-scale events, even the Elastic Load Balancing load balancers can be pre-warmed by working with your local solutions architect or AWS Support.

Scheduled Scaling

Sometimes you know exactly when you will need to increase or decrease the number of instances in your group, simply because that need arises on a predictable schedule. Examples include periodic events such as end-of-month, end-of-quarter, or end-of-year processing, and also other predictable, recurring events. Scheduled scaling means that scaling actions are performed automatically as a function of time and date.

> Recurring events such as end-of-month, quarter, or year processing, or scheduled and recurring automated load and performance testing, can be anticipated and Auto Scaling can be ramped up appropriately at the time of the scheduled event.

Dynamic Scaling

Dynamic scaling lets you define parameters that control the Auto Scaling process in a scaling policy. For example, you might create a policy that adds more Amazon EC2 instances to the web tier when the network bandwidth, measured by Amazon CloudWatch, reaches a certain threshold.

Auto Scaling Components

Auto Scaling has several components that need to be configured to work properly: a *launch configuration*, an *Auto Scaling group*, and an optional *scaling policy*.

Launch Configuration

A *launch configuration* is the template that Auto Scaling uses to create new instances, and it is composed of the configuration name, *Amazon Machine Image (AMI)*, Amazon EC2 instance type, security group, and instance key pair. Each Auto Scaling group can have only one launch configuration at a time.

The CLI command that follows will create a launch configuration with the following attributes:

Name: myLC

AMI: ami-0535d66c

Instance type: m3.medium

Security groups: sg-f57cde9d

Instance key pair: myKeyPair

```
> aws autoscaling create-launch-configuration --launch-configuration-name myLC
--image-id ami-0535d66c --instance-type m3.medium --security-groups sg-f57cde9d
--key-name myKeyPair
```

Security groups for instances launched in EC2-Classic may be referenced by security group name such as "SSH" or "Web" if that is what they are named, or you can reference the security group IDs, such as sg-f57cde9d. If you launched the instances in Amazon VPC, which is recommended, you must use the security group IDs to reference the security groups you want associated with the instances in an Auto Scaling launch configuration.

The default limit for launch configurations is 100 per region. If you exceed this limit, the call to create-launch-configuration will fail. You may view and update this limit by running describe-account-limits at the command line, as shown here.

```
> aws autoscaling describe-account-limits
```

Auto Scaling may cause you to reach limits of other services, such as the default number of Amazon EC2 instances you can currently launch within a region, which is 20. When building more complex architectures with AWS, it is important to keep in mind the service limits for all AWS Cloud services you are using.

When you run a command using the CLI and it fails, check your syntax first. If that checks out, verify the limits for the command you are attempting, and check to see that you have not exceeded a limit. Some limits can be raised and usually defaulted to a reasonable value to limit a race condition, an errant script running in a loop, or other similar automation that might cause unintended high usage and billing of AWS resources. AWS service limits can be viewed in the AWS General Reference Guide under AWS Service Limits. You can raise your limits by creating a support case at the AWS Support Center online and then choosing Service Limit Increase under Regarding. Then fill in the appropriate service and limit to increase value in the online form.

Auto Scaling Group

An Auto Scaling group is a collection of Amazon EC2 instances managed by the Auto Scaling service. Each Auto Scaling group contains configuration options that control when Auto Scaling should launch new instances and terminate existing instances. An Auto Scaling group must contain a name and a minimum and maximum number of instances that can be in the group. You can optionally specify desired capacity, which is the number of instances that the group must have at all times. If you don't specify a desired capacity, the default desired capacity is the minimum number of instances that you specify.

The CLI command that follows will create an Auto Scaling group that references the previous launch configuration and includes the following specifications:

Name: myASG

Launch configuration: myLC

Availability Zones: us-east-1a and us-east-1c

Minimum size: 1

Desired capacity: 3

Maximum capacity: 10

Load balancers: myELB

```
> aws autoscaling create-auto-scaling-group --auto-scaling-group-name myASG
--launch-configuration-name myLC --availability-zones us-east-1a, us-east-1c
--min-size 1 --max-size 10 --desired-capacity 3 --load-balancer-names myELB
```

Figure 5.1 depicts deployed AWS resources after a load balancer named myELB is created and the launch configuration myLC and Auto Scaling Group myASG are set up.

FIGURE 5.1   Auto Scaling group behind an Elastic Load Balancing load balancer

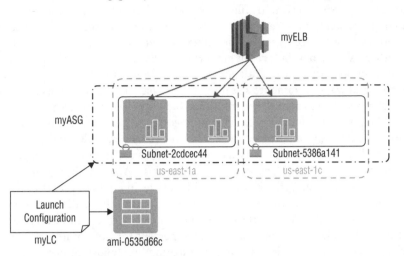

An Auto Scaling group can use either On-Demand or Spot Instances as the Amazon EC2 instances it manages. On-Demand is the default, but Spot Instances can be used by referencing a maximum bid price in the launch configuration (–spot-price "0.15") associated with the Auto Scaling group. You may change the bid price by creating a new launch configuration with the new bid price and then associating it with your Auto Scaling group. If instances are available at or below your bid price, they will be launched in your Auto Scaling group. Spot Instances in an Auto Scaling group follow the same guidelines as Spot Instances outside an Auto Scaling group and require applications that are flexible and can tolerate Amazon EC2 instances that are terminated with short notice, for example, when the Spot price rises above the bid price you set in the launch configuration. A launch configuration can reference On-Demand Instances or Spot Instances, but not both.

Spot On!

Auto Scaling supports using cost-effective Spot Instances. This can be very useful when you are hosting sites where you want to provide additional compute capacity but are price constrained. An example is a "freemium" site model where you may offer some basic functionality to users for free and additional functionality for premium users who pay for use. Spot Instances can be used for providing the basic functionality when available by referencing a maximum bid price in the launch configuration (–spot-price "0.15") associated with the Auto Scaling group.

Scaling Policy

You can associate Amazon CloudWatch alarms and *scaling policies* with an Auto Scaling group to adjust Auto Scaling dynamically. When a threshold is crossed, Amazon

CloudWatch sends alarms to trigger changes (scaling in or out) to the number of Amazon EC2 instances currently receiving traffic behind a load balancer. After the Amazon CloudWatch alarm sends a message to the Auto Scaling group, Auto Scaling executes the associated policy to scale your group. The policy is a set of instructions that tells Auto Scaling whether to scale out, launching new Amazon EC2 instances referenced in the associated launch configuration, or to scale in and terminate instances.

There are several ways to configure a scaling policy: You can increase or decrease by a specific number of instances, such as adding two instances; you can target a specific number of instances, such as a maximum of five total Amazon EC2 instances; or you can adjust based on a percentage. You can also scale by steps and increase or decrease the current capacity of the group based on a set of scaling adjustments that vary based on the size of the alarm threshold trigger.

You can associate more than one scaling policy with an Auto Scaling group. For example, you can create a policy using the trigger for CPU utilization, called *CPULoad*, and the CloudWatch metric *CPUUtilization* to specify scaling out if CPU utilization is greater than 75 percent for two minutes. You could attach another policy to the same Auto Scaling group to scale in if CPU utilization is less than 40 percent for 20 minutes.

The following CLI commands will create the scaling policy just described.

```
> aws autoscaling put-scaling-policy --auto-scaling-group-name myASG
--policy-name CPULoadScaleOut --scaling-adjustment 1 --adjustment-type
ChangeInCapacity --cooldown 30

> aws autoscaling put-scaling-policy --auto-scaling-group-name myASG
--policy-name CPULoadScaleIn --scaling-adjustment -1 --adjustment-type
ChangeInCapacity --cooldown 600
```

The following CLI commands will associate Amazon CloudWatch alarms for scaling out and scaling in with the scaling policy, as shown in Figure 5.2. In this example, the Amazon CloudWatch alarms reference the scaling policy by Amazon Resource Name (ARN).

FIGURE 5.2   Auto Scaling group with policy

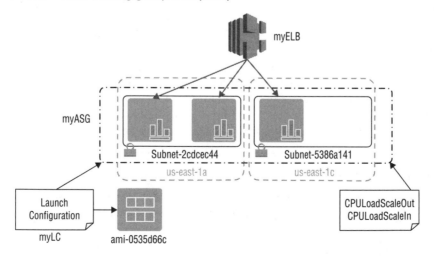

```
> aws cloudwatch put-metric-alarm --alarm name capacityAdd --metric-name
CPUUtilization --namespace AWS/EC2 --statistic Average --period 300 --threshold 75
--comparison-operator GreaterThanOrEqualToThreshold --dimensions
"Name=AutoScalingGroupName, Value=myASG" --evaluation-periods 1 --alarm-actions
arn:aws:autoscaling:us-east-1:123456789012:scalingPolicy:12345678-90ab-cdef-
1234567890ab:autoScalingGroupName/myASG:policyName/CPULoadScaleOut --unit Percent
```

```
> aws cloudwatch put-metric-alarm --alarm name capacityReduce --metric-name
CPUUtilization --namespace AWS/EC2 --statistic Average --period 1200 --threshold 40
--comparison-operator GreaterThanOrEqualToThreshold --dimensions
"Name=AutoScalingGroupName, Value=myASG" --evaluation-periods 1 --alarm-actions
arn:aws:autoscaling:us-east-1:123456789011:scalingPolicy:11345678-90ab-cdef-
1234567890ab:autoScalingGroupName/myASG:policyName/CPULoadScaleIn --unit Percent
```

If the scaling policy defined in the previous paragraph is associated with the Auto Scaling group named myASG, and the CPU utilization is over 75 percent for more than five minutes, as shown in Figure 5.3, a new Amazon EC2 instance will be launched and attached to the load balancer named myELB.

FIGURE 5.3   Amazon CloudWatch alarm triggering scaling out

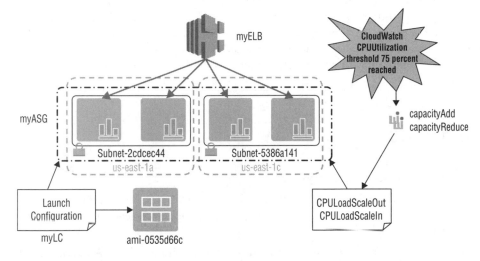

A recommended best practice is to scale out quickly and scale in slowly so you can respond to bursts or spikes but avoid inadvertently terminating Amazon EC2 instances too quickly, only having to launch more Amazon EC2 instances if the burst is sustained. Auto Scaling also supports a *cooldown period*, which is a configurable setting that determines when to suspend scaling activities for a short time for an Auto Scaling group.

If you start an Amazon EC2 instance, you will be billed for one full hour of running time. Partial instance hours consumed are billed as full hours. This means that if you have a permissive scaling policy that launches, terminates, and relaunches many instances an hour, you are billing a full hour for each and every instance you launch, even if you terminate some of those instances in less than hour. A recommended best practice for cost effectiveness is to scale out quickly when needed but scale in more slowly to avoid having to relaunch new and separate Amazon EC2 instances for a spike in workload demand that fluctuates up and down within minutes but generally continues to need more resources within an hour.

    Scale out quickly; scale in slowly.

It is important to consider bootstrapping for Amazon EC2 instances launched using Auto Scaling. It takes time to configure each newly launched Amazon EC2 instance before the instance is healthy and capable of accepting traffic. Instances that start and are available for load faster can join the capacity pool more quickly. Furthermore, instances that are more stateless instead of stateful will more gracefully enter and exit an Auto Scaling group.

Rolling Out a Patch at Scale

In large deployments of Amazon EC2 instances, Auto Scaling can be used to make rolling out a patch to your instances easy. The launch configuration associated with the Auto Scaling group may be modified to reference a new AMI and even a new Amazon EC2 instance if needed. Then you can deregister or terminate instances one at a time or in small groups, and the new Amazon EC2 instances will reference the new patched AMI.

Summary

This chapter introduced three services:

- Elastic Load Balancing, which is used to distribute traffic across a group of Amazon EC2 instances in one or more Availability Zones to achieve greater levels of fault tolerance for your applications.

- Amazon CloudWatch, which monitors resources and applications. Amazon CloudWatch is used to collect and track metrics, create alarms that send notifications, and make changes to resources being monitored based on rules you define.

- Auto Scaling, which allows you to automatically scale your Amazon EC2 capacity out and in using criteria that you define.

These three services can be used very effectively together to create a highly available application with a resilient architecture on AWS.

Exam Essentials

Understand what the Elastic Load Balancing service provides.   Elastic Load Balancing is a highly available service that distributes traffic across Amazon EC2 instances and includes options that provide flexibility and control of incoming requests to Amazon EC2 instances.

Know the types of load balancers the Elastic Load Balancing service provides and when to use each one.   An Internet-facing load balancer is, as the name implies, a load balancer that takes requests from clients over the Internet and distributes them to Amazon EC2 instances that are registered with the load balancer.

An internal load balancer is used to route traffic to your Amazon EC2 instances in VPCs with private subnets.

An HTTPS load balancer is used when you want to encrypt data between your load balancer and the clients that initiate HTTPS sessions and for connections between your load balancer and your back-end instances.

Know the types of listeners the Elastic Load Balancing service provides and the use case and requirements for using each one.   A listener is a process that checks for connection requests. It is configured with a protocol and a port for front-end (client to load balancer) connections and a protocol and a port for back-end (load balancer to back-end instance) connections.

Understand the configuration options for Elastic Load Balancing.   Elastic Load Balancing allows you to configure many aspects of the load balancer, including idle connection time-out, cross-zone load balancing, connection draining, proxy protocol, sticky sessions, and health checks.

Know what an Elastic Load Balancing health check is and why it is important.   Elastic Load Balancing supports health checks to test the status of the Amazon EC2 instances behind an Elastic Load Balancing load balancer.

Understand what the Amazon CloudWatch service provides and what use cases there are for using it.   Amazon CloudWatch is a service that you can use to monitor your AWS resources and your applications in real time. With Amazon CloudWatch, you can collect and track metrics, create alarms that send notifications, and make changes to the resources being monitored based on rules you define.

For example, you might choose to monitor CPU utilization to decide when to add or remove Amazon EC2 instances in an application tier. Or, if a particular application-specific metric that is not visible to AWS is the best indicator for assessing your scaling needs, you can perform a PUT request to push that metric into Amazon CloudWatch. You can then use this custom metric to manage capacity.

Know the differences between the two types of monitoring—basic and detailed—for Amazon CloudWatch.   Amazon CloudWatch offers basic or detailed monitoring for supported AWS products. Basic monitoring sends data points to Amazon CloudWatch every five minutes for a limited number of preselected metrics at no charge. Detailed monitoring sends data points to Amazon CloudWatch every minute and allows data aggregation for an additional charge. If you want to use detailed monitoring, you must enable it—basic is the default.

Understand Auto Scaling and why it is an important advantage of the AWS Cloud. A distinct advantage of deploying applications to the cloud is the ability to launch and then release servers in response to variable workloads. Provisioning servers on demand and then releasing them when they are no longer needed can provide significant cost savings for workloads that are not steady state.

Know when and why to use Auto Scaling. Auto Scaling is a service that allows you to scale your Amazon EC2 capacity automatically by scaling out and scaling in according to criteria that you define. With Auto Scaling, you can ensure that the number of running Amazon EC2 instances increases during demand spikes or peak demand periods to maintain application performance and decreases automatically during demand lulls or troughs to minimize costs.

Know the supported Auto Scaling plans. Auto Scaling has several schemes or plans that you can use to control how you want Auto Scaling to perform. The Auto Scaling plans are named Maintain Current Instant Levels, Manual Scaling, Scheduled Scaling, and Dynamic Scaling.

Understand how to build an Auto Scaling launch configuration and an Auto Scaling group and what each is used for. A launch configuration is the template that Auto Scaling uses to create new instances and is composed of the configuration name, AMI, Amazon EC2 instance type, security group, and instance key pair.

Know what a scaling policy is and what use cases to use it for. A scaling policy is used by Auto Scaling with CloudWatch alarms to determine when your Auto Scaling group should scale out or scale in. Each CloudWatch alarm watches a single metric and sends messages to Auto Scaling when the metric breaches a threshold that you specify in your policy.

Understand how Elastic Load Balancing, Amazon CloudWatch, and Auto Scaling are used together to provide dynamic scaling. Elastic Load Balancing, Amazon CloudWatch, and Auto Scaling can be used together to create a highly available application with a resilient architecture on AWS.

Exercises

For assistance in completing the following exercises, refer to the Elastic Load Balancing Developer Guide located at `http://docs.aws.amazon.com/ElasticLoadBalancing/latest/DeveloperGuide/elastic-load-balancing.html`, the Amazon CloudWatch Developer Guide at `http://docs.aws.amazon.com/AmazonCloudWatch/latest/DeveloperGuide/WhatIsCloudWatch.html`, and the Auto Scaling User Guide at `http://docs.aws.amazon.com/autoscaling/latest/userguide/WhatIsAutoScaling.html`.

EXERCISE 5.1

Create an Elastic Load Balancing Load Balancer

In this exercise, you will use the AWS Management Console to create an Elastic Load Balancing load balancer.

1. Launch an Amazon EC2 instance using an AMI with a web server on it, or install and configure a web server.

2. Create a static page to display and a health check page that returns HTTP 200. Configure the Amazon EC2 instance to accept traffic over port 80.

3. Register the Amazon EC2 instance with the Elastic Load Balancing load balancer, and configure it to use the health check page to evaluate the health of the instance.

EXERCISE 5.2

Use an Amazon CloudWatch Metric

1. Launch an Amazon EC2 instance.

2. Use an existing Amazon CloudWatch metric to monitor a value.

EXERCISE 5.3

Create a Custom Amazon CloudWatch Metric

1. Create a custom Amazon CloudWatch metric for memory consumption.

2. Use the CLI to PUT values into the metric.

EXERCISE 5.4

Create a Launch Configuration and Auto Scaling Group

1. Using the AWS Management Console, create a launch configuration using an existing AMI.

2. Create an Auto Scaling group using this launch configuration with a group size of four and spanning two Availability Zones. Do not use a scaling policy. Keep the group at its initial size.

3. Manually terminate an Amazon EC2 instance, and observe Auto Scaling launch a new Amazon EC2 instance.

EXERCISE 5.5

Create a Scaling Policy

1. Create an Amazon Cloud Watch metric and alarm for CPU utilization using the AWS Management Console.

2. Using the Auto Scaling group from Exercise 5.4, edit the Auto Scaling group to include a policy that uses the CPU utilization alarm.

3. Drive CPU utilization on the monitored Amazon EC2 instance(s) up to observe Auto Scaling.

EXERCISE 5.6

Create a Web Application That Scales

1. Create a small web application architected with an Elastic Load Balancing load balancer, an Auto Scaling group spanning two Availability Zones that uses an Amazon CloudWatch metric, and an alarm attached to a scaling policy used by the Auto Scaling group.

2. Verify that Auto Scaling is operating correctly by removing instances and driving the metric up and down to force Auto Scaling.

Review Questions

1. Which of the following are required elements of an Auto Scaling group? (Choose 2 answers)

   A. Minimum size

   B. Health checks

   C. Desired capacity

   D. Launch configuration

2. You have created an Elastic Load Balancing load balancer listening on port 80, and you registered it with a single Amazon Elastic Compute Cloud (Amazon EC2) instance also listening on port 80. A client makes a request to the load balancer with the correct protocol and port for the load balancer. In this scenario, how many connections does the balancer maintain?

   A. 1

   B. 2

   C. 3

   D. 4

3. How long does Amazon CloudWatch keep metric data?

   A. 1 day

   B. 2 days

   C. 1 week

   D. 2 weeks

4. Which of the following are the minimum required elements to create an Auto Scaling launch configuration?

   A. Launch configuration name, Amazon Machine Image (AMI), and instance type

   B. Launch configuration name, AMI, instance type, and key pair

   C. Launch configuration name, AMI, instance type, key pair, and security group

   D. Launch configuration name, AMI, instance type, key pair, security group, and block device mapping

5. You are responsible for the application logging solution for your company's existing applications running on multiple Amazon EC2 instances. Which of the following is the best approach for aggregating the application logs within AWS?

   A. Amazon CloudWatch custom metrics

   B. Amazon CloudWatch Logs Agent

   C. An Elastic Load Balancing listener

   D. An internal Elastic Load Balancing load balancer

6. Which of the following must be configured on an Elastic Load Balancing load balancer to accept incoming traffic?

A. A port

B. A network interface

C. A listener

D. An instance

7. You create an Auto Scaling group in a new region that is configured with a minimum size value of 10, a maximum size value of 100, and a desired capacity value of 50. However, you notice that 30 of the Amazon Elastic Compute Cloud (Amazon EC2) instances within the Auto Scaling group fail to launch. Which of the following is the cause of this behavior?

A. You cannot define an Auto Scaling group larger than 20.

B. The Auto Scaling group maximum value cannot be more than 20.

C. You did not attach an Elastic Load Balancing load balancer to the Auto Scaling group.

D. You have not raised your default Amazon EC2 capacity (20) for the new region.

8. You want to host multiple Hypertext Transfer Protocol Secure (HTTPS) websites on a fleet of Amazon EC2 instances behind an Elastic Load Balancing load balancer with a single X.509 certificate. How must you configure the Secure Sockets Layer (SSL) certificate so that clients connecting to the load balancer are not presented with a warning when they connect?

A. Create one SSL certificate with a Subject Alternative Name (SAN) value for each website name.

B. Create one SSL certificate with the Server Name Indication (SNI) value checked.

C. Create multiple SSL certificates with a SAN value for each website name.

D. Create SSL certificates for each Availability Zone with a SAN value for each website name.

9. Your web application front end consists of multiple Amazon Compute Cloud (Amazon EC2) instances behind an Elastic Load Balancing load balancer. You have configured the load balancer to perform health checks on these Amazon EC2 instances. If an instance fails to pass health checks, which statement will be true?

A. The instance is replaced automatically by the load balancer.

B. The instance is terminated automatically by the load balancer.

C. The load balancer stops sending traffic to the instance that failed its health check.

D. The instance is quarantined by the load balancer for root cause analysis.

10. In the basic monitoring package for Amazon Elastic Compute Cloud (Amazon EC2), what Amazon CloudWatch metrics are available?

A. Web server visible metrics such as number of failed transaction requests

B. Operating system visible metrics such as memory utilization

C. Database visible metrics such as number of connections

D. Hypervisor visible metrics such as CPU utilization

11. A cell phone company is running dynamic-content television commercials for a contest. They want their website to handle traffic spikes that come after a commercial airs. The website is interactive, offering personalized content to each visitor based on location, purchase history, and the current commercial airing. Which architecture will configure Auto Scaling to scale out to respond to spikes of demand, while minimizing costs during quiet periods?

A. Set the minimum size of the Auto Scaling group so that it can handle high traffic volumes without needing to scale out.

B. Create an Auto Scaling group large enough to handle peak traffic loads, and then stop some instances. Configure Auto Scaling to scale out when traffic increases using the stopped instances, so new capacity will come online quickly.

C. Configure Auto Scaling to scale out as traffic increases. Configure the launch configuration to start new instances from a preconfigured Amazon Machine Image (AMI).

D. Use Amazon CloudFront and Amazon Simple Storage Service (Amazon S3) to cache changing content, with the Auto Scaling group set as the origin. Configure Auto Scaling to have sufficient instances necessary to initially populate CloudFront and Amazon ElastiCache, and then scale in after the cache is fully populated.

12. For an application running in the ap-northeast-1 region with three Availability Zones (ap-northeast-1a, ap-northeast-1b, and ap-northeast-1c), which instance deployment provides high availability for the application that normally requires nine running Amazon Elastic Compute Cloud (Amazon EC2) instances but can run on a minimum of 65 percent capacity while Auto Scaling launches replacement instances in the remaining Availability Zones?

A. Deploy the application on four servers in ap-northeast-1a and five servers in ap-northeast-1b, and keep five stopped instances in ap-northeast-1a as reserve.

B. Deploy the application on three servers in ap-northeast-1a, three servers in ap-northeast-1b, and three servers in ap-northeast-1c.

C. Deploy the application on six servers in ap-northeast-1b and three servers in ap-northeast-1c.

D. Deploy the application on nine servers in ap-northeast-1b, and keep nine stopped instances in ap-northeast-1a as reserve.

13. Which of the following are characteristics of the Auto Scaling service on AWS? (Choose 3 answers)

A. Sends traffic to healthy instances

B. Responds to changing conditions by adding or terminating Amazon Elastic Compute Cloud (Amazon EC2) instances

C. Collects and tracks metrics and sets alarms

D. Delivers push notifications

E. Launches instances from a specified Amazon Machine Image (AMI)

F. Enforces a minimum number of running Amazon EC2 instances

14. Why is the launch configuration referenced by the Auto Scaling group instead of being part of the Auto Scaling group?

   A. It allows you to change the Amazon Elastic Compute Cloud (Amazon EC2) instance type and Amazon Machine Image (AMI) without disrupting the Auto Scaling group.

   B. It facilitates rolling out a patch to an existing set of instances managed by an Auto Scaling group.

   C. It allows you to change security groups associated with the instances launched without having to make changes to the Auto Scaling group.

   D. All of the above

   E. None of the above

15. An Auto Scaling group may use: (Choose 2 answers)

   A. On-Demand Instances

   B. Stopped instances

   C. Spot Instances

   D. On-premises instances

   E. Already running instances if they use the same Amazon Machine Image (AMI) as the Auto Scaling group's launch configuration and are not already part of another Auto Scaling group

16. Amazon CloudWatch supports which types of monitoring plans? (Choose 2 answers)

   A. Basic monitoring, which is free

   B. Basic monitoring, which has an additional cost

   C. Ad hoc monitoring, which is free

   D. Ad hoc monitoring, which has an additional cost

   E. Detailed monitoring, which is free

   F. Detailed monitoring, which has an additional cost

17. Elastic Load Balancing health checks may be: (Choose 3 answers)

   A. A ping

   B. A key pair verification

   C. A connection attempt

   D. A page request

   E. An Amazon Elastic Compute Cloud (Amazon EC2) instance status check

18. When an Amazon Elastic Compute Cloud (Amazon EC2) instance registered with an Elastic Load Balancing load balancer using connection draining is deregistered or unhealthy, which of the following will happen? (Choose 2 answers)

   A. Immediately close all existing connections to that instance.

   B. Keep the connections open to that instance, and attempt to complete in-flight requests.

    C. Redirect the requests to a user-defined error page like "Oops this is embarrassing" or "Under Construction."

    D. Forcibly close all connections to that instance after a timeout period.

    E. Leave the connections open as long as the load balancer is running.

19. Elastic Load Balancing supports which of the following types of load balancers? (Choose 3 answers)

    A. Cross-region

    B. Internet-facing

    C. Interim

    D. Itinerant

    E. Internal

    F. Hypertext Transfer Protocol Secure (HTTPS) using Secure Sockets Layer (SSL)

20. Auto Scaling supports which of the following plans for Auto Scaling groups? (Choose 3 answers)

    A. Predictive

    B. Manual

    C. Preemptive

    D. Scheduled

    E. Dynamic

    F. End-user request driven

    G. Optimistic

AWS Identity and Access Management (IAM)

THE AWS CERTIFIED SOLUTIONS ARCHITECT ASSOCIATE EXAM OBJECTIVES COVERED IN THIS CHAPTER MAY INCLUDE, BUT ARE NOT LIMITED TO, THE FOLLOWING:

Domain 2.0: Implementation/Deployment

✓ **2.1 Identify the appropriate techniques and methods using Amazon EC2, Amazon S3, Elastic Beanstalk, CloudFormation, Amazon Virtual Private Cloud (VPC), and AWS Identity and Access Management (IAM) to code and implement a cloud solution.**

Content may include the following:

- Configure IAM policies and best practices

Domain 3.0: Data Security

✓ **3.1 Recognize and implement secure practices for optimum cloud deployment and maintenance.**

Content may include the following:

- AWS Identity and Access Management (IAM)

Introduction

In this chapter, you will learn how *AWS Identity and Access Management (IAM)* secures interactions with the AWS resources in your account, including:

- Which principals interact with AWS through the AWS Management Console, Command Line Interface (CLI), and Software Development Kits (SDKs)
- How each principal is authenticated
- How IAM policies are written to specify the access privileges of principals
- How IAM policies are associated with principals
- How to secure your infrastructure further through Multi-Factor Authentication (MFA) and key rotation
- How IAM roles can be used to delegate permissions and federate users
- How to resolve multiple, possibly conflicting IAM permissions

IAM is a powerful service that allows you to control how people and programs are allowed to manipulate your AWS infrastructure. IAM uses traditional identity concepts such as users, groups, and access control policies to control who can use your AWS account, what services and resources they can use, and how they can use them. The control provided by IAM is granular enough to limit a single user to the ability to perform a single action on a specific resource from a specific IP address during a specific time window. Applications can be granted access to AWS resources whether they are running on-premises or in the cloud. This flexibility creates a very powerful system that will give you all the power you need to ensure that your AWS account users have the ability to meet your business needs while addressing all of the security concerns of your organization.

This chapter will cover the different principals that can interact with AWS and how they are authenticated. It will then discuss how to write policies that define permitted access to services, actions, and resources and associate these policies with authenticated principals. Finally, it will cover additional features of IAM that will help you secure your infrastructure, including MFA, rotating keys, federation, resolving multiple permissions, and using IAM roles.

As important as it is to know what IAM is exactly, it is equally important to understand what it is not:

- First, IAM is not an identity store/authorization system for your applications. The permissions that you assign are permissions to manipulate AWS infrastructure, not permissions within your application. If you are migrating an existing on-premises application that already has its own user repository and authentication/authorization mechanism, then that should continue to work when you deploy on AWS and is probably the right choice. If your application identities are based on Active Directory, your on-premises Active Directory can be extended into the cloud to continue to fill that need. A great solution for using Active Directory in the cloud is AWS Directory Service, which is an Active Directory-compatible directory service that can work on its own or integrate with your on-premises Active Directory. Finally, if you are working with a mobile app, consider *Amazon Cognito* for identity management for mobile applications.

- Second, IAM is not operating system identity management. Remember that under the shared responsibility model, you are in control of your operating system console and configuration. Whatever mechanism you currently use to control access to your server infrastructure will continue to work on Amazon Elastic Compute Cloud (Amazon EC2) instances, whether that is managing individual machine login accounts or a directory service such as Active Directory or Lightweight Directory Access Protocol (LDAP). You can run an Active Directory or LDAP server on Amazon EC2, or you can extend your on-premises system into the cloud. AWS Directory Service will also work well to provide Active Directory functionality in the cloud as a service, whether standalone or integrated with your existing Active Directory.

Table 6.1 summarizes the role that different authentication systems can play in your AWS environment.

TABLE 6.1   Authentication Technologies

Use Case	Technology Solutions
Operating System Access	Active Directory
	LDAP
	Machine-specific accounts
Application Access	Active Directory
	Application User Repositories
	Amazon Cognito
AWS Resources	IAM

IAM is controlled like most other AWS Cloud services:

- Through the *AWS Management Console*—Like other services, the AWS Management Console is the easiest way to start learning about and manipulating a service.
- With the *CLI*—As you learn the system, you can start scripting repeated tasks using the CLI.
- Via the *AWS SDKs*—Eventually you may start writing your own tools and complex processes by manipulating IAM directly through the REST API via one of several SDKs.

All of these methods work to control IAM just as they work with other services. In addition, the AWS Partner Network (APN) includes a rich ecosystem of tools to manage and extend IAM.

Principals

The first IAM concept to understand is principals. A *principal* is an IAM entity that is allowed to interact with AWS resources. A principal can be permanent or temporary, and it can represent a human or an application. There are three types of principals: root users, IAM users, and roles/temporary security tokens.

Root User

When you first create an AWS account, you begin with only a single sign-in principal that has complete access to all AWS Cloud services and resources in the account. This principal is called the *root user*. As long as you have an open account with AWS, the root user for that relationship will persist. The root user can be used for both console and programmatic access to AWS resources.

The root user is similar in concept to the UNIX root or Windows Administrator account—it has full privileges to do anything in the account, including closing the account. It is strongly recommended that you do not use the root user for your everyday tasks, even the administrative ones. Instead, adhere to the best practice of using the root user only to create your first IAM user and then securely locking away the root user credentials.

IAM Users

Users are persistent identities set up through the IAM service to represent individual people or applications. You may create separate IAM users for each member of your operations team so they can interact with the console and use the CLI. You might also create dev, test, and production users for applications that need to access AWS Cloud services (although you will see later in this chapter that IAM roles may be a better solution for that use case).

IAM users can be created by principals with IAM administrative privileges at any time through the AWS Management Console, CLI, or SDKs. Users are persistent in that there is no expiration period; they are permanent entities that exist until an *IAM administrator* takes an action to delete them.

 Users are an excellent way to enforce the principle of least privilege; that is, the concept of allowing a person or process interacting with your AWS resources to perform exactly the tasks they need but nothing else. Users can be associated with very granular policies that define these permissions. Policies will be covered in a later section.

Roles/Temporary Security Tokens

Roles and temporary security tokens are very important for advanced IAM usage, but many AWS users find them confusing. Roles are used to grant specific privileges to specific actors for a set duration of time. These actors can be authenticated by AWS or some trusted external system. When one of these actors assumes a role, AWS provides the actor with a temporary security token from the *AWS Security Token Service (STS)* that the actor can use to access AWS Cloud services. Requesting a temporary security token requires specifying how long the token will exist before it expires. The range of a temporary security token lifetime is 15 minutes to 36 hours.

Roles and temporary security tokens enable a number of use cases:

- *Amazon EC2 Roles*—Granting permissions to applications running on an Amazon EC2 instance.

- *Cross-Account Access*—Granting permissions to users from other AWS accounts, whether you control those accounts or not.

- *Federation*—Granting permissions to users authenticated by a trusted external system.

Amazon EC2 Roles

Granting permissions to an application is always tricky, as it usually requires configuring the application with some sort of credential upon installation. This leads to issues around securely storing the credential prior to use, how to access it safely during installation, and how to secure it in the configuration. Suppose that an application running on an Amazon EC2 instance needs to access an Amazon Simple Storage Service (Amazon S3) bucket. A policy granting permission to read and write that bucket can be created and assigned to an IAM user, and the application can use the access key for that IAM user to access the Amazon S3 bucket. The problem with this approach is that the access key for the user must be accessible to the application, probably by storing it in some sort of configuration file. The process for obtaining the access key and storing it encrypted in the configuration is usually complicated and a hindrance to agile development. Additionally, the access key is at risk when being passed around. Finally, when the time comes to rotate the access key, the rotation involves performing that whole process again.

Using IAM roles for Amazon EC2 removes the need to store AWS credentials in a configuration file.

An alternative is to create an IAM role that grants the required access to the Amazon S3 bucket. When the Amazon EC2 instance is launched, the role is assigned to the instance. When the application running on the instance uses the Application Programming Interface (API) to access the Amazon S3 bucket, it assumes the role assigned to the instance and obtains a temporary token that it sends to the API. The process of obtaining the temporary token and passing it to the API is handled automatically by most of the AWS SDKs, allowing the application to make a call to access the Amazon S3 bucket without worrying about authentication. In addition to being easy for the developer, this removes any need to store an access key in a configuration file. Also, because the API access uses a temporary token, there is no fixed access key that must be rotated.

Cross-Account Access

Another common use case for IAM roles is to grant access to AWS resources to IAM users in other AWS accounts. These accounts may be other AWS accounts controlled by your company or outside agents like customers or suppliers. You can set up an IAM role with the permissions you want to grant to users in the other account, then users in the other account can assume that role to access your resources. This is highly recommended as a best practice, as opposed to distributing access keys outside your organization.

Federation

Many organizations already have an identity repository outside of AWS and would rather leverage that repository than create a new and largely duplicate repository of IAM users. Similarly, web-based applications may want to leverage web-based identities such as Facebook, Google, or Login with Amazon. *IAM Identity Providers* provide the ability to federate these outside identities with IAM and assign privileges to those users authenticated outside of IAM.

IAM can integrate with two different types of outside *Identity Providers (IdP)*. For federating web identities such as Facebook, Google, or Login with Amazon, IAM supports integration via OpenID Connect (OIDC). This allows IAM to grant privileges to users authenticated with some of the major web-based IdPs. For federating internal identities, such as Active Directory or LDAP, IAM supports integration via Security Assertion Markup Language 2.0 (SAML). A SAML-compliant IdP such as Active Directory Federation Services (ADFS) is used to federate the internal directory to IAM. (Instructions for configuring many compatible products can be found on the AWS website.) In each case, federation works by returning a temporary token associated with a role to the IdP for the authenticated identity to use for calls to the AWS API. The actual role returned is determined via information received from the IdP, either attributes of the user in the on-premises identity store or the user name and authenticating service of the web identity store.

The three types of principals and their general traits are listed in Table 6.2.

TABLE 6.2   Traits of AWS Principals

Principal	Traits
Root User	Cannot be limited Permanent
IAM Users	Access controlled by policy Durable Can be removed by IAM administrator
Roles/Temporary Security Tokens	Access controlled by policy Temporary Expire after specific time interval

Authentication

There are three ways that IAM *authenticates* a principal:

- *User Name/Password*—When a principal represents a human interacting with the console, the human will provide a user name/password pair to verify their identity. IAM allows you to create a password policy enforcing password complexity and expiration.

- *Access Key*—An access key is a combination of an access key ID (20 characters) and an access secret key (40 characters). When a program is manipulating the AWS infrastructure via the API, it will use these values to sign the underlying REST calls to the services. The AWS SDKs and tools handle all the intricacies of signing the REST calls, so using an access key will almost always be a matter of providing the values to the SDK or tool.

- *Access Key/Session Token*—When a process operates under an assumed role, the temporary security token provides an access key for authentication. In addition to the access key (remember that it consists of two parts), the token also includes a *session token*. Calls to AWS must include both the two-part access key and the session token to authenticate.

It is important to note that when an IAM user is created, it has neither an access key nor a password, and the IAM administrator can set up either or both. This adds an extra layer of security in that console users cannot use their credentials to run a program that accesses your AWS infrastructure.

Figure 6.1 shows a summary of the different authentication methods.

FIGURE 6.1   Different identities authenticating with AWS

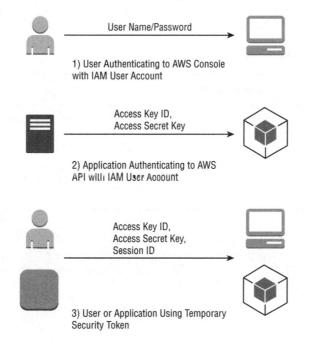

User Name/Password

1) User Authenticating to AWS Console
with IAM User Account

Access Key ID,
Access Secret Key

2) Application Authenticating to AWS
API with IAM User Account

Access Key ID,
Access Secret Key,
Session ID

3) User or Application Using Temporary
Security Token

Authorization

After IAM has authenticated a principal, it must then manage the access of that principal to protect your AWS infrastructure. The process of specifying exactly what actions a principal can and cannot perform is called *authorization*. Authorization is handled in IAM by defining specific privileges in *policies* and associating those policies with principals.

Policies

Understanding how access management works under IAM begins with understanding policies. A *policy* is a JSON document that fully defines a set of permissions to access and manipulate AWS resources. Policy documents contain one or more permissions, with each permission defining:

- *Effect*—A single word: Allow or Deny.

- *Service*—For what service does this permission apply? Most AWS Cloud services support granting access through IAM, including IAM itself.

- *Resource*—The resource value specifies the specific AWS infrastructure for which this permission applies. This is specified as an *Amazon Resource Name (ARN)*. The format for an ARN varies slightly between services, but the basic format is:

  ```
  "arn:aws:service:region:account-id:[resourcetype:]resource"
  ```

For some services, wildcard values are allowed; for instance, an Amazon S3 ARN could have a resource of foldername* to indicate all objects in the specified folder. Table 6.3 displays some sample ARNs.

TABLE 6.3 Sample ARNs

Resource	ARN Format
Amazon S3 Bucket	arn:aws:s3:us-east-1:123456789012:my_corporate_bucket/*
IAM User	arn:aws:iam:us-east-1:123456789012:user/David
Amazon DynamoDB Table	arn:aws:dynamodb:us-east-1:123456789012:table/tablename

- *Action*—The action value specifies the subset of actions within a service that the permission allows or denies. For instance, a permission may grant access to any read-based action for Amazon S3. A set of actions can be specified with an enumerated list or by using wildcards (Read*).

- *Condition*—The condition value optionally defines one or more additional restrictions that limit the actions allowed by the permission. For instance, the permission might contain a condition that limits the ability to access a resource to calls that come from a specific IP address range. Another condition could restrict the permission only to apply during a specific time interval. There are many types of permissions that allow a rich variety of functionality that varies between services. See the IAM documentation for lists of supported conditions for each service.

A sample policy is shown in the following listing. This policy allows a principal to list the objects in a specific bucket and to retrieve those objects, but only if the call comes from a specific IP address.

```
{
    "Version": "2012-10-17",
    "Statement": [
        {
            "Sid": "Stmt1441716043000",
            "Effect": "Allow",      <- This policy grants access
            "Action": [             <- Allows identities to list
                "s3:GetObject",     <- and get objects in
                "s3:ListBucket"     <- the S3 bucket
            ],
            "Condition": {
                "IpAddress": {                      <- Only from a specific
                    "aws:SourceIp": "192.168.0.1"   <- IP Address
                }
            },
            "Resource": [
                "arn:aws:s3:::my_public_bucket/*"   <- Only this bucket
            ]
        }
    ]
}
```

Associating Policies with Principals

There are several ways to associate a policy with an IAM user; this section will only cover the most common.

A policy can be associated directly with an IAM user in one of two ways:

- *User Policy*—These policies exist only in the context of the user to which they are attached. In the console, a user policy is entered into the user interface on the IAM user page.

▪ *Managed Policies*—These policies are created in the Policies tab on the IAM page (or through the CLI, and so forth) and exist independently of any individual user. In this way, the same policy can be associated with many users or groups of users. There are a large number of predefined managed policies that you can review on the Policies tab of the IAM page in the AWS Management Console. In addition, you can write your own policies specific to your use cases.

 Using predefined managed policies ensures that when new permissions are added for new features, your users will still have the correct access.

The other common method for associating policies with users is with the IAM groups feature. Groups simplify managing permissions for large numbers of users. After a policy is assigned to a group, any user who is a member of that group assumes those permissions. This makes it simpler to assign policies to an entire team in your organization. For instance, if you create an "Operations" group with every IAM user for your operations team assigned to that group, then it is a simple matter to associate the needed permissions to the group, and all of the team's IAM users will assume those permissions. New IAM users can then be assigned directly to the group.

This is a much simpler management process than having to review what policies a new IAM user for the operations team should receive and manually adding those policies to the user. There are two ways a policy can be associated with an IAM group:

▪ *Group Policy*—These policies exist only in the context of the group to which they are attached. In the AWS Management Console, a group policy is entered into the user interface on the IAM Group page.

▪ *Managed Policies*—In the same way that managed policies (discussed in the "Authorization" section) can be associated with IAM users, they can also be associated with IAM groups.

Figure 6.2 shows the different ways that polices can be associated with an IAM User.

FIGURE 6.2   Associating IAM users with policies

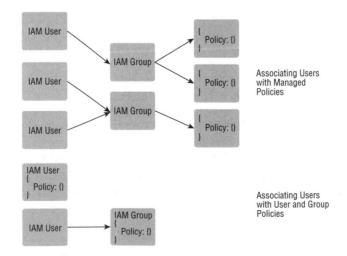

A good first step is to use the root user to create a new IAM group called "IAM Administrators" and assign the managed policy, "IAMFullAccess." Then create a new IAM user called "Administrator," assign a password, and add it to the IAM Administrators group. At this point, you can log off as the root user and perform all further administration with the IAM user account.

The final way an actor can be associated with a policy is by assuming a role. In this case, the actor can be:

- An authenticated IAM user (person or process). In this case, the IAM user must have the rights to assume the role.

- A person or process authenticated by a trusted service outside of AWS, such as an on-premises LDAP directory or a web authentication service. In this situation, an AWS Cloud service will assume the role on the actor's behalf and return a token to the actor.

After an actor has assumed a role, it is provided with a temporary security token associated with the policies of that role. The token contains all the information required to authenticate API calls. This information includes a standard access key plus an additional session token required for authenticating calls under an assumed role.

Other Key Features

Beyond the critical concepts of principals, authentication, and authorization, there are several other features of the IAM service that are important to understand to realize the full benefits of IAM.

Multi-Factor Authentication (MFA)

Multi-Factor Authentication (MFA) can add an extra layer of security to your infrastructure by adding a second method of authentication beyond just a password or access key. With MFA, authentication also requires entering a One-Time Password (OTP) from a small device. The MFA device can be either a small hardware device you carry with you or a virtual device via an app on your smart phone (for example, the AWS Virtual MFA app).

MFA requires you to verify your identity with both something you *know* and something you *have*.

MFA can be assigned to any IAM user account, whether the account represents a person or application. When a person using an IAM user configured with MFA attempts to access the AWS Management Console, after providing their password they will be prompted to enter the current code displayed on their MFA device before being granted access. An application using an IAM user configured with MFA must query the application user to provide the current code, which the application will then pass to the API.

It is strongly recommended that AWS customers add MFA protection to their root user.

Rotating Keys

The security risk of any credential increases with the age of the credential. To this end, it is a security best practice to *rotate access keys* associated with your IAM users. IAM facilitates this process by allowing two active access keys at a time. The process to rotate keys can be conducted via the console, CLI, or SDKs:

1. Create a new access key for the user.
2. Reconfigure all applications to use the new access key.
3. Disable the original access key (disabling instead of deleting at this stage is critical, as it allows rollback to the original key if there are issues with the rotation).
4. Verify the operation of all applications.
5. Delete the original access key.

 Access keys should be rotated on a regular schedule.

Resolving Multiple Permissions

Occasionally, multiple permissions will be applicable when determining whether a principal has the privilege to perform some action. These permissions may come from multiple policies associated with a principal or resource policies attached to the AWS resource in question. It is important to know how conflicts between these permissions are resolved:

1. Initially the request is denied by default.
2. All the appropriate policies are evaluated; if there is an explicit "deny" found in any policy, the request is denied and evaluation stops.
3. If no explicit "deny" is found and an explicit "allow" is found in any policy, the request is allowed.
4. If there are no explicit "allow" or "deny" permissions found, then the default "deny" is maintained and the request is denied.

The only exception to this rule is if an `AssumeRole` call includes a role and a policy, the policy cannot expand the privileges of the role (for example, the policy cannot override any permission that is denied by default in the role).

Summary

IAM is a powerful service that gives you the ability to control which people and applications can access your AWS account at a very granular level. Because the root user in an AWS account cannot be limited, you should set up IAM users and temporary security tokens for your people and processes to interact with AWS.

Policies define what actions can and cannot be taken. Policies are associated with IAM users either directly or through group membership. A temporary security token is associated with a policy by assuming an IAM role. You can write your own policies or use one of the managed policies provided by AWS.

Common use cases for IAM roles include federating identities from external IdPs, assigning privileges to an Amazon EC2 instance where they can be assumed by applications running on the instance, and cross-account access.

IAM user accounts can be further secured by rotating keys, implementing MFA, and adding conditions to policies. MFA ensures that authentication is based on something you have in addition to something you know, and conditions can add further restrictions such as limiting client IP address ranges or setting a particular time interval.

Exam Essentials

Know the different principals in IAM. The three principals that can authenticate and interact with AWS resources are the root user, IAM users, and roles. The root user is associated with the actual AWS account and cannot be restricted in any way. IAM users are persistent identities that can be controlled through IAM. Roles allow people or processes the ability to operate temporarily with a different identity. People or processes assume a role by being granted a temporary security token that will expire after a specified period of time.

Know how principals are authenticated in IAM. When you log in to the AWS Management Console as an IAM user or root user, you use a user name/password combination. A program that accesses the API with an IAM user or root user uses a two-part access key. A temporary security token authenticates with an access key plus an additional session token unique to that temporary security token.

Know the parts of a policy. A policy is a JSON document that defines one or more permissions to interact with AWS resources. Each permission includes the effect, service, action, and resource. It may also include one or more conditions. AWS makes many predefined policies available as managed policies.

Know how a policy is associated with a principal. An authenticated principal is associated with zero to many policies. For an IAM user, these policies may be attached directly to the user account or attached to an IAM group of which the user account is a member. A temporary security token is associated with policies by assuming an IAM role.

Understand MFA.   MFA increases the security of an AWS account by augmenting the password (something you know) with a rotating OTP from a small device (something you have), ensuring that anyone authenticating the account has both knowledge of the password and possession of the device. AWS supports both Gemalto hardware MFA devices and a number of virtual MFA apps.

Understand key rotation.   To protect your AWS infrastructure, access keys should be rotated regularly. AWS allows two access keys to be valid simultaneously to make the rotation process straightforward: Generate a new access key, configure your application to use the new access key, test, disable the original access key, test, delete the original access key, and test again.

Understand IAM roles and federation.   IAM roles are prepackaged sets of permissions that have no credentials. Principals can assume a role and then use the associated permissions. When a temporary security token is created, it assumes a role that defines the permissions assigned to the token. When an Amazon EC2 instance is associated with an IAM role, SDK calls acquire a temporary security token based on the role associated with the instance and use that token to access AWS resources.
Roles are the basis for federating external IdPs with AWS. You configure an IAM IdP to interact with the external IdP, the authenticated identity from the IdP is mapped to a role, and a temporary security token is returned that has assumed that role. AWS supports both SAML and OIDC IdPs.

Know how to resolve conflicting permissions.   Resolving multiple permissions is relatively straightforward. If an action on a resource has not been explicitly allowed by a policy, it is denied. If two policies contradict each other; that is, if one policy allows an action on a resource and another policy denies that action, the action is denied. While this sounds improbable, it may occur due to scope differences in a policy. One policy may expose an entire fleet of Amazon EC2 instances, and a second policy may explicitly lock down one particular instance.

Exercises

For assistance in completing the following exercises, refer to the IAM User Guide at http://docs.aws.amazon.com/IAM/latest/UserGuide/.

EXERCISE 6.1

Create an IAM Group

In this exercise, you will create a group for all IAM administrator users and assign the proper permissions to the new group. This will allow you to avoid assigning policies directly to a user later in these exercises.

1. Log in as the root user.

2. Create an IAM group called Administrators.

3. Attach the managed policy, IAMFullAccess, to the Administrators group.

EXERCISE 6.2

Create a Customized Sign-In Link and Password Policy

In this exercise, you will set up your account with some basic IAM safeguards. The password policy is a recommended security practice, and the sign-in link makes it easier for your users to log in to the AWS Management Console.

1. Customize a sign-in link, and write down the new link name in full.

2. Create a password policy for your account.

EXERCISE 6.3

Create an IAM User

In this exercise, you will create an IAM user who can perform all administrative IAM functions. Then you will log in as that user so that you no longer need to use the root user login. Using the root user login only when explicitly required is a recommended security practice (along with adding MFA to your root user).

1. While logged in as the root user, create a new IAM user called Administrator.

2. Add your new user to the Administrators group.

3. On the Details page for the administrator user, create a password.

4. Log out as the root user.

5. Use the customized sign-in link to sign in as Administrator.

EXERCISE 6.4

Create and Use an IAM Role

In this exercise, you will create an IAM role, associate it with a new instance, and verify that applications running on the instance assume the permissions of the role. IAM roles allow you to avoid storing access keys on your Amazon EC2 instances.

1. While signed in as administrator, create an Amazon EC2-type role named S3Client.

2. Attach the managed policy, AmazonS3ReadOnlyAccess, to S3Client.

3. Launch an Amazon Linux EC2 instance with the new role attached (Amazon Linux AMIs come with CLI installed).

4. SSH into the new instance, and use the CLI to list the contents of an Amazon S3 bucket.

EXERCISE 6.5

Rotate Keys

In this exercise, you will go through the process of rotating access keys, a recommended security practice.

1. Select the administrator, and create a two-part access key.

2. Download the access key.

3. Download and install the CLI to your desktop.

4. Configure the CLI to use the access key with the AWS Configure command.

5. Use the CLI to list the contents of an Amazon S3 bucket.

6. Return to the console, and create a new access key for the administrator account.

7. Download the access key, and reconfigure the CLI to use the new access key.

8. In the console, make the original access key inactive.

9. Confirm that you are using the new access key by once again listing the contents of the Amazon S3 bucket.

10. Delete the original access key.

EXERCISE 6.6

Set Up MFA

In this exercise, you will add MFA to your IAM administrator. You will use a virtual MFA application for your phone. MFA is a security recommendation on powerful accounts such as IAM administrators.

1. Download the AWS Virtual MFA app to your phone.

2. Select the administrator user, and manage the MFA device.

3. Go through the steps to activate a Virtual MFA device.

4. Log off as administrator.

5. Log in as administrator, and enter the MFA value to complete the authentication process.

EXERCISE 6.7

Resolve Conflicting Permissions

In this exercise, you will add a policy to your IAM administrator user with a conflicting permission. You will then attempt actions that verify how IAM resolves conflicting permissions.

1. Use the policy generator to create a new policy.

2. Create the policy with Effect: Deny; AWS Service: Amazon S3; Actions: *; and ARN: *.

3. Attach the new policy to the Administrators group.

4. Use the CLI to attempt to list the contents of an Amazon S3 bucket. The policy that allows access and the policy that denies access should resolve to deny access.

Review Questions

1. Which of the following methods will allow an application using an AWS SDK to be authenticated as a principal to access AWS Cloud services? (Choose 2 answers)

   A. Create an IAM user and store the user name and password for the user in the application's configuration.

   B. Create an IAM user and store both parts of the access key for the user in the application's configuration.

   C. Run the application on an Amazon EC2 instance with an assigned IAM role.

   D. Make all the API calls over an SSL connection.

2. Which of the following are found in an IAM policy? (Choose 2 answers)

   A. Service Name

   B. Region

   C. Action

   D. Password

3. Your AWS account administrator left your company today. The administrator had access to the root user and a personal IAM administrator account. With these accounts, he generated other IAM accounts and keys. Which of the following should you do today to protect your AWS infrastructure? (Choose 4 answers)

   A. Change the password and add MFA to the root user.

   B. Put an IP restriction on the root user.

   C. Rotate keys and change passwords for IAM accounts.

   D. Delete all IAM accounts.

   E. Delete the administrator's personal IAM account.

   F. Relaunch all Amazon EC2 instances with new roles.

4. Which of the following actions can be authorized by IAM? (Choose 2 answers)

   A. Installing ASP.NET on a Windows Server

   B. Launching an Amazon Linux EC2 instance

   C. Querying an Oracle database

   D. Adding a message to an Amazon Simple Queue Service (Amazon SQS) queue

5. Which of the following are IAM security features? (Choose 2 answers)

   A. Password policies

   B. Amazon DynamoDB global secondary indexes

   C. MFA

   D. Consolidated Billing

6. Which of the following are benefits of using Amazon EC2 roles? (Choose 2 answers)
   - **A.** No policies are required.
   - **B.** Credentials do not need to be stored on the Amazon EC2 instance.
   - **C.** Key rotation is not necessary.
   - **D.** Integration with Active Directory is automatic.

7. Which of the following are based on temporary security tokens? (Choose 2 answers)
   - **A.** Amazon EC2 roles
   - **B.** MFA
   - **C.** Root user
   - **D.** Federation

8. Your security team is very concerned about the vulnerability of the IAM administrator user accounts (the accounts used to configure all IAM features and accounts). What steps can be taken to lock down these accounts? (Choose 3 answers)
   - **A.** Add multi-factor authentication (MFA) to the accounts.
   - **B.** Limit logins to a particular U.S. state.
   - **C.** Implement a password policy on the AWS account.
   - **D.** Apply a source IP address condition to the policy that only grants permissions when the user is on the corporate network.
   - **E.** Add a CAPTCHA test to the accounts.

9. You want to grant the individuals on your network team the ability to fully manipulate Amazon EC2 instances. Which of the following accomplish this goal? (Choose 2 answers)
   - **A.** Create a new policy allowing EC2:* actions, and name the policy **NetworkTeam**.
   - **B.** Assign the managed policy, EC2FullAccess, to a group named NetworkTeam, and assign all the team members' IAM user accounts to that group.
   - **C.** Create a new policy that grants EC2:* actions on all resources, and assign that policy to each individual's IAM user account on the network team.
   - **D.** Create a NetworkTeam IAM group, and have each team member log in to the AWS Management Console using the user name/password for the group.

10. What is the format of an IAM policy?
   - **A.** XML
   - **B.** Key/value pairs
   - **C.** JSON
   - **D.** Tab-delimited text

Chapter 7

Databases and AWS

THE AWS CERTIFIED SOLUTIONS ARCHITECT ASSOCIATE EXAM OBJECTIVES COVERED IN THIS CHAPTER MAY INCLUDE, BUT ARE NOT LIMITED TO, THE FOLLOWING:

Domain 1.0: Designing highly available, cost-efficient, fault-tolerant, and scalable systems

✓ **1.1 Identify and recognize cloud architecture considerations, such as fundamental components and effective designs.**

Content may include the following:

- Planning and design

- Architectural trade-off decisions (Amazon Relational Database Service [Amazon RDS] vs. installing on Amazon Elastic Compute Cloud [Amazon EC2])

- Best practices for AWS architecture

- Recovery Time Objective (RTO) and Recovery Point Objective (RPO) Disaster Recovery (DR) design

- Elasticity and scalability

Domain 3.0: Data Security

✓ **3.1 Recognize and implement secure practices for optimum cloud deployment and maintenance.**

Content may include the following:

- AWS administration and security services

- Design patterns

✓ **3.2 Recognize critical disaster recovery techniques and their implementation.**

This chapter will cover essential database concepts and introduce three of Amazon's managed database services: Amazon Relational Database Service (Amazon RDS), Amazon DynamoDB, and Amazon Redshift. These managed services simplify the setup and operation of relational databases, NoSQL databases, and data warehouses.

This chapter focuses on key topics you need to understand for the exam, including:

- The differences among a relational database, a NoSQL database, and a data warehouse

- The benefits and tradeoffs between running a database on Amazon EC2 or on Amazon RDS

- How to deploy database engines into the cloud

- How to back up and recover your database and meet your Recovery Point Objective (RPO) and Recovery Time Objective (RTO) requirements

- How to build highly available database architectures

- How to scale your database compute and storage vertically

- How to select the right type of storage volume

- How to use read replicas to scale horizontally

- How to design and scale an Amazon DynamoDB table

- How to read and write from an Amazon DynamoDB table

- How to use secondary indexes to speed queries

- How to design an Amazon Redshift table

- How to load and query an Amazon Redshift data warehouse

- How to secure your databases, tables, and clusters

Database Primer

Almost every application relies on a database to store important data and records for its users. A database engine allows your application to access, manage, and search large volumes of data records. In a well-architected application, the database will need to meet the performance demands, the availability needs, and the recoverability characteristics of the system.

Database systems and engines can be grouped into two broad categories: Relational Database Management Systems (RDBMS) and NoSQL (or non-relational) databases. It is not uncommon to build an application using a combination of RDBMS and NoSQL databases. A strong understanding of essential database concepts, Amazon RDS, and Amazon DynamoDB are required to pass this exam.

Relational Databases

The most common type of database in use today is the *relational database*. The relational database has roots going back to the 1970s when Edgar F. Codd, working for IBM, developed the concepts of the relational model. Today, relational databases power all types of applications from social media apps, e-commerce websites, and blogs to complex enterprise applications. Commonly used relational database software packages include MySQL, PostgreSQL, Microsoft SQL Server, and Oracle.

Relational databases provide a common interface that lets users read and write from the database using commands or queries written using *Structured Query Language (SQL)*. A relational database consists of one or more tables, and a table consists of columns and rows similar to a spreadsheet. A database column contains a specific attribute of the record, such as a person's name, address, and telephone number. Each attribute is assigned a data type such as text, number, or date, and the database engine will reject invalid inputs.

A database row comprises an individual record, such as the details about a student who attends a school. Consider the example in Table 7.1.

TABLE 7.1 Students Table

StudentID	FirstName	LastName	Gender	Age
1001	Joe	Dusty	M	29
1002	Andrea	Romanov	F	20
1003	Ben	Johnson	M	30
1004	Beth	Roberts	F	30

This is an example of a basic table that would sit in a relational database. There are five fields with different data types:

StudentID = Number or integer

FirstName = String

LastName = String

Gender = String (Character Length = 1)

Age = Integer

This sample table has four records, with each record representing an individual student. Each student has a StudentID field, which is usually a unique number per student. A unique number that identifies each student can be called a *primary key*.

One record in a table can relate to a record in another table by referencing the primary key of a record. This pointer or reference is called a foreign key. For example, the Grades table that records scores for each student would have its own primary key and an additional column known as a foreign key that refers to the primary key of the student record. By referencing the primary keys of other tables, relational databases minimize duplication of data in associated tables. With relational databases, it is important to note that the structure of the table (such as the number of columns and data type of each column) must be defined prior to data being added to the table.

A relational database can be categorized as either an *Online Transaction Processing (OLTP)* or *Online Analytical Processing (OLAP)* database system, depending on how the tables are organized and how the application uses the relational database. OLTP refers to transaction-oriented applications that are frequently writing and changing data (for example, data entry and e-commerce). OLAP is typically the domain of data warehouses and refers to reporting or analyzing large data sets. Large applications often have a mix of both OLTP and OLAP databases.

Amazon Relational Database Service (Amazon RDS) significantly simplifies the setup and maintenance of OLTP and OLAP databases. Amazon RDS provides support for six popular relational database engines: MySQL, Oracle, PostgreSQL, Microsoft SQL Server, MariaDB, and Amazon Aurora. You can also choose to run nearly any database engine using Windows or Linux Amazon Elastic Compute Cloud (Amazon EC2) instances and manage the installation and administration yourself.

Data Warehouses

A *data warehouse* is a central repository for data that can come from one or more sources. This data repository is often a specialized type of relational database that can be used for reporting and analysis via OLAP. Organizations typically use data warehouses to compile reports and search the database using highly complex queries.

Data warehouses are also typically updated on a batch schedule multiple times per day or per hour, compared to an OLTP relational database that can be updated thousands of times per second. Many organizations split their relational databases into two different databases: one database as their main production database for OLTP transactions, and the other database as their data warehouse for OLAP. OLTP transactions occur frequently and are relatively simple. OLAP transactions occur much less frequently but are much more complex.

Amazon RDS is often used for OLTP workloads, but it can also be used for OLAP. *Amazon Redshift* is a high-performance data warehouse designed specifically for OLAP use cases. It is also common to combine Amazon RDS with Amazon Redshift in the same application and periodically extract recent transactions and load them into a reporting database.

NoSQL Databases

NoSQL databases have gained significant popularity in recent years because they are often simpler to use, more flexible, and can achieve performance levels that are difficult or impossible with traditional relational databases. Traditional relational databases are difficult to scale beyond a single server without significant engineering and cost, but a NoSQL architecture allows for horizontal scalability on commodity hardware.

NoSQL databases are non-relational and do not have the same table and column semantics of a relational database. NoSQL databases are instead often key/value stores or document stores with flexible schemas that can evolve over time or vary. Contrast that to a relational database, which requires a very rigid schema.

Many of the concepts of NoSQL architectures trace their foundational concepts back to whitepapers published in 2006 and 2007 that described distributed systems like Dynamo at Amazon. Today, many application teams use Hbase, MongoDB, Cassandra, CouchDB, Riak, and *Amazon DynamoDB* to store large volumes of data with high transaction rates. Many of these database engines support clustering and scale horizontally across many machines for performance and fault tolerance. A common use case for NoSQL is managing user session state, user profiles, shopping cart data, or time-series data.

You can run any type of NoSQL database on AWS using Amazon EC2, or you can choose a managed service like Amazon DynamoDB to deal with the heavy lifting involved with building a distributed cluster spanning multiple data centers.

Amazon Relational Database Service (Amazon RDS)

Amazon RDS is a service that simplifies the setup, operations, and scaling of a relational database on AWS. With Amazon RDS, you can spend more time focusing on the application and the schema and let Amazon RDS offload common tasks like backups, patching, scaling, and replication.

Amazon RDS helps you to streamline the installation of the database software and also the provisioning of infrastructure capacity. Within a few minutes, Amazon RDS can launch one of many popular database engines that is ready to start taking SQL transactions. After the initial launch, Amazon RDS simplifies ongoing maintenance by automating common administrative tasks on a recurring basis.

With Amazon RDS, you can accelerate your development timelines and establish a consistent operating model for managing relational databases. For example, Amazon RDS makes it easy to replicate your data to increase availability, improve durability, or scale up or beyond a single database instance for read-heavy database workloads.

Amazon RDS exposes a database endpoint to which client software can connect and execute SQL. Amazon RDS does not provide shell access to Database (DB) Instances, and it restricts access to certain system procedures and tables that require advanced privileges.

With Amazon RDS, you can typically use the same tools to query, analyze, modify, and administer the database. For example, current Extract, Transform, Load (ETL) tools and reporting tools can connect to Amazon RDS databases in the same way with the same drivers, and often all it takes to reconfigure is changing the hostname in the connection string.

Database (DB) Instances

The Amazon RDS service itself provides an Application Programming Interface (API) that lets you create and manage one or more *DB Instances*. A DB Instance is an isolated database environment deployed in your private network segments in the cloud. Each DB Instance runs and manages a popular commercial or open source database engine on your behalf. Amazon RDS currently supports the following database engines: MySQL, PostgreSQL, MariaDB, Oracle, SQL Server, and Amazon Aurora.

You can launch a new DB Instance by calling the CreateDBInstance API or by using the AWS Management Console. Existing DB Instances can be changed or resized using the ModifyDBInstance API. A DB Instance can contain multiple different databases, all of which you create and manage within the DB Instance itself by executing SQL commands with the Amazon RDS endpoint. The different databases can be created, accessed, and managed using the same SQL client tools and applications that you use today.

The compute and memory resources of a DB Instance are determined by its DB Instance class. You can select the DB Instance class that best meets your needs for compute and memory. The range of DB Instance classes extends from a db.t2.micro with 1 virtual CPU (vCPU) and 1 GB of memory, up to a db.r3.8xlarge with 32 vCPUs and 244 GB of memory. As your needs change over time, you can change the instance class and the balance of compute of memory, and Amazon RDS will migrate your data to a larger or smaller instance class. Independent from the DB Instance class that you select, you can also control the size and performance characteristics of the storage used.

Amazon RDS supports a large variety of engines, versions, and feature combinations. Check the Amazon RDS documentation to determine support for specific features. Many features and common configuration settings are exposed and managed using *DB parameter groups* and *DB option groups*. A DB parameter group acts as a container for engine configuration values that can be applied to one or more DB Instances. You may change the DB parameter group for an existing instance, but a reboot is required. A DB option group acts as a container for engine features, which is empty by default. In order to enable specific features of a DB engine (for example, Oracle Statspack, Microsoft SQL Server Mirroring), you create a new DB option group and configure the settings accordingly.

> **TIP**
> Existing databases can be migrated to Amazon RDS using native tools and techniques that vary depending on the engine. For example with MySQL, you can export a backup using mysqldump and import the file into Amazon RDS MySQL. You can also use the AWS Database Migration Service, which gives you a graphical interface that simplifies the migration of both schema and data between databases. AWS Database Migration Service also helps convert databases from one database engine to another.

Operational Benefits

Amazon RDS increases the operational reliability of your databases by applying a very consistent deployment and operational model. This level of consistency is achieved in part by limiting the types of changes that can be made to the underlying infrastructure and through the extensive use of automation. For example with Amazon RDS, you cannot use Secure Shell (SSH) to log in to the host instance and install a custom piece of software. You can, however, connect using SQL administrator tools or use DB option groups and DB parameter groups to change the behavior or feature configuration for a DB Instance. If you want full control of the Operating System (OS) or require elevated permissions to run, then consider installing your database on Amazon EC2 instead of Amazon RDS.

Amazon RDS is designed to simplify the common tasks required to operate a relational database in a reliable manner. It's useful to compare the responsibilities of an administrator when operating a relational database in your data center, on Amazon EC2, or with Amazon RDS (see Table 7.2).

TABLE 7.2   Comparison of Operational Responsibilities

Responsibility	Database On-Premise	Database on Amazon EC2	Database on Amazon RDS
App Optimization	You	You	You
Scaling	You	You	AWS
High Availability	You	You	AWS
Backups	You	You	AWS
DB Engine Patches	You	You	AWS
Software Installation	You	You	AWS
OS Patches	You	You	AWS
OS Installation	You	AWS	AWS
Server Maintenance	You	AWS	AWS
Rack and Stack	You	AWS	AWS
Power and Cooling	You	AWS	AWS

Database Engines

Amazon RDS supports six database engines: MySQL, PostgreSQL, MariaDB, Oracle, SQL Server, and Amazon Aurora. Features and capabilities vary slightly depending on the engine that you select.

MySQL

MySQL is one of the most popular open source databases in the world, and it is used to power a wide range of applications, from small personal blogs to some of the largest websites in the world. As of the time of this writing, Amazon RDS for MySQL currently supports MySQL 5.7, 5.6, 5.5, and 5.1. The engine is running the open source Community Edition with InnoDB as the default and recommended database storage engine. Amazon RDS MySQL allows you to connect using standard MySQL tools such as MySQL Workbench or SQL Workbench/J. Amazon RDS MySQL supports *Multi-AZ* deployments for high availability and *read replicas* for horizontal scaling.

PostgreSQL

PostgreSQL is a widely used open source database engine with a very rich set of features and advanced functionality. Amazon RDS supports DB Instances running several versions of PostgreSQL. As of the time of this writing, Amazon RDS supports multiple releases of PostgreSQL, including 9.5.x, 9.4.x, and 9.3.x. Amazon RDS PostgreSQL can be managed using standard tools like pgAdmin and supports standard JDBC/ODBC drivers. Amazon RDS PostgreSQL also supports Multi-AZ deployment for high availability and read replicas for horizontal scaling.

MariaDB

Amazon RDS recently added support for DB Instances running MariaDB. MariaDB is a popular open source database engine built by the creators of MySQL and enhanced with enterprise tools and functionality. MariaDB adds features that enhance the performance, availability, and scalability of MySQL. As of the time of this writing, AWS supports MariaDB version 10.0.17. Amazon RDS fully supports the XtraDB storage engine for MariaDB DB Instances and, like Amazon RDS MySQL and PostgreSQL, has support for Multi-AZ deployment and read replicas.

Oracle

Oracle is one of the most popular relational databases used in the enterprise and is fully supported by Amazon RDS. As of the time of this writing, Amazon RDS supports DB Instances running several editions of Oracle 11g and Oracle 12c. Amazon RDS supports access to schemas on a DB Instance using any standard SQL client application, such as Oracle SQL Plus.

Amazon RDS Oracle supports three different editions of the popular database engine: Standard Edition One, Standard Edition, and Enterprise Edition. Table 7.3 outlines some of the major differences between editions:

TABLE 7.3   Amazon RDS Oracle Editions Compared

Edition	Performance	Multi-AZ	Encryption
Standard One	++++	Yes	KMS
Standard	++++++++	Yes	KMS
Enterprise	++++++++	Yes	KMS and TDE

Microsoft SQL Server

Microsoft SQL Server is another very popular relational database used in the enterprise. Amazon RDS allows Database Administrators (DBAs) to connect to their SQL Server DB Instance in the cloud using native tools like SQL Server Management Studio. As of the time of this writing, Amazon RDS provides support for several versions of Microsoft SQL Server, including SQL Server 2008 R2, SQL Server 2012, and SQL Server 2014.

Amazon RDS SQL Server also supports four different editions of SQL Server: Express Edition, Web Edition, Standard Edition, and Enterprise Edition. Table 7.4 highlights the relative performance, availability, and encryption differences among these editions.

TABLE 7.4   Amazon RDS SQL Server Editions Compared

Edition	Performance	Multi-AZ	Encryption
Express	+	No	KMS
Web	++++	No	KMS
Standard	++++	Yes	KMS
Enterprise	++++++++	Yes	KMS and TDE

Licensing

Amazon RDS Oracle and Microsoft SQL Server are commercial software products that require appropriate licenses to operate in the cloud. AWS offers two licensing models: *License Included* and *Bring Your Own License (BYOL)*.

License Included   In the License Included model, the license is held by AWS and is included in the Amazon RDS instance price. For Oracle, License Included provides licensing for Standard Edition One. For SQL Server, License Included provides licensing for SQL Server Express Edition, Web Edition, and Standard Edition.

Bring Your Own License (BYOL)   In the BYOL model, you provide your own license. For Oracle, you must have the appropriate Oracle Database license for the DB Instance class and Oracle Database edition you want to run. You can bring over Standard Edition One, Standard Edition, and Enterprise Edition.

For SQL Server, you provide your own license under the Microsoft License Mobility program. You can bring over Microsoft SQL Standard Edition and also Enterprise Edition. You are responsible for tracking and managing how licenses are allocated.

Amazon Aurora

Amazon Aurora offers enterprise-grade commercial database technology while offering the simplicity and cost effectiveness of an open source database. This is achieved by redesigning the internal components of MySQL to take a more service-oriented approach.

Like other Amazon RDS engines, Amazon Aurora is a fully managed service, is MySQL-compatible out of the box, and provides for increased reliability and performance over standard MySQL deployments. Amazon Aurora can deliver up to five times the performance of MySQL without requiring changes to most of your existing web applications. You can use the same code, tools, and applications that you use with your existing MySQL databases with Amazon Aurora.

When you first create an Amazon Aurora instance, you create a DB cluster. A DB cluster has one or more instances and includes a cluster volume that manages the data for those instances. An Amazon Aurora cluster volume is a virtual database storage volume that spans multiple Availability Zones, with each Availability Zone having a copy of the cluster data. An Amazon Aurora DB cluster consists of two different types of instances:

Primary Instance   This is the main instance, which supports both read and write workloads. When you modify your data, you are modifying the primary instance. Each Amazon Aurora DB cluster has one primary instance.

Amazon Aurora Replica   This is a secondary instance that supports only read operations. Each DB cluster can have up to 15 Amazon Aurora Replicas in addition to the primary instance. By using multiple Amazon Aurora Replicas, you can distribute the read workload among various instances, increasing performance. You can also locate your Amazon Aurora Replicas in multiple Availability Zones to increase your database availability.

Storage Options

Amazon RDS is built using Amazon Elastic Block Store (Amazon EBS) and allows you to select the right storage option based on your performance and cost requirements. Depending on the database engine and workload, you can scale up to 4 to 6TB in provisioned storage and up to 30,000 IOPS. Amazon RDS supports three storage types: Magnetic, General Purpose (Solid State Drive [SSD]), and Provisioned IOPS (SSD). Table 7.5 highlights the relative size, performance, and cost differences between types.

TABLE 7.5 Amazon RDS Storage Types

	Magnetic	General Purpose (SSD)	Provisioned IOPS (SSD)
Size	+++	+++++	+++++
Performance	+	+++	+++++
Cost	++	+++	+++++

Magnetic   Magnetic storage, also called standard storage, offers cost-effective storage that is ideal for applications with light I/O requirements.

General Purpose (SSD)   General purpose (SSD)-backed storage, also called gp2, can provide faster access than magnetic storage. This storage type can provide burst performance to meet spikes and is excellent for small- to medium-sized databases.

Provisioned IOPS (SSD)   Provisioned IOPS (SSD) storage is designed to meet the needs of I/O-intensive workloads, particularly database workloads, that are sensitive to storage performance and consistency in random access I/O throughput.

For most applications, General Purpose (SSD) is the best option and provides a good mix of lower-cost and higher-performance characteristics.

Backup and Recovery

Amazon RDS provides a consistent operational model for backup and recovery procedures across the different database engines. Amazon RDS provides two mechanisms for backing up the database: automated backups and manual snapshots. By using a combination of both techniques, you can design a backup recovery model to protect your application data.

Each organization typically will define a *Recovery Point Objective (RPO)* and *Recovery Time Objective (RTO)* for important applications based on the criticality of the application and the expectations of the users. It's common for enterprise systems to have an RPO measured in minutes and an RTO measured in hours or even days, while some critical applications may have much lower tolerances.

RPO is defined as the maximum period of data loss that is acceptable in the event of a failure or incident. For example, many systems back up transaction logs every 15 minutes to allow them to minimize data loss in the event of an accidental deletion or hardware failure.

RTO is defined as the maximum amount of downtime that is permitted to recover from backup and to resume processing. For large databases in particular, it can take hours to restore from a full backup. In the event of a hardware failure, you can reduce your RTO to minutes by failing over to a secondary node. You should create a recovery plan that, at a minimum, lets you recover from a recent backup.

Automated Backups

An *automated backup* is an Amazon RDS feature that continuously tracks changes and backs up your database. Amazon RDS creates a storage volume snapshot of your DB Instance, backing up the entire DB Instance and not just individual databases. You can set the backup retention period when you create a DB Instance. One day of backups will be retained by default, but you can modify the retention period up to a maximum of 35 days. Keep in mind that when you delete a DB Instance, all automated backup snapshots are deleted and cannot be recovered. Manual snapshots, however, are not deleted.

Automated backups will occur daily during a configurable 30-minute maintenance window called the backup window. Automated backups are kept for a configurable number of days, called the *backup retention period*. You can restore your DB Instance to any specific time during this retention period, creating a new DB Instance.

Manual DB Snapshots

In addition to automated backups, you can perform manual *DB snapshots* at any time. A DB snapshot is initiated by you and can be created as frequently as you want. You can then restore the DB Instance to the specific state in the DB snapshot at any time. DB snapshots can be created with the Amazon RDS console or the `CreateDBSnapshot` action. Unlike automated snapshots that are deleted after the retention period, manual DB snapshots are kept until you explicitly delete them with the Amazon RDS console or the `DeleteDBSnapshot` action.

> For busy databases, use Multi-AZ to minimize the performance impact of a snapshot. During the backup window, storage I/O may be suspended while your data is being backed up, and you may experience elevated latency. This I/O suspension typically lasts for the duration of the snapshot. This period of I/O suspension is shorter for Multi-AZ DB deployments because the backup is taken from the standby, but latency can occur during the backup process.

Recovery

Amazon RDS allows you to recover your database quickly whether you are performing automated backups or manual DB snapshots. You cannot restore from a DB snapshot to an existing DB Instance; a new DB Instance is created when you restore. When you restore a DB Instance, only the default DB parameter and security groups are associated with the restored instance. As soon as the restore is complete, you should associate any custom DB parameter or security groups used by the instance from which you restored. When using automated backups, Amazon RDS combines the daily backups performed during your predefined maintenance window in conjunction with transaction logs to enable you to restore your DB Instance to any point during your retention period, typically up to the last five minutes.

High Availability with Multi-AZ

One of the most powerful features of Amazon RDS is Multi-AZ deployments, which allows you to create a database cluster across multiple Availability Zones. Setting up a relational database to run in a highly available and fault-tolerant fashion is a challenging task. With Amazon RDS Multi-AZ, you can reduce the complexity involved with this common administrative task; with a single option, Amazon RDS can increase the availability of your database using replication. Multi-AZ lets you meet the most demanding RPO and RTO targets by using synchronous replication to minimize RPO and fast failover to minimize RTO to minutes.

Multi-AZ allows you to place a secondary copy of your database in another Availability Zone for disaster recovery purposes. Multi-AZ deployments are available for all types of Amazon RDS database engines. When you create a Multi-AZ DB Instance, a primary instance is created in one Availability Zone and a secondary instance is created in another Availability Zone. You are assigned a database instance endpoint such as the following:

```
my_app_db.ch6fe7ykq1zd.us-west-2.rds.amazonaws.com
```

This endpoint is a Domain Name System (DNS) name that AWS takes responsibility for resolving to a specific IP address. You use this DNS name when creating the connection to your database. Figure 7.1 illustrates a typical Multi-AZ deployment spanning two Availability Zones.

FIGURE 7.1 Multi-AZ Amazon RDS architecture

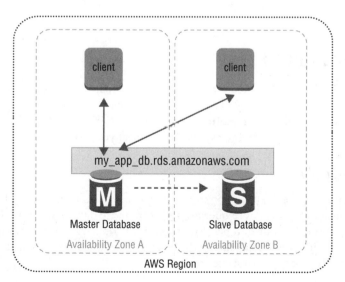

Amazon RDS automatically replicates the data from the master database or primary instance to the slave database or secondary instance using synchronous replication. Each Availability Zone runs on its own physically distinct, independent infrastructure and is engineered to be highly reliable. Amazon RDS detects and automatically recovers from the most common failure scenarios for Multi-AZ deployments so that you can resume database operations as quickly as possible without administrative intervention. Amazon RDS automatically performs a failover in the event of any of the following:

- Loss of availability in primary Availability Zone
- Loss of network connectivity to primary database
- Compute unit failure on primary database
- Storage failure on primary database

Amazon RDS will automatically fail over to the standby instance without user intervention. The DNS name remains the same, but the Amazon RDS service changes the CNAME to point to the standby. The primary DB Instance switches over automatically to the standby replica if there was an Availability Zone service disruption, if the primary DB Instance fails, or if the instance type is changed. You can also perform a manual failover of the DB Instance. Failover between the primary and the secondary instance is fast, and the time automatic failover takes to complete is typically one to two minutes.

> It is important to remember that Multi-AZ deployments are for disaster recovery only; they are not meant to enhance database performance. The standby DB Instance is not available to offline queries from the primary master DB Instance. To improve database performance using multiple DB Instances, use read replicas or other DB caching technologies such as Amazon ElastiCache.

Scaling Up and Out

As the number of transactions increase to a relational database, scaling up, or vertically, by getting a larger machine allows you to process more reads and writes. Scaling out, or horizontally, is also possible, but it is often more difficult. Amazon RDS allows you to scale compute and storage vertically, and for some DB engines, you can scale horizontally.

Vertical Scalability

Adding additional compute, memory, or storage resources to your database allows you to process more transactions, run more queries, and store more data. Amazon RDS makes it easy to scale up or down your database tier to meet the demands of your application. Changes can be scheduled to occur during the next maintenance window or to begin immediately using the ModifyDBInstance action.

To change the amount of compute and memory, you can select a different DB Instance class of the database. After you select a larger or smaller DB Instance class, Amazon RDS automates the migration process to a new class with only a short disruption and minimal effort.

You can also increase the amount of storage, the storage class, and the storage performance for an Amazon RDS Instance. Each database instance can scale from 5GB up to 6TB in provisioned storage depending on the storage type and engine. Storage for Amazon RDS can be increased over time as needs grow with minimal impact to the running database. Storage expansion is supported for all of the database engines except for SQL Server.

Horizontal Scalability with Partitioning

A relational database can be scaled vertically only so much before you reach the maximum instance size. Partitioning a large relational database into multiple instances or shards is a common technique for handling more requests beyond the capabilities of a single instance.

Partitioning, or *sharding*, allows you to scale horizontally to handle more users and requests but requires additional logic in the application layer. The application needs to decide how to route database requests to the correct shard and becomes limited in the types of queries that can be performed across server boundaries. NoSQL databases like Amazon DynamoDB or Cassandra are designed to scale horizontally.

Horizontal Scalability with Read Replicas

Another important scaling technique is to use *read replicas* to offload read transactions from the primary database and increase the overall number of transactions. Amazon RDS supports read replicas that allow you to scale out elastically beyond the capacity constraints of a single DB Instance for read-heavy database workloads.

There are a variety of use cases where deploying one or more read replica DB Instances is helpful. Some common scenarios include:

- Scale beyond the capacity of a single DB Instance for read-heavy workloads.

- Handle read traffic while the source DB Instance is unavailable. For example, due to I/O suspension for backups or scheduled maintenance, you can direct read traffic to a replica.

- Offload reporting or data warehousing scenarios against a replica instead of the primary DB Instance.

For example, a blogging website may have very little write activity except for the occasional comment, and the vast majority of database activity will be read-only. By offloading some or all of the read activity to one or more read replicas, the primary database instance can focus on handling the writes and replicating the data out to the replicas.

Read replicas are currently supported in Amazon RDS for MySQL, PostgreSQL, MariaDB, and Amazon Aurora. Amazon RDS uses the MySQL, MariaDB, and PostgreSQL DB engines' built-in replication functionality to create a special type of DB Instance, called a read replica, from a source DB Instance. Updates made to the source DB Instance are asynchronously copied to the read replica. You can reduce the load on your source DB Instance by routing read queries from your applications to the read replica.

> You can create one or more replicas of a database within a single AWS Region or across multiple AWS Regions. To enhance your disaster recovery capabilities or reduce global latencies, you can use cross-region read replicas to serve read traffic from a region closest to your global users or migrate your databases across AWS Regions.

[handwritten margin notes: IAM policy, Private subnet, SS, NACL, Pwd rotation & complexity, @rest ENC, KMS or TDE, @motion ENC, SSL]

Security

Securing your Amazon RDS DB Instances and relational databases requires a comprehensive plan that addresses the many layers commonly found in database-driven systems. This includes the infrastructure resources, the database, and the network.

Protect access to your infrastructure resources using AWS Identity and Access Management (IAM) policies that limit which actions AWS administrators can perform. For example, some key administrator actions that can be controlled in IAM include CreateDBInstance and DeleteDBInstance.

Another security best practice is to deploy your Amazon RDS DB Instances into a private subnet within an Amazon Virtual Private Cloud (Amazon VPC) that limits network access to the DB Instance. Before you can deploy into an Amazon VPC, you must first create a *DB subnet group* that predefines which subnets are available for Amazon RDS deployments. Further, restrict network access using network Access Control Lists (ACLs) and security groups to limit inbound traffic to a short list of source IP addresses.

At the database level, you will also need to create users and grant them permissions to read and write to your databases. Access to the database is controlled using the database engine-specific access control and user management mechanisms. Create users at the database level with strong passwords that you rotate frequently.

Finally, protect the confidentiality of your data in transit and at rest with multiple encryption capabilities provided with Amazon RDS. Security features vary slightly from one engine to another, but all engines support some form of in-transit encryption and also at-rest encryption. You can securely connect a client to a running DB Instance using Secure Sockets Layer (SSL) to protect data in transit. Encryption at rest is possible for all engines using the Amazon Key Management Service (KMS) or *Transparent Data Encryption (TDE)*. All logs, backups, and snapshots are encrypted for an encrypted Amazon RDS instance.

Amazon Redshift

Amazon Redshift is a fast, powerful, fully managed, petabyte-scale data warehouse service in the cloud. Amazon Redshift is a relational database designed for OLAP scenarios and optimized for high-performance analysis and reporting of very large datasets. Traditional data warehouses are difficult and expensive to manage, especially for large datasets. Amazon Redshift not only significantly lowers the cost of a data warehouse, but it also makes it easy to analyze large amounts of data very quickly.

Amazon Redshift gives you fast querying capabilities over structured data using standard SQL commands to support interactive querying over large datasets. With connectivity via ODBC or JDBC, Amazon Redshift integrates well with various data loading, reporting, data mining, and analytics tools. Amazon Redshift is based on industry-standard PostgreSQL, so most existing SQL client applications will work with only minimal changes.

Amazon Redshift manages the work needed to set up, operate, and scale a data warehouse, from provisioning the infrastructure capacity to automating ongoing administrative tasks such as backups and patching. Amazon Redshift automatically monitors your nodes and drives to help you recover from failures.

Clusters and Nodes

The key component of an Amazon Redshift data warehouse is a *cluster*. A cluster is composed of a leader node and one or more compute nodes. The client application interacts directly only with the leader node, and the compute nodes are transparent to external applications.

Amazon Redshift currently has support for six different node types and each has a different mix of CPU, memory, and storage. The six node types are grouped into two categories: Dense Compute and Dense Storage. The Dense Compute node types support clusters up to 326TB using fast SSDs, while the Dense Storage nodes support clusters up to 2PB using large magnetic disks. Each cluster consists of one leader node and one or more compute nodes. Figure 7.2 shows the internal components of an Amazon Redshift data warehouse cluster.

FIGURE 7.2   Amazon Redshift cluster architecture

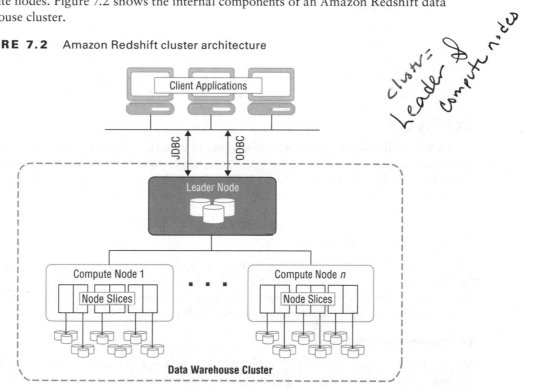

Each cluster contains one or more databases. User data for each table is distributed across the compute nodes. Your application or SQL client communicates with Amazon Redshift using standard JDBC or ODBC connections with the leader node, which in turn coordinates query execution with the compute nodes. Your application does not interact directly with the compute nodes.

The disk storage for a compute node is divided into a number of slices. The number of slices per node depends on the node size of the cluster and typically varies between 2 and 16. The nodes all participate in parallel query execution, working on data that is distributed as evenly as possible across the slices.

You can increase query performance by adding multiple nodes to a cluster. When you submit a query, Amazon Redshift distributes and executes the query in parallel across all of a cluster's compute nodes. Amazon Redshift also spreads your table data across all compute nodes in a cluster based on a *distribution strategy* that you specify. This partitioning of data across multiple compute resources allows you to achieve high levels of performance.

Amazon Redshift allows you to resize a cluster to add storage and compute capacity over time as your needs evolve. You can also change the node type of a cluster and keep the overall size the same. Whenever you perform a resize operation, Amazon Redshift will create a new cluster and migrate data from the old cluster to the new one. During a resize operation, the database will become read-only until the operation is finished.

Table Design

Each Amazon Redshift cluster can support one or more databases, and each database can contain many tables. Like most SQL-based databases, you can create a table using the CREATE TABLE command. This command specifies the name of the table, the columns, and their data types. In addition to columns and data types, the Amazon Redshift CREATE TABLE command also supports specifying compression encodings, distribution strategy, and sort keys.

Data Types

Amazon Redshift columns support a wide range of data types. This includes common numeric data types like INTEGER, DECIMAL, and DOUBLE, text data types like CHAR and VARCHAR, and date data types like DATE and TIMESTAMP. Additional columns can be added to a table using the ALTER TABLE command; however, existing columns cannot be modified.

Compression Encoding

One of the key performance optimizations used by Amazon Redshift is data compression. When loading data for the first time into an empty table, Amazon Redshift will automatically sample your data and select the best compression scheme for each column. Alternatively, you can specify compression encoding on a per-column basis as part of the CREATE TABLE command.

Distribution Strategy

One of the primary decisions when creating a table in Amazon Redshift is how to distribute the records across the nodes and slices in a cluster. You can configure the distribution style of a table to give Amazon Redshift hints as to how the data should be partitioned to best meet your query patterns. When you run a query, the optimizer shifts the rows to the compute nodes as needed to perform any joins and aggregates. The goal in selecting a table distribution style is to minimize the impact of the redistribution step by putting the data where it needs to be before the query is performed.

The data distribution style that you select for your database has a big impact on query performance, storage requirements, data loading, and maintenance. By choosing the best distribution strategy for each table, you can balance your data distribution and significantly improve overall system performance. When creating a table, you can choose between one of three distribution styles: EVEN, KEY, or ALL.

EVEN distribution   This is the default option and results in the data being distributed across the slices in a uniform fashion regardless of the data.

KEY distribution   With KEY distribution, the rows are distributed according to the values in one column. The leader node will store matching values close together and increase query performance for joins.

ALL distribution   With ALL, a full copy of the entire table is distributed to every node. This is useful for lookup tables and other large tables that are not updated frequently.

Sort Keys

Another important decision to make during the creation of a table is whether to specify one or more columns as sort keys. Sorting enables efficient handling of range-restricted predicates. If a query uses a range-restricted predicate, the query processor can rapidly skip over large numbers of blocks during table scans.

The sort keys for a table can be either compound or interleaved. A compound sort key is more efficient when query predicates use a prefix, which is a subset of the sort key columns in order. An interleaved sort key gives equal weight to each column in the sort key, so query predicates can use any subset of the columns that make up the sort key, in any order.

Loading Data

Amazon Redshift supports standard SQL commands like INSERT and UPDATE to create and modify records in a table. For bulk operations, however, Amazon Redshift provides the COPY command as a much more efficient alternative than repeatedly calling INSERT.

A COPY command can load data into a table in the most efficient manner, and it supports multiple types of input data sources. The fastest way to load data into Amazon Redshift is doing bulk data loads from flat files stored in an Amazon Simple Storage Service (Amazon S3) bucket or from an Amazon DynamoDB table.

When loading data from Amazon S3, the COPY command can read from multiple files at the same time. Amazon Redshift can distribute the workload to the nodes and perform the load process in parallel. Instead of having one single large file with your data, you can enable parallel processing by having a cluster with multiple nodes and multiple input files.

After each bulk data load that modifies a significant amount of data, you will need to perform a VACUUM command to reorganize your data and reclaim space after deletes. It is also recommended to run an ANALYZE command to update table statistics.

Data can also be exported out of Amazon Redshift using the UNLOAD command. This command can be used to generate delimited text files and store them in Amazon S3.

[handwritten margin note: Vacuum = re-org & reclaim]

Querying Data

Amazon Redshift allows you to write standard SQL commands to query your tables. By supporting commands like SELECT to query and join tables, analysts can quickly become productive using Amazon Redshift or integrate it easily. For complex queries, you can analyze the query plan to better optimize your access pattern. You can monitor the performance of the cluster and specific queries using Amazon CloudWatch and the Amazon Redshift web console.

For large Amazon Redshift clusters supporting many users, you can configure Workload Management (WLM) to queue and prioritize queries. WLM allows you define multiple queues and set the concurrency level for each queue. For example, you might want to have one queue set up for long-running queries and limit the concurrency and another queue for short-running queries and allow higher levels of concurrency.

Snapshots

Similar to Amazon RDS, you can create point-in-time snapshots of your Amazon Redshift cluster. A snapshot can then be used to restore a copy or create a clone of your original Amazon Redshift cluster. Snapshots are durably stored internally in Amazon S3 by Amazon Redshift.

Amazon Redshift supports both automated snapshots and manual snapshots. With automated snapshots, Amazon Redshift will periodically take snapshots of your cluster and keep a copy for a configurable retention period. You can also perform manual snapshots and share them across regions or even with other AWS accounts. Manual snapshots are retained until you explicitly delete them.

Security

Securing your Amazon Redshift cluster is similar to securing other databases running in the cloud. Your security plan should include controls to protect the infrastructure resources, the database schema, the records in the table, and network access. By addressing security at every level, you can securely operate an Amazon Redshift data warehouse in the cloud.

The first layer of security comes at the infrastructure level using IAM policies that limit the actions AWS administrators can perform. With IAM, you can create policies that grant other AWS users the permission to create and manage the lifecycle of a cluster, including scaling, backup, and recovery operations.

At the network level, Amazon Redshift clusters can be deployed within the private IP address space of your Amazon VPC to restrict overall network connectivity. Fine-grained network access can be further restricted using security groups and network ACLs at the subnet level.

In addition to controlling infrastructure access at the infrastructure level, you must protect access at the database level. When you initially create an Amazon Redshift cluster, you will create a master user account and password. The master account can be used to log in to the Amazon Redshift database and to create more users and groups. Each database user can be granted permission to schemas, tables, and other database objects. These permissions are independent from the IAM policies used to control access to the infrastructure resources and the Amazon Redshift cluster configuration.

Protecting the data stored in Amazon Redshift is another important aspect of your security design. Amazon Redshift supports encryption of data in transit using SSL-encrypted connections, and also encryption of data at rest using multiple techniques. To encrypt data at rest, Amazon Redshift integrates with KMS and AWS CloudHSM for encryption key management services. Encryption at rest and in transit assists in meeting compliance requirements, such as for the Health Insurance Portability and Accountability Act (HIPAA) or the Payment Card Industry Data Security Standard (PCI DSS), and provides additional protections for your data.

Amazon DynamoDB

Amazon DynamoDB is a fully managed NoSQL database service that provides fast and low-latency performance that scales with ease. Amazon DynamoDB lets you offload the administrative burdens of operating a distributed NoSQL database and focus on the application. Amazon DynamoDB significantly simplifies the hardware provisioning, setup and configuration, replication, software patching, and cluster scaling of NoSQL databases.

Amazon DynamoDB is designed to simplify database and cluster management, provide consistently high levels of performance, simplify scalability tasks, and improve reliability with automatic replication. Developers can create a table in Amazon DynamoDB and write an unlimited number of items with consistent latency.

Amazon DynamoDB can provide consistent performance levels by automatically distributing the data and traffic for a table over multiple partitions. After you configure a certain read or write capacity, Amazon DynamoDB will automatically add enough infrastructure capacity to support the requested throughput levels. As your demand changes over time, you can adjust the read or write capacity after a table has been created, and Amazon DynamoDB will add or remove infrastructure and adjust the internal partitioning accordingly.

To help maintain consistent, fast performance levels, all table data is stored on high-performance SSD disk drives. Performance metrics, including transactions rates, can be monitored using Amazon CloudWatch. In addition to providing high-performance levels, Amazon DynamoDB also provides automatic high-availability and durability protections by replicating data across multiple Availability Zones within an AWS Region.

Data Model

The basic components of the Amazon DynamoDB data model include *tables*, items, and attributes. As depicted in Figure 7.3, a table is a collection of items and each item is a collection of one or more attributes. Each item also has a primary key that uniquely identifies the item.

FIGURE 7.3   Table, items, attributes relationship

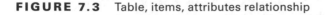

In a relational database, a table has a predefined schema such as the table name, primary key, list of its column names, and their data types. All records stored in the table must have the same set of columns. In contrast, Amazon DynamoDB only requires that a table have a primary key, but it does not require you to define all of the attribute names and data types in advance. Individual items in an Amazon DynamoDB table can have any number of attributes, although there is a limit of 400KB on the item size.

Each attribute in an item is a name/value pair. An attribute can be a single-valued or multi-valued set. For example, a book item can have title and authors attributes. Each book has one title but can have many authors. The multi-valued attribute is a set; duplicate values are not allowed. Data is stored in Amazon DynamoDB in key/value pairs such as the following:

```
{
    Id = 101
    ProductName = "Book 101 Title"
    ISBN = "123-1234567890"
    Authors = [ "Author 1", "Author 2" ]
    Price = 2.88
    Dimensions = "8.5 x 11.0 x 0.5"
    PageCount = 500
    InPublication = 1
    ProductCategory = "Book"
}
```

Applications can connect to the Amazon DynamoDB service endpoint and submit requests over HTTP/S to read and write items to a table or even to create and delete tables. DynamoDB provides a web service API that accepts requests in JSON format. While you could program directly against the web service API endpoints, most developers choose to use the AWS Software Development Kit (SDK) to interact with their items and tables. The AWS SDK is available in many different languages and provides a simplified, high-level programming interface.

Data Types

Amazon DynamoDB gives you a lot of flexibility with your database schema. Unlike a traditional relational database that requires you to define your column types ahead of time, DynamoDB only requires a primary key attribute. Each item that is added to the table can then add additional attributes. This gives you flexibility over time to expand your schema without having to rebuild the entire table and deal with record version differences with application logic.

When you create a table or a secondary index, you must specify the names and data types of each primary key attribute (partition key and sort key). Amazon DynamoDB supports a wide range of data types for attributes. Data types fall into three major categories: Scalar, Set, or Document.

Scalar Data Types   A scalar type represents exactly one value. Amazon DynamoDB supports the following five scalar types:

String   Text and variable length characters up to 400KB. Supports Unicode with UTF8 encoding

Number   Positive or negative number with up to 38 digits of precision

Binary   Binary data, images, compressed objects up to 400KB in size

Boolean   Binary flag representing a true or false value

Null   Represents a blank, empty, or unknown state. String, Number, Binary, Boolean cannot be empty.

Set Data Types   Sets are useful to represent a unique list of one or more scalar values. Each value in a set needs to be unique and must be the same data type. Sets do not guarantee order. Amazon DynamoDB supports three set types: String Set, Number Set, and Binary Set.

String Set   Unique list of String attributes

Number Set   Unique list of Number attributes

Binary Set   Unique list of Binary attributes

Document Data Types   Document type is useful to represent multiple nested attributes, similar to the structure of a JSON file. Amazon DynamoDB supports two document types: List and Map. Multiple Lists and Maps can be combined and nested to create complex structures.

List   Each List can be used to store an ordered list of attributes of different data types.

Map   Each Map can be used to store an unordered list of key/value pairs. Maps can be used to represent the structure of any JSON object.

Primary Key

When you create a table, you must specify the primary key of the table in addition to the table name. Like a relational database, the primary key uniquely identifies each item in the table. A primary key will point to exactly one item. Amazon DynamoDB supports two types of primary keys, and this configuration cannot be changed after a table has been created:

Partition Key   The primary key is made of one attribute, a partition (or hash) key. Amazon DynamoDB builds an unordered hash index on this primary key attribute.

Partition and Sort Key   The primary key is made of two attributes. The first attribute is the partition key and the second one is the sort (or range) key. Each item in the table is uniquely identified by the combination of its partition and sort key values. It is possible for two items to have the same partition key value, but those two items must have different sort key values.

Furthermore, each primary key attribute must be defined as type string, number, or binary. Amazon DynamoDB uses the partition key to distribute the request to the right partition.

If you are performing many reads or writes per second on the same primary key, you will not be able to fully use the compute capacity of the Amazon DynamoDB cluster. A best practice is to maximize your through-put by distributing requests across the full range of partition keys.

Provisioned Capacity

When you create an Amazon DynamoDB table, you are required to provision a certain amount of read and write capacity to handle your expected workloads. Based on your configuration settings, DynamoDB will then provision the right amount of infrastructure capacity to meet your requirements with sustained, low-latency response times. Overall capacity is measured in read and write capacity units. These values can later be scaled up or down by using an `UpdateTable` action.

Each operation against an Amazon DynamoDB table will consume some of the provisioned capacity units. The specific amount of capacity units consumed depends largely on the size of the item, but also on other factors. For read operations, the amount of capacity consumed also depends on the read consistency selected in the request. Read more about eventual and strong consistency later in this chapter.

For example, given a table without a local secondary index, you will consume 1 capacity unit if you read an item that is 4KB or smaller. Similarly, for write operations you will consume 1 capacity unit if you write an item that is 1KB or smaller. This means that if you read an item that is 110KB, you will consume 28 capacity units, or 110 / 4 = 27.5 rounded up to 28. For read operations that are strongly consistent, they will use twice the number of capacity units, or 56 in this example.

You can use Amazon CloudWatch to monitor your Amazon DynamoDB capacity and make scaling decisions. There is a rich set of metrics, including `ConsumedReadCapacityUnits` and `ConsumedWriteCapacityUnits`. If you do exceed your provisioned capacity for a period of time, requests will be throttled and can be retried later. You can monitor and alert on the `ThrottledRequests` metric using Amazon CloudWatch to notify you of changing usage patterns.

Secondary Indexes

When you create a table with a partition and sort key (formerly known as a hash and range key), you can optionally define one or more secondary indexes on that table. A secondary index lets you query the data in the table using an alternate key, in addition to queries against the primary key. Amazon DynamoDB supports two different kinds of indexes:

Global Secondary Index   The *global secondary index* is an index with a partition and sort key that can be different from those on the table. You can create or delete a global secondary index on a table at any time.

Local Secondary Index   The *local secondary index* is an index that has the same partition key attribute as the primary key of the table, but a different sort key. You can only create a local secondary index when you create a table.

[handwritten: only 1 local secondary index! Multiple global secondary indexes.]

Secondary indexes allow you to search a large table efficiently and avoid an expensive scan operation to find items with specific attributes. These indexes allow you to support different query access patterns and use cases beyond what is possible with only a primary key. While a table can only have one local secondary index, you can have multiple global secondary indexes.

Amazon DynamoDB updates each secondary index when an item is modified. These updates consume write capacity units. For a local secondary index, item updates will consume write capacity units from the main table, while global secondary indexes maintain their own provisioned throughput settings separate from the table.

Writing and Reading Data

After you create a table with a primary key and indexes, you can begin writing and reading items to the table. Amazon DynamoDB provides multiple operations that let you create, update, and delete individual items. Amazon DynamoDB also provides multiple querying options that let you search a table or an index or retrieve back a specific item or a batch of items.

Writing Items

Amazon DynamoDB provides three primary API actions to create, update, and delete items: `PutItem`, `UpdateItem`, and `DeleteItem`. Using the `PutItem` action, you can create a new item with one or more attributes. Calls to `PutItem` will update an existing item if the primary key already exists. `PutItem` only requires a table name and a primary key; any additional attributes are optional.

The UpdateItem action will find existing items based on the primary key and replace the attributes. This operation can be useful to only update a single attribute and leave the other attributes unchanged. UpdateItem can also be used to create items if they don't already exist. Finally, you can remove an item from a table by using DeleteItem and specifying a specific primary key.

The UpdateItem action also provides support for atomic counters. *Atomic counters* allow you to increment and decrement a value and are guaranteed to be consistent across multiple concurrent requests. For example, a counter attribute used to track the overall score of a mobile game can be updated by many clients at the same time.

These three actions also support conditional expressions that allow you to perform validation before an action is applied. For example, you can apply a conditional expression on PutItem that checks that certain conditions are met before the item is created. This can be useful to prevent accidental overwrites or to enforce some type of business logic checks.

Reading Items

After an item has been created, it can be retrieved through a direct lookup by calling the GetItem action or through a search using the Query or Scan action. GetItem allows you to retrieve an item based on its primary key. All of the item's attributes are returned by default, and you have the option to select individual attributes to filter down the results.

If a primary key is composed of a partition key, the entire partition key needs to be specified to retrieve the item. If the primary key is a composite of a partition key and a sort key, GetItem will require both the partition and sort key as well. Each call to GetItem consumes read capacity units based on the size of the item and the consistency option selected.

By default, a GetItem operation performs an eventually consistent read. You can optionally request a strongly consistent read instead; this will consume additional read capacity units, but it will return the most up-to-date version of the item.

Eventual Consistency

When reading items from Amazon DynamoDB, the operation can be either eventually consistent or strongly consistent. Amazon DynamoDB is a distributed system that stores multiple copies of an item across an AWS Region to provide high availability and increased durability. When an item is updated in Amazon DynamoDB, it starts replicating across multiple servers. Because Amazon DynamoDB is a distributed system, the replication can take some time to complete. Because of this we refer to the data as being eventually consistent, meaning that a read request immediately after a write operation might not show the latest change. In some cases, the application needs to guarantee that the data is the latest and Amazon DynamoDB offers an option for strongly consistent reads.

Eventually Consistent Reads   When you read data, the response might not reflect the results of a recently completed write operation. The response might include some stale data. Consistency across all copies of the data is usually reached within a second; if you repeat your read request after a short time, the response returns the latest data.

Strongly Consistent Reads   When you issue a strongly consistent read request, Amazon DynamoDB returns a response with the most up-to-date data that reflects updates by all prior related write operations to which Amazon DynamoDB returned a successful response. A strongly consistent read might be less available in the case of a network delay or outage. You can request a strongly consistent read result by specifying optional parameters in your request.

Batch Operations

Amazon DynamoDB also provides several operations designed for working with large batches of items, including `BatchGetItem` and `BatchWriteItem`. Using the `BatchWriteItem` action, you can perform up to 25 item creates or updates with a single operation. This allows you to minimize the overhead of each individual call when processing large numbers of items.

Searching Items

Amazon DynamoDB also gives you two operations, Query and Scan, that can be used to search a table or an index. A Query operation is the primary search operation you can use to find items in a table or a secondary index using only primary key attribute values. Each Query requires a partition key attribute name and a distinct value to search. You can optionally provide a sort key value and use a comparison operator to refine the search results. Results are automatically sorted by the primary key and are limited to 1MB.

In contrast to a Query, a Scan operation will read every item in a table or a secondary index. By default, a Scan operation returns all of the data attributes for every item in the table or index. Each request can return up to 1MB of data. Items can be filtered out using expressions, but this can be a resource-intensive operation. If the result set for a Query or a Scan exceeds 1MB, you can page through the results in 1MB increments.

> For most operations, performing a Query operation instead of a Scan operation will be the most efficient option. Performing a Scan operation will result in a full scan of the entire table or secondary index, then it filters out values to provide the desired result. Use a Query operation when possible and avoid a Scan on a large table or index for only a small number of items.

Scaling and Partitioning

Amazon DynamoDB is a fully managed service that abstracts away most of the complexity involved in building and scaling a NoSQL cluster. You can create tables that can scale up to hold a virtually unlimited number of items with consistent low-latency performance. An Amazon DynamoDB table can scale horizontally through the use of partitions to meet the storage and performance requirements of your application. Each individual partition represents a unit of compute and storage capacity. A well-designed application will take the partition structure of a table into account to distribute read and write transactions evenly and achieve high transaction rates at low latencies.

Amazon DynamoDB stores items for a single table across multiple partitions, as represented in Figure 7.4. Amazon DynamoDB decides which partition to store the item in based on the partition key. The partition key is used to distribute the new item among all of the available partitions, and items with the same partition key will be stored on the same partition.

FIGURE 7.4   Table partitioning

Table

Partition 1   Partition 2

As the number of items in a table grows, additional partitions can be added by splitting an existing partition. The provisioned throughput configured for a table is also divided evenly among the partitions. Provisioned throughput allocated to a partition is entirely dedicated to that partition, and there is no sharing of provisioned throughput across partitions.

When a table is created, Amazon DynamoDB configures the table's partitions based on the desired read and write capacity. One single partition can hold about 10GB of data and supports a maximum of 3,000 read capacity units or 1,000 write capacity units. For partitions that are not fully using their provisioned capacity, Amazon DynamoDB provides some burst capacity to handle spikes in traffic. A portion of your unused capacity will be reserved to handle bursts for short periods.

As storage or capacity requirements change, Amazon DynamoDB can split a partition to accommodate more data or higher provisioned request rates. After a partition is split, however, it cannot be merged back together. Keep this in mind when planning to increase provisioned capacity temporarily and then lower it again. With each additional partition added, its share of the provisioned capacity is reduced.

To achieve the full amount of request throughput provisioned for a table, keep your workload spread evenly across the partition key values. Distributing requests across partition key values distributes the requests across partitions. For example, if a table has 10,000 read capacity units configured but all of the traffic is hitting one partition key, you will not be able to get more than the 3,000 maximum read capacity units that one partition can support.

To maximize Amazon DynamoDB throughput, create tables with a partition key that has a large number of distinct values and ensure that the values are requested fairly uniformly. Adding a random element that can be calculated or hashed is one common technique to improve partition distribution.

Security

Amazon DynamoDB gives you granular control over the access rights and permissions for users and administrators. Amazon DynamoDB integrates with the IAM service to provide strong control over permissions using policies. You can create one or more policies that allow or deny specific operations on specific tables. You can also use conditions to restrict access to individual items or attributes.

All operations must first be authenticated as a valid user or user session. Applications that need to read and write from Amazon DynamoDB need to obtain a set of temporary or permanent access control keys. While these keys could be stored in a configuration file, a best practice is for applications running on AWS to use IAM Amazon EC2 instance profiles to manage credentials. IAM Amazon EC2 instance profiles or roles allow you to avoid storing sensitive keys in configuration files that must then be secured.

· IAM policies
w/ conditions
· Instance profile
w/ IAM

For mobile applications, a best practice is to use a combination of web identity federation with the AWS Security Token Service (AWS STS) to issue temporary keys that expire after a short period.

Amazon DynamoDB also provides support for fine-grained access control that can restrict access to specific items within a table or even specific attributes within an item. For example, you may want to limit a user to only access his or her items within a table and prevent access to items associated with a different user. Using conditions in an IAM policy allows you to restrict which actions a user can perform, on which tables, and to which attributes a user can read or write.

Amazon DynamoDB Streams

A common requirement for many applications is to keep track of recent changes and then perform some kind of processing on the changed records. Amazon DynamoDB Streams makes it easy to get a list of item modifications for the last 24-hour period. For example, you might need to calculate metrics on a rolling basis and update a dashboard, or maybe synchronize two tables or log activity and changes to an audit trail. With Amazon DynamoDB Streams, these types of applications become easier to build.

Amazon DynamoDB Streams allows you to extend application functionality without modifying the original application. By reading the log of activity changes from the stream, you can build new integrations or support new reporting requirements that weren't part of the original design.

Each item change is buffered in a time-ordered sequence or stream that can be read by other applications. Changes are logged to the stream in near real-time and allow you to respond quickly or chain together a sequence of events based on a modification.

Streams can be enabled or disabled for an Amazon DynamoDB table using the AWS Management Console, Command Line Interface (CLI), or SDK. A stream consists of stream records. Each stream record represents a single data modification in the Amazon

DynamoDB table to which the stream belongs. Each stream record is assigned a sequence number, reflecting the order in which the record was published to the stream.

Stream records are organized into groups, also referred to as *shards*. Each shard acts as a container for multiple stream records and contains information on accessing and iterating through the records. Shards live for a maximum of 24 hours and, with fluctuating load levels, could be split one or more times before they are eventually closed.

> **T/P**
>
> To build an application that reads from a shard, it is recommended to use the Amazon DynamoDB Streams Kinesis Adapter. The Kinesis Client Library (KCL) simplifies the application logic required to process reading records from streams and shards.

Summary

In this chapter, you learned the basic concepts of relational databases, data warehouses, and NoSQL databases. You also learned about the benefits and features of AWS managed database services Amazon RDS, Amazon Redshift, and Amazon DynamoDB.

Amazon RDS manages the heavy lifting involved in administering a database infrastructure and software and lets you focus on building the relational schemas that best fit your use case and the performance tuning to optimize your queries.

Amazon RDS supports popular open-source and commercial database engines and provides a consistent operational model for common administrative tasks. Increase your availability by running a master-slave configuration across Availability Zones using Multi-AZ deployment. Scale your application and increase your database read performance using read replicas.

Amazon Redshift allows you to deploy a data warehouse cluster that is optimized for analytics and reporting workloads within minutes. Amazon Redshift distributes your records using columnar storage and parallelizes your query execution across multiple compute nodes to deliver fast query performance. Amazon Redshift clusters can be scaled up or down to support large, petabyte-scale databases using SSD or magnetic disk storage.

Connect to Amazon Redshift clusters using standard SQL clients with JDBC/ODBC drivers and execute SQL queries using many of the same analytics and ETL tools that you use today. Load data into your Amazon Redshift clusters using the COPY command to bulk import flat files stored in Amazon S3, then run standard SELECT commands to search and query the table.

Back up both your Amazon RDS databases and Amazon Redshift clusters using automated and manual snapshots to allow for point-in-time recovery. Secure your Amazon RDS and Amazon Redshift databases using a combination of IAM, database-level access control, network-level access control, and data encryption techniques.

Amazon DynamoDB simplifies the administration and operations of a NoSQL database in the cloud. Amazon DynamoDB allows you to create tables quickly that can scale to an unlimited number of items and configure very high levels of provisioned read and write capacity.

Amazon DynamoDB tables provide a flexible data storage mechanism that only requires a primary key and allows for one or more attributes. Amazon DynamoDB supports both simple scalar data types like String and Number, and also more complex structures using List and Map. Secure your Amazon DynamoDB tables using IAM and restrict access to items and attributes using fine-grained access control.

Amazon DynamoDB will handle the difficult task of cluster and partition management and provide you with a highly available database table that replicates data across Availability Zones for increased durability. Track and process recent changes by tapping into Amazon DynamoDB Streams.

Exam Essentials

Know what a relational database is.   A relational database consists of one or more tables. Communication to and from relational databases usually involves simple SQL queries, such as "Add a new record," or "What is the cost of product *x*?" These simple queries are often referred to as OLTP.

Understand which databases are supported by Amazon RDS.   Amazon RDS currently supports six relational database engines:

- Microsoft SQL Server
- MySQL Server
- Oracle
- PostgreSQL
- MariaDB
- Amazon Aurora

Understand the operational benefits of using Amazon RDS.   Amazon RDS is a managed service provided by AWS. AWS is responsible for patching, antivirus, and management of the underlying guest OS for Amazon RDS. Amazon RDS greatly simplifies the process of setting a secondary slave with replication for failover and setting up read replicas to offload queries.

Remember that you cannot access the underlying OS for Amazon RDS DB instances.   You cannot use Remote Desktop Protocol (RDP) or SSH to connect to the underlying OS. If you need to access the OS, install custom software or agents, or want to use a database engine not supported by Amazon RDS, consider running your database on Amazon EC2 instead.

Know that you can increase availability using Amazon RDS Multi-AZ deployment.   Add fault tolerance to your Amazon RDS database using Multi-AZ deployment. You can quickly set up a secondary DB Instance in another Availability Zone with Multi-AZ for rapid failover.

Understand the importance of RPO and RTO.   Each application should set RPO and RTO targets to define the amount of acceptable data loss and also the amount of time required to recover from an incident. Amazon RDS can be used to meet a wide range of RPO and RTO requirements.

Understand that Amazon RDS handles Multi-AZ failover for you.   If your primary Amazon RDS Instance becomes unavailable, AWS fails over to your secondary instance in another Availability Zone automatically. This failover is done by pointing your existing database endpoint to a new IP address. You do not have to change the connection string manually; AWS handles the DNS change automatically.

Remember that Amazon RDS read replicas are used for scaling out and increased performance.   This replication feature makes it easy to scale out your read-intensive databases. Read replicas are currently supported in Amazon RDS for MySQL, PostgreSQL, and Amazon Aurora. You can create one or more replicas of a database within a single AWS Region or across multiple AWS Regions. Amazon RDS uses native replication to propagate changes made to a source DB Instance to any associated read replicas. Amazon RDS also supports cross-region read replicas to replicate changes asynchronously to another geography or AWS Region.

Know what a NoSQL database is.   NoSQL databases are non-relational databases, meaning that you do not have to have an existing table created in which to store your data. NoSQL databases come in the following formats:

- Document databases
- Graph stores
- Key/value stores
- Wide-column stores

Remember that Amazon DynamoDB is AWS NoSQL service.   You should remember that for NoSQL databases, AWS provides a fully managed service called Amazon DynamoDB. Amazon DynamoDB is an extremely fast NoSQL database with predictable performance and high scalability. You can use Amazon DynamoDB to create a table that can store and retrieve any amount of data and serve any level of request traffic. Amazon DynamoDB automatically spreads the data and traffic for the table over a sufficient number of partitions to handle the request capacity specified by the customer and the amount of data stored, while maintaining consistent and fast performance.

Know what a data warehouse is.   A data warehouse is a central repository for data that can come from one or more sources. This data repository would be used for query and analysis using OLAP. An organization's management typically uses a data warehouse to compile reports on specific data. Data warehouses are usually queried with highly complex queries.

Remember that Amazon Redshift is AWS data warehouse service.   You should remember that Amazon Redshift is Amazon's data warehouse service. Amazon Redshift organizes the data by column instead of storing data as a series of rows. Because only the columns involved in the queries are processed and columnar data is stored sequentially on the storage media, column-based systems require far fewer I/Os, which greatly improves query performance. Another advantage of columnar data storage is the increased compression, which can further reduce overall I/O.

Exercises

In order to pass the exam, you should practice deploying databases and creating tables using Amazon RDS, Amazon DynamoDB, and Amazon Redshift. Remember to delete any resources you provision to minimize any charges.

EXERCISE 7.1

Create a MySQL Amazon RDS Instance

1. Log in to the AWS Management Console, and navigate to the Amazon RDS Console.

2. Launch a new Amazon RDS DB Instance, and select MySQL Community Edition instance as the database engine.

3. Configure the DB Instance to use Multi-AZ and General Purpose (SSD) storage.

   Warning: This is not eligible for AWS Free Tier; you will incur a small charge by provisioning this instance.

4. Set the DB Instance identifier and database name to **MySQL123**, and configure the master username and password.

5. Validate the configuration settings, and launch the DB Instance.

6. Return to the list of the Amazon RDS instances. You will see the status of your Amazon RDS database as Creating. It may take up to 20 minutes to create your new Amazon RDS instance.

You have provisioned your first Amazon RDS instance using Multi-AZ.

EXERCISE 7.2

Simulate a Failover from One AZ to Another

In this exercise, you will use Multi-AZ failover to simulate a failover from one Availability Zone to another.

1. In the Amazon RDS Console, view the list of DB Instances.

2. Find your DB Instance called MySQL123, and check its status. When its status is Available, proceed to the next step.

3. Select the instance, and issue a Reboot command from the actions menu.

4. Confirm the reboot.

You have now simulated a failover from one Availability Zone to another using Multi-AZ failover. The failover should take approximately two or three minutes.

EXERCISE 7.3

Create a Read Replica

In this exercise, you will create a read replica of your existing MySQL123 DB server.

1. In the Amazon RDS Console, view the list of DB Instances.

2. Find your DB Instance called MySQL123, and check its status. When its status is Available, proceed to the next step.

3. Select the instance, and issue a Create Read Replica command from the list of actions.

4. Configure the name of the read replica and any other settings. Create the replica.

5. Wait for the replica to be created, which can typically take several minutes. When it is complete, delete both the MySQL123 and MySQLReadReplica databases by clicking the checkboxes next to them, clicking the Instance Actions drop-down box, and then clicking Delete.

In the preceding exercises, you created a new Amazon RDS MySQL instance with Multi-AZ enabled. You then simulated a failover from one Availability Zone to another by rebooting the primary instance. After that, you scaled your Amazon RDS instance out by creating a read replica of the primary database. Delete the DB Instance.

EXERCISE 7.4

Read and Write from a DynamoDB Table

In this exercise, you will create an Amazon DynamoDB table and then read and write to it using the AWS Management Console.

1. Log in to the AWS Management Console, and view the Amazon DynamoDB console.

2. Create a new table named **UserProfile** with a partition key of userID of type String.

3. After the table has been created, view the list of items in the table.

4. Using the Amazon DynamoDB console, create and save a new item in the table. Set the userID to U01, and append another String attribute called **name** with a value of Joe.

5. Perform a scan on the table to retrieve the new item.

You have now created a simple Amazon DynamoDB table, put a new item, and retrieved it using Scan. Delete the DynamoDB table.

EXERCISE 7.5

Launch a Redshift Cluster

In this exercise, you will create a data warehouse using Amazon Redshift and then read and write to it using the AWS Management Console.

1. Log in to the AWS Management Console, and view the Amazon Redshift Console.

2. Create a new cluster, configuring the database name, username, and password.

3. Configure the cluster to be single node using one SSD-backed storage node.

4. Launch the cluster into an Amazon VPC using the appropriate security group.

5. Install and configure SQL Workbench on your local computer, and connect to the new cluster.

6. Create a new table and load data using the COPY command.

You have now created an Amazon Redshift cluster and connected to it using a standard SQL client. Delete the cluster when you have completed the exercise.

Review Questions

1. Which AWS database service is best suited for traditional Online Transaction Processing (OLTP)?

   A. Amazon Redshift

   B. Amazon Relational Database Service (Amazon RDS)

   C. Amazon Glacier

   D. Elastic Database

2. Which AWS database service is best suited for non-relational databases?

   A. Amazon Redshift

   B. Amazon Relational Database Service (Amazon RDS)

   C. Amazon Glacier

   D. Amazon DynamoDB

3. You are a solutions architect working for a media company that hosts its website on AWS. Currently, there is a single Amazon Elastic Compute Cloud (Amazon EC2) Instance on AWS with MySQL installed locally to that Amazon EC2 Instance. You have been asked to make the company's production environment more resilient and to increase performance. You suggest that the company split out the MySQL database onto an Amazon RDS Instance with Multi-AZ enabled. This addresses the company's increased resiliency requirements. Now you need to suggest how you can increase performance. Ninety-nine percent of the company's end users are magazine subscribers who will be reading additional articles on the website, so only one percent of end users will need to write data to the site. What should you suggest to increase performance?

   A. Alter the connection string so that if a user is going to write data, it is written to the secondary copy of the Multi-AZ database.

   B. Alter the connection string so that if a user is going to write data, it is written to the primary copy of the Multi-AZ database.

   C. Recommend that the company use read replicas, and distribute the traffic across multiple read replicas.

   D. Migrate the MySQL database to Amazon Redshift to take advantage of columnar storage and maximize performance.

4. Which AWS Cloud service is best suited for Online Analytics Processing (OLAP)?

   A. Amazon Redshift

   B. Amazon Relational Database Service (Amazon RDS)

   C. Amazon Glacier

   D. Amazon DynamoDB

5. You have been using Amazon Relational Database Service (Amazon RDS) for the last year to run an important application with automated backups enabled. One of your team members is performing routine maintenance and accidentally drops an important table, causing an outage. How can you recover the missing data while minimizing the duration of the outage?

A. Perform an undo operation and recover the table.

B. Restore the database from a recent automated DB snapshot.

C. Restore only the dropped table from the DB snapshot.

D. The data cannot be recovered.

6. Which Amazon Relational Database Service (Amazon RDS) database engines support Multi-AZ?

A. All of them

B. Microsoft SQL Server, MySQL, and Oracle

C. Oracle, Amazon Aurora, and PostgreSQL

D. MySQL

7. Which Amazon Relational Database Service (Amazon RDS) database engines support read replicas?

A. Microsoft SQL Server and Oracle

B. MySQL, MariaDB, PostgreSQL, and Aurora

C. Aurora, Microsoft SQL Server, and Oracle

D. MySQL and PostgreSQL

8. Your team is building an order processing system that will span multiple Availability Zones. During testing, the team wanted to test how the application will react to a database failover. How can you enable this type of test?

A. Force a Multi-AZ failover from one Availability Zone to another by rebooting the primary instance using the Amazon RDS console.

B. Terminate the DB instance, and create a new one. Update the connection string.

C. Create a support case asking for a failover.

D. It is not possible to test a failover.

9. You are a system administrator whose company has moved its production database to AWS. Your company monitors its estate using Amazon CloudWatch, which sends alarms using Amazon Simple Notification Service (Amazon SNS) to your mobile phone. One night, you get an alert that your primary Amazon Relational Database Service (Amazon RDS) Instance has gone down. You have Multi-AZ enabled on this instance. What should you do to ensure the failover happens quickly?

A. Update your Domain Name System (DNS) to point to the secondary instance's new IP address, forcing your application to fail over to the secondary instance.

B. Connect to your server using Secure Shell (SSH) and update your connection strings so that your application can communicate to the secondary instance instead of the failed primary instance.

C. Take a snapshot of the secondary instance and create a new instance using this snapshot, then update your connection string to point to the new instance.

D. No action is necessary. Your connection string points to the database endpoint, and AWS automatically updates this endpoint to point to your secondary instance.

10. You are working for a small organization without a dedicated database administrator on staff. You need to install Microsoft SQL Server Enterprise edition quickly to support an accounting back office application on Amazon Relational Database Service (Amazon RDS). What should you do?

A. Launch an Amazon RDS DB Instance, and select Microsoft SQL Server Enterprise Edition under the Bring Your Own License (BYOL) model.

B. Provision SQL Server Enterprise Edition using the License Included option from the Amazon RDS Console.

C. SQL Server Enterprise edition is only available via the Command Line Interface (CLI). Install the command-line tools on your laptop, and then provision your new Amazon RDS Instance using the CLI.

D. You cannot use SQL Server Enterprise edition on Amazon RDS. You should install this on to a dedicated Amazon Elastic Compute Cloud (Amazon EC2) Instance.

11. You are building the database tier for an enterprise application that gets occasional activity throughout the day. Which storage type should you select as your default option?

A. Magnetic storage

B. General Purpose Solid State Drive (SSD)

C. Provisioned IOPS (SSD)

D. Storage Area Network (SAN)-attached

12. You are designing an e-commerce web application that will scale to potentially hundreds of thousands of concurrent users. Which database technology is best suited to hold the session state for large numbers of concurrent users?

A. Relational database using Amazon Relational Database Service (Amazon RDS)

B. NoSQL database table using Amazon DynamoDB

C. Data warehouse using Amazon Redshift

D. Amazon Simple Storage Service (Amazon S3)

13. Which of the following techniques can you use to help you meet Recovery Point Objective (RPO) and Recovery Time Objective (RTO) requirements? (Choose 3 answers)

A. DB snapshots

B. DB option groups

C. Read replica

D. Multi-AZ deployment

14. When using Amazon Relational Database Service (Amazon RDS) Multi-AZ, how can you offload read requests from the primary? (Choose 2 answers)

    A. Configure the connection string of the clients to connect to the secondary node and perform reads while the primary is used for writes.

    B. Amazon RDS automatically sends writes to the primary and sends reads to the secondary.

    C. Add a read replica DB instance, and configure the client's application logic to use a read-replica.

    D. Create a caching environment using ElastiCache to cache frequently used data. Update the application logic to read/write from the cache.

15. You are building a large order processing system and are responsible for securing the database. Which actions will you take to protect the data? (Choose 3 answers)

    A. Adjust AWS Identity and Access Management (IAM) permissions for administrators.

    B. Configure security groups and network Access Control Lists (ACLs) to limit network access.

    C. Configure database users, and grant permissions to database objects.

    D. Install anti-virus software on the Amazon RDS DB Instance.

16. Your team manages a popular website running Amazon Relational Database Service (Amazon RDS) MySQL back end. The Marketing department has just informed you about an upcoming television commercial that will drive thousands of new visitors to the website. How can you prepare your database to handle the load? (Choose 3 answers)

    A. Vertically scale the DB Instance by selecting a more powerful instance class.

    B. Create read replicas to offload read requests and update your application.

    C. Upgrade the storage from Magnetic volumes to General Purpose Solid State Drive (SSD) volumes.

    D. Upgrade to Amazon Redshift for faster columnar storage.

17. You are building a photo management application that maintains metadata on millions of images in an Amazon DynamoDB table. When a photo is retrieved, you want to display the metadata next to the image. Which Amazon DynamoDB operation will you use to retrieve the metadata attributes from the table?

    A. Scan operation

    B. Search operation

    C. Query operation

    D. Find operation

18. You are creating an Amazon DynamoDB table that will contain messages for a social chat application. This table will have the following attributes: Username (String), Timestamp (Number), Message (String). Which attribute should you use as the partition key? The sort key?

   A. Username, Timestamp

   B. Username, Message

   C. Timestamp, Message

   D. Message, Timestamp

19. Which of the following statements about Amazon DynamoDB tables are true? (Choose 2 answers)

   A. Global secondary indexes can only be created when the table is being created.

   B. Local secondary indexes can only be created when the table is being created.

   C. You can only have one global secondary index.

   D. You can only have one local secondary index.

20. Which of the following workloads are a good fit for running on Amazon Redshift? (Choose 2 answers)

   A. Transactional database supporting a busy e-commerce order processing website

   B. Reporting database supporting back-office analytics

   C. Data warehouse used to aggregate multiple disparate data sources

   D. Manage session state and user profile data for thousands of concurrent users

SQS, SWF, and SNS

THE AWS CERTIFIED SOLUTIONS ARCHITECT ASSOCIATE EXAM OBJECTIVES COVERED IN THIS CHAPTER MAY INCLUDE, BUT ARE NOT LIMITED TO, THE FOLLOWING:

1   Domain 1.0: Designing highly available, cost-efficient, fault-tolerant, scalable systems

✓ **1.1   Identify and recognize cloud architecture considerations, such as fundamental components and effective designs.**

Content may include the following:

- How to design cloud services

- Planning and design

- Monitoring and logging

- Familiarity with:

  - Best practices for AWS architecture

  - Architectural trade-off decisions (e.g., high availability vs. cost, Amazon Relational Database Service [Amazon RDS] vs. installing your own database on Amazon Elastic Compute Cloud [Amazon EC2])

  - Elasticity and scalability (e.g., Auto Scaling, Amazon Simple Queue Service [Amazon SQS], Elastic Load Balancing, Amazon CloudFront)

Domain 2.0: Implementation/Deployment

✓ **2.1   Identify the appropriate techniques and methods using Amazon EC2, Amazon Simple Storage Service (Amazon S3), AWS Elastic Beanstalk, AWS CloudFormation, AWS OpsWorks, Amazon VPC, and AWS Identity and Access Management (IAM) to code and implement a cloud solution.**

Domain 4.0: Troubleshooting

Content may include the following:

- General troubleshooting information and questions

There are a number of services under the Application and Mobile Services section of the AWS Management Console. At the time of writing this chapter, application services include Amazon Simple Queue Service (Amazon SQS), Amazon Simple Workflow Service (Amazon SWF), Amazon AppStream, Amazon Elastic Transcoder, Amazon Simple Email Service (Amazon SES), Amazon CloudSearch, and Amazon API Gateway. Mobile services include Amazon Cognito, Amazon Simple Notification Service (Amazon SNS), AWS Device Farm, and Amazon Mobile Analytics. This chapter focuses on the core services you are required to be familiar with to pass the exam: Amazon SQS, Amazon SWF, and Amazon SNS.

Amazon Simple Queue Service (Amazon SQS)

Amazon SQS is a fast, reliable, scalable, and fully managed message queuing service. Amazon SQS makes it simple and cost effective to decouple the components of a cloud application. You can use Amazon SQS to transmit any volume of data, at any level of throughput, without losing messages or requiring other services to be continuously available.

With Amazon SQS, you can offload the administrative burden of operating and scaling a highly available messaging cluster while paying a low price for only what you use. Using Amazon SQS, you can store application messages on reliable and scalable infrastructure, enabling you to move data between distributed components to perform different tasks as needed.

An *Amazon SQS queue* is basically a buffer between the application components that receive data and those components that process the data in your system. If your processing servers cannot process the work fast enough (perhaps due to a spike in traffic), the work is queued so that the processing servers can get to it when they are ready. This means that work is not lost due to insufficient resources.

Amazon SQS ensures delivery of each message at least once and supports multiple readers and writers interacting with the same queue. A single queue can be used simultaneously by many distributed application components, with no need for those components to coordinate with one another to share the queue. Although most of the time each message will be delivered to your application exactly once, you should design your system to be *idempotent* (that is, it must not be adversely affected if it processes the same message more than once).

Amazon SQS is engineered to be highly available and to deliver messages reliably and efficiently; however, the service does not guarantee First In, First Out (FIFO) delivery of messages. For many distributed applications, each message can stand on its own and, if all messages are delivered, the order is not important. If your system requires that order be preserved, you can place sequencing information in each message so that you can reorder the messages when they are retrieved from the queue.

Message Lifecycle

The diagram and process shown in Figure 8.1 describes the lifecycle of an Amazon SQS message, called Message A, from creation to deletion. Assume that a queue already exists.

FIGURE 8.1 Message lifecycle

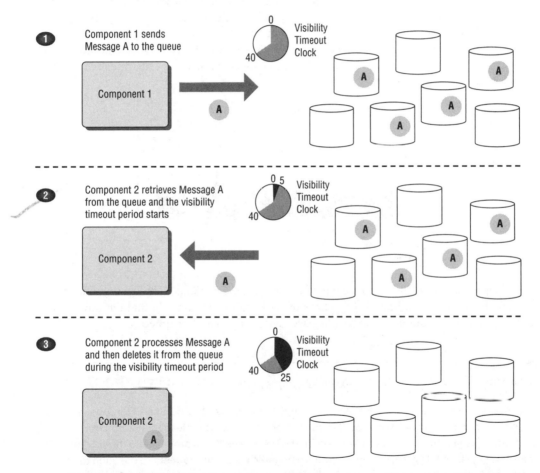

1. Component 1 sends Message A to a queue, and the message is redundantly distributed across the Amazon SQS servers.
2. When Component 2 is ready to process a message, it retrieves messages from the queue, and Message A is returned. While Message A is being processed, it remains in the queue and is not returned to subsequently receive requests for the duration of the visibility timeout.

3. Component 2 deletes Message A from the queue to prevent the message from being received and processed again after the visibility timeout expires.

Delay Queues and Visibility Timeouts

Delay queues allow you to postpone the delivery of new messages in a queue for a specific number of seconds. If you create a delay queue, any message that you send to that queue will be invisible to consumers for the duration of the delay period. To create a delay queue, use CreateQueue and set the DelaySeconds attribute to any value between 0 and 900 (15 minutes). You can also turn an existing queue into a delay queue by using SetQueueAttributes to set the queue's DelaySeconds attribute. The default value for DelaySeconds is 0.

Delay queues are similar to visibility timeouts in that both features make messages unavailable to consumers for a specific period of time. The difference is that a delay queue hides a message when it is first added to the queue, whereas a visibility timeout hides a message only after that message is retrieved from the queue. Figure 8.2 illustrates the functioning of a visibility timeout.

FIGURE 8.2   Diagram of visibility timeout

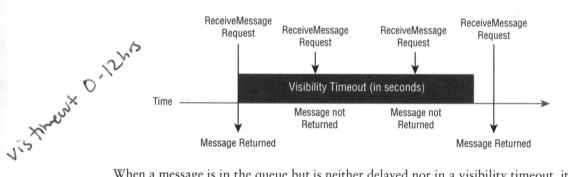

When a message is in the queue but is neither delayed nor in a visibility timeout, it is considered to be "in flight." You can have up to 120,000 messages in flight at any given time. Amazon SQS supports up to 12 hours' maximum visibility timeout.

Separate Throughput from Latency

Like many other AWS Cloud services, Amazon SQS is accessed through HTTP request-response, and a typical Amazon SQS request-response takes a bit less than 20ms from Amazon Elastic Compute Cloud (Amazon EC2). This means that from a single thread, you can, on average, issue 50+ Application Programming Interface (API) requests per second (a bit fewer for batch API requests, but those do more work). The throughput scales horizontally, so the more threads and hosts you add, the higher the throughput. Using this scaling model, some AWS customers have queues that process thousands of messages every second.

Queue Operations, Unique IDs, and Metadata

The defined operations for Amazon SQS queues are CreateQueue, ListQueues, DeleteQueue, SendMessage, SendMessageBatch, ReceiveMessage, DeleteMessage, DeleteMessageBatch, PurgeQueue, ChangeMessageVisibility, ChangeMessageVisibilityBatch, SetQueueAttributes, GetQueueAttributes, GetQueueUrl, ListDeadLetterSourceQueues, AddPermission, and RemovePermission. Only the AWS account owner or an AWS identity that has been granted the proper permissions can perform operations.

Your messages are identified via a globally unique ID that Amazon SQS returns when the message is delivered to the queue. The ID isn't required in order to perform any further actions on the message, but it's useful for tracking whether a particular message in the queue has been received. When you receive a message from the queue, the response includes a receipt handle, which you must provide when deleting the message.

Queue and Message Identifiers

Amazon SQS uses three identifiers that you need to be familiar with: queue URLs, message IDs, and receipt handles.

When creating a new queue, you must provide a queue name that is unique within the scope of all of your queues. Amazon SQS assigns each queue an identifier called a *queue URL*, which includes the queue name and other components that Amazon SQS determines. Whenever you want to perform an action on a queue, you must provide its queue URL.

Amazon SQS assigns each message a unique ID that it returns to you in the SendMessage response. This identifier is useful for identifying messages, but note that to delete a message, you need the message's receipt handle instead of the message ID. The maximum length of a message ID is 100 characters.

Each time you receive a message from a queue, you receive a receipt handle for that message. The handle is associated with the act of receiving the message, not with the message itself. As stated previously, to delete the message or to change the message visibility, you must provide the receipt handle and not the message ID. This means you must always receive a message before you can delete it (that is, you can't put a message into the queue and then recall it). The maximum length of a receipt handle is 1,024 characters.

Message Attributes

Amazon SQS provides support for *message attributes*. Message attributes allow you to provide structured *metadata* items (such as timestamps, geospatial data, signatures, and identifiers) about the message. Message attributes are optional and separate from, but sent along with, the message body. The receiver of the message can use this information to help decide how to handle the message without having to process the message body first. Each message can have up to 10 attributes. To specify message attributes, you can use the AWS Management Console, AWS Software Development Kits (SDKs), or a query API.

Long Polling

When your application queries the Amazon SQS queue for messages, it calls the function `ReceiveMessage`. `ReceiveMessage` will check for the existence of a message in the queue and return immediately, either with or without a message. If your code makes periodic calls to the queue, this pattern is sufficient. If your SQS client is just a loop that repeatedly checks for new messages, however, then this pattern becomes problematic, as the constant calls to `ReceiveMessage` burn CPU cycles and tie up a thread.

In this situation, you will want to use *long polling*. With long polling, you send a `WaitTimeSeconds` argument to `ReceiveMessage` of up to 20 seconds. If there is no message in the queue, then the call will wait up to `WaitTimeSeconds` for a message to appear before returning. If a message appears before the time expires, the call will return the message right away. Long polling drastically reduces the amount of load on your client.

Dead Letter Queues

Amazon SQS provides support for *dead letter queues*. A dead letter queue is a queue that other (source) queues can target to send messages that for some reason could not be successfully processed. A primary benefit of using a dead letter queue is the ability to sideline and isolate the unsuccessfully processed messages. You can then analyze any messages sent to the dead letter queue to try to determine the cause of failure.

Messages can be sent to and received from a dead letter queue, just like any other Amazon SQS queue. You can create a dead letter queue from the Amazon SQS API and the Amazon SQS console.

Access Control

While IAM can be used to control the interactions of different AWS identities with queues, there are often times when you will want to expose queues to other accounts. These situations may include:

- You want to grant another AWS account a particular type of access to your queue (for example, `SendMessage`).

- You want to grant another AWS account access to your queue for a specific period of time.

- You want to grant another AWS account access to your queue only if the requests come from your Amazon EC2 instances.

- You want to deny another AWS account access to your queue.

While close coordination between accounts may allow these types of actions through the use of IAM roles, that level of coordination is frequently unfeasible.

Amazon SQS Access Control allows you to assign policies to queues that grant specific interactions to other accounts without that account having to assume IAM roles from your account. These policies are written in the same JSON language as IAM. For example, the following sample policy gives the developer with AWS account number 111122223333 the SendMessage permission for the queue named 444455556666/queue1 in the US East (N. Virginia) region.

```
{
"Version": "2012&#x02013;10-17",
"Id": "Queue1_Policy_UUID",
"Statement": [
{
"Sid":"Queue1_SendMessage",
"Effect": "Allow",
"Principal": {
"AWS": "111122223333"
},
"Action": "sqs:SendMessage",
"Resource": "arn:aws:sqs:us-east-1:444455556666:queue1"
}
]
}
```

Tradeoff Message Durability and Latency

Amazon SQS does not return success to a SendMessage API call until the message is durably stored in Amazon SQS. This makes the programming model very simple with no doubt about the safety of messages, unlike the situation with an asynchronous messaging model. If you don't need a durable messaging system, however, you can build an asynchronous, client-side batching on top of Amazon SQS libraries that delays enqueue of messages to Amazon SQS and transmits a set of messages in a batch. Please be aware that with a client-side batching approach, you could potentially lose messages when your client process or client host dies for any reason.

Amazon Simple Workflow Service (Amazon SWF)

Amazon SWF makes it easy to build applications that coordinate work across distributed components. In Amazon SWF, a task represents a logical unit of work that is performed by a component of your application. Coordinating tasks across the application involves managing inter-task dependencies, scheduling, and concurrency in accordance with the logical flow of the application. Amazon SWF gives you full control over implementing and coordinating tasks without worrying about underlying complexities such as tracking their progress and maintaining their state.

When using Amazon SWF, you implement workers to perform *tasks*. These workers can run either on cloud infrastructure, such as Amazon EC2, or on your own premises. You can create long-running tasks that might fail, time out, or require restarts, or tasks that can complete with varying throughput and latency. Amazon SWF stores tasks, assigns them to workers when they are ready, monitors their progress, and maintains their state, including details on their completion. To coordinate tasks, you write a program that gets the latest state of each task from Amazon SWF and uses it to initiate subsequent tasks. Amazon SWF maintains an application's execution state durably so that the application is resilient to failures in individual components. With Amazon SWF, you can implement, deploy, scale, and modify these application components independently.

Workflows

Using Amazon SWF, you can implement distributed, asynchronous applications as *workflows*. Workflows coordinate and manage the execution of activities that can be run asynchronously across multiple computing devices and that can feature both sequential and parallel processing.

When designing a workflow, analyze your application to identify its component tasks, which are represented in Amazon SWF as activities. The workflow's coordination logic determines the order in which activities are executed.

Workflow Domains

Domains provide a way of scoping Amazon SWF resources within your AWS account. You must specify a domain for all the components of a workflow, such as the workflow type and activity types. It is possible to have more than one workflow in a domain; however, workflows in different domains cannot interact with one another.

Workflow History

The workflow history is a detailed, complete, and consistent record of every event that occurred since the workflow execution started. An event represents a discrete change in your workflow execution's state, such as scheduled and completed activities, task timeouts, and signals.

Actors

Amazon SWF consists of a number of different types of programmatic features known as *actors*. Actors can be workflow starters, deciders, or activity workers. These actors communicate with Amazon SWF through its API. You can develop actors in any programming language.

A workflow starter is any application that can initiate workflow executions. For example, one workflow starter could be an e-commerce website where a customer places an order. Another workflow starter could be a mobile application where a customer orders takeout food or requests a taxi.

Activities within a workflow can run sequentially, in parallel, synchronously, or asynchronously. The logic that coordinates the tasks in a workflow is called the *decider*. The decider schedules the activity tasks and provides input data to the activity workers. The decider also processes events that arrive while the workflow is in progress and closes the workflow when the objective has been completed.

An *activity worker* is a single computer process (or thread) that performs the activity tasks in your workflow. Different types of activity workers process tasks of different activity types, and multiple activity workers can process the same type of task. When an activity worker is ready to process a new activity task, it polls Amazon SWF for tasks that are appropriate for that activity worker. After receiving a task, the activity worker processes the task to completion and then returns the status and result to Amazon SWF. The activity worker then polls for a new task.

Tasks

Amazon SWF provides activity workers and deciders with work assignments, given as one of three types of tasks: activity tasks, AWS Lambda tasks, and decision tasks.

An activity task tells an activity worker to perform its function, such as to check inventory or charge a credit card. The activity task contains all the information that the activity worker needs to perform its function.

An AWS Lambda task is similar to an activity task, but executes an AWS Lambda function instead of a traditional Amazon SWF activity. For more information about how to define an AWS Lambda task, see the AWS documentation on AWS Lambda tasks.

A decision task tells a decider that the state of the workflow execution has changed so that the decider can determine the next activity that needs to be performed. The decision task contains the current workflow history.

Amazon SWF schedules a decision task when the workflow starts and whenever the state of the workflow changes, such as when an activity task completes. Each decision task contains a paginated view of the entire workflow execution history. The decider analyzes the workflow execution history and responds back to Amazon SWF with a set of decisions that specify what should occur next in the workflow execution. Essentially, every decision task gives the decider an opportunity to assess the workflow and provide direction back to Amazon SWF.

Task Lists

Task lists provide a way of organizing the various tasks associated with a workflow. You could think of task lists as similar to dynamic queues. When a task is scheduled in Amazon SWF, you can specify a queue (task list) to put it in. Similarly, when you poll Amazon SWF for a task, you determine which queue (task list) to get the task from.

Task lists provide a flexible mechanism to route tasks to workers as your use case necessitates. Task lists are dynamic in that you don't need to register a task list or explicitly create it through an action—simply scheduling a task creates the task list if it doesn't already exist.

Long Polling

Deciders and activity workers communicate with Amazon SWF using long polling. The decider or activity worker periodically initiates communication with Amazon SWF, notifying Amazon SWF of its availability to accept a task, and then specifies a task list to get tasks from. Long polling works well for high-volume task processing. Deciders and activity workers can manage their own capacity.

Object Identifiers

Amazon SWF objects are uniquely identified by workflow type, activity type, decision and activity tasks, and workflow execution:

- A registered workflow type is identified by its domain, name, and version. Workflow types are specified in the call to `RegisterWorkflowType`.

- A registered activity type is identified by its domain, name, and version. Activity types are specified in the call to `RegisterActivityType`.

- Each decision task and activity task is identified by a unique task token. The task token is generated by Amazon SWF and is returned with other information about the task in the response from `PollForDecisionTask` or `PollForActivityTask`. Although the token is most commonly used by the process that received the task, that process could pass the token to another process, which could then report the completion or failure of the task.

- A single execution of a workflow is identified by the domain, workflow ID, and run ID. The first two are parameters that are passed to `StartWorkflowExecution`. The run ID is returned by `StartWorkflowExecution`.

Workflow Execution Closure

After you start a workflow execution, it is open. An open workflow execution can be closed as completed, canceled, failed, or timed out. It can also be continued as a new execution, or it can be terminated. The decider, the person administering the workflow, or Amazon SWF can close a workflow execution.

Lifecycle of a Workflow Execution

From the start of a workflow execution to its completion, Amazon SWF interacts with actors by assigning them appropriate tasks: either activity tasks or decision tasks.

Figure 8.3 shows the lifecycle of an order-processing workflow execution from the perspective of components that act on it.

FIGURE 8.3   Amazon SWF workflow illustration

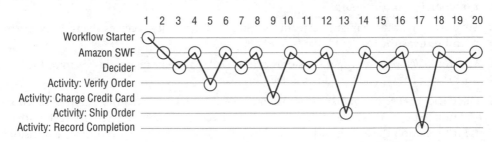

The following 20 steps describe the workflow detailed in Figure 8.3:

1. A workflow starter calls an Amazon SWF action to start the workflow execution for an order, providing order information.

2. Amazon SWF receives the start workflow execution request and then schedules the first decision task.

3. The decider receives the task from Amazon SWF, reviews the history, and applies the coordination logic to determine that no previous activities occurred. It then makes a decision to schedule the Verify Order activity with the information the activity worker needs to process the task and returns the decision to Amazon SWF.

4. Amazon SWF receives the decision, schedules the Verify Order activity task, and waits for the activity task to complete or time out.

5. An activity worker that can perform the Verify Order activity receives the task, performs it, and returns the results to Amazon SWF.

6. Amazon SWF receives the results of the Verify Order activity, adds them to the workflow history, and schedules a decision task.

7. The decider receives the task from Amazon SWF, reviews the history, applies the coordination logic, makes a decision to schedule a Charge Credit Card activity task with information the activity worker needs to process the task, and returns the decision to Amazon SWF.

8. Amazon SWF receives the decision, schedules the Charge Credit Card activity task, and waits for it to complete or time out.

9. An activity worker activity receives the Charge Credit Card task, performs it, and returns the results to Amazon SWF.

10. Amazon SWF receives the results of the Charge Credit Card activity task, adds them to the workflow history, and schedules a decision task.

11. The decider receives the task from Amazon SWF, reviews the history, applies the coordination logic, makes a decision to schedule a Ship Order activity task with the information the activity worker needs to perform the task, and returns the decision to Amazon SWF.

12. Amazon SWF receives the decision, schedules a Ship Order activity task, and waits for it to complete or time out.

13. An activity worker that can perform the Ship Order activity receives the task, performs it, and returns the results to Amazon SWF.

14. Amazon SWF receives the results of the Ship Order activity task, adds them to the workflow history, and schedules a decision task.

15. The decider receives the task from Amazon SWF, reviews the history, applies the coordination logic, makes a decision to schedule a Record Completion activity task with the information the activity worker needs, performs the task, and returns the decision to Amazon SWF.

16. Amazon SWF receives the decision, schedules a Record Completion activity task, and waits for it to complete or time out.

17. An activity worker Record Completion receives the task, performs it, and returns the results to Amazon SWF.

18. Amazon SWF receives the results of the Record Completion activity task, adds them to the workflow history, and schedules a decision task.

19. The decider receives the task from Amazon SWF, reviews the history, applies the coordination logic, makes a decision to close the workflow execution, and returns the decision along with any results to Amazon SWF.

20. Amazon SWF closes the workflow execution and archives the history for future reference.

Amazon Simple Notification Service (Amazon SNS)

Amazon SNS is a web service for mobile and enterprise messaging that enables you to set up, operate, and send notifications. It is designed to make web-scale computing easier for developers. Amazon SNS follows the publish-subscribe (pub-sub) messaging paradigm, with notifications being delivered to clients using a push mechanism that eliminates the need to check periodically (or poll) for new information and updates. For example, you can send notifications to Apple, Android, Fire OS, and Windows devices. In China, you can send messages to Android devices with Baidu Cloud Push. You can use Amazon SNS to send Short Message Service (SMS) messages to mobile device users in the United States or to email recipients worldwide.

Amazon SNS consists of two types of clients: publishers and subscribers (sometimes known as producers and consumers). Publishers communicate to subscribers asynchronously by sending a message to a topic. A topic is simply a logical access point/communication channel that contains a list of subscribers and the methods used to communicate to them. When you send a message to a topic, it is automatically forwarded to each subscriber of that topic using the communication method configured for that subscriber.

Figure 8.4 shows this process at a high level. A publisher issues a message on a topic. The message is then delivered to the subscribers of that topic using different methods, such as Amazon SQS, HTTP, HTTPS, email, SMS, and AWS Lambda.

FIGURE 8.4   Diagram of topic delivery

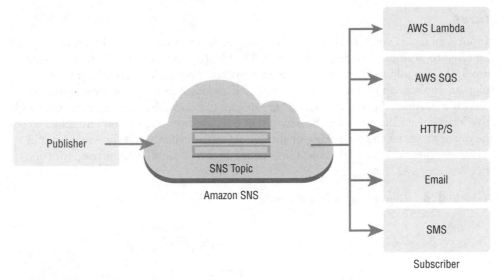

When using Amazon SNS, you (as the owner) create a topic and control access to it by defining policies that determine which publishers and subscribers can communicate with the topic and via which technologies. Publishers send messages to topics that they created or that they have permission to publish to. Instead of including a specific destination address in each message, a publisher sends a message to the topic, and Amazon SNS delivers the message to each subscriber for that topic. Each topic has a unique name that identifies the Amazon SNS endpoint where publishers post messages and subscribers register for notifications. Subscribers receive all messages published to the topics to which they subscribe, and all subscribers to a topic receive the same messages.

Common Amazon SNS Scenarios

Amazon SNS can support a wide variety of needs, including monitoring applications, workflow systems, time-sensitive information updates, mobile applications, and any other application that generates or consumes notifications. For example, you can use Amazon SNS to relay events in workflow systems among distributed computer applications, move data between data stores, or update records in business systems. Event updates and notifications concerning validation, approval, inventory changes, and shipment status are immediately delivered to relevant system components and end users. Another example use for Amazon SNS is to relay time-critical events to mobile applications and devices. Because

Amazon SNS is both highly reliable and scalable, it provides significant advantages to developers who build applications that rely on real-time events.

To help illustrate, the following sections describe some common Amazon SNS scenarios, including fanout scenarios, application and system alerts, push email and text messaging, and mobile push notifications.

Fanout

A fanout scenario is when an Amazon SNS message is sent to a topic and then replicated and pushed to multiple Amazon SQS queues, HTTP endpoints, or email addresses (see Figure 8.5). This allows for parallel asynchronous processing. For example, you can develop an application that sends an Amazon SNS message to a topic whenever an order is placed for a product. Then the Amazon SQS queues that are subscribed to that topic will receive identical notifications for the new order. An Amazon EC2 instance attached to one of the queues handles the processing or fulfillment of the order, while an Amazon EC2 instance attached to a parallel queue sends order data to a data warehouse application/service for analysis.

FIGURE 8.5   Diagram of fanout scenario

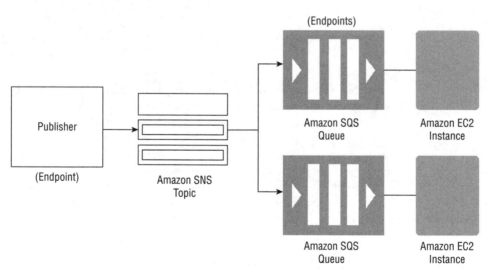

Another way to use fanout is to replicate data sent to your production environment and integrate it with your development environment. Expanding upon the previous example, you can subscribe yet another queue to the same topic for new incoming orders. Then, by attaching this new queue to your development environment, you can continue to improve and test your application using data received from your production environment.

Application and System Alerts

Application and system alerts are SMS and/or email notifications that are triggered by predefined thresholds. For example, because many AWS Cloud services use Amazon SNS, you can receive immediate notification when an event occurs, such as a specific change to your Auto Scaling group in AWS.

Push Email and Text Messaging

Push email and text messaging are two ways to transmit messages to individuals or groups via email and/or SMS. For example, you can use Amazon SNS to push targeted news headlines to subscribers by email or SMS. Upon receiving the email or SMS text, interested readers can then choose to learn more by visiting a website or launching an application.

Mobile Push Notifications

Mobile push notifications enable you to send messages directly to mobile applications. For example, you can use Amazon SNS for sending notifications to an application, indicating that an update is available. The notification message can include a link to download and install the update.

Summary

In this chapter, you learned about the core application and mobile services that you will be tested on in your AWS Certified Solutions Architect – Associate exam.

Amazon SQS is a unique service designed by Amazon to help you decouple your infrastructure. Using Amazon SQS, you can store messages on reliable and scalable infrastructure as they travel between distributed components of your applications that perform different tasks, without losing messages or requiring each component to be continuously available.

Understand Amazon SQS queue operations, unique IDs, and metadata. Be familiar with queue and message identifiers such as queue URLs, message IDs, and receipt handles. Understand related concepts such as delay queues, message attributes, long polling, message timers, dead letter queues, access control, and the overall message lifecycle.

Amazon SWF allows you to create applications that coordinate work across distributed components. Amazon SWF is driven by tasks, which are logical units of work that different components of your application perform. To manage tasks across your application, you need to be aware of inter-task dependencies, scheduling of tasks, and using tasks concurrently. Amazon SWF simplifies the coordination of workflow tasks, giving you full control over their implementation without worrying about underlying complexities such as tracking their progress and maintaining their state.

You must be familiar with the following Amazon SWF components and the lifecycle of a workflow execution:

- Workers, starters, and deciders
- Workflows
- Workflow history
- Actors

- Tasks
- Domains
- Object identifiers
- Task lists
- Workflow execution closure
- Long polling

Amazon SNS is a push notification service that lets you send individual or multiple messages to large numbers of recipients. Amazon SNS consists of two types of clients: publishers and subscribers (sometimes known as producers and consumers). Publishers communicate to subscribers asynchronously by sending a message to a topic. A topic is simply a logical access point/communication channel that contains a list of subscribers and the methods used to communicate to them. When you send a message to a topic, it is automatically forwarded to each subscriber of that topic using the communication method configured for that subscriber.

Amazon SNS can support a wide variety of needs, including monitoring applications, workflow systems, time-sensitive information updates, mobile applications, and any other application that generates or consumes notifications. Understand some common Amazon SNS scenarios, including:

- Fanout
- Application and system alerts
- Push email and text messaging
- Mobile push notifications

Exam Essentials

Know how to use Amazon SQS.   Amazon SQS is a unique service designed by Amazon to help you to decouple your infrastructure. Using Amazon SQS, you can store messages on reliable and scalable infrastructure as they travel between your servers. This allows you to move data between distributed components of your applications that perform different tasks without losing messages or requiring each component always to be available.

Understand Amazon SQS visibility timeouts.   Visibility timeout is a period of time during which Amazon SQS prevents other components from receiving and processing a message because another component is already processing it. By default, the message visibility timeout is set to 30 seconds, and the maximum that it can be is 12 hours.

Know how to use Amazon SQS long polling.   Long polling allows your Amazon SQS client to poll an Amazon SQS queue. If nothing is there, ReceiveMessage waits between 1 and 20 seconds. If a message arrives in that time, it is returned to the caller as soon as possible. If a message does not arrive in that time, you need to execute the ReceiveMessage function again. This helps you avoid polling in tight loops and prevents you from burning through CPU cycles, keeping costs low.

Know how to use Amazon SWF. Amazon SWF allows you to make applications that coordinate work across distributed components. Amazon SWF is driven by tasks, which are logical units of work that part of your application performs. To manage tasks across your application, you need to be aware of inter-task dependencies, scheduling of tasks, and using tasks concurrently. This is where Amazon SWF can help you. It gives you full control over implementing tasks and coordinating them without worrying about underlying complexities such as tracking their progress and maintaining their state.

Know the basics of an Amazon SWF workflow. A workflow is a collection of activities (coordinated by logic) that carry out a specific goal. For example, a workflow receives a customer order and takes whatever actions are necessary to fulfill it. Each workflow runs in an AWS resource called a domain, which controls the scope of the workflow. An AWS account can have multiple domains, each of which can contain multiple workflows, but workflows in different domains cannot interact.

Understand the different Amazon SWF actors. Amazon SWF interacts with a number of different types of programmatic actors. Actors can be activity workers, workflow starters, or deciders.

Understand Amazon SNS basics. Amazon SNS is a push notification service that lets you send individual or multiple messages to large numbers of recipients. Amazon SNS consists of two types of clients: publishers and subscribers (sometimes known as producers and consumers). Publishers communicate to subscribers asynchronously by sending a message to a topic.

Know the different protocols used with Amazon SNS. You can use the following protocols with Amazon SNS: HTTP, HTTPS, SMS, email, email-JSON, Amazon SQS, and AWS Lambda.

Exercises

In this section, you create a topic and subscription in Amazon SNS and then publish a message to your topic.

EXERCISE 8.1

Create an Amazon SNS Topic

In this exercise, you will create an Amazon SNS message.

1. Open a browser, and navigate to the AWS Management Console. Sign in to your AWS account.

2. Navigate to Mobile Services and then Amazon SNS to load the Amazon SNS dashboard.

3. Create a new topic, and use `MyTopic` for both the topic name and the display name.

4. Note that an Amazon Resource Name (ARN) is specified immediately.

Congratulations! You have created your first topic.

EXERCISE 8.2

Create a Subscription to Your Topic

In this exercise, you will create a subscription to the newly created topic using your email address. Then you confirm your email address.

1. In the Amazon SNS dashboard of the AWS Management Console, navigate to Topics.

2. Select the ARN that you just created. Create a Subscription with the protocol of Email, and enter your email address.

3. Create the Subscription.

4. The service sends a confirmation email to your email address. Before this subscription can go live, you need to click on the link in the email that AWS sent you to confirm your email address. Check your email, and confirm your address.

Congratulations! You have now confirmed your email address and created a subscription to a topic.

EXERCISE 8.3

Publish to a Topic

In this exercise, you will publish a message to your newly created topic.

1. In the Amazon SNS dashboard of the AWS Management Console, navigate to Topics.

2. Navigate to the ARN link for your newly created topic.

3. Update the subject with My Test Message, leave the message format to set to Raw, and use a Time to Live (TTL) field to 300.

4. Publish the message.

5. You should receive an email from your topic name with the subject that you speci-fied. If you do not receive this email, check your junk folder.

Congratulations! In this exercise, you created a new topic, added a new subscription, and then published a message to your new topic. Note the different formats in which you can publish messages, including HTTP and AWS Lambda. Delete your newly created topic and subscriptions after you are finished.

EXERCISE 8.4

Create Queue

1. In the AWS Management Console, navigate to Application Services and then to Amazon SQS to load the Amazon SQS dashboard.

2. Create a new queue with **input** as the queue name, 60 seconds for the default visibility, and 5 minutes for the message retention period. Leave the remaining default values for this exercise.

3. Create the queue.

Congratulations! In this exercise, you created a new queue. You will publish to this queue in the following exercise.

EXERCISE 8.5

Subscribe Queue to SNS Topic

1. In the AWS Management Console, navigate to Application Services and then to Amazon SQS to load the Amazon SQS dashboard.

2. Subscribe your queue to your Amazon SNS topic.

3. Now return to the Amazon SNS dashboard (in the AWS Management Console under Mobile Services).

4. Publish to your new topic, and use the defaults.

5. Return to the Amazon SQS dashboard (in the AWS Management Console under Application Services).

6. You will notice there is "1 Message Available" in the input queue. Check the input box to the left of the input queue name.

7. Start polling for messages. You should see the Amazon SNS message in your queue.

8. Click the More Details link to see the details of the message.

9. Review your message, and click Close.

10. Delete your message.

Congratulations! In this exercise, you subscribed your input queue to an Amazon SNS topic and viewed your message in your Amazon SQS queue in addition to receiving the message in subscribed email.

Review Questions

1. Which of the following is not a supported Amazon Simple Notification Service (Amazon SNS) protocol?

    A. HTTPS

    B. AWS Lambda

    C. Email-JSON

    D. Amazon DynamoDB

2. When you create a new Amazon Simple Notification Service (Amazon SNS) topic, which of the following is created automatically?

    A. An Amazon Resource Name (ARN)

    B. A subscriber

    C. An Amazon Simple Queue Service (Amazon SQS) queue to deliver your Amazon SNS topic

    D. A message

3. Which of the following are features of Amazon Simple Notification Service (Amazon SNS)? (Choose 3 answers)

    A. Publishers

    B. Readers

    C. Subscribers

    D. Topic

4. What is the default time for an Amazon Simple Queue Service (Amazon SQS) visibility timeout?

    A. 30 seconds

    B. 60 seconds

    C. 1 hour

    D. 12 hours

5. What is the longest time available for an Amazon Simple Queue Service (Amazon SQS) visibility timeout?

    A. 30 seconds

    B. 60 seconds

    C. 1 hour

    D. 12 hours

6. Which of the following options are valid properties of an Amazon Simple Queue Service (Amazon SQS) message? (Choose 2 answers)

    A. Destination

    B. Message ID

    C. Type

    D. Body

7. You are a solutions architect who is working for a mobile application company that wants to use Amazon Simple Workflow Service (Amazon SWF) for their new takeout ordering application. They will have multiple workflows that will need to interact. What should you advise them to do in structuring the design of their Amazon SWF environment?

    A. Use multiple domains, each containing a single workflow, and design the workflows to interact across the different domains.

    B. Use a single domain containing multiple workflows. In this manner, the workflows will be able to interact.

    C. Use a single domain with a single workflow and collapse all activities to within this single workflow.

    D. Workflows cannot interact with each other; they would be better off using Amazon Simple Queue Service (Amazon SQS) and Amazon Simple Notification Service (Amazon SNS) for their application.

8. In Amazon Simple Workflow Service (Amazon SWF), which of the following are actors? (Choose 3 answers)

    A. Activity workers

    B. Workflow starters

    C. Deciders

    D. Activity tasks

9. You are designing a new application, and you need to ensure that the components of your application are not tightly coupled. You are trying to decide between the different AWS Cloud services to use to achieve this goal. Your requirements are that messages between your application components may not be delivered more than once, tasks must be completed in either a synchronous or asynchronous fashion, and there must be some form of application logic that decides what do when tasks have been completed. What application service should you use?

    A. Amazon Simple Queue Service (Amazon SQS)

    B. Amazon Simple Workflow Service (Amazon SWF)

    C. Amazon Simple Storage Service (Amazon S3)

    D. Amazon Simple Email Service (Amazon SES)

10. How does Amazon Simple Queue Service (Amazon SQS) deliver messages?

    A. Last In, First Out (LIFO)

    B. First In, First Out (FIFO)

    C. Sequentially

    D. Amazon SQS doesn't guarantee delivery of your messages in any particular order.

11. Of the following options, what is an efficient way to fanout a single Amazon Simple Notification Service (Amazon SNS) message to multiple Amazon Simple Queue Service (Amazon SQS) queues?

    A. Create an Amazon SNS topic using Amazon SNS. Then create and subscribe multiple Amazon SQS queues sent to the Amazon SNS topic.

    B. Create one Amazon SQS queue that subscribes to multiple Amazon SNS topics.

    C. Amazon SNS allows exactly one subscriber to each topic, so fanout is not possible.

    D. Create an Amazon SNS topic using Amazon SNS. Create an application that subscribes to that topic and duplicates the message. Send copies to multiple Amazon SQS queues.

12. Your application polls an Amazon Simple Queue Service (Amazon SQS) queue frequently and returns immediately, often with empty ReceiveMessageResponses. What is one thing that can be done to reduce Amazon SQS costs?

    A. Pricing on Amazon SQS does not include a cost for service requests; therefore, there is no concern.

    B. Increase the timeout value for short polling to wait for messages longer before returning a response.

    C. Change the message visibility value to a higher number.

    D. Use long polling by supplying a WaitTimeSeconds of greater than 0 seconds when calling ReceiveMessage.

13. What is the longest time available for an Amazon Simple Queue Service (Amazon SQS) long polling timeout?

    A. 10 seconds

    B. 20 seconds

    C. 30 seconds

    D. 1 hour

14. What is the longest configurable message retention period for Amazon Simple Queue Service (Amazon SQS)?

    A. 30 minutes

    B. 4 days

    C. 30 seconds

    D. 14 days

15. What is the default message retention period for Amazon Simple Queue Service (Amazon SQS)?

    A. 30 minutes

    B. 4 days

    C. 30 seconds

    D. 14 days

16. Amazon Simple Notification Service (Amazon SNS) is a push notification service that lets you send individual or multiple messages to large numbers of recipients. What types of clients are supported?

   A. Java and JavaScript clients that support publisher and subscriber types

   B. Producers and consumers supported by C and C++ clients

   C. Mobile and AMQP support for publisher and subscriber client types

   D. Publisher and subscriber client types

17. In Amazon Simple Workflow Service (Amazon SWF), a decider is responsible for what?

   A. Executing each step of the work

   B. Defining work coordination logic by specifying work sequencing, timing, and failure conditions

   C. Executing your workflow

   D. Registering activities and workflow with Amazon SWF

18. Can an Amazon Simple Notification Service (Amazon SNS) topic be recreated with a previously used topic name?

   A. Yes. The topic name should typically be available after 24 hours after the previous topic with the same name has been deleted.

   B. Yes. The topic name should typically be available after 1–3 hours after the previous topic with the same name has been deleted.

   C. Yes. The topic name should typically be available after 30–60 seconds after the previous topic with the same name has been deleted.

   D. At this time, this feature is not supported.

19. What should you do in order to grant a different AWS account permission to your Amazon Simple Queue Service (Amazon SQS) queue?

   A. Share credentials to your AWS account and have the other account's applications use your account's credentials to access the Amazon SQS queue.

   B. Create a user for that account in AWS Identity and Access Management (IAM) and establish an IAM policy that grants access to the queue.

   C. Create an Amazon SQS policy that grants the other account access.

   D. Amazon Virtual Private Cloud (Amazon VPC) peering must be used to achieve this.

20. Can an Amazon Simple Notification Service (Amazon SNS) message be deleted after being published to a topic?

   A. Only if a subscriber(s) has/have not read the message yet

   B. Only if the Amazon SNS recall message parameter has been set

   C. No. After a message has been successfully published to a topic, it cannot be recalled.

   D. Yes. However it can be deleted only if the subscribers are Amazon SQS queues.

Domain Name System (DNS) and Amazon Route 53

THE AWS CERTIFIED SOLUTIONS ARCHITECT EXAM TOPICS COVERED IN THIS CHAPTER MAY INCLUDE, BUT ARE NOT LIMITED TO, THE FOLLOWING:

Domain 1.0: Designing highly available, cost-efficient, fault-tolerant, scalable systems

✓ **1.1 Identify and recognize cloud architecture considerations, such as fundamental components and effective designs.**

Content may include the following:

- How to design cloud services

- Planning and design

- Monitoring and logging

- Familiarity with:

    - Best practices for AWS architecture

    - Developing to client specifications, including pricing/cost (for example, on-demand vs. reserved vs. spot; RTO and RPO DR design)

    - Architectural trade-off decisions (for example, high availability vs. cost, Amazon Relational Database Service [RDS] vs. installing your own database on Amazon Elastic Compute Cloud—EC2)

    - Elasticity and scalability (for example, auto-scaling, SQS, ELB, CloudFront)

Domain 3.0: Data Security

✓ **3.1   Recognize and implement secure procedures for optimum cloud deployment and maintenance.**

✓ **3.2   Recognize critical disaster-recovery techniques and their implementation.**

- Amazon Route 53

Domain Name System (DNS)

The *Domain Name System (DNS)* is sometimes a difficult concept to understand because it is so ubiquitously used in making the Internet work. Before we get into the details, let's start with a simple analogy. The *Internet Protocol (IP)* address of your website is like your phone number—it could change if you move to a new area (at least your land line could change). DNS is like the phonebook. If someone wants to call you at your new house or location, they might look you up by name in the phonebook. If their phonebook hasn't been updated since you moved, however, they might call your old house. When a visitor wants to access your website, their computer takes the domain name typed in (www.amazon .com, for example) and looks up the IP address for that domain using DNS.

More specifically, DNS is a globally-distributed service that is foundational to the way people use the Internet. DNS uses a hierarchical name structure, and different levels in the hierarchy are each separated with a dot (.). Consider the domain names www.amazon .com and aws.amazon.com. In both these examples, com is the Top-Level Domain (TLD) and amazon is the Second-Level Domain (SLD). There can be any number of lower levels (for example, www and aws) below the SLD.

Computers use the DNS hierarchy to translate human readable names (for example, www.amazon.com) into the IP addresses (for example, 192.0.2.1) that computers use to connect to one another. Every time you use a domain name, a DNS service must translate the name into the corresponding IP address. In summary, if you've used the Internet, you've used DNS.

Amazon Route 53 is an *authoritative DNS system*. An authoritative DNS system provides an update mechanism that developers use to manage their public DNS names. It then answers DNS queries, translating domain names into IP addresses so that computers can communicate with each other.

This chapter is intended to provide you with a baseline understanding of DNS and the Amazon Route 53 service that is designed to help users find your website or application over the Internet.

Domain Name System (DNS) Concepts

This section of the chapter defines DNS terms, describes how DNS works, and explains commonly used *record types*.

Top-Level Domains (TLDs)

A *Top-Level Domain (TLD)* is the most general part of the domain. The TLD is the farthest portion to the right (as separated by a dot). Common TLDs are .com, .net, .org, .gov, .edu, and .io.

TLDs are at the top of the hierarchy in terms of domain names. Certain parties are given management control over TLDs by the Internet Corporation for Assigned Names and Numbers (ICANN). These parties can then distribute domain names under the TLD, usually through a domain registrar. These domains are registered with the Network Information Center (InterNIC), a service of ICANN, which enforces the uniqueness of domain names across the Internet. Each domain name becomes registered in a central database, known as the WhoIS database.

Domain Names

A *domain name* is the human-friendly name that we are used to associating with an Internet resource. For instance, amazon.com is a domain name. Some people will say that the amazon portion is the domain, but we can generally refer to the combined form as the domain name.

The URL aws.amazon.com is associated with the servers owned by AWS. The DNS allows users to reach the AWS servers when they type aws.amazon.com into their browsers.

IP Addresses

An *IP address* is a network addressable location. Each IP address must be unique within its network. For public websites, this network is the entire Internet.

IPv4 addresses, the most common form of addresses, consist of four sets of numbers separated by a dot, with each set having up to three digits. For example, 111.222.111.222 could be a valid IPv4 IP address. With DNS, we map a name to that address so that you do not have to remember a complicated set of numbers for each place you want to visit on a network.

Due to the tremendous growth of the Internet and the number of devices connected to it, the IPv4 address range has quickly been depleted. IPv6 was created to solve this depletion issue, and it has an address space of 128 bits, which allows for 340,282,366,920,938,463, 463,374,607,431,768,211,456, or 340 undecillion, unique addresses. For human beings, this number is difficult to imagine, so consider this: If each IPv4 address were one grain of sand, you would have enough addresses to fill approximately one dump truck with sand. If each IPv6 address were one grain of sand, you would have enough sand to equal the approximate size of the sun. Today, most devices and networks still communicate using IPv4, but migration to IPv6 is proceeding gradually over time.

Hosts

Within a domain, the domain owner can define individual *hosts*, which refer to separate computers or services accessible through a domain. For instance, most domain owners make their web servers accessible through the base domain (example.com) and also through the host definition www (as in www.example.com).

You can have other host definitions under the general domain, such as Application Program Interface (API) access through an API host (api.example.com) or File Transfer

Protocol (FTP) access with a host definition of FTP or files (ftp.example.com or files .example.com). The host names can be arbitrary if they are unique for the domain.

Subdomains

DNS works in a hierarchal manner and allows a large domain to be partitioned or extended into multiple subdomains. TLDs can have many subdomains under them. For instance, zappos.com and audible.com are both subdomains of the .com TLD (although they are typically just called domains). The zappos or audible portion can be referred to as an SLD.

Likewise, each SLD can have subdomains located under it. For instance, the URL for the history department of a school could be www.history.school.edu. The history portion is a subdomain.

The difference between a host name and a *subdomain* is that a host defines a computer or resource, while a subdomain extends the parent domain. Subdomains are a method of subdividing the domain itself.

Whether talking about subdomains or hosts, you can see that the left-most portions of a domain are the most specific. This is how DNS works: from most to least specific as you read from left to right.

Fully Qualified Domain Name (FQDN)

Domain locations in a DNS can be relative to one another and, as such, can be somewhat ambiguous. A *Fully Qualified Domain Name (FQDN)*, also referred to as an absolute domain name, specifies a domain's location in relation to the absolute root of the DNS.

This means that the FQDN specifies each parent domain including the TLD. A proper FQDN ends with a dot, indicating the root of the DNS hierarchy. For example, mail .amazon.com is an FQDN. Sometimes, software that calls for an FQDN does not require the ending dot, but it is required to conform to ICANN standards.

In Figure 9.1, you can see that the entire string is the FQDN, which is composed of the domain name, subdomain, root, TLD, SLD and host.

FIGURE 9.1   FQDN components

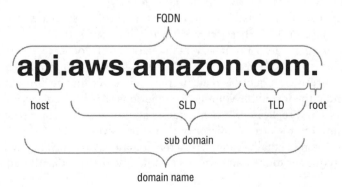

Name Servers

A *name server* is a computer designated to translate domain names into IP addresses. These servers do most of the work in the DNS. Because the total number of domain translations is too much for any one server, each server may redirect requests to other name servers or delegate responsibility for the subset of subdomains for which they are responsible.

Name servers can be authoritative, meaning that they give answers to queries about domains under their control. Otherwise, they may point to other servers or serve cached copies of other name servers' data.

Zone Files

A *zone file* is a simple text file that contains the mappings between domain names and IP addresses. This is how a DNS server finally identifies which IP address should be contacted when a user requests a certain domain name.

> *Zone files reside in name servers and generally define the resources available under a specific domain, or the place where one can go to get that information.*

Top-Level Domain (TLD) Name Registrars

Because all of the names in a given domain must be unique, there needs to be a way to organize them so that domain names aren't duplicated. This is where *domain name registrars* come in. A domain name registrar is an organization or commercial entity that manages the reservation of Internet domain names. A domain name registrar must be accredited by a generic TLD (gTLD) registry and/or a country code TLD (ccTLD) registry. The management is done in accordance with the guidelines of the designated domain name registries.

Steps Involved in Domain Name System (DNS) Resolution

When you type a domain name into your browser, your computer first checks its host file to see if it has that domain name stored locally. If it does not, it will check its DNS cache to see if you have visited the site before. If it still does not have a record of that domain name, it will contact a DNS server to resolve the domain name.

DNS is, at its core, a hierarchical system. At the top of this system are root servers. ICANN delegates the control of these servers to various organizations.

As of this writing, there are 13 root servers in operation. Root servers handle requests for information about TLDs. When a request comes in for a domain that a lower-level name server cannot resolve, a query is made to the root server for the domain.

In order to handle the incredible volume of resolutions that happen every day, these root servers are mirrored and replicated. When requests are made to a certain root server, the request will be routed to the nearest mirror of that root server.

The root servers won't actually know where the domain is hosted. They will, however, be able to direct the requester to the name servers that handle the specifically-requested TLD.

For example, if a request for www.wikipedia.org is made to the root server, it will check its zone files for a listing that matches that domain name, but it will not find one in its records. It will instead find a record for the .org TLD and give the requesting entity the address of the name server responsible for .org addresses.

Top-Level Domain (TLD) Servers

After a root server returns the IP address of the appropriate server that is responsible for the TLD of a request, the requester then sends a new request to that address.

To continue the example from the previous section, the requesting entity would send a request to the name server responsible for knowing about .org domains to see if it can locate www.wikipedia.org.

Once again, when the name server searches its zone files for a www.wikipedia.org listing, it will not find one in its records. However, it will find a listing for the IP address of the name server responsible for wikipedia.org. This is getting much closer to the correct IP address.

Domain-Level Name Servers

At this point, the requester has the IP address of the name server that is responsible for knowing the actual IP address of the resource. It sends a new request to the name server asking, once again, if it can resolve www.wikipedia.org.

The name server checks its zone files, and it finds a zone file associated with wikipedia.org. Inside of this file, there is a record that contains the IP address for the .www host. The name server returns the final address to the requester.

Resolving Name Servers

In the previous scenario, we referred to a requester. What is the requester in this situation?

In almost all cases, the requester will be what is called a *resolving name server,* which is a server that is configured to ask other servers questions. Its primary function is to act as an intermediary for a user, caching previous query results to improve speed and providing the addresses of appropriate root servers to resolve new requests.

A user will usually have a few resolving name servers configured on their computer system. The resolving name servers are typically provided by an Internet Service Provider (ISP) or other organization. There are several public resolving DNS servers that you can query. These can be configured in your computer either automatically or manually.

When you type a URL in the address bar of your browser, your computer first looks to see if it can find the resource's location locally. It checks the host file on the computer and any locally stored cache. It then sends the request to the resolving name server and waits to receive the IP address of the resource.

The resolving name server then checks its cache for the answer. If it doesn't find it, it goes through the steps outlined in the previous sections.

Resolving name servers compress the requesting process for the end user. The clients simply have to know to ask the resolving name servers where a resource is located, and the resolving name servers will do the work to investigate and return the final answer.

More About Zone Files

Zone files are the way that name servers store information about the domains they know. The more zone files that a name server has, the more requests it will be able to answer authoritatively. Most requests to the average name server, however, are for domains that are not in the local zone file.

If the server is configured to handle recursive queries, like a resolving name server, it will find the answer and return it. Otherwise, it will tell the requesting entity where to look next.

A zone file describes a DNS zone, which is a subset of the entire DNS. Zone files are generally used to configure a single domain, and they can contain a number of records that define where resources are for the domain in question.

The zone file's $ORIGIN directive is a parameter equal to the zone's highest level of authority by default. If a zone file is used to configure the example.com domain, the $ORIGIN would be set to example.com.

This parameter is either configured at the top of the zone file or defined in the DNS server's configuration file that references the zone file. Either way, this parameter defines what authoritative records the zone governs.

Similarly, the $TTL directive configures the default Time to Live (TTL) value for resource records in the zone. This value defines the length of time that previously queried results are available to a caching name server before they expire.

Record Types

Each zone file contains records. In its simplest form, a *record* is a single mapping between a resource and a name. These can map a domain name to an IP address or define resources for the domain, such as name servers or mail servers. This section describes each record type in detail.

Start of Authority (SOA) Record

A *Start of Authority (SOA) record* is mandatory in all zone files, and it identifies the base DNS information about the domain. Each zone contains a single SOA record.

The SOA record stores information about the following:

- The name of the DNS server for that zone
- The administrator of the zone
- The current version of the data file
- The number of seconds that a secondary name server should wait before checking for updates
- The number of seconds that a secondary name server should wait before retrying a failed zone transfer
- The maximum number of seconds that a secondary name server can use data before it must either be refreshed or expire
- The default TTL value (in seconds) for resource records in the zone

A and AAAA

Both types of address records map a host to an IP address. The A record is used to map a host to an IPv4 IP address, while AAAA records are used to map a host to an IPv6 address.

Canonical Name (CNAME)

A *Canonical Name (CNAME) record* is a type of resource record in the DNS that defines an alias for the CNAME for your server (the domain name defined in an A or AAAA record).

Mail Exchange (MX)

*Mail Exchange (MX) record*s are used to define the mail servers used for a domain and ensure that email messages are routed correctly. The MX record should point to a host defined by an A or AAAA record and not one defined by a CNAME.

Name Server (NS)

*Name Server (NS) record*s are used by TLD servers to direct traffic to the DNS server that contains the authoritative DNS records.

Pointer (PTR)

A *Pointer (PTR) record* is essentially the reverse of an A record. PTR records map an IP address to a DNS name, and they are mainly used to check if the server name is associated with the IP address from where the connection was initiated.

Sender Policy Framework (SPF)

*Sender Policy Framework (SPF) record*s are used by mail servers to combat spam. An SPF record tells a mail server what IP addresses are authorized to send an email from your domain name. For example, if you wanted to ensure that only your mail server sends emails from your company's domain, such as example.com, you would create an SPF record with the IP address of your mail server. That way, an email sent from your domain, such as marketing@example.com, would need to have an originating IP address of your company mail server in order to be accepted. This prevents people from spoofing emails from your domain name.

Text (TXT)

*Text (TXT) record*s are used to hold text information. This record provides the ability to associate some arbitrary and unformatted text with a host or other name, such as human readable information about a server, network, data center, and other accounting information.

Service (SRV)

A *Service (SRV) record* is a specification of data in the DNS defining the location (the host name and port number) of servers for specified services. The idea behind SRV is that, given a domain name (for example, example.com) and a service name (for example, web [HTTP], which runs on a protocol [TCP]), a DNS query may be issued to find the host name that provides such a service for the domain, which may or may not be within the domain.

Amazon Route 53 Overview

Now that you have a foundational understanding of DNS and the different DNS record types, you can explore Amazon Route 53. *Amazon Route 53* is a highly available and scalable cloud DNS web service that is designed to give developers and businesses an extremely reliable and cost-effective way to route end users to Internet applications.

Amazon Route 53 performs three main functions:

- *Domain registration*—Amazon Route 53 lets you register domain names, such as example.com.

- *DNS service*—Amazon Route 53 translates friendly domain names like www.example.com into IP addresses like 192.0.2.1. Amazon Route 53 responds to DNS queries using a global network of authoritative DNS servers, which reduces latency. To comply with DNS standards, responses sent over User Datagram Protocol (UDP) are limited to 512 bytes in size. Responses exceeding 512 bytes are truncated, and the resolver must re-issue the request over TCP.

- *Health checking*—Amazon Route 53 sends automated requests over the Internet to your application to verify that it's reachable, available, and functional.

You can use any combination of these functions. For example, you can use Amazon Route 53 as both your registrar and your DNS service, or you can use Amazon Route 53 as the DNS service for a domain that you registered with another domain registrar.

Domain Registration

If you want to create a website, you first need to register the domain name. If you already registered a domain name with another registrar, you have the option to transfer the domain registration to Amazon Route 53. It isn't required to use Amazon Route 53 as your DNS service or to configure health checking for your resources.

Amazon Route 53 supports domain registration for a wide variety of generic TLDs (for example, .com and .org) and geographic TLDs (for example, .be and .us). For a complete list of supported TLDs, refer to the Amazon Route 53 Developer Guide at https://docs .aws.amazon.com/Route53/latest/DeveloperGuide/.

Domain Name System (DNS) Service

As stated previously, Amazon Route 53 is an authoritative DNS service that routes Internet traffic to your website by translating friendly domain names into IP addresses. When someone enters your domain name in a browser or sends you an email, a DNS request is forwarded to the nearest Amazon Route 53 DNS server in a global network of authoritative DNS servers. Amazon Route 53 responds with the IP address that you specified.

If you register a new domain name with Amazon Route 53, Amazon Route 53 will be automatically configured as the DNS service for the domain, and a *hosted zone* will be created for your domain. You add resource record sets to the hosted zone, which define how you want Amazon Route 53 to respond to DNS queries for your domain (for example, with the IP address for a web server, the IP address for the nearest Amazon CloudFront edge location, or the IP address for an Elastic Load Balancing load balancer).

If you registered your domain with another domain registrar, that registrar is probably providing the DNS service for your domain. You can transfer DNS service to Amazon Route 53, with or without transferring registration for the domain.

If you're using Amazon CloudFront, Amazon Simple Storage Service (Amazon S3), or Elastic Load Balancing, you can configure Amazon Route 53 to route Internet traffic to those resources.

Hosted Zones

A *hosted zone* is a collection of resource record sets hosted by Amazon Route 53. Like a traditional DNS zone file, a hosted zone represents resource record sets that are managed together under a single domain name. Each hosted zone has its own metadata and configuration information.

There are two types of hosted zones: private and public. A *private hosted zone* is a container that holds information about how you want to route traffic for a domain and its subdomains within one or more Amazon Virtual Private Clouds (Amazon VPCs). A *public hosted zone* is a container that holds information about how you want to route traffic on the Internet for a domain (for example, example.com) and its subdomains (for example, apex.example.com and acme.example.com).

The resource record sets contained in a hosted zone must share the same suffix. For example, the example.com hosted zone can contain resource record sets for the www.example.com and www.aws.example.com subdomains, but it cannot contain resource record sets for a www.example.ca subdomain.

You can use Amazon S3 to host your static website at the hosted zone (for example, domain.com) and redirect all requests to a subdomain (for example, www.domain.com). Then, in Amazon Route 53, you can create an alias resource record that sends requests for the root domain to the Amazon S3 bucket.

Use an alias record, not a CNAME, for your hosted zone. CNAMEs are not allowed for hosted zones in Amazon Route 53.

Do not use A records for subdomains (for example, www.domain.com), as they refer to hardcoded IP addresses. Instead, use Amazon Route 53 alias records or traditional CNAME records to always point to the right resource, wherever your site is hosted, even when the physical server has changed its IP address.

Supported Record Types

Amazon Route 53 supports the following DNS resource record types. When you access Amazon Route 53 using the API, you will see examples of how to format the Value element for each record type. Supported record types include:

- A
- AAAA
- CNAME
- MX
- NS
- PTR
- SOA
- SPF
- SRV
- TXT
- Routing Policies

When you create a resource record set, you choose a *routing policy*, which determines how Amazon Route 53 responds to queries. Routing policy options are simple, weighted, latency-based, failover, and geolocation. When specified, Amazon Route 53 evaluates a resource's relative weight, the client's network latency to the resource, or the client's geographical location when deciding which resource to send back in a DNS response.

Routing policies can be associated with health checks, so resource health status is considered before it even becomes a candidate in a conditional decision tree. A description of possible routing policies and more on health checking is covered in this section.

Simple

This is the default routing policy when you create a new resource. Use a simple routing policy when you have a single resource that performs a given function for your domain (for example, one web server that serves content for the example.com website). In this case, Amazon Route 53 responds to DNS queries based only on the values in the resource record set (for example, the IP address in an A record).

Weighted

With weighted DNS, you can associate multiple resources (such as Amazon Elastic Compute Cloud [Amazon EC2] instances or Elastic Load Balancing load balancers) with a single DNS name.

Use the weighted routing policy when you have multiple resources that perform the same function (such as web servers that serve the same website), and you want Amazon Route 53 to route traffic to those resources in proportions that you specify. For example, you may use this for load balancing between different AWS regions or to test new versions of your website (you can send 10 percent of traffic to the test environment and 90 percent of traffic to the older version of your website).

To create a group of weighted resource record sets, you need to create two or more resource record sets that have the same DNS name and type. You then assign each resource record set a unique identifier and a relative weight.

When processing a DNS query, Amazon Route 53 searches for a resource record set or a group of resource record sets that have the same name and DNS record type (such as an A record). Amazon Route 53 then selects one record from the group. The probability of any resource record set being selected is governed by the following formula:

$$\frac{Weight\ for\ a\ given\ resource\ record\ set}{Sum\ of\ the\ weights\ for\ the\ resource\ record\ sets\ in\ the\ group}$$

Latency-Based

Latency-based routing allows you to route your traffic based on the lowest network latency for your end user (for example, using the AWS region that will give them the fastest response time).

Use the latency routing policy when you have resources that perform the same function in multiple AWS Availability Zones or regions and you want Amazon Route 53 to respond to DNS queries using the resources that provide the best latency. For example, suppose you have Elastic Load Balancing load balancers in the U.S. West (Oregon) region and in the Asia Pacific (Singapore) region, and you created a latency resource record set in Amazon Route 53 for each load balancer. A user in London enters the name of your domain in a browser, and DNS routes the request to an Amazon Route 53 name server. Amazon Route 53 refers to its data on latency between London and the Singapore region and between London and the Oregon region. If latency is lower between London and the Oregon region, Amazon Route 53 responds to the user's request with the IP address of your load balancer in Oregon. If latency is lower between London and the Singapore region, Amazon Route 53 responds with the IP address of your load balancer in Singapore.

Failover

Use a failover routing policy to configure active-passive failover, in which one resource takes all the traffic when it's available and the other resource takes all the traffic when the first resource isn't available. Note that you can't create failover resource record sets for private hosted zones.

For example, you might want your primary resource record set to be in U.S. West (N. California) and your secondary, Disaster Recovery (DR), resource(s) to be in U.S. East (N. Virginia). Amazon Route 53 will monitor the health of your primary resource endpoints using a health check.

A health check tells Amazon Route 53 how to send requests to the endpoint whose health you want to check: which protocol to use (HTTP, HTTPS, or TCP), which IP address and port to use, and, for HTTP/HTTPS health checks, a domain name and path.

After you have configured a health check, Amazon will monitor the health of your selected DNS endpoint. If your health check fails, then failover routing policies will be applied and your DNS will fail over to your DR site.

Geolocation

Geolocation routing lets you choose where Amazon Route 53 will send your traffic based on the geographic location of your users (the location from which DNS queries originate). For example, you might want all queries from Europe to be routed to a fleet of Amazon EC2 instances that are specifically configured for your European customers, with local languages and pricing in Euros.

You can also use geolocation routing to restrict distribution of content to only the locations in which you have distribution rights. Another possible use is for balancing load across endpoints in a predictable, easy-to-manage way so that each user location is consistently routed to the same endpoint.

You can specify geographic locations by continent, by country, or even by state in the United States. You can also create separate resource record sets for overlapping geographic regions, and priority goes to the smallest geographic region. For example, you might have one resource record set for Europe and one for the United Kingdom. This allows you to route some queries for selected countries (in this example, the United Kingdom) to one resource and to route queries for the rest of the continent (in this example, Europe) to a different resource.

Geolocation works by mapping IP addresses to locations. You should be cautious, however, as some IP addresses aren't mapped to geographic locations. Even if you create geolocation resource record sets that cover all seven continents, Amazon Route 53 will receive some DNS queries from locations that it can't identify.

In this case, you can create a default resource record set that handles both queries from IP addresses that aren't mapped to any location and queries that come from locations for which you haven't created geolocation resource record sets. If you don't create a default resource record set, Amazon Route 53 returns a "no answer" response for queries from those locations.

You cannot create two geolocation resource record sets that specify the same geographic location. You also cannot create geolocation resource record sets that have the same values for "Name" and "Type" as the "Name" and "Type" of non-geolocation resource record sets.

More on Health Checking

Amazon Route 53 health checks monitor the health of your resources such as web servers and email servers. You can configure Amazon CloudWatch alarms for your health checks so that you receive notification when a resource becomes unavailable. You can also configure Amazon Route 53 to route Internet traffic away from resources that are unavailable.

Health checks and DNS failover are major tools in the Amazon Route 53 feature set that help make your application highly available and resilient to failures. If you deploy an application in multiple Availability Zones and multiple AWS regions, with Amazon Route 53 health checks attached to every endpoint, Amazon Route 53 can send back a list of healthy endpoints only. Health checks can automatically switch to a healthy endpoint with minimal disruption to your clients and without any configuration changes. You can use this automatic recovery scenario in active-active or active-passive setups, depending on whether your additional endpoints are always hit by live traffic or only after all primary endpoints have failed. Using health checks and automatic failovers, Amazon Route 53 improves your service uptime, especially when compared to the traditional monitor-alert-restart approach of addressing failures.

Amazon Route 53 health checks are not triggered by DNS queries; they are run periodically by AWS, and results are published to all DNS servers. This way, name servers can be aware of an unhealthy endpoint and route differently within approximately 30 seconds of a problem (after three failed tests in a row), and new DNS results will be known to clients a minute later (assuming your TTL is 60 seconds), bringing complete recovery time to about a minute and a half in total in this scenario.

The 2014 AWS re:Invent session SDD408, "Amazon Route 53 Deep Dive: Delivering Resiliency, Minimizing Latency," introduced a set of best practices for Amazon Route 53. Explore those best practices to help you get started using Amazon Route 53 as a building block to deliver highly-available and resilient applications on AWS.

Amazon Route 53 Enables Resiliency

When pulling these concepts together to build an application that is highly available and resilient to failures, consider these building blocks:

- In every AWS region, an Elastic Load Balancing load balancer is set up with cross-zone load balancing and connection draining. This distributes the load evenly across all instances in all Availability Zones, and it ensures requests in flight are fully served before an Amazon EC2 instance is disconnected from an Elastic Load Balancing load balancer for any reason.

- Each Elastic Load Balancing load balancer delegates requests to Amazon EC2 instances running in multiple Availability Zones in an auto-scaling group. This protects the application from Availability Zone outages, ensures that a minimal amount of instances is always running, and responds to changes in load by properly scaling each group's Amazon EC2 instances.

- Each Elastic Load Balancing load balancer has health checks defined to ensure that it delegates requests only to healthy instances.

- Each Elastic Load Balancing load balancer also has an Amazon Route 53 health check associated with it to ensure that requests are routed only to load balancers that have healthy Amazon EC2 instances.

- The application's production environment (for example, `prod.domain.com`) has Amazon Route 53 alias records that point to Elastic Load Balancing load balancers. The production environment also uses a latency-based routing policy that is associated with Elastic Load Balancing health checks. This ensures that requests are routed to a healthy load balancer, thereby providing minimal latency to a client.

- The application's failover environment (for example, `fail.domain.com`) has an Amazon Route 53 alias record that points to an Amazon CloudFront distribution of an Amazon S3 bucket hosting a static version of the application.

- The application's subdomain (for example, `www.domain.com`) has an Amazon Route 53 alias record that points to `prod.domain.com` (as primary target) and `fail.domain.com` (as secondary target) using a failover routing policy. This ensures `www.domain.com` routes to the production load balancers if at least one of them is healthy or the "fail whale" if all of them appear to be unhealthy.

- The application's hosted zone (for example, `domain.com`) has an Amazon Route 53 alias record that redirects requests to `www.domain.com` using an Amazon S3 bucket of the same name.

- Application content (both static and dynamic) can be served using Amazon Cloud-Front. This ensures that the content is delivered to clients from Amazon CloudFront edge locations spread all over the world to provide minimal latency. Serving dynamic content from a Content Delivery Network (CDN), where it is cached for short periods of time (that is, several seconds), takes the load off of the application and further improves its latency and responsiveness.

- The application is deployed in multiple AWS regions, protecting it from a regional outage.

Summary

In this chapter, you learned the fundamentals of DNS, which is the methodology that computers use to convert human-friendly domain names (for example, `amazon.com`) into IP addresses (such as `192.0.2.1`).

DNS starts with TLDs (for example, `.com`, `.edu`). The Internet Assigned Numbers Authority (IANA) controls the TLDs in a root zone database, which is essentially a database of all available TLDs.

DNS names are registered with a domain registrar. A registrar is an authority that can assign domain names directly under one or more TLDs. These domains are registered with InterNIC, a service of ICANN, which enforces the uniqueness of domain names across the Internet. Each domain name becomes registered in a central database, known as the WhoIS database.

DNS consists of a number of different record types, including but not limited to the following:

- A
- AAAA
- CNAME

- MX
- NS
- PTR
- SOA
- SPF
- TXT

Amazon Route 53 is a highly available and highly scalable AWS-provided DNS service. Amazon Route 53 connects user requests to infrastructure running on AWS (for example, Amazon EC2 instances and Elastic Load Balancing load balancers). It can also be used to route users to infrastructure outside of AWS.

With Amazon Route 53, your DNS records are organized into hosted zones that you configure with the Amazon Route 53 API. A hosted zone simply stores records for your domain. These records can consist of A, CNAME, MX, and other supported record types.

Amazon Route 53 allows you to have several different routing policies, including the following:

- *Simple*—Most commonly used when you have a single resource that performs a given function for your domain

- *Weighted*—Used when you want to route a percentage of your traffic to one particular resource or resources

- *Latency-Based*—Used to route your traffic based on the lowest latency so that your users get the fastest response times

- *Failover*—Used for DR and to route your traffic from your resources in a primary location to a standby location

- *Geolocation*—Used to route your traffic based on your end user's location

Remember to pull these concepts together to build an application that is highly available and resilient to failures. Use Elastic Load Balancing load balancers across Availability Zones with connection draining enabled, use health checks defined to ensure that the application delegates requests only to healthy Amazon EC2 instances, and use a latency-based routing policy with Elastic Load Balancing health checks to ensure requests are routed with minimal latency to clients. Use Amazon CloudFront edge locations to spread content all over the world with minimal client latency. Deploy the application in multiple AWS regions, protecting it from a regional outage.

Exam Essentials

Understand what DNS is.   DNS is the methodology that computers use to convert human-friendly domain names (for example, `amazon.com`) into IP addresses (such as `192.0.2.1`).

Know how DNS registration works.   Domains are registered with domain registrars that in turn register the domain name with InterNIC, a service of ICANN. ICANN enforces uniqueness of domain names across the Internet. Each domain name becomes registered in a central database known as the WhoIS database. Domains are defined by their TLDs. TLDs are controlled by IANA in a root zone database, which is essentially a database of all available TLDs.

Remember the steps involved in DNS resolution.   Your browser asks the resolving DNS server what the IP address is for amazon.com. The resolving server does not know the address, so it asks a root server the same question. There are 13 root servers around the world, and these are managed by ICANN. The root server replies that it does not know the answer to this, but it can give an address to a TLD server that knows about .com domain names. The resolving server then contacts the TLD server. The TLD server does not know the address of the domain name either, but it does know the address of the resolving name server. The resolving server then queries the resolving name server. The resolving name server contains the authoritative records and sends these to the resolving server, which then saves these records locally so it does not have to perform these steps again in the near future. The resolving name server returns this information to the user's web browser, which also caches the information.

Remember the different record types.   DNS consists of the following different record types: A (address record), AAAA (IPv6 address record), CNAME (canonical name record or alias), MX (mail exchange record), NS (name server record), PTR (pointer record), SOA (start of authority record), SPF (sender policy framework), SRV (service locator), and TXT (text record). You should know the differences among each record type.

Remember the different routing policies.   With Amazon Route 53, you can have different routing policies. The simple routing policy is most commonly used when you have a single resource that performs a given function for your domain. Weighted routing is used when you want to route a percentage of your traffic to a particular resource or resources. Latency-based routing is used to route your traffic based on the lowest latency so that your users get the fastest response times. Failover routing is used for DR and to route your traffic from a primary resource to a standby resource. Geolocation routing is used to route your traffic based on your end user's location.

Exercises

In this section, you explore the different types of DNS routing policies that you can create using AWS. For specific step-by-step instructions, refer to the Amazon Route 53 information and documentation at http://aws.amazon.com/route53/. You will need your own domain name to complete this section, and you should be aware that Amazon Route 53 is not AWS Free Tier eligible. Hosting a zone on Amazon Route 53 should cost you a minimal amount per month per hosted zone, and additional charges will be levied depending on the routing policy you use. For current information on Amazon Route 53 pricing, refer to http://aws .amazon.com/route53/pricing/.

EXERCISE 9.1

Create a New Zone

1. Log in to the AWS Management Console.

2. Navigate to Amazon Route 53, and create a hosted zone.

3. Enter your domain name, and create your new zone file.

4. In the new zone file, you will see the SOA record and name servers. You will need to log in to your domain registrar's website, and update the name servers with your AWS name servers.

5. After you update your name servers with your domain registrars, Amazon Route 53 will be configured to serve DNS requests for your domain.

You have now created your first Amazon Route 53 zone.

EXERCISE 9.2

Create Two Web Servers in Two Different Regions

In this exercise, you will create two new Amazon EC2 web servers in different AWS regions. You will use these in the following exercises when setting up Amazon Route 53 to access the web servers.

Create an Amazon EC2 Instance

1. Log in to the AWS Management Console.

2. Change your region to Asia Pacific (Sydney).

3. In the Compute section, load the Amazon EC2 dashboard. Launch an instance, and select the first Amazon Linux Amazon Machine Image (AMI).

4. Select the instance type, and configure your instance details. Take a close look at the different options available to you, and change your instance's storage device settings as necessary.

5. Name the instance **Sydney,** and add a security group that allows HTTP.

6. Launch your new Amazon EC2 instance, and verify that it has launched properly.

Connect to Your Amazon EC2 Instance

7. Navigate to the Amazon EC2 instance in the AWS Management Console, and copy the public IP address to your clipboard.

8. Using a Secure Shell (SSH) client of your choice, connect to your Amazon EC2 instance using the public IP address, the user name ec2-user, and your private key.

EXERCISE 9.2 *(continued)*

9. When prompted about the authenticity of the host, type **Yes**, and continue.

10. You should now be connected to your Amazon EC2 instance. Elevate your privileges to root by typing **#sudo su**.

11. While you're logged in as the root user to your Amazon EC2 instance, run the following command to install Apache httpd:

    #yum install httpd -y

12. After the installation has completed, run the command #service httpd start followed by #chkconfig httpd on.

13. Navigate to the EC2 instance, and type: **cd /var/www/html**

14. Type **#nano index.html** and press Enter.

15. In Nano, type **This is the Sydney Server** and then press Ctrl+X.

16. Type **Y** to confirm that you want to save the changes, and then press Enter.

17. Type **#ls**. You should now see your newly created index.html file.

18. In your browser, navigate to http://yourpublicipaddress/index.html.

You should now see your "This is the Sydney Server" home page. If you do not see this, check your security group to make sure you allowed access for port 80.

Create an Elastic Load Balancing Load Balancer

19. Return to the AWS Management Console, and navigate to the Amazon EC2 dashboard.

20. Create a load balancer named Sydney, leaving the settings at their default values.

21. Create your security group, and allow all traffic in on port 80.

22. Configure health check, leaving the settings at their default values.

23. Select your newly added instance. Add tags here if you want to tag your instances.

24. Click Create to provision your load balancer.

Create These Resources in a Second Region

25. Return to the AWS Management Console, and change your region to South America (Sao Paulo).

26. Repeat the three procedures in this section to add a second Amazon EC2 instance and a load balancer in this new region.

You have now created two web servers in different regions of the world and placed these regions behind Elastic Load Balancing load balancers.

EXERCISE 9.3

Create an Alias A Record with a Simple Routing Policy

1. Log in to the AWS Management Console, and navigate to the Amazon Route 53 dashboard.

2. Select your newly-created zone domain name, and create a record set with the name
   `A - IPv4 Address`

3. Create an alias, leaving your routing policy set to Simple.

4. In your web browser, navigate to your domain name. You should now see a welcome screen for the Sydney region. If you do not see this, check that your Amazon EC2 instance is attached to your load balancer and that the instance is in service. If the instance is not in service, this means that it is failing its health check. Check that Apache HTTP Server (HTTPD) is running and that your `index.html` document is accessible.

You have now created your first Alias A record for the zone apex using the simple routing policy.

EXERCISE 9.4

Create a Weighted Routing Policy

1. Return to the AWS Management Console, and navigate to the Amazon Route 53 dashboard.

2. Navigate to hosted zones, and select your newly-created zone domain name.

3. Create a record set with type set to developer. This will create a subdomain of `developer.yourdomainname.com`.

4. Select your Sydney load balancer. Change the routing policy to Weighted with a value of 50 and a type of Sydney. Leave the other values at their defaults. Click Create. You will now see your newly-created DNS entry.

5. Create another record set with type set to developer. This will add a new record with the same name you created earlier. Both records will work together.

6. Select your Sao Paulo load balancer. Change the routing policy to Weighted with a value of 50 and type of Sao Paulo. Leave the other values at their defaults. Click Create. You will now see your newly-created DNS entry.

7. Test your DNS by visiting `http://developer.yourdomainname.com` and refreshing the page. You should be accessing the Sydney server 50 percent of the time and the Sao Paulo server the other 50 percent of the time.

You have now created a weighted DNS routing policy. You can continue to experiment with other routing policies by following the documentation at `http://docs.aws.amazon .com/Route53/latest/DeveloperGuide/routing-policy.html`.

EXERCISE 9.5

Create a Hosted Zone for Amazon Virtual Private Cloud (Amazon VPC)

Amazon VPC details are covered in Chapter 4, "Amazon Virtual Private Cloud (Amazon VPC)."

Create a Private Hosted Zone

1. Return to the AWS Management Console, and navigate to the Amazon Route 53 dashboard.

2. Create a hosted zone, and enter your private domain name.

3. Select the default Amazon VPC that you used in Exercise 9.2 to deploy the first server in the Asia Pacific (Sydney) region. Click Create. This will create a new zone file.

Verify Amazon VPC Configuration

4. Return to the AWS Management Console, and change your region to Asia Pacific (Sydney).

5. In the Amazon VPC dashboard, choose your Amazon VPC.

6. Click on the default Amazon VPC from the list. Ensure that both DNS resolution and DNS host names are enabled. These settings need to use private hosted zones.

Create Resource Record Sets

7. Return to the AWS Management Console, and navigate to the Amazon Route 53 dashboard.

8. Select your newly-created private zone domain name, and create a record set.

9. Enter the name you want to give to your Amazon EC2 instance (for example, **webserver1**), and select IPv4 address with no alias.

10. Enter the internal IP address of your Amazon EC2 instance that you noted in Exercise 9.2.

11. Leave your routing policy set to Simple, and click Create.

Connect to Your Amazon EC2 Instance

12. On the Amazon EC2 instances screen, wait until you see your virtual machine's instance state as running. Copy the public IP address to your clipboard.

13. Using an SSH client of your choice, connect to your Amazon EC2 instance using the public IP address, the user name ec2-user, and your private key. For example, if you're using Terminal in OSX, you would type the following command:

    ```
    ssh ec2-user@publicipaddresshere -i MyPrivateKey.pem
    ```

14. When prompted about the authenticity of the host, type **Yes** and continue. You should now be connected to your Amazon EC2 instance.

15. While you're logged in to your Amazon EC2 instance, run the following command to check if the host names in Amazon Route 53 are resolving:

   `nslookup webserver1.yourprivatehostedzone.com`

16. You should receive a non-authoritative answer with the host name and IP address for the record set that you created in Amazon Route 53.

You have now created a private hosted zone in Amazon Route 53 and associated it with an Amazon VPC. You can continue to add instances in Amazon VPC and create resource record sets for them in Amazon Route 53. These new instances would be able to inter-communicate with the instances in the same Amazon VPC using the domain name that you created.

Remember to delete your Amazon EC2 instances and Elastic Load Balancing load balancers after you've finished experimenting with your different routing policies. You may also want to delete the zone if you are no longer using it.

Review Questions

1. Which type of record is commonly used to route traffic to an IPv6 address?

    A. An A record

    B. A CNAME

    C. An AAAA record

    D. An MX record

2. Where do you register a domain name?

    A. With your local government authority

    B. With a domain registrar

    C. With InterNIC directly

    D. With the Internet Assigned Numbers Authority (IANA)

3. You have an application that for legal reasons must be hosted in the United States when U.S. citizens access it. The application must be hosted in the European Union when citizens of the EU access it. For all other citizens of the world, the application must be hosted in Sydney. Which routing policy should you choose in order to achieve this?

    A. Latency-based routing

    B. Simple routing

    C. Geolocation routing

    D. Failover routing

4. Which type of DNS record should you use to resolve an IP address to a domain name?

    A. An A record

    B. A C Name

    C. An SPF record

    D. A PTR record

5. You host a web application across multiple AWS regions in the world, and you need to configure your DNS so that your end users will get the fastest network performance possible. Which routing policy should you apply?

    A. Geolocation routing

    B. Latency-based routing

    C. Simple routing

    D. Weighted routing

6. Which DNS record should you use to configure the transmission of email to your intended mail server?

    A. SPF records

    B. A records

    C. MX records

    D. SOA record

7. Which DNS records are commonly used to stop email spoofing and spam?

    A. MX records

    B. SPF records

    C. A records

    D. C names

8. You are rolling out A and B test versions of a web application to see which version results in the most sales. You need 10 percent of your traffic to go to version A, 10 percent to go to version B, and the rest to go to your current production version. Which routing policy should you choose to achieve this?

    A. Simple routing

    B. Weighted routing

    C. Geolocation routing

    D. Failover routing

9. Which DNS record must all zones have by default?

    A. SPF

    B. TXT

    C. MX

    D. SOA

10. Your company has its primary production site in Western Europe and its DR site in the Asia Pacific. You need to configure DNS so that if your primary site becomes unavailable, you can fail DNS over to the secondary site. Which DNS routing policy would best achieve this?

    A. Weighted routing

    B. Geolocation routing

    C. Simple routing

    D. Failover routing

11. Which type of DNS record should you use to resolve a domain name to another domain name?

    A. An A record

    B. A CNAME record

    C. An SPF record

    D. A PTR record

12. Which is a function that Amazon Route 53 does not perform?

    A. Domain registration

    B. DNS service

    C. Load balancing

    D. Health checks

13. Which DNS record can be used to store human-readable information about a server, network, and other accounting data with a host?

A. A TXT record

B. An MX record

C. An SPF record

D. A PTR record

14. Which resource record set would not be allowed for the hosted zone `example.com`?

A. `www.example.com`

B. `www.aws.example.com`

C. `www.example.ca`

D. `www.beta.example.com`

15. Which port number is used to serve requests by DNS?

A. 22

B. 53

C. 161

D. 389

16. Which protocol is primarily used by DNS to serve requests?

A. Transmission Control Protocol (TCP)

B. Hyper Text Transfer Protocol (HTTP)

C. File Transfer Protocol (FTP)

D. User Datagram Protocol (UDP)

17. Which protocol is used by DNS when response data size exceeds 512 bytes?

A. Transmission Control Protocol (TCP)

B. Hyper Text Transfer Protocol (HTTP)

C. File Transfer Protocol (FTP)

D. User Datagram Protocol (UDP)

18. What are the different hosted zones that can be created in Amazon Route 53?

1. Public hosted zone

2. Global hosted zone

3. Private hosted zone

A. 1 and 2

B. 1 and 3

C. 2 and 3

D. 1, 2, and 3

19. Amazon Route 53 cannot route queries to which AWS resource?

    A. Amazon CloudFront distribution

    B. Elastic Load Balancing load balancer

    C. Amazon EC2

    D. AWS OpsWorks

20. When configuring Amazon Route 53 as your DNS service for an existing domain, which is the first step that needs to be performed?

    A. Create hosted zones.

    B. Create resource record sets.

    C. Register a domain with Amazon Route 53.

    D. Transfer domain registration from current registrar to Amazon Route 53.

Chapter

10

Amazon ElastiCache

THE AWS CERTIFIED SOLUTIONS ARCHITECT ASSOCIATE EXAM OBJECTIVES COVERED IN THIS CHAPTER MAY INCLUDE, BUT ARE NOT LIMITED TO, THE FOLLOWING:

Domain 1.0: Designing highly available, cost-efficient, fault-tolerant, and scalable systems

✓ **Identify and recognize cloud architecture considerations, such as fundamental components and effective designs.**

Content may include the following:

- Planning and design
- Architectural trade-off decisions
- Best practices for AWS architecture
- Elasticity and scalability

Domain 3.0: Data Security

✓ **3.1   Recognize and implement secure practices for optimum cloud deployment and maintenance.**

Content may include the following:

- AWS administration and security services

✓ **3.2   Recognize critical disaster recovery techniques and their implementation.**

Introduction

This chapter focuses on building high-performance applications using in-memory caching technologies and Amazon ElastiCache. By using the Amazon ElastiCache service, you can offload the heavy lifting involved in the deployment and operation of cache environments running Memcached or Redis. It focuses on key topics you need to understand for the exam, including:

- How to improve application performance using caching
- How to launch cache environments in the cloud
- What are the basic differences and use cases for Memcached and Redis?
- How to scale your cluster vertically
- How to scale your Memcached cluster horizontally using additional cache nodes
- How to scale your Redis cluster horizontally using replication groups
- How to back up and recover your Redis cluster
- How to apply a layered security model

In-Memory Caching

One of the common characteristics of a successful application is a fast and responsive user experience. Research has shown that users will get frustrated and leave a website or app when it is slow to respond. In 2007, testing of Amazon.com's retail site showed that for every 100ms increase in load times, sales decreased by 1%. Round-trips back and forth to a database and its underlying storage can add significant delays and are often the top contributor to application latency.

Caching frequently-used data is one of the most important performance optimizations you can make in your applications. Compared to retrieving data from an in-memory cache, querying a database is an expensive operation. By storing or moving frequently accessed data in-memory, application developers can significantly improve the performance and responsiveness of read-heavy applications. For example, the application session state for a large website can be stored in an in-memory caching engine, instead of storing the session data in the database.

For many years, developers have been building applications that use cache engines like Memcached or Redis to store data in-memory to get blazing fast application performance. Memcached is a simple-to-use in-memory key/value store that can be used to store arbitrary types of data. It is one of the most popular cache engines. Redis is a flexible in-memory data structure store that can be used as a cache, database, or even as a message broker. Amazon ElastiCache allows developers to easily deploy and manage cache environments running either Memcached or Redis.

Amazon ElastiCache

Amazon ElastiCache is a web service that simplifies the setup and management of distributed in-memory caching environments. This service makes it easy and cost effective to provide a high-performance and scalable caching solution for your cloud applications. You can use Amazon ElastiCache in your applications to speed the deployment of cache clusters and reduce the administration required for a distributed cache environment.

With Amazon ElastiCache, you can choose from a Memcached or Redis protocol-compliant cache engine and quickly launch a cluster within minutes. Because Amazon ElastiCache is a managed service, you can start using the service today with very few or no modifications to your existing applications that use Memcached or Redis. Because Amazon ElastiCache is protocol-compliant with both of these engines, you only need to change the endpoint in your configuration files.

Using Amazon ElastiCache, you can implement any number of caching patterns. The most common pattern is the cache-aside pattern depicted in Figure 10.1. In this scenario, the app server checks the cache first to see if it contains the data it needs. If the data does not exist in the cache node, it will query the database and serialize and write the query results to the cache. The next user request will then be able to read the data directly from the cache instead of querying the database.

While it is certainly possible to build and manage a cache cluster yourself on Amazon Elastic Compute Cloud (Amazon EC2), Amazon ElastiCache allows you to offload the heavy lifting of installation, patch management, and monitoring to AWS so you can focus on your application instead. Amazon ElastiCache also provides a number of features to enhance the reliability of critical deployments. While it is rare, the underlying Amazon EC2 instances can become impaired. Amazon ElastiCache can automatically detect and recover from the failure of a cache node. With the Redis engine, Amazon ElastiCache makes it easy to set up read replicas and fail over from the primary to a replica in the event of a problem.

FIGURE 10.1 Common caching architecture

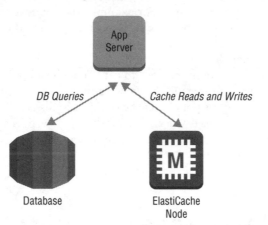

Data Access Patterns

Retrieving a flat key from an in-memory cache will always be faster than the most optimized database query. You should evaluate the access pattern of the data before you decide to store it in cache. A good example of something to cache is the list of products in a catalog. For a busy website, the list of items could be retrieved thousands of times per second. While it makes sense to cache the most heavily requested items, you can also benefit from caching items that are not frequently requested.

There are also some data items that should not be cached. For example, if you generate a unique page every request, you probably should not cache the page results. However, even though the page changes every time, it does make sense to cache the components of the page that do not change.

Cache Engines

Amazon ElastiCache allows you to quickly deploy clusters of two different types of popular cache engines: Memcached and Redis. At a high level, Memcached and Redis may seem similar, but they support a variety of different use cases and provide different functionality.

Memcached   Memcached provides a very simple interface that allows you to write and read objects into in-memory key/value data stores. With Amazon ElastiCache, you can elastically grow and shrink a cluster of Memcached nodes to meet your demands. You can partition your cluster into shards and support parallelized operations for very high performance throughput. Memcached deals with objects as blobs that can be retrieved using a unique key. What you put into the object is up to you, and it is typically the serialized results from a database query. This could be simple string values or binary data.

Amazon ElastiCache supports a number of recent versions of Memcached. As of early 2016, the service supports Memcached version 1.4.24, and also older versions going back to 1.4.5. When a new version of Memcached is released, Amazon ElastiCache simplifies the upgrade process by allowing you to spin up a new cluster with the latest version.

Redis   In late 2013, Amazon ElastiCache added support to deploy Redis clusters. At the time of this writing, the service supports the deployment of Redis version 2.8.24, and also a number of older versions. Beyond the object support provided in Memcached, Redis supports a rich set of data types likes strings, lists, and sets.

Unlike Memcached, Redis supports the ability to persist the in-memory data onto disk. This allows you to create snapshots that back up your data and then recover or replicate from the backups. Redis clusters also can support up to five read replicas to offload read requests. In the event of failure of the primary node, a read replica can be promoted and become the new master using Multi-AZ replication groups.

Redis also has advanced features that make it easy to sort and rank data. Some common use cases include building a leaderboard for a mobile application or serving as a high-speed message broker in a distributed system. With a Redis cluster, you can leverage a publish and subscribe messaging abstraction that allows you to decouple the components of your applications. A publish and subscribe messaging architecture gives you the flexibility to change how you consume the messages in the future without affecting the component that is producing the messages in the first place.

Nodes and Clusters

Each deployment of Amazon ElastiCache consists of one or more *nodes* in a *cluster*. There are many different types of nodes available to choose from based on your use case and the necessary resources. A single Memcached cluster can contain up to 20 nodes. Redis clusters are always made up of a single node; however, multiple clusters can be grouped into a *Redis replication group.*

The individual node types are derived from a subset of the Amazon EC2 instance type families, like t2, m3, and r3. The specific node types may change over time, but today they range from a t2.micro node type with 555MB of memory up to an r3.8xlarge with 237GB of memory, with many choices in between. The t2 cache node family is ideal for development and low-volume applications with occasional bursts, but certain features may not be available. The m3 family is a good blend of compute and memory, while the r3 family is optimized for memory-intensive workloads.

Depending on your needs, you may choose to have a few large nodes or many smaller nodes in your cluster or replication group. As demand for your application changes, you may also add or remove nodes from time to time. Each node type comes with a preconfigured amount of memory, with a small amount of the memory allocated to the caching engine and operating system itself.

Design for Failure

While it is unlikely, you should plan for the potential failure of an individual cache node. For Memcached clusters, you can decrease the impact of the failure of a cache node by using a larger number of nodes with a smaller capacity, instead of a few large nodes.

In the event that Amazon ElastiCache detects the failure of a node, it will provision a replacement and add it back to the cluster. During this time, your database will experience increased load, because any requests that would have been cached will now need to be read from the database. For Redis clusters, Amazon ElastiCache will detect failure and replace the primary node. If a Multi-AZ replication group is enabled, a read replica can be automatically promoted to primary.

Memcached Auto Discovery

For Memcached clusters partitioned across multiple nodes, Amazon ElastiCache supports *Auto Discovery* with the provided client library. Auto Discovery simplifies your application code by no longer needing awareness of the infrastructure topology of the cache cluster in your application layer.

Using Auto Discovery

The Auto Discovery client gives your applications the ability to identify automatically all of the nodes in a cache cluster and to initiate and maintain connections to all of these nodes. The Auto Discovery client is available for .NET, Java, and PHP platforms.

Scaling

Amazon ElastiCache allows you to adjust the size of your environment to meet the needs of workloads as they evolve over time. Adding additional cache nodes allows you to easily expand horizontally and meet higher levels of read or write performance. You can also select different classes of cache nodes to scale vertically.

Horizontal Scaling   Amazon ElastiCache also adds additional functionality that allows you to scale horizontally the size of your cache environment. This functionality differs depending on the cache engine you have selected. With Memcached, you can partition your data and scale horizontally to 20 nodes or more. With Auto Discovery, your application can discover Memcached nodes that are added or removed from a cluster.

A Redis cluster consists of a single cache node that is handling read and write transactions. Additional clusters can be created and grouped into a Redis replication group. While you can only have one node handling write commands, you can have up to five read replicas handling read-only requests.

Vertical Scaling   Support for vertical scaling is more limited with Amazon ElastiCache. If you like to change the cache node type and scale the compute resources vertically, the service does not directly allow you to resize your cluster in this manner. You can, however, quickly spin up a new cluster with the desired cache node types and start redirecting traffic to the new cluster. It's important to understand that a new Memcached cluster always starts empty, while a Redis cluster can be initialized from a backup.

Replication and Multi-AZ

Replication is a useful technique to provide rapid recovery in the event of a node failure, and also to serve up very high volumes of read queries beyond the capabilities of a single node. Amazon ElastiCache clusters running Redis support both of these design requirements. Unlike Redis, cache clusters running Memcached are standalone in-memory services without any redundant data protection services.

Cache clusters running Redis support the concept of *replication groups*. A replication group consists of up to six clusters, with five of them designated as read replicas. This allows you to scale horizontally by writing code in your application to offload reads to one of the five clones (see Figure 10.2).

FIGURE 10.2   Redis replication group

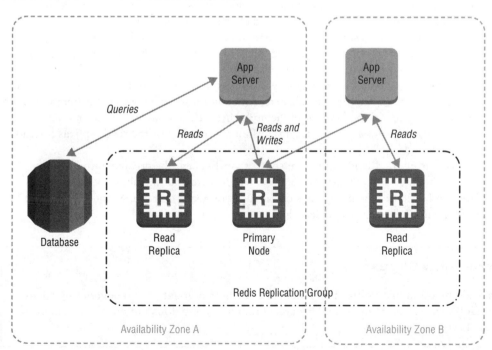

Multi-AZ Replication Groups

You can also create a *Multi-AZ replication group* that allows you to increase availability and minimize the loss of data. Multi-AZ simplifies the process of dealing with a failure by automating the replacement and failover from the primary node.

In the event the primary node fails or can't be reached, Multi-AZ will select and promote a read replica to become the new primary, and a new node will be provisioned to replace the failed one. Amazon ElastiCache will then update the Domain Name System (DNS) entry of the new primary node to allow your application to continue processing without any configuration change and with only a short disruption.

Understand That Replication Is Asynchronous

It's important to keep in mind that replication between the clusters is performed asynchronously and there will be a small delay before data is available on all cluster nodes.

Backup and Recovery

Amazon ElastiCache clusters running Redis allow you to persist your data from in-memory to disk and create a *snapshot*. Each snapshot is a full clone of the data that can be used to recover to a specific point in time or to create a copy for other purposes. Snapshots cannot be created for clusters using the Memcached engine because it is a purely in-memory key/value store and always starts empty. Amazon ElastiCache uses the native backup capabilities of Redis and will generate a standard Redis database backup file that gets stored in Amazon Simple Storage Service (Amazon S3).

Snapshots require compute and memory resources to perform and can potentially have a performance impact on heavily used clusters. Amazon ElastiCache will try different backup techniques depending on the amount of memory currently available. A best practice is to set up a replication group and perform a snapshot against one of the read replicas instead of the primary node.

In addition to manually initiated snapshots, snapshots can be created automatically based on a schedule. You can also configure a window for the snapshot operation to be completed and specify how many days of backups you want to store. Manual snapshots are stored indefinitely until you delete them.

Backup Redis Clusters

Use a combination of automatic and manual snapshots to meet your recovery objectives for your Redis cluster. Memcached is purely in-memory and does not have native backup capabilities.

Whether the snapshot was created automatically or manually, the snapshot can then be used to create a new cluster at any time. By default, the new cluster will have the same configuration as the source cluster, but you can override these settings. You can also restore from an RDB file generated from any other compatible Redis cluster.

Access Control

Access to your Amazon ElastiCache cluster is controlled primarily by restricting inbound network access to your cluster. Inbound network traffic is restricted through the use of security groups. Each security group defines one or more inbound rules that restrict the source traffic. When deployed inside of a Virtual Private Cloud (VPC), each node will be issued a private IP address within one or more subnets that you select. Individual nodes can never be accessed from the Internet or from Amazon EC2 instances outside the VPC. You can further restrict network ingress at the subnet level by modifying the network Access Control Lists (ACLs).

Access to manage the configuration and infrastructure of the cluster is controlled separately from access to the actual Memcached or Redis service endpoint. Using the AWS Identity and Access Management (IAM) service, you can define policies that control which AWS users can manage the Amazon ElastiCache infrastructure itself.

Some of the key actions an administrator can perform include `CreateCacheCluster`, `ModifyCacheCluster`, or `DeleteCacheCluster`. Redis clusters also support `CreateReplicationGroup` and `CreateSnapshot` actions, among others.

Summary

In this chapter, you learned about caching environments within the cloud using Amazon ElastiCache. You can quickly launch clusters running Memcached or Redis to store frequently used data in-memory. Caching can speed up the response time of your applications, reduce load on your back-end data stores, and improve the user experience.

With Amazon ElastiCache, you can offload the administrative tasks for provisioning and operating clusters and focus on the application. Each cache *cluster* contains one or more *nodes*. Select from a range of *node types* to give the right mix of compute and memory resources for your use case.

You can expand both Memcached and Redis clusters vertically by selecting a larger or smaller node type to match your needs. With Amazon ElastiCache and the Memcached engine, you can also scale your cluster horizontally by adding or removing nodes. With Amazon ElastiCache and the Redis engine, you can also scale horizontally by creating a *replication group* that will automatically replicate across multiple read replicas.

Streamline your backup and recovery process for Redis clusters with Amazon ElastiCache's consistent operational model. While Memcached clusters are in-memory only and cannot be persisted, Redis clusters support both automated and manual *snapshots*. A snapshot can then be restored to recover from a failure or to clone an environment.

You can secure your cache environments at the network level with security groups and network ACLs, and at the infrastructure level using IAM policies. Security groups will serve as your primary access control mechanism to restrict inbound access for active clusters.

You should analyze your data usage patterns and identify frequently run queries or other expensive operations that could be candidates for caching. You can relieve pressure from your database by offloading read requests to the cache tier. Data elements that are accessed on every page load, or with every request but do not change, are often prime candidates for caching. Even data that changes frequently can often benefit from being cached with very large request volumes.

Exam Essentials

Know how to use Amazon ElastiCache.   Improve the performance of your application by deploying Amazon ElastiCache clusters as part of your application and offloading read requests for frequently accessed data. Use the cache-aside pattern in your application first to check the cache for your query results before checking the database.

Understand when to use a specific cache engine.   Amazon ElastiCache gives you the choice of cache engine to suit your requirements. Use Memcached when you need a simple, in-memory object store that can be easily partitioned and scaled horizontally. Use Redis when you need to back up and restore your data, need many clones or read replicas, or are looking for advanced functionality like sort and rank or leaderboards that Redis natively supports.

Understand how to scale a Redis cluster horizontally.   An Amazon ElastiCache cluster running Redis can be scaled horizontally first by creating a replication group, then by creating additional clusters and adding them to the replication group.

Understand how to scale a Memcached cluster horizontally.   An Amazon ElastiCache cluster running Memcached can be scaled horizontally by adding or removing additional cache nodes to the cluster. The Amazon ElastiCache client library supports Auto Discovery and can discover new nodes added or removed from the cluster without having to hardcode the list of nodes.

Know how to back up your Amazon ElastiCache cluster.   You can create a snapshot to back up your Amazon ElastiCache clusters running the Redis engine. Snapshots can be created automatically on a daily basis or manually on demand. Amazon ElastiCache clusters running Memcached do not support backup and restore natively.

Exercises

In this section, you will create a cache cluster using Amazon ElastiCache, expand the cluster with additional nodes, and finally create a replication group with an Amazon ElastiCache Redis cluster.

EXERCISE 10.1

Create an Amazon ElastiCache Cluster Running Memcached

In this exercise, you will create an Amazon ElastiCache cluster using the Memcached engine.

1. While signed into the AWS Management Console, open the Amazon ElastiCache service dashboard.

2. Begin the launch and configuration process to create a new Amazon ElastiCache cluster.

3. Select the Memcached cache engine, and configure the cluster name, number of nodes, and node type.

4. Optionally configure the security group and maintenance window as needed.

5. Review the cluster configuration, and begin provisioning the cluster.

6. Connect to the cluster with any Memcached client using the DNS name of the cluster.

You have now created your first Amazon ElastiCache cluster.

EXERCISE 10.2

Expand the Size of a Memcached Cluster

In this exercise, you will expand the size of an existing Amazon ElastiCache Memcached cluster.

1. Launch a Memcached cluster using the steps defined in Exercise 10.1.

2. Go to the Amazon ElastiCache dashboard, and view the details of your existing cluster.

3. View the list of nodes currently provisioned, and then add one additional node by increasing the number of nodes.

4. Apply the configuration change, and wait for the new node to finish the provisioning process.

5. Verify that the new node has been created, and connect to the node using a Memcached client.

In this exercise, you have horizontally scaled an existing Amazon ElastiCache cluster by adding a cache node.

EXERCISE 10.3

Create an Amazon ElastiCache Cluster and Redis Replication Group

In this exercise, you will create an Amazon ElastiCache cluster using Redis nodes, create a replication group, and set up a read replica.

1. Sign in to the AWS Management Console, and navigate to the Amazon ElastiCache service dashboard.

2. Begin the configuration and launch process for a new Amazon ElastiCache cluster.

3. Select the Redis cache engine, and then configure a replication group and the node type.

4. Configure a read replica by setting the number of read replicas to 1, and verify that Enable Replication and Multi-AZ are selected.

5. Adjust the Availability Zones for the primary and read replica clusters, security groups, and maintenance window, as needed.

6. Review the cluster configuration, and begin provisioning the cluster.

7. Connect to the primary node and the read replica node with a Redis client library. Perform a simple set operation on the primary node, and then perform a get operation with the same key on the replica.

You have now created an Amazon ElastiCache cluster using the Redis engine and configured a read replica.

Review Questions

1. Which of the following objects are good candidates to store in a cache? (Choose 3 answers)

    A. Session state

    B. Shopping cart

    C. Product catalog

    D. Bank account balance

2. Which of the following cache engines are supported by Amazon ElastiCache? (Choose 2 answers)

    A. MySQL

    B. Memcached

    C. Redis

    D. Couchbase

3. How many nodes can you add to an Amazon ElastiCache cluster running Memcached?

    A. 1

    B. 5

    C. 20

    D. 100

4. How many nodes can you add to an Amazon ElastiCache cluster running Redis?

    A. 1

    B. 5

    C. 20

    D. 100

5. An application currently uses Memcached to cache frequently used database queries. Which steps are required to migrate the application to use Amazon ElastiCache with minimal changes? (Choose 2 answers)

    A. Recompile the application to use the Amazon ElastiCache libraries.

    B. Update the configuration file with the endpoint for the Amazon ElastiCache cluster.

    C. Configure a security group to allow access from the application servers.

    D. Connect to the Amazon ElastiCache nodes using Secure Shell (SSH) and install the latest version of Memcached.

6. How can you back up data stored in Amazon ElastiCache running Redis? (Choose 2 answers)

    A. Create an image of the Amazon Elastic Compute Cloud (Amazon EC2) instance.

    B. Configure automatic snapshots to back up the cache environment every night.

    C.   Create a snapshot manually.

    D.   Redis clusters cannot be backed up.

7. How can you secure an Amazon ElastiCache cluster? (Choose 3 answers)

    A.   Change the Memcached root password.

    B.   Restrict Application Programming Interface (API) actions using AWS Identity and Access Management (IAM) policies.

    C.   Restrict network access using security groups.

    D.   Restrict network access using a network Access Control List (ACL).

8. You are working on a mobile gaming application and are building the leaderboard feature to track the top scores across millions of users. Which AWS services are best suited for this use case?

    A.   Amazon Redshift

    B.   Amazon ElastiCache using Memcached

    C.   Amazon ElastiCache using Redis

    D.   Amazon Simple Storage Service (S3)

9. You have built a large web application that uses Amazon ElastiCache using Memcached to store frequent query results. You plan to expand both the web fleet and the cache fleet multiple times over the next year to accommodate increased user traffic. How do you minimize the amount of changes required when a scaling event occurs?

    A.   Configure AutoDiscovery on the client side

    B.   Configure AutoDiscovery on the server side

    C.   Update the configuration file each time a new cluster

    D.   Use an Elastic Load Balancer to proxy the requests

10. Which cache engines does Amazon ElastiCache support? (Choose 2 answers)

    A.   Memcached

    B.   Redis

    C.   Membase

    D.   Couchbase

Chapter

11

Additional Key Services

THE AWS CERTIFIED SOLUTIONS ARCHITECT ASSOCIATE EXAM TOPICS OBJECTIVES COVERED IN THIS CHAPTER MAY INCLUDE, BUT ARE NOT LIMITED TO, THE FOLLOWING:

Domain 1.0: Designing highly available, cost-efficient, fault-tolerant, and scalable systems

✓ **1.1   Identify and recognize cloud architecture considerations, such as fundamental components and effective designs.**

Content may include the following:

- How to design cloud services

- Planning and design

- Monitoring and logging

Domain 2.0: Implementation/Deployment

✓ **2.1   Identify the appropriate techniques and methods using Amazon Elastic Compute Cloud (Amazon EC2), Amazon Simple Storage Service (Amazon S3), AWS Elastic Beanstalk, AWS CloudFormation, AWS OpsWorks, Amazon Virtual Private Cloud (Amazon VPC), and AWS Identity and Access Management (IAM) to code and implement a cloud solution.**

Content may include the following:

- Configure services to support compliance requirements in the cloud

- Launch instances across the AWS global infrastructure

Domain 3.0: Data Security

✓ **3.1 Recognize and implement secure practices for optimum cloud deployment and maintenance.**

Content may include the following:

- AWS platform compliance
- AWS security attributes (customer workloads down to physical layer)
- AWS administration and security services
- AWS CloudTrail
- Ingress vs. egress filtering and which AWS cloud services and features fit
- Encryption solutions (e.g., key services)
- AWS Trusted Advisor

✓ **3.2 Recognize critical disaster recovery techniques and their implementation.**

Content may include the following:

- AWS Import/Export
- AWS Storage Gateway

Introduction

Because Solutions Architects are often involved in solutions across a wide variety of business verticals and use cases, it is important to understand the basics of all AWS cloud service offerings. This chapter focuses on additional key AWS services that you should know at a high level to be successful on the exam. These services are grouped into four categories: Storage and Content Delivery, Security, Analytics, and DevOps.

Before architecting any system, foundational practices that influence security should be in place; for example, providing directories that contain organizational information or how encryption protects data by way of rendering it unintelligible to unauthorized access. As a Solutions Architect, understanding the AWS cloud services available to support an organization's directories and encryption are important because they support objectives such as identity management or complying with regulatory obligations.

Architecting analytical solutions is critical because the amount of data that companies need to understand continues to grow to record sizes. AWS provides analytic services that can scale to very large data stores efficiently and cost-effectively. Understanding these services allows Solutions Architects to build virtually any big data application and support any workload regardless of volume, velocity, and variety of data.

DevOps becomes an important concept as the pace of innovation accelerates and customer needs rapidly evolve, forcing businesses to become increasingly agile. Time to market is key, and to facilitate overall business goals, IT departments need to be agile. Understanding the DevOps options that are available on AWS will help Solutions Architects meet the demands of agile businesses that need IT operations to deploy applications in a consistent, repeatable, and reliable manner.

Understanding these additional services will not only help in your exam preparation, but it will also help you establish a foundation for growing as a Solutions Architect on the AWS platform.

Storage and Content Delivery

This section covers two additional storage and content delivery services that are important for a Solutions Architect to understand: Amazon CloudFront and AWS Storage Gateway.

Amazon CloudFront

Amazon CloudFront is a global Content Delivery Network (CDN) service. It integrates with other AWS products to give developers and businesses an easy way to distribute content to end users with low latency, high data transfer speeds, and no minimum usage commitments.

Overview

A *Content Delivery Network (CDN)* is a globally distributed network of caching servers that speed up the downloading of web pages and other content. CDNs use Domain Name System (DNS) *geo-location* to determine the geographic location of each request for a web page or other content, then they serve that content from edge caching servers closest to that location instead of the original web server. A CDN allows you to increase the scalability of a website or mobile application easily in response to peak traffic spikes. In most cases, using a CDN is completely transparent—end users simply experience better website performance, while the load on your original website is reduced.

Amazon CloudFront is AWS CDN. It can be used to deliver your web content using Amazon's global network of *edge locations*. When a user requests content that you're serving with Amazon CloudFront, the user is routed to the edge location that provides the lowest latency (time delay), so content is delivered with the best possible performance. If the content is already in the edge location with the lowest latency, Amazon CloudFront delivers it immediately. If the content is not currently in that edge location, Amazon CloudFront retrieves it from the *origin server*, such as an Amazon Simple Storage Service (Amazon S3) bucket or a web server, which stores the original, definitive versions of your files.

Amazon CloudFront is optimized to work with other AWS cloud services as the origin server, including Amazon S3 buckets, Amazon S3 static websites, Amazon Elastic Compute Cloud (Amazon EC2), and Elastic Load Balancing. Amazon CloudFront also works seamlessly with any non-AWS origin server, such as an existing on-premises web server. Amazon CloudFront also integrates with Amazon Route 53.

Amazon CloudFront supports all content that can be served over HTTP or HTTPS. This includes any popular static files that are a part of your web application, such as HTML files, images, JavaScript, and CSS files, and also audio, video, media files, or software downloads. Amazon CloudFront also supports serving dynamic web pages, so it can actually be used to deliver your entire website. Finally, Amazon CloudFront supports media *streaming*, using both HTTP and RTMP.

Amazon CloudFront Basics

There are three core concepts that you need to understand in order to start using CloudFront: distributions, origins, and cache control. With these concepts, you can easily use CloudFront to speed up delivery of static content from your websites.

Distributions To use Amazon CloudFront, you start by creating a *distribution*, which is identified by a DNS domain name such as d111111abcdef8.cloudfront.net. To serve files from Amazon CloudFront, you simply use the distribution domain name in place of your website's domain name; the rest of the file paths stay unchanged. You can use the Amazon

CloudFront distribution domain name as-is, or you can create a user-friendly DNS name in your own domain by creating a CNAME record in Amazon Route 53 or another DNS service. The CNAME is automatically redirected to your Amazon CloudFront distribution domain name.

Origins   When you create a distribution, you must specify the DNS domain name of the *origin*—the Amazon S3 bucket or HTTP server—from which you want Amazon CloudFront to get the definitive version of your objects (web files). For example:

- **Amazon S3 bucket:** `myawsbucket.s3.amazonaws.com`

- **Amazon EC2 instance:** `ec2-203-0-113-25.compute-1.amazonaws.com`

- **Elastic Load Balancing load balancer:** `my-load-balancer-1234567890.us-west-2.elb.amazonaws.com`

- **Website URL:** `mywebserver.mycompanydomain.com`

Cache Control   Once requested and served from an edge location, objects stay in the cache until they expire or are evicted to make room for more frequently requested content. By default, objects expire from the cache after 24 hours. Once an object expires, the next request results in Amazon CloudFront forwarding the request to the origin to verify that the object is unchanged or to fetch a new version if it has changed.

Optionally, you can control how long objects stay in an Amazon CloudFront cache before expiring. To do this, you can choose to use Cache-Control headers set by your origin server or you can set the minimum, maximum, and default *Time to Live (TTL)* for objects in your Amazon CloudFront distribution.

You can also remove copies of an object from all Amazon CloudFront edge locations at any time by calling the *invalidation* Application Program Interface (API). This feature removes the object from every Amazon CloudFront edge location regardless of the expiration period you set for that object on your origin server. The invalidation feature is designed to be used in unexpected circumstances, such as to correct an error or to make an unanticipated update to a website, not as part of your everyday workflow.

Instead of invalidating objects manually or programmatically, it is a best practice to use a version identifier as part of the object (file) path name. For example:

- **Old file:** `assets/v1/css/narrow.css`

- **New file:** `assets/v2/css/narrow.css`

When using versioning, users always see the latest content through Amazon CloudFront when you update your site without using invalidation. Old versions will expire from the cache automatically.

Amazon CloudFront Advanced Features

CloudFront can do much more than simply serve static web files. To start using CloudFront's advanced features, you will need to understand how to use cache behaviors, and how to restrict access to sensitive content.

Dynamic Content, Multiple Origins, and Cache Behaviors   Serving static assets, such as described previously, is a common way to use a CDN. An Amazon CloudFront distribution, however, can easily be set up to serve dynamic content in addition to static content and to use more than one origin server. You control which requests are served by which origin and how requests are cached using a feature called *cache behaviors*.

A cache behavior lets you configure a variety of Amazon CloudFront functionalities for a given URL path pattern for files on your website. For example see Figure 11.1. One cache behavior applies to all PHP files in a web server (dynamic content), using the path pattern `*.php`, while another behavior applies to all JPEG images in another origin server (static content), using the path pattern `*.jpg`.

FIGURE 11.1   Delivering static and dynamic content

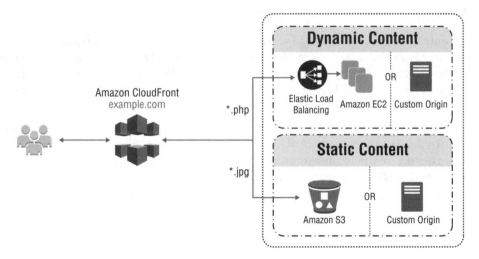

The functionality you can configure for each cache behavior includes the following:

- The path pattern
- Which origin to forward your requests to
- Whether to forward query strings to your origin
- Whether accessing the specified files requires signed URLs
- Whether to require HTTPS access
- The amount of time that those files stay in the Amazon CloudFront cache (regardless of the value of any Cache-Control headers that your origin adds to the files)

Cache behaviors are applied in order; if a request does not match the first path pattern, it drops down to the next path pattern. Normally the last path pattern specified is * to match all files.

Whole Website   Using cache behaviors and multiple origins, you can easily use Amazon CloudFront to serve your whole website and to support different behaviors for different client devices.

Private Content   In many cases, you may want to restrict access to content in Amazon CloudFront to only selected requestors, such as paid subscribers or to applications or users in your company network. Amazon CloudFront provides several mechanisms to allow you to serve private content. These include:

Signed URLs   Use URLs that are valid only between certain times and optionally from certain IP addresses.

Signed Cookies   Require authentication via public and private key pairs.

Origin Access Identities (OAI)   Restrict access to an Amazon S3 bucket only to a special Amazon CloudFront user associated with your distribution. This is the easiest way to ensure that content in a bucket is only accessed by Amazon CloudFront.

Use Cases

There are several use cases where Amazon CloudFront is an excellent choice, including, but not limited to:

Serving the Static Assets of Popular Websites   Static assets such as images, CSS, and JavaScript traditionally make up the bulk of requests to typical websites. Using Amazon CloudFront will speed up the user experience and reduce load on the website itself.

Serving a Whole Website or Web Application   Amazon CloudFront can serve a whole website containing both dynamic and static content by using multiple origins, cache behaviors, and short TTLs for dynamic content.

Serving Content to Users Who Are Widely Distributed Geographically   Amazon CloudFront will improve site performance, especially for distant users, and reduce the load on your origin server.

Distributing Software or Other Large Files   Amazon CloudFront will help speed up the download of these files to end users.

Serving Streaming Media   Amazon CloudFront helps serve streaming media, such as audio and video.

There are also use cases where CloudFront is not appropriate, including:

All or Most Requests Come From a Single Location   If all or most of your requests come from a single geographic location, such as a large corporate campus, you will not take advantage of multiple edge locations.

All or Most Requests Come Through a Corporate VPN   Similarly, if your users connect via a corporate Virtual Private Network (VPN), even if they are distributed, user requests appear to CloudFront to originate from one or a few locations. These use cases will generally not see benefit from using Amazon CloudFront.

AWS Storage Gateway

AWS Storage Gateway is a service connecting an on-premises software appliance with cloud-based storage to provide seamless and secure integration between an organization's on-premises IT environment and AWS storage infrastructure. The service enables you to store data securely on the AWS cloud in a scalable and cost-effective manner. AWS Storage Gateway supports industry-standard storage protocols that work with your existing applications. It provides low-latency performance by caching frequently accessed data on-premises while encrypting and storing all of your data in Amazon S3 or Amazon Glacier.

Overview

AWS Storage Gateway's software appliance is available for download as a Virtual Machine (VM) image that you install on a host in your data center and then register with your AWS account through the AWS Management Console. The storage associated with the appliance is exposed as an iSCSI device that can be mounted by your on-premises applications.

There are three configurations for AWS Storage Gateway: Gateway-Cached volumes, Gateway-Stored volumes, and Gateway-Virtual Tape Libraries (VTL).

Gateway-Cached Volumes   *Gateway-Cached volumes* allow you to expand your local storage capacity into Amazon S3. All data stored on a Gateway-Cached volume is moved to Amazon S3, while recently read data is retained in local storage to provide low-latency access. While each volume is limited to a maximum size of 32TB, a single gateway can support up to 32 volumes for a maximum storage of 1 PB.

Point-in-time snapshots can be taken to back up your AWS Storage Gateway. These snapshots are performed incrementally, and only the data that has changed since the last snapshot is stored.

All Gateway-Cached volume data and snapshot data is transferred to Amazon S3 over encrypted Secure Sockets Layer (SSL) connections. It is encrypted at rest in Amazon S3 using Server-Side Encryption (SSE). However, you cannot directly access this data with the Amazon S3 API or other tools such as the Amazon S3 console; instead you must access it through the AWS Storage Gateway service.

Gateway-Stored Volumes   *Gateway-Stored volumes* allow you to store your data on your on-premises storage and asynchronously back up that data to Amazon S3. This provides low-latency access to all data, while also providing off-site backups taking advantage of the durability of Amazon S3. The data is backed up in the form of Amazon Elastic Block Store (Amazon EBS) snapshots. While each volume is limited to a maximum size of 16TB, a single gateway can support up to 32 volumes for a maximum storage of 512TB.

Similar to Gateway-Cached volumes, you can take snapshots of your Gateway-Stored volumes. The gateway stores these snapshots in Amazon S3 as *Amazon EBS snapshots*. When you take a new snapshot, only the data that has changed since your last snapshot is stored. You can initiate snapshots on a scheduled or one-time basis. Because these snapshots are stored as Amazon EBS snapshots, you can create a new Amazon EBS volume from a Gateway-Stored volume.

All Gateway-Stored volume data and snapshot data is transferred to Amazon S3 over encrypted SSL connections. It is encrypted at rest in Amazon S3 using SSE. However, you cannot access this data with the Amazon S3 API or other tools such as the Amazon S3 console.

If your on-premises appliance or even entire data center becomes unavailable, the data in AWS Storage Gateway can still be retrieved. If it's only the appliance that is unavailable, a new appliance can be launched in the data center and attached to the existing AWS Storage Gateway. A new appliance can also be launched in another data center or even on an Amazon EC2 instance on the cloud.

Gateway Virtual Tape Libraries (VTL)   Gateway-VTL offers a durable, cost-effective solution to archive your data on the AWS cloud. The VTL interface lets you leverage your existing tape-based backup application infrastructure to store data on virtual tape cartridges that you create on your Gateway-VTL.

A virtual tape is analogous to a physical tape cartridge, except the data is stored on the AWS cloud. Tapes are created blank through the console or programmatically and then filled with backed up data. A gateway can contain up to 1,500 tapes (1 PB) of total tape data. Virtual tapes appear in your gateway's VTL, a virtualized version of a physical tape library. Virtual tapes are discovered by your backup application using its standard media inventory procedure.

When your tape software ejects a tape, it is archived on a Virtual Tape Shelf (VTS) and stored in Amazon Glacier. You're allowed 1 VTS per AWS region, but multiple gateways in the same region can share a VTS.

Use Cases

There are several use cases where AWS Storage Gateway is an excellent choice, including, but not limited to:

- Gateway-Cached volumes enable you to expand local storage hardware to Amazon S3, allowing you to store much more data without drastically increasing your storage hardware or changing your storage processes.

- Gateway-Stored volumes provide seamless, asynchronous, and secure backup of your on-premises storage without new processes or hardware.

- Gateway-VTLs enable you to keep your current tape backup software and processes while storing your data more cost-effectively and simply on the cloud.

Security

Cloud security at AWS is the highest priority. AWS customers benefit from data centers and network architectures built to meet the requirements of the most security-sensitive organizations.

An advantage of the AWS cloud is that it allows customers to scale and innovate while maintaining a secure environment. Cloud security is much like security in your on-premises data centers, only without the costs of maintaining facilities and hardware. In the cloud, you don't have to manage physical servers or storage devices. Instead, you use software-based security tools to monitor and protect the flow of information into and of out of your cloud resources.

This section will focus on four AWS services that are directly related to the specific security purposes: AWS Directory Service for identity management, AWS Key Management Service (KMS), AWS CloudHSM for key management, and AWS CloudTrail for auditing.

AWS Directory Service

AWS Directory Service is a managed service offering that provides directories that contain information about your organization, including users, groups, computers, and other resources.

Overview

You can choose from three directory types:

- AWS Directory Service for Microsoft Active Directory (Enterprise Edition), also referred to as Microsoft AD

- Simple AD

- AD Connector

As a managed offering, AWS Directory Service is designed to reduce identity management tasks, thereby allowing you to focus more of your time and resources on your business. There is no need to build out your own complex, highly-available directory topology because each directory is deployed across multiple Availability Zones, and monitoring automatically detects and replaces domain controllers that fail. In addition, data replication and automated daily snapshots are configured for you. There is no software to install, and AWS handles all of the patching and software updates.

AWS Directory Service for Microsoft Active Directory (Enterprise Edition)   AWS Directory Service for Microsoft Active Directory (Enterprise Edition) is a managed *Microsoft Active Directory* hosted on the AWS cloud. It provides much of the functionality offered by Microsoft Active Directory plus integration with AWS applications. With the additional Active Directory functionality, you can, for example, easily set up trust relationships with your existing Active Directory domains to extend those directories to AWS cloud services.

Simple AD   Simple AD is a Microsoft Active Directory-compatible directory from AWS Directory Service that is powered by Samba 4. Simple AD supports commonly used Active Directory features such as user accounts, group memberships, domain-joining Amazon EC2 instances running Linux and Microsoft Windows, Kerberos-based Single Sign-On (SSO), and group policies. This makes it even easier to manage Amazon EC2 instances running Linux and Windows and deploy Windows applications on the AWS cloud.

Many of the applications and tools you use today that require Microsoft Active Directory support can be used with Simple AD. User accounts in Simple AD can also access AWS applications, such as Amazon WorkSpaces, Amazon WorkDocs, or Amazon WorkMail. They can also use AWS IAM roles to access the AWS Management Console and manage AWS resources. Finally, Simple AD provides daily automated snapshots to enable point-in-time recovery.

Note that you cannot set up trust relationships between Simple AD and other Active Directory domains. Other features not supported at the time of this writing by Simple AD include DNS dynamic update, schema extensions, Multi-Factor Authentication (MFA), communication over Lightweight Directory Access Protocol (LDAP), PowerShell AD cmdlets, and the transfer of *Flexible Single-Master Operations (FSMO)* roles.

AD Connector   AD Connector is a proxy service for connecting your on-premises Microsoft Active Directory to the AWS cloud without requiring complex directory synchronization or the cost and complexity of hosting a federation infrastructure.

AD Connector forwards sign-in requests to your Active Directory domain controllers for authentication and provides the ability for applications to query the directory for data. After setup, your users can use their existing corporate credentials to log on to AWS applications, such as Amazon WorkSpaces, Amazon WorkDocs, or Amazon WorkMail. With the proper IAM permissions, they can also access the AWS Management Console and manage AWS resources such as Amazon EC2 instances or Amazon S3 buckets. You can also use AD Connector to enable MFA by integrating it with your existing *Remote Authentication Dial-Up Service (RADIUS)*-based MFA infrastructure to provide an additional layer of security when users access AWS applications.

With AD Connector, you continue to manage your Active Directory as usual. For example, adding new users, adding new groups, or updating passwords are all accomplished using standard directory administration tools with your on-premises directory. Thus, in addition to providing a streamlined experience for your users, AD Connector enables consistent enforcement of your existing security policies, such as password expiration, password history, and account lockouts, whether users are accessing resources on-premises or on the AWS cloud.

Use Cases

AWS Directory Service provides multiple ways to use Microsoft Active Directory with other AWS cloud services. You can choose the directory service with the features you need at a cost that fits your budget.

AWS Directory Service for Microsoft Active Directory (Enterprise Edition)   This Directory Service is your best choice if you have more than 5,000 users and need a trust relationship set up between an AWS-hosted directory and your on-premises directories.

Simple AD   In most cases, Simple AD is the least expensive option and your best choice if you have 5,000 or fewer users and don't need the more advanced Microsoft Active Directory features.

AD Connector   AD Connector is your best choice when you want to use your existing on-premises directory with AWS cloud services.

AWS Key Management Service (KMS) and AWS CloudHSM

Key management is the management of *cryptographic keys* within a *cryptosystem*. This includes dealing with the generation, exchange, storage, use, and replacement of keys.

Overview

AWS offers two services that provide you with the ability to manage your own *symmetric* or *asymmetric* cryptographic keys:

- **AWS KMS:** A service enabling you to generate, store, enable/disable, and delete symmetric keys
- **AWS CloudHSM:** A service providing you with secure cryptographic key storage by making Hardware Security Modules (HSMs) available on the AWS cloud

AWS Key Management Service (AWS KMS)   *AWS KMS* is a managed service that makes it easy for you to create and control the encryption keys used to encrypt your data. AWS KMS lets you create keys that can never be exported from the service and that can be used to encrypt and decrypt data based on policies you define.

By using AWS KMS, you gain more control over access to data you encrypt. You can use the key management and cryptographic features directly in your applications or through AWS cloud services that are integrated with AWS KMS. Whether you are writing applications for AWS or using AWS cloud services, AWS KMS enables you to maintain control over who can use your keys and gain access to your encrypted data.

> **Customer Managed Keys**   AWS KMS uses a type of key called a *Customer Master Key (CMK)* to encrypt and decrypt data. CMKs are the fundamental resources that AWS KMS manages. They can be used inside of AWS KMS to encrypt or decrypt up to 4 KB of data directly. They can also be used to encrypt generated *data keys* that are then used to encrypt or decrypt larger amounts of data outside of the service. CMKs can never leave AWS KMS unencrypted, but data keys can leave the service unencrypted.

> **Data Keys**   You use data keys to encrypt large data objects within your own application outside AWS KMS. When you call GenerateDataKey, AWS KMS returns a plaintext version of the key and ciphertext that contains the key encrypted under the specified CMK. AWS KMS tracks which CMK was used to encrypt the data key. You use the plaintext data key in your application to encrypt data, and you typically store the encrypted key alongside your encrypted data. Security best practices suggest that you should remove the plaintext key from memory as soon as is practical after use. To decrypt data in your application, pass the encrypted data key to the Decrypt function. AWS KMS uses the

associated CMK to decrypt and retrieve your plaintext data key. Use the plaintext key to decrypt your data, and then remove the key from memory.

Envelope Encryption   AWS KMS uses *envelope encryption* to protect data. AWS KMS creates a data key, encrypts it under a CMK, and returns plaintext and encrypted versions of the data key to you. You use the plaintext key to encrypt data and store the encrypted key alongside the encrypted data. The key should be removed from memory as soon as is practical after use. You can retrieve a plaintext data key only if you have the encrypted data key and you have permission to use the corresponding master key.

Encryption Context   All AWS KMS cryptographic operations accept an optional key/value map of additional contextual information called an *encryption context*. The specified context must be the same for both the encrypt and decrypt operations or decryption will not succeed. The encryption context is logged, can be used for additional auditing, and is available as context in the AWS policy language for fine-grained policy-based authorization.

AWS CloudHSM   AWS CloudHSM helps you meet corporate, contractual, and regulatory compliance requirements for data security by using dedicated HSM appliances within the AWS cloud. An *HSM* is a hardware appliance that provides secure key storage and cryptographic operations within a tamper-resistant hardware module. HSMs are designed to securely store cryptographic key material and use the key material without exposing it outside the cryptographic boundary of the appliance.

The recommended configuration for using AWS CloudHSM is to use two HSMs configured in a high-availability configuration, as illustrated in Figure 11.2.

FIGURE 11.2   High availability CloudHSM architecture

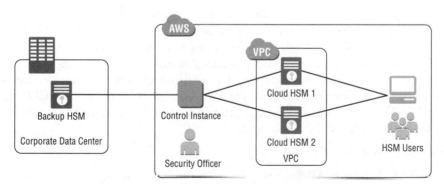

AWS CloudHSM allows you to protect your encryption keys within HSMs that are designed and validated to government standards for secure key management. You can securely generate, store, and manage the cryptographic keys used for data encryption in a way that ensures that only you have access to the keys. AWS CloudHSM helps you comply with strict key management requirements within the AWS cloud without sacrificing application performance.

Use Cases

The AWS key management services address several security needs that would require extensive effort to deploy and manage otherwise, including, but not limited to:

Scalable Symmetric Key Distribution   Symmetric encryption algorithms require that the same key be used for both encrypting and decrypting the data. This is problematic because transferring the key from the sender to the receiver must be done either through a known secure channel or some "out of band" process.

Government-Validated Cryptography   Certain types of data (for example, Payment Card Industry—PCI—or health information records) must be protected with cryptography that has been validated by an outside party as conforming to the algorithm(s) asserted by the claiming party.

AWS CloudTrail

AWS CloudTrail provides visibility into user activity by recording API calls made on your account. AWS CloudTrail records important information about each API call, including the name of the API, the identity of the caller, the time of the API call, the request parameters, and the response elements returned by the AWS service. This information helps you to track changes made to your AWS resources and to troubleshoot operational issues. AWS CloudTrail makes it easier to ensure compliance with internal policies and regulatory standards.

Overview

AWS CloudTrail captures AWS API calls and related events made by or on behalf of an AWS account and delivers log files to an Amazon S3 bucket that you specify. Optionally, you can configure AWS CloudTrail to deliver events to a log group monitored by Amazon CloudWatch Logs. You can also choose to receive Amazon Simple Notification Service (Amazon SNS) notifications each time a log file is delivered to your bucket. You can create a *trail* with the AWS CloudTrail console, the AWS Command Line Interface (CLI), or the AWS CloudTrail API. A trail is a configuration that enables logging of the AWS API activity and related events in your account.

You can create two types of trails:

A Trail That Applies to All Regions   When you create a trail that applies to all AWS regions, AWS CloudTrail creates the same trail in each region, records the log files in each region, and delivers the log files to the single Amazon S3 bucket (and optionally to the Amazon CloudWatch Logs log group) that you specify. This is the default option when you create a trail using the AWS CloudTrail console. If you choose to receive Amazon SNS notifications for log file deliveries, one Amazon SNS topic will suffice for all regions. If you choose to have AWS CloudTrail send events from a trail that applies to all regions to an Amazon CloudWatch Logs log group, events from all regions will be sent to the single log group.

A Trail That Applies to One Region   You specify a bucket that receives events only from that region. The bucket can be in any region that you specify. If you create additional individual trails that apply to specific regions, you can have those trails deliver event logs to a single Amazon S3 bucket.

By default, your log files are encrypted using Amazon S3 SSE. You can store your log files in your bucket for as long as you want, but you can also define Amazon S3 lifecycle rules to archive or delete log files automatically.

AWS CloudTrail typically delivers log files within 15 minutes of an API call. In addition, the service publishes new log files multiple times an hour, usually about every five minutes. These log files contain API calls from all of the account's services that support AWS CloudTrail.

   Enable AWS CloudTrail on all of your AWS accounts. Instead of configuring a trail for one region, you should enable trails for all regions.

Use Cases

AWS CloudTrail is beneficial for several use cases:

External Compliance Audits   Your business must demonstrate compliance to a set of regulations pertinent to some or all data being transmitted, processed, and stored within your AWS accounts. Events from AWS CloudTrail can be used to show the degree to which you are compliant with the regulations.

Unauthorized Access to Your AWS Account   AWS CloudTrail records all sign-on attempts to your AWS account, including AWS Management Console login attempts, AWS Software Development Kit (SDK) API calls, and AWS CLI API calls. Routine examination of AWS CloudTrail events will provide the needed information to determine if your AWS account is being targeted for unauthorized access.

Analytics

Analytics, and the associated big data that it requires, presents a unique list of challenges to a Solutions Architect. The big data must be ingested at a very high rate, stored in very high volume, and processed with a tremendous amount of compute. Often, the need to perform analytics on the big data is sporadic, with a great deal of compute infrastructure needed regularly for very small time periods. The cloud, with its easy access to compute and nearly limitless storage capacity, is ideally suited to address these analytics challenges. This section covers several AWS cloud services that will help you address analytics and big data issues on the exam.

Amazon Kinesis

Amazon Kinesis is a platform for handling massive streaming data on AWS, offering powerful services to make it easy to load and analyze streaming data and also providing the ability for you to build custom streaming data applications for specialized needs.

Overview

Amazon Kinesis is a streaming data platform consisting of three services addressing different real-time streaming data challenges:

- **Amazon Kinesis Firehose:** A service enabling you to load massive volumes of streaming data into AWS

- **Amazon Kinesis Streams:** A service enabling you to build custom applications for more complex analysis of streaming data in real time

- **Amazon Kinesis Analytics:** A service enabling you to easily analyze streaming data real time with standard SQL

Each of these services can scale to handle virtually limitless data streams.

Amazon Kinesis Firehose   *Amazon Kinesis Firehose* receives stream data and stores it in Amazon S3, Amazon Redshift, or *Amazon Elasticsearch.* You do not need to write any code; just create a delivery stream and configure the destination for your data. Clients write data to the stream using an AWS API call and the data is automatically sent to the proper destination. The various destination options are shown in Figure 11.3.

FIGURE 11.3   Amazon Kinesis Firehose

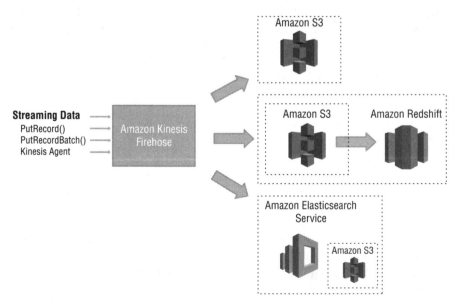

When configured to save a stream to Amazon S3, Amazon Kinesis Firehose sends the data directly to Amazon S3. For an Amazon Redshift destination, the data is first written to Amazon S3, and then an Amazon Redshift COPY command is executed to load the data into Amazon Redshift. Amazon Kinesis Firehose can also write data out to Amazon Elasticsearch, with the option to back the data up concurrently to Amazon S3.

Amazon Kinesis Streams   *Amazon Kinesis Streams* enable you to collect and process large streams of data records in real time. Using AWS SDKs, you can create an *Amazon Kinesis Streams application* that processes the data as it moves through the stream. Because response time for data intake and processing is in near real time, the processing is typically lightweight. Amazon Kinesis Streams can scale to support nearly limitless data streams by distributing incoming data across a number of *shards*. If any shard becomes too busy, it can be further divided into more shards to distribute the load further. The processing is then executed on consumers, which read data from the shards and run the Amazon Kinesis Streams application. This architecture is shown in Figure 11.4.

FIGURE 11.4   Amazon Kinesis Streams

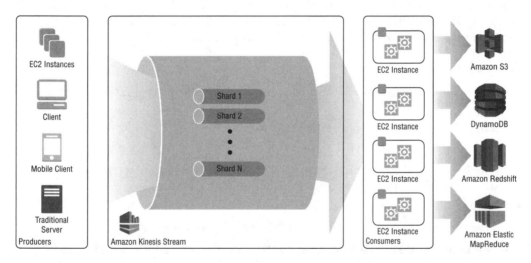

Amazon Kinesis Analytics   At the time of this writing, Amazon Kinesis Analytics has been announced but not yet released.

Use Cases

The Amazon Kinesis services support many strategic workloads that would otherwise require extensive effort to deploy and manage, including, but not limited to:

Data Ingestion   The first challenge with a huge stream of data is accepting it reliably. Whether it is user data from highly trafficked websites, input data from thousands of monitoring devices, or any other sources of huge streams, Amazon Kinesis Firehose is an excellent choice to ensure that all of your data is successfully stored in your AWS infrastructure.

Real-Time Processing of Massive Data Streams   Companies often need to act on knowledge gleaned from a big data stream right away, whether to feed a dashboard application, alter advertising strategies based on social media trends, allocate assets based on real-time situations, or a host of other scenarios. Amazon Kinesis Streams enables you to gather this knowledge from the data in your stream on a real-time basis.

It's good to remember that while Amazon Kinesis is ideally suited for ingesting and processing streams of data, it is less appropriate for batch jobs such as nightly *Extract, Transform, Load (ETL)* processes. For those types of workloads, consider AWS Data Pipeline, which is described later in this chapter.

Amazon Elastic MapReduce (Amazon EMR)

Amazon Elastic MapReduce (Amazon EMR) provides you with a fully managed, on-demand Hadoop framework. Amazon EMR reduces the complexity and up-front costs of setting up Hadoop and, combined with the scale of AWS, gives you the ability to spin up large Hadoop clusters instantly and start processing within minutes.

Overview

When you launch an Amazon EMR cluster, you specify several options, the most important being:

- The instance type of the nodes in your cluster

- The number of nodes in your cluster

- The version of Hadoop you want to run (Amazon EMR supports several recent versions of Apache Hadoop, and also several versions of MapR Hadoop.)

- Additional tools or applications like Hive, Pig, Spark, or Presto

There are two types of storage that can be used with Amazon EMR:

Hadoop Distributed File System (HDFS)   *HDFS* is the standard file system that comes with Hadoop. All data is replicated across multiple instances to ensure durability. Amazon EMR can use Amazon EC2 instance storage or Amazon EBS for HDFS. When a cluster is shut down, instance storage is lost and the data does not persist. HDFS can also make use of Amazon EBS storage, trading in the cost effectiveness of instance storage for the ability to shut down a cluster without losing data.

EMR File System (EMRFS)   *EMRFS* is an implementation of HDFS that allows clusters to store data on Amazon S3. EMRFS allows you to get the durability and low cost of Amazon S3 while preserving your data even if the cluster is shut down.

A key factor driving the type of storage a cluster uses is whether the cluster is persistent or transient. A *persistent cluster* continues to run 24×7 after it is launched. Persistent clusters are appropriate when continuous analysis is going to be run on the data. For persistent clusters, HDFS is a common choice. Persistent clusters take advantage of the low latency of HDFS, especially on instance storage, when constant operation means no data lost when shutting down a cluster. In other situations, big data workloads are frequently run inconsistently, and it can be cost-effective to turn the cluster off when not in use. Clusters that are started when needed and then immediately stopped when done are called *transient clusters*. EMRFS is well suited for transient clusters, as the data persists independent of the lifetime of the cluster. You can also choose to use a combination of local HDFS and EMRFS to meet your workload needs.

Because Amazon EMR is an instance of Apache Hadoop, you can use the extensive ecosystem of tools that work on top of Hadoop, such as Hive, Pig, and Spark. Many of these tools are natively supported and can be included automatically when you launch your cluster, while others can be installed through *bootstrap* actions.

Use Cases

Amazon EMR is well suited for a large number of use cases, including, but not limited to:

Log Processing   Amazon EMR can be used to process logs generated by web and mobile applications. Amazon EMR helps customers turn petabytes of unstructured or semi-structured data into useful insights about their applications or users.

Clickstream Analysis   Amazon EMR can be used to analyze *clickstream* data in order to segment users and understand user preferences. Advertisers can also analyze clickstreams and advertising impression logs to deliver more effective ads.

Genomics and Life Sciences   Amazon EMR can be used to process vast amounts of genomic data and other large scientific datasets quickly and efficiently. Processes that require years of compute can be completed in a day when scaled across large clusters.

AWS Data Pipeline

AWS Data Pipeline is a web service that helps you reliably process and move data between different AWS compute and storage services, and also on-premises data sources, at specified intervals. With AWS Data Pipeline, you can regularly access your data where it's stored, transform and process it at scale, and efficiently transfer the results to AWS services such as Amazon S3, Amazon Relational Database Service (Amazon RDS), Amazon DynamoDB, and Amazon EMR.

Overview

Everything in AWS Data Pipeline starts with the pipeline itself. A pipeline schedules and runs tasks according to the pipeline definition. The scheduling is flexible and can run every 15 minutes, every day, every week, and so forth.

The pipeline interacts with data stored in data nodes. Data nodes are locations where the pipeline reads input data or writes output data, such as Amazon S3, a MySQL database, or an Amazon Redshift cluster. Data nodes can be on AWS or on your premises.

The pipeline will execute *activities* that represent common scenarios, such as moving data from one location to another, running Hive queries, and so forth. Activities may require additional resources to run, such as an Amazon EMR cluster or an Amazon EC2 instance. In these situations, AWS Data Pipeline will automatically launch the required resources and tear them down when the activity is completed.

Distributed data flows often have dependencies; just because an activity is scheduled to run does not mean that there is data waiting to be processed. For situations like this, AWS Data Pipeline supports preconditions, which are conditional statements that must be true before an activity can run. These include scenarios such as whether an Amazon S3 key is present, whether an Amazon DynamoDB table contains any data, and so forth.

If an activity fails, retry is automatic. The activity will continue to retry up to the limit you configure. You can define actions to take in the event when the activity reaches that limit without succeeding.

Use Cases

AWS Data Pipeline can be used for virtually any batch mode ETL process. A simple example is shown in Figure 11.5.

FIGURE 11.5 Example pipeline

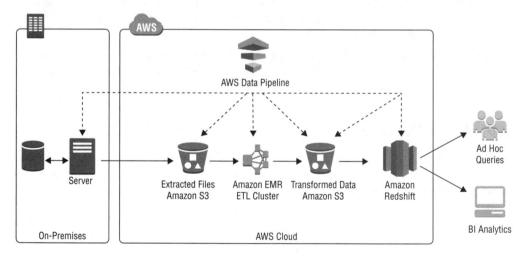

The pipeline in Figure 11.5 is performing the following workflow:

- Every hour an activity begins to extract log data from on-premises storage to Amazon S3. A precondition checks that there is data to be transferred before actually starting the activity.

- The next activity launches a transient Amazon EMR cluster that uses the extracted dataset as input, validates and transforms it, and then outputs the data to an Amazon S3 bucket.

- The final activity moves the transformed data from Amazon S3 to Amazon Redshift via an Amazon Redshift `COPY` command.

AWS Data Pipeline is best for regular batch processes instead of for continuous data streams; use Amazon Kinesis for data streams.

AWS Import/Export

One key challenge of big data on the AWS cloud is getting huge datasets to the cloud in the first place, or retrieving them back to on-premises when necessary. Regardless of how much bandwidth you configure out of your data center, there are times when there is more data to transfer than can move over the connection in a reasonable period of time. AWS Import/Export is a service that accelerates transferring large amounts of data into and out of AWS using physical storage appliances, bypassing the Internet. The data is copied to a device at the source (your data center or an AWS region), shipped via standard shipping mechanisms, and then copied to the destination (your data center or an AWS region).

Overview

AWS Import/Export has two features that support shipping data into and out of your AWS infrastructure: AWS Import/Export Snowball (AWS Snowball) and AWS Import/Export Disk.

AWS Snowball   AWS Snowball uses Amazon-provided shippable storage appliances shipped through UPS. Each AWS Snowball is protected by AWS KMS and made physically rugged to secure and protect your data while the device is in transit. At the time of this writing, AWS Snowballs come in two sizes: 50TB and 80TB, and the availability of each varies by region.

AWS Snowball provides the following features:

- You can import and export data between your on-premises data storage locations and Amazon S3.

- Encryption is enforced, protecting your data at rest and in physical transit.

- You don't have to buy or maintain your own hardware devices.

- You can manage your jobs through the AWS Snowball console.

- The AWS Snowball is its own shipping container, and the shipping label is an *E Ink display* that automatically shows the correct address when the AWS Snowball is ready to ship. You can drop it off with UPS, no box required.

With AWS Snowball, you can import or export terabytes or even petabytes of data.

AWS Import/Export Disk   AWS Import/Export Disk supports transfers data directly onto and off of storage devices you own using the Amazon high-speed internal network.

Important things to understand about AWS Import/Export Disk include:

- You can import your data into Amazon Glacier and Amazon EBS, in addition to Amazon S3.
- You can export data from Amazon S3.
- Encryption is optional and not enforced.
- You buy and maintain your own hardware devices.
- You can't manage your jobs through the AWS Snowball console.
- Unlike AWS Snowball, AWS Import/Export Disk has an upper limit of 16TB.

Use Cases

AWS Import/Export can be used for just about any situation where you have more data to move than you can get through your Internet connection in a reasonable time, including, but not limited to:

Storage Migration   When companies shut down a data center, they often need to move massive amounts of storage to another location. AWS Import/Export is a suitable technology for this requirement.

Migrating Applications   Migrating an application to the cloud often involves moving huge amounts of data. This can be accelerated using AWS Import/Export.

DevOps

As organizations created increasingly complex software applications, IT development teams evolved their software creation practices for more flexibility, moving from waterfall models to agile or lean development practices. This change also propagated to operations teams, which blurred the lines between traditional development and operations teams. AWS provides a flexible environment that facilitated the successes of organizations like Netflix, Airbnb, General Electric, and many others that embraced DevOps. This section reviews elements of AWS cloud services that support DevOps practices.

AWS OpsWorks

AWS OpsWorks is a configuration management service that helps you configure and operate applications using Chef. AWS OpsWorks will work with applications of any level of complexity and is independent of any particular architectural pattern. You can define an application's architecture and the specification of each component, including package installation, software configuration, and resources such as storage.

AWS OpsWorks supports both Linux or Windows servers, including existing Amazon EC2 instances or servers running in your own data center. This allows organizations to use a single configuration management service to deploy and operate applications across hybrid architectures.

Overview

Many solutions on AWS usually involve groups of resources, such as Amazon EC2 instances and Amazon RDS instances, which must be created and managed collectively. For example, these architectures typically require application servers, database servers, load balancers, and so on. This group of resources is typically called a *stack*. A simple application server stack might be arranged something like in Figure 11.6.

FIGURE 11.6   Simple application server stack

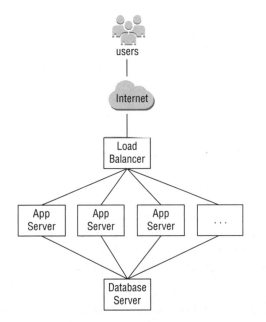

In addition to creating the instances and installing the necessary packages, you typically need a way to distribute applications to the application servers, monitor the stack's performance, manage security and permissions, and so on. AWS OpsWorks provides a simple and flexible way to create and manage stacks and applications. Figure 11.7 depicts how a simple application server stack might look with AWS OpsWorks. Although relatively simple, this stack shows the key AWS OpsWorks features.

FIGURE 11.7 Simple application server stack with AWS OpsWorks

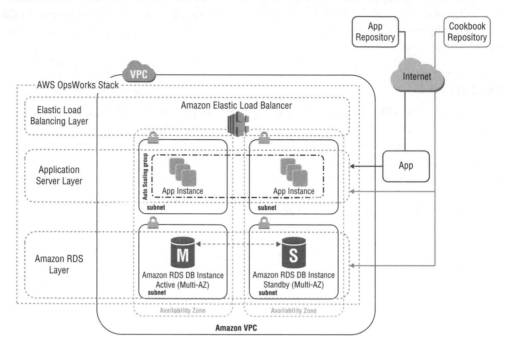

The *stack* is the core AWS OpsWorks component. It is basically a container for AWS resources—Amazon EC2 instances, Amazon RDS database instances, and so on—that have a common purpose and make sense to be logically managed together. The stack helps you manage these resources as a group and defines some default configuration settings, such as the Amazon EC2 instances' operating system and AWS region. If you want to isolate some stack components from direct user interaction, you can run the stack in an Amazon Virtual Private Cloud (Amazon VPC). Each stack lets you grant users permission to access the stack and specify what actions they can take.

> **NOTE**
> You can use AWS OpsWorks or IAM to manage user permissions. Note that the two options are not mutually exclusive; it is sometimes desirable to use both.

You define the elements of a stack by adding one or more layers. A *layer* represents a set of resources that serve a particular purpose, such as load balancing, web applications, or hosting a database server. You can customize or extend layers by modifying the default configurations or adding Chef recipes to perform tasks such as installing additional packages. Layers give you complete control over which packages are installed, how they are configured, how applications are deployed, and more.

Layers depend on Chef recipes to handle tasks such as installing packages on instances, deploying applications, and running scripts. One of the key AWS OpsWorks features is a set of lifecycle events that automatically run a specified set of recipes at the appropriate time on each instance.

An instance represents a single computing resource, such as an Amazon EC2 instance. It defines the resource's basic configuration, such as operating system and size. Other configuration settings, such as Elastic IP addresses or Amazon EBS volumes, are defined by the instance's layers. The layer's recipes complete the configuration by performing tasks, such as installing and configuring packages and deploying applications.

You store applications and related files in a repository, such as an Amazon S3 bucket or Git repo. Each application is represented by an *app*, which specifies the application type and contains the information that is needed to deploy the application from the repository to your instances, such as the repository URL and password. When you deploy an app, AWS OpsWorks triggers a Deploy event, which runs the Deploy recipes on the stack's instances.

Using the concepts of stacks, layers, and apps, you can model and visualize your application and resources in an organized fashion.

Finally, AWS OpsWorks sends all of your resource metrics to Amazon CloudWatch, making it easy to view graphs and set alarms to help you troubleshoot and take automated action based on the state of your resources. AWS OpsWorks provides many custom metrics, such as CPU idle, memory total, average load for one minute, and more. Each instance in the stack has detailed monitoring to provide insights into your workload.

Use Cases

AWS OpsWorks supports many DevOps efforts, including, but not limited to:

Host Multi-Tier Web Applications   AWS OpsWorks lets you model and visualize your application with layers that define how to configure a set of resources that are managed together. Because AWS OpsWorks uses the Chef framework, you can bring your own recipes or leverage hundreds of community-built configurations.

Support Continuous Integration   AWS OpsWorks supports DevOps principles, such as continuous integration. Everything in your environment can be automated.

AWS CloudFormation

AWS CloudFormation is a service that helps you model and set up your AWS resources so that you can spend less time managing those resources and more time focusing on your applications that run in AWS. AWS CloudFormation allows organizations to deploy, modify, and update resources in a controlled and predictable way, in effect applying version control to AWS infrastructure the same way one would do with software.

Overview

AWS CloudFormation gives developers and systems administrators an easy way to create and manage a collection of related AWS resources, provisioning and updating them in an orderly and predictable fashion. When you use AWS CloudFormation, you work with *templates* and *stacks*.

You create AWS CloudFormation templates to define your AWS resources and their properties. A *template* is a text file whose format complies with the JSON standard. AWS CloudFormation uses these templates as blueprints for building your AWS resources.

> When you use AWS CloudFormation, you can reuse your template to set up your resources consistently and repeatedly. Just describe your resources once, and then provision the same resources over and over in multiple regions.

When you use AWS CloudFormation, you manage related resources as a single unit called a stack. You create, update, and delete a collection of resources by creating, updating, and deleting stacks. All of the resources in a stack are defined by the stack's AWS CloudFormation template. Suppose you created a template that includes an Auto Scaling group, Elastic Load Balancing load balancer, and an Amazon RDS database instance. To create those resources, you create a stack by submitting your template that defines those resources, and AWS CloudFormation handles all of the provisioning for you. After all of the resources have been created, AWS CloudFormation reports that your stack has been created. You can then start using the resources in your stack. If stack creation fails, AWS CloudFormation rolls back your changes by deleting the resources that it created.

Often you will need to launch stacks from the same template, but with minor variations, such as within a different Amazon VPC or using AMIs from a different region. These variations can be addressed using parameters. You can use parameters to customize aspects of your template at runtime, when the stack is built. For example, you can pass the Amazon RDS database size, Amazon EC2 instance types, database, and web server port numbers to AWS CloudFormation when you create a stack. By leveraging template parameters, you can use a single template for many infrastructure deployments with different configuration values. For example, your Amazon EC2 instance types, Amazon CloudWatch alarm thresholds, and Amazon RDS read-replica settings may differ among AWS regions if you receive more customer traffic in the United States than in Europe. You can use template parameters to tune the settings and thresholds in each region separately and still be sure that the application is deployed consistently across the regions.

Figure 11.8 depicts the AWS CloudFormation workflow for creating stacks.

FIGURE 11.8   Creating a stack workflow

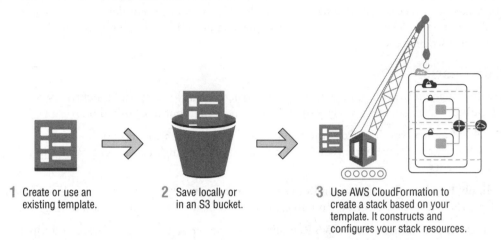

1 Create or use an existing template.

2 Save locally or in an S3 bucket.

3 Use AWS CloudFormation to create a stack based on your template. It constructs and configures your stack resources.

Because environments are dynamic in nature, you inevitably will need to update your stack's resources from time to time. There is no need to create a new stack and delete the old one; you can simply modify the existing stack's template. To update a stack, create a *change set* by submitting a modified version of the original stack template, different input parameter values, or both. AWS CloudFormation compares the modified template with the original template and generates a change set. The change set lists the proposed changes. After reviewing the changes, you can execute the change set to update your stack. Figure 11.9 depicts the workflow for updating a stack.

FIGURE 11.9   Updating a stack workflow

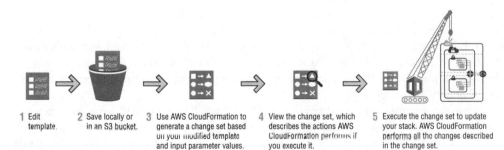

1 Edit template.

2 Save locally or in an S3 bucket.

3 Use AWS CloudFormation to generate a change set based on your modified template and input parameter values.

4 View the change set, which describes the actions AWS CloudFormation performs if you execute it.

5 Execute the change set to update your stack. AWS CloudFormation performs all the changes described in the change set.

When the time comes and you need to delete a stack, AWS CloudFormation deletes the stack and all of the resources in that stack.

> If you want to delete a stack but still retain some resources in that stack, you can use a deletion policy to retain those resources. If a resource has no deletion policy, AWS CloudFormation deletes the resource by default.

After all of the resources have been deleted, AWS CloudFormation signals that your stack has been successfully deleted. If AWS CloudFormation cannot delete a resource, the stack will not be deleted. Any resources that haven't been deleted will remain until you can successfully delete the stack.

Use Case

By allowing you to replicate your entire infrastructure stack easily and quickly, AWS CloudFormation enables a variety of use cases, including, but not limited to:

Quickly Launch New Test Environments   AWS CloudFormation lets testing teams quickly create a clean environment to run tests without disturbing ongoing efforts in other environments.

Reliably Replicate Configuration Between Environments   Because AWS CloudFormation scripts the entire environment, human error is eliminated when creating new stacks.

Launch Applications in New AWS Regions   A single script can be used across multiple regions to launch stacks reliably in different markets.

AWS Elastic Beanstalk

AWS Elastic Beanstalk is the fastest and simplest way to get an application up and running on AWS. Developers can simply upload their application code, and the service automatically handles all of the details, such as resource provisioning, load balancing, Auto Scaling, and monitoring.

Overview

AWS comprises dozens of building block services, each of which exposes an area of functionality. While the variety of services offers flexibility for how organizations want to manage their AWS infrastructure, it can be challenging to figure out which services to use and how to provision them. With AWS Elastic Beanstalk, you can quickly deploy and manage applications on the AWS cloud without worrying about the infrastructure that runs those applications. AWS Elastic Beanstalk reduces management complexity without restricting choice or control.

There are key components that comprise AWS Elastic Beanstalk and work together to provide the necessary services to deploy and manage applications easily in the cloud. An *AWS Elastic Beanstalk application* is the logical collection of these AWS Elastic Beanstalk components, which includes environments, versions, and environment configurations. In AWS Elastic Beanstalk, an application is conceptually similar to a folder.

An *application version* refers to a specific, labeled iteration of deployable code for a web application. An application version points to an Amazon S3 object that contains the deployable code. Applications can have many versions and each application version is unique. In a running environment, organizations can deploy any application version they already uploaded to the application, or they can upload and immediately deploy a new application version. Organizations might upload multiple application versions to test differences between one version of their web application and another.

An *environment* is an application version that is deployed onto AWS resources. Each environment runs only a single application version at a time; however, the same version or different versions can run in as many environments at the same time as needed. When an environment is created, AWS Elastic Beanstalk provisions the resources needed to run the application version that is specified.

An *environment configuration* identifies a collection of parameters and settings that define how an environment and its associated resources behave. When an environment's configuration settings are updated, AWS Elastic Beanstalk automatically applies the changes to existing resources or deletes and deploys new resources depending on the type of change.

When an AWS Elastic Beanstalk environment is launched, the environment tier, platform, and environment type are specified. The environment tier that is chosen determines whether AWS Elastic Beanstalk provisions resources to support a web application that handles HTTP(S) requests or an application that handles background-processing tasks. An environment tier whose web application processes web requests is known as a *web server tier*. An environment tier whose application runs background jobs is known as a *worker tier*.

At the time of this writing, AWS Elastic Beanstalk provides platform support for the programming languages Java, Node.js, PHP, Python, Ruby, and Go with support for the web containers Tomcat, Passenger, Puma, and Docker.

Use Cases

A company provides a website for prospective home buyers, sellers, and renters to browse home and apartment listings for more than 110 million homes. The website processes more than three million new images daily. It receives more than 17,000 image requests per second on its website during peak traffic from both desktop and mobile clients.

The company was looking for ways to be more agile with deployments and empower its developers to focus more on writing code instead of spending time managing and configuring servers, databases, load balancers, firewalls, and networks. It began using AWS Elastic Beanstalk as the service for deploying and scaling the web applications and services. Developers were empowered to upload code to AWS Elastic Beanstalk, which then automatically handled the deployment, from capacity provisioning, load balancing, and Auto Scaling, to application health monitoring.

Because the company ingests data in a haphazard way, running feeds that dump a ton of work into the image processing system all at once, it needs to scale up its image converter fleet to meet peak demand. The company determined that an AWS Elastic Beanstalk worker fleet to run a Python Imaging Library with custom code was the simplest way to meet the requirement. This eliminated the need to have a number of static instances or, worse, trying to write their own Auto Scaling configuration.

By making the move to AWS Elastic Beanstalk, the company was able to reduce operating costs while increasing agility and scalability for its image processing and delivery system.

Key Features

AWS Elastic Beanstalk provides several management features that ease deployment and management of applications on AWS. Organizations have access to built-in Amazon CloudWatch monitoring metrics such as average CPU utilization, request count, and average latency. They can receive email notifications through Amazon SNS when application health changes or application servers are added or removed. Server logs for the application servers can be accessed without needing to log in. Organizations can even elect to have updates applied automatically to the underlying platform running the application such as the AMI, operating system, language and framework, and application or proxy server.

Additionally, developers retain full control over the AWS resources powering their application and can perform a variety of functions by simply adjusting the configuration settings. These include settings such as:

- Selecting the most appropriate Amazon EC2 instance type that matches the CPU and memory requirements of their application

- Choosing the right database and storage options such as Amazon RDS, Amazon DynamoDB, Microsoft SQL Server, and Oracle

- Enabling login access to Amazon EC2 instances for immediate and direct troubleshooting

- Enhancing application security by enabling HTTPS protocol on the load balancer

- Adjusting application server settings (for example, JVM settings) and passing environment variables

- Adjust Auto Scaling settings to control the metrics and thresholds used to determine when to add or remove instances from an environment

With AWS Elastic Beanstalk, organizations can deploy an application quickly while retaining as much control as they want to have over the underlying infrastructure.

AWS Trusted Advisor

AWS Trusted Advisor draws upon best practices learned from the aggregated operational history of serving over a million AWS customers. AWS Trusted Advisor inspects your AWS environment and makes recommendations when opportunities exist to save money, improve system availability and performance, or help close security gaps. You can view the overall status of your AWS resources and savings estimations on the AWS Trusted Advisor dashboard.

 NOTE   AWS Trusted Advisor is accessed in the AWS Management Console. Additionally, programmatic access to AWS Trusted Advisor is available with the AWS Support API.

AWS Trusted Advisor provides best practices in four categories: cost optimization, security, fault tolerance, and performance improvement. The status of the check is shown by using color coding on the dashboard page, as depicted in Figure 11.10.

FIGURE 11.10   AWS Trusted Advisor Console dashboard

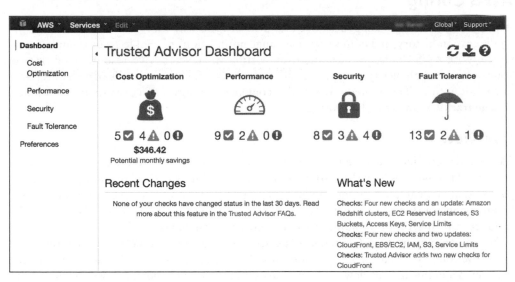

The color coding reflects the following information:

- *Red*: Action recommended

- *Yellow*: Investigation recommended

- *Green*: No problem detected

For each check, you can review a detailed description of the recommended best practice, a set of alert criteria, guidelines for action, and a list of useful resources on the topic.

All AWS customers have access to four AWS Trusted Advisor checks at no cost. The four standard AWS Trusted Advisor checks are:

Service Limits   Checks for usage that is more than 80 percent of the service limit. These values are based on a snapshot, so current usage might differ and can take up to 24 hours to reflect changes.

Security Groups–Specific Ports Unrestricted   Checks security groups for rules that allow unrestricted access (0.0.0.0/0) to specific ports

IAM Use   Checks for your use of AWS IAM

MFA on Root Account   Checks the root account and warns if MFA is not enabled

Customers with a Business or Enterprise AWS Support plan can view all AWS Trusted Advisor checks—over 50 checks.

There may be occasions when a particular check is not relevant to some resources in your AWS environment. You have the ability to exclude items from a check and optionally restore them later at any time. AWS Trusted Advisor acts like a customized cloud expert, and it helps organizations provision their resources by following best practices while identifying inefficiencies, waste, potential cost savings, and security issues.

AWS Config

AWS Config is a fully managed service that provides you with an AWS resource inventory, configuration history, and configuration change notifications to enable security and governance. With AWS Config, you can discover existing and deleted AWS resources, determine your overall compliance against rules, and dive into configuration details of a resource at any point in time. These capabilities enable compliance auditing, security analysis, resource change tracking, and troubleshooting.

Overview

AWS Config provides a detailed view of the configuration of AWS resources in your AWS account. This includes how the resources are related and how they were configured in the past so that you can see how the configurations and relationships change over time. AWS Config defines a resource as an entity you can work with in AWS, such as an Amazon EC2 instance, an Amazon EBS volume, a security group, or an Amazon VPC.

When you turn on AWS Config, it first discovers the supported AWS resources that exist in your account and generates a *configuration item* for each resource. A configuration item represents a point-in-time view of the various attributes of a supported AWS resource that exists in your account. The components of a configuration item include metadata, attributes, relationships, current configuration, and related events.

AWS Config will generate configuration items when the configuration of a resource changes, and it maintains historical records of the configuration items of your resources from the time you start the *configuration recorder.* The configuration recorder stores the configurations of the supported resources in your account as configuration items. By default, AWS Config creates configuration items for every supported resource in the region. If you don't want AWS Config to create configuration items for all supported resources, you can specify the resource types that you want it to track.

Organizations often need to assess the overall compliance and risk status from a configuration perspective, view compliance trends over time, and pinpoint which configuration change caused a resource to drift out of compliance. An *AWS Config Rule* represents desired configuration settings for specific AWS resources or for an entire AWS account. While AWS Config continuously tracks your resource configuration changes, it checks whether these changes violate any of the conditions in your rules. If a resource violates a rule, AWS Config flags the resource and the rule as noncompliant and notifies you through Amazon SNS.

AWS Config makes it easy to track resource configuration without the need for up-front investments and while avoiding the complexity of installing and updating agents for data collection or maintaining large databases. Once AWS Config is enabled, organizations can view continuously updated details of all configuration attributes associated with AWS resources.

Use Cases

Some of the infrastructure management tasks AWS Config enables include:

Discovery AWS Config will discover resources that exist in your account, record their current configuration, and capture any changes to these configurations. AWS Config will also retain configuration details for resources that have been deleted. A comprehensive snapshot of all resources and their configuration attributes provides a complete inventory of resources in your account.

Change Management   When your resources are created, updated, or deleted, AWS Config streams these configuration changes to Amazon SNS so that you are notified of all configuration changes. AWS Config represents relationships between resources, so you can assess how a change to one resource may affect other resources.

Continuous Audit and Compliance   AWS Config and AWS Config Rules are designed to help you assess compliance with internal policies and regulatory standards by providing visibility into the configuration of a resource at any time and evaluating relevant configuration changes against rules that you can define.

Troubleshooting   Using AWS Config, you can quickly troubleshoot operational issues by identifying the recent configuration changes to your resources.

Security and Incident Analysis   Properly configured resources improve your security posture. Data from AWS Config enables you to monitor the configurations of your resources continuously and evaluate these configurations for potential security weaknesses. After a potential security event, AWS Config enables you to examine the configuration of your resources at any single point in the past.

Key Features

In the past, organizations needed to poll resource APIs and maintain their own external database for change management. AWS Config resolves this previous need and automatically records resource configuration information and will evaluate any rules that are triggered by a change. The configuration of the resource and its overall compliance against rules are presented in a dashboard.

AWS Config integrates with AWS CloudTrail, a service that records AWS API calls for an account and delivers API usage log files to an Amazon S3 bucket. If the configuration change of a resource was the result of an API call, AWS Config also records the AWS CloudTrail event ID that corresponds to the API call that changed the resource's configuration. Organizations can then leverage the AWS CloudTrail logs to obtain details of the API call that was made—including who made the API call, at what time, and from which IP address—to use for troubleshooting purposes.

When a configuration change is made to a resource or when the compliance of an AWS Config rule changes, a notification message is delivered that contains the updated configuration of the resource or compliance state of the rule and key information such as the old and new values for each changed attribute. Additionally, AWS Config sends notifications when a *Configuration History* file is delivered to Amazon S3 and when the customer initiates a *Configuration Snapshot*. These messages are all streamed to an Amazon SNS topic that you specify.

Organizations can use the AWS Management Console, API, or AWS CLI to obtain details of what a resource's configuration looked like at any point in the past. AWS Config will also automatically deliver a history file to the Amazon S3 bucket you specify every six hours that contains all changes to your resource configurations.

Summary

In this chapter, you learned about additional key AWS cloud services, many of which will be covered on your AWS Certified Solutions Architect – Associate exam. These services are grouped into four categories of services: storage and content delivery, security, analytics, and DevOps.

In the storage and content delivery group, we covered Amazon CloudFront and AWS Storage Gateway. Amazon CloudFront is a global CDN service. It integrates with other AWS products to give developers and businesses an easy way to distribute content to end users with low latency, high data transfer speeds, and no minimum usage commitments. AWS Storage Gateway is a service that connects an on-premises software appliance with cloud-based storage. It provides seamless and secure integration between an organization's on-premises IT environment and AWS storage infrastructure. The AWS Storage Gateway appliance maintains frequently accessed data on-premises while encrypting and storing all of your data in Amazon S3 or Amazon Glacier.

The services we covered in security focused on Identity Management (AWS Directory Service), Key Management (AWS KMS AWS CloudHSM), and Audit (AWS CloudTrail). AWS Directory Service is a managed service offering, providing directories that contain information about your organization, including users, groups, computers, and other resources. AWS Directory Service is offered in three types: AWS Directory Service for Microsoft Active Directory (Enterprise Edition), Simple AD, and AD Connector.

Key management is the management of cryptographic keys within a cryptosystem. This includes dealing with the generation, exchange, storage, use, and replacement of keys. AWS KMS is a managed service that makes it easy for you to create and control the encryption keys used to encrypt your data. AWS KMS lets you create keys that can never be exported from the service and that can be used to encrypt and decrypt data based on policies you define. AWS CloudHSM helps you meet corporate, contractual, and regulatory compliance requirements for data security by using dedicated HSM appliances within the AWS cloud. An HSM is a hardware appliance that provides secure key storage and cryptographic operations within a tamper-resistant hardware module.

Rounding out the security services is AWS CloudTrail. AWS CloudTrail provides visibility into user activity by recording API calls made on your account. AWS CloudTrail records important information about each API call, including the name of the API, the identity of the caller, the time of the API call, the request parameters, and the response elements returned by the AWS service. This information helps you to track changes made to your AWS resources and to troubleshoot operational issues.

The analytics services covered help you overcome the unique list of challenges associated with big data in today's IT world. Amazon Kinesis is a platform for handling massive streaming data on AWS, offering powerful services to make it easy to load and analyze streaming data and also providing the ability for you to build custom streaming data applications for specialized needs. Amazon EMR provides you with a fully managed, on-demand Hadoop framework. The reduction of complexity and up-front costs combined with the scale of AWS means you can instantly spin up large Hadoop clusters and start processing within minutes.

To supplement the big data challenges, orchestrating data movement comes with its own challenges. AWS Data Pipeline is a web service that helps you reliably process and move data between different AWS compute and storage services, and also on-premises data sources, at specified intervals. With AWS Data Pipeline, you can regularly access your data where it's stored, transform and process it at scale, and efficiently transfer the results to AWS services such as Amazon S3, Amazon RDS, Amazon DynamoDB, and Amazon EMR. Additionally, AWS Import/Export helps when you're faced with the challenge of getting huge datasets into AWS in the first place or retrieving them back to on-premises when necessary. AWS Import/Export is a service that accelerates transferring large amounts of data into and out of AWS using physical storage appliances, bypassing the Internet. The data is copied to a device at the source, shipped via standard shipping mechanisms, and then copied to the destination.

AWS continues to evolve services in support of organizations embracing DevOps. Services such as AWS OpsWorks, AWS CloudFormation, AWS Elastic Beanstalk, and AWS Config are leading the way for DevOps on AWS. AWS OpsWorks provides a configuration management service that helps you configure and operate applications using Chef. AWS OpsWorks works with applications of any level of complexity and is independent of any particular architectural pattern. AWS CloudFormation allows organizations to deploy, modify, and update resources in a controlled and predictable way, in effect applying version control to AWS infrastructure the same way one would do with software. AWS Elastic Beanstalk allows developers to simply upload their application code, and the service automatically handles all of the details such as resource provisioning, load balancing, Auto Scaling, and monitoring. AWS Config delivers a fully managed service that provides you with an AWS resource inventory, configuration history, and configuration change notifications to enable security and governance. With AWS Config, organizations have the information necessary for compliance auditing, security analysis, resource change tracking, and troubleshooting.

The key additional services covered in this chapter will help you form a knowledge base to understand the necessities for the exam. As you continue to grow as a Solutions Architect, diving deeper into the AWS cloud services as a whole will expand your ability to define well architected solutions across a wide variety of business verticals and use cases.

Exam Essentials

Know the basic use cases for Amazon CloudFront.   Know when to use Amazon CloudFront (for popular static and dynamic content with geographically distributed users) and when not to (all users at a single location or connecting through a corporate VPN).

Know how Amazon CloudFront works.   Amazon CloudFront optimizes downloads by using geolocation to identify the geographical location of users, then serving and caching content at the edge location closest to each user to maximize performance.

Know how to create an Amazon CloudFront distribution and what types of origins are supported.   To create a distribution, you specify an origin and the type of distribution, and Amazon CloudFront creates a new domain name for the distribution. Origins supported include Amazon S3 buckets or static Amazon S3 websites and HTTP servers located in Amazon EC2 or in your own data center.

Know how to use Amazon CloudFront for dynamic content and multiple origins.   Understand how to specify multiple origins for different types of content and how to use cache behaviors and path strings to control what content is served by which origin.

Know what mechanisms are available to serve private content through Amazon CloudFront.   Amazon CloudFront can serve private content using Amazon S3 Origin Access Identifiers, signed URLs, and signed cookies.

Know the three configurations of AWS storage gateway and their use cases.   Gateway-Cached volumes expand your on-premises storage into Amazon S3 and cache frequently used files locally. Gateway-Stored values keep all your data available locally at all times and also replicate it asynchronously to Amazon S3. Gateway-VTL enables you to keep your current backup tape software and processes while eliminating physical tapes by storing your data in the cloud.

Understand the value of AWS Directory Service.   AWS Directory Service is designed to reduce identity management tasks, thereby allowing you to focus more of your time and resources on your business.

Know the AWS Directory Service Directory types.   AWS Directory Service offers three directory types:

- AWS Directory Service for Microsoft Active Directory (Enterprise Edition), also referred to as Microsoft AD
- Simple AD
- AD Connector

Know when you should use AWS Directory Service for Microsoft Active Directory.   You should use Microsoft Active Directory if you have more than 5,000 users or need a trust relationship set up between an AWS hosted directory and your on-premises directories.

Understand key management.   Key management is the management of cryptographic keys within a cryptosystem. This includes dealing with the generation, exchange, storage, use, and replacement of keys.

Understand when you should use AWS KMS.   AWS KMS is a managed service that makes it easy for you to create and control the symmetric encryption keys used to encrypt your data. AWS KMS lets you create keys that can never be exported from the service and which can be used to encrypt and decrypt data based on policies you define.

Understand when you should use AWS CloudHSM.   AWS CloudHSM helps you meet corporate, contractual, and regulatory compliance requirements for data security by using dedicated hardware security module appliances within the AWS cloud.

Understand the value of AWS CloudTrail.   AWS CloudTrail provides visibility into user activity by recording API calls made on your account. This helps you to track changes made to your AWS resources and to troubleshoot operational issues. AWS CloudTrail makes it easier to ensure compliance with internal policies and regulatory standards.

Know the three services of Amazon Kinesis and their use cases.   Amazon Kinesis Firehose allows you to load massive volumes of streaming data into AWS. Amazon Kinesis Analytics enables you to easily analyze streaming data real time with standard SQL. Amazon Kinesis Streams enables you to build custom applications that process or analyze streaming data real time for specialized needs.

Know what service Amazon EMR provides.   Amazon EMR provides a managed Hadoop service on AWS that allows you to spin up large Hadoop clusters in minutes.

Know the difference between persistent and transient clusters.   Persistent clusters run continuously, so they do not lose data stored on instance-based HDFS. Transient clusters are launched for a specific task, then terminated, so they access data on Amazon S3 via EMRFS.

Know the use cases for Amazon EMR.   Amazon EMR is useful for big data analytics in virtually any industry, including, but not limited to, log processing, clickstream analysis, and genomics and life sciences.

Know the use cases for AWS Data Pipeline.   AWS Data Pipeline can manage batch ETL processes at scale on the cloud, accessing data both in AWS and on-premises. It can take advantage of AWS cloud services by spinning up resources required for the process, such as Amazon EC2 instances or Amazon EMR clusters.

Know the types of AWS Import/Export services and the possible sources/destinations of each.   AWS Snowball is Amazon shippable appliances supplied ready to ship. It can transfer data to and from your on-premises storage and to and from Amazon S3. AWS Import/Export Disk uses your storage devices and, in addition to transferring data in and out of your on-premises storage, can import data to Amazon S3, Amazon EBS, and Amazon S3; it can only export data from Amazon S3.

Understand the basics of AWS OpsWorks.   AWS OpsWorks is a configuration management service that helps you configure and operate applications of all shapes and sizes using Chef. You can define an application's architecture and the specification of each component including package installation, software configuration, and resources such as storage.

Understand the value of AWS CloudFormation.   AWS CloudFormation is a service that helps you model and set up your AWS resources. AWS CloudFormation allows organizations to deploy, modify, and update resources in a controlled and predictable way, in effect applying version control to AWS infrastructure the same way you would do with software.

Understand the value of AWS Elastic Beanstalk. AWS Elastic Beanstalk is the fastest and simplest way to get an application up and running on AWS. Developers can simply upload their application code, and the service automatically handles all the details such as resource provisioning, load balancing, Auto Scaling, and monitoring.

Understand the components of AWS Elastic Beanstalk. An AWS Elastic Beanstalk application is the logical collection of environments, versions, and environment configurations. In AWS Elastic Beanstalk, an application is conceptually similar to a folder.

Understand the value of AWS Config. AWS Config is a fully managed service that provides organizations with an AWS resource inventory, configuration history, and configuration change notifications to enable security and governance. With AWS Config, organizations can discover existing and deleted AWS resources, determine their overall compliance against rules and dive into configuration details of a resource at any point in time. These capabilities enable compliance auditing, security analysis, resource change tracking, and troubleshooting.

Review Questions

1. What origin servers are supported by Amazon CloudFront? (Choose 3 answers)

   A. An Amazon Route 53 Hosted Zone

   B. An Amazon Simple Storage Service (Amazon S3) bucket

   C. An HTTP server running on Amazon Elastic Compute Cloud (Amazon EC2)

   D. An Amazon EC2 Auto Scaling Group

   E. An HTTP server running on-premises

2. Which of the following are good use cases for Amazon CloudFront? (Choose 2 answers)

   A. A popular software download site that supports users around the world, with dynamic content that changes rapidly

   B. A corporate website that serves training videos to employees. Most employees are located in two corporate campuses in the same city.

   C. A heavily used video and music streaming service that requires content to be delivered only to paid subscribers

   D. A corporate HR website that supports a global workforce. Because the site contains sensitive data, all users must connect through a corporate Virtual Private Network (VPN).

3. You have a web application that contains both static content in an Amazon Simple Storage Service (Amazon S3) bucket—primarily images and CSS files—and also dynamic content currently served by a PHP web app running on Amazon Elastic Compute Cloud (Amazon EC2). What features of Amazon CloudFront can be used to support this application with a single Amazon CloudFront distribution? (Choose 2 answers)

   A. Multiple Origin Access Identifiers

   D. Multiple signed URLs

   C. Multiple origins

   D. Multiple edge locations

   E. Multiple cache behaviors

4. You are building a media-sharing web application that serves video files to end users on both PCs and mobile devices. The media files are stored as objects in an Amazon Simple Storage Service (Amazon S3) bucket, but are to be delivered through Amazon CloudFront. What is the simplest way to ensure that only Amazon CloudFront has access to the objects in the Amazon S3 bucket?

   A. Create Signed URLs for each Amazon S3 object.

   B. Use an Amazon CloudFront Origin Access Identifier (OAI).

   C. Use public and private keys with signed cookies.

   D. Use an AWS Identity and Access Management (IAM) bucket policy.

5. Your company data center is completely full, but the sales group has determined a need to store 200TB of product video. The videos were created over the last several years, with the most recent being accessed by sales the most often. The data must be accessed locally, but there is no space in the data center to install local storage devices to store this data. What AWS cloud service will meet sales' requirements?

   A. AWS Storage Gateway Gateway-Stored volumes

   B. Amazon Elastic Compute Cloud (Amazon EC2) instances with attached Amazon EBS Volumes

   C. AWS Storage Gateway Gateway-Cached volumes

   D. AWS Import/Export Disk

6. Your company wants to extend their existing Microsoft Active Directory capability into an Amazon Virtual Private Cloud (Amazon VPC) without establishing a trust relationship with the existing on-premises Active Directory. Which of the following is the best approach to achieve this goal?

   A. Create and connect an AWS Directory Service AD Connector.

   B. Create and connect an AWS Directory Service Simple AD.

   C. Create and connect an AWS Directory Service for Microsoft Active Directory (Enterprise Edition).

   D. None of the above

7. Which of the following are AWS Key Management Service (AWS KMS) keys that will never exit AWS unencrypted?

   A. AWS KMS data keys

   B. Envelope encryption keys

   C. AWS KMS Customer Master Keys (CMKs)

   D. A and C

8. Which cryptographic method is used by AWS Key Management Service (AWS KMS) to encrypt data?

   A. Password-based encryption

   B. Asymmetric

   C. Shared secret

   D. Envelope encryption

9. Which AWS service records Application Program Interface (API) calls made on your account and delivers log files to your Amazon Simple Storage Service (Amazon S3) bucket?

   A. AWS CloudTrail

   B. Amazon CloudWatch

   C. Amazon Kinesis

   D. AWS Data Pipeline

10. You are trying to decrypt ciphertext with AWS KMS and the decryption operation is failing. Which of the following are possible causes? (Choose 2 answers)

    A. The private key does not match the public key in the ciphertext.

    B. The plaintext was encrypted along with an encryption context, and you are not providing the identical encryption context when calling the Decrypt API.

    C. The ciphertext you are trying to decrypt is not valid.

    D. You are not providing the correct symmetric key to the Decrypt API.

11. Your company has 30 years of financial records that take up 15TB of on-premises storage. It is regulated that you maintain these records, but in the year you have worked for the company no one has ever requested any of this data. Given that the company data center is already filling the bandwidth of its Internet connection, what is an alternative way to store the data on the most appropriate cloud storage?

    A. AWS Import/Export to Amazon Simple Storage Service (Amazon S3)

    B. AWS Import/Export to Amazon Glacier

    C. Amazon Kinesis

    D. Amazon Elastic MapReduce (AWS EMR)

12. Your company collects information from the point of sale registers at all of its franchise locations. Each month these processes collect 200TB of information stored in Amazon Simple Storage Service (Amazon S3). Analytics jobs taking 24 hours are performed to gather knowledge from this data. Which of the following will allow you to perform these analytics in a cost-effective way?

    A. Copy the data to a persistent Amazon Elastic MapReduce (Amazon EMR) cluster, and run the MapReduce jobs.

    B. Create an application that reads the information of the Amazon S3 bucket and runs it through an Amazon Kinesis stream.

    C. Run a transient Amazon EMR cluster, and run the MapReduce jobs against the data directly in Amazon S3.

    D. Launch a d2.8xlarge (32 vCPU, 244GB RAM) Amazon Elastic Compute Cloud (Amazon EC2) instance, and run an application to read and process each object sequentially.

13. Which service allows you to process nearly limitless streams of data in flight?

    A. Amazon Kinesis Firehose

    B. Amazon Elastic MapReduce (Amazon EMR)

    C. Amazon Redshift

    D. Amazon Kinesis Streams

14. What combination of services enable you to copy daily 50TB of data to Amazon storage, process the data in Hadoop, and store the results in a large data warehouse?

    A. Amazon Kinesis, Amazon Data Pipeline, Amazon Elastic MapReduce (Amazon EMR), and Amazon Elastic Compute Cloud (Amazon EC2)

    B. Amazon Elastic Block Store (Amazon EBS), Amazon Data Pipeline, Amazon EMR, and Amazon Redshift

   C. Amazon Simple Storage Service (Amazon S3), Amazon Data Pipeline, Amazon EMR, and Amazon Redshift

   D. Amazon S3, Amazon Simple Workflow, Amazon EMR, and Amazon DynamoDB

15. Your company has 50,000 weather stations around the country that send updates every 2 seconds. What service will enable you to ingest this stream of data and store it to Amazon Simple Storage Service (Amazon S3) for future processing?

   A. Amazon Simple Queue Service (Amazon SQS)

   B. Amazon Kinesis Firehose

   C. Amazon Elastic Compute Cloud (Amazon EC2)

   D. Amazon Data Pipeline

16. Your organization uses Chef heavily for its deployment automation. What AWS cloud service provides integration with Chef recipes to start new application server instances, configure application server software, and deploy applications?

   A. AWS Elastic Beanstalk

   B. Amazon Kinesis

   C. AWS OpsWorks

   D. AWS CloudFormation

17. A firm is moving its testing platform to AWS to provide developers with instant access to clean test and development environments. The primary requirement for the firm is to make environments easily reproducible and fungible. What service will help the firm meet their requirements?

   A. AWS CloudFormation

   B. AWS Config

   C. Amazon Redshift

   D. AWS Trusted Advisor

18. Your company's IT management team is looking for an online tool to provide recommendations to save money, improve system availability and performance, and to help close security gaps. What can help the management team?

   A. Cloud-init

   B. AWS Trusted Advisor

   C. AWS Config

   D. Configuration Recorder

19. Your company works with data that requires frequent audits of your AWS environment to ensure compliance with internal policies and best practices. In order to perform these audits, you need access to historical configurations of your resources to evaluate relevant configuration changes. Which service will provide the necessary information for your audits?

   A. AWS Config

   B. AWS Key Management Service (AWS KMS)

C. AWS CloudTrail

D. AWS OpsWorks

20. All of the website deployments are currently done by your company's development team. With a surge in website popularity, the company is looking for ways to be more agile with deployments. What AWS cloud service can help the developers focus more on writing code instead of spending time managing and configuring servers, databases, load balancers, firewalls, and networks?

A. AWS Config

B. AWS Trusted Advisor

C. Amazon Kinesis

D. AWS Elastic Beanstalk

Security on AWS

THE AWS CERTIFIED SOLUTIONS ARCHITECT EXAM TOPICS COVERED IN THIS CHAPTER MAY INCLUDE, BUT ARE NOT LIMITED TO, THE FOLLOWING:

Domain 3.0: Data Security

✓ **3.1 Recognize and implement secure practices for optimum cloud deployment and maintenance.**

Content may include the following:

- AWS shared responsibility model
- AWS platform compliance
- AWS security attributes (customer workloads down to physical layer)
- AWS administration and security services
- AWS Identity and Access Management (IAM)
- Amazon Virtual Private Cloud (Amazon VPC)
- AWS CloudTrail
- Ingress vs. egress filtering, and which AWS services and features fit
- Core Amazon Elastic Compute Cloud (Amazon EC2) and Amazon Simple Storage Service (Amazon S3) security feature sets
- Incorporating common conventional security products (Firewall, Virtual Private Network [VPN])
- Denial of Service (DoS) mitigation
- Encryption solutions (e.g., key services)
- Complex access controls (building sophisticated security groups, Access Control Lists [ACLs], etc.)

Introduction

Cloud security is the first priority at AWS. All AWS customers benefit from a data center and network architecture that is built to satisfy the requirements of the most security-sensitive organizations. AWS and its partners offer tools and features to help you meet your security objectives around visibility, auditability, controllability, and agility. This means that you can have the security you need, but without the capital outlay and at a much lower operational overhead than in an on-premises or a traditional data center environment. This chapter will cover the relevant security topics that are within scope of the AWS Certified Solutions Architect – Associate exam.

Shared Responsibility Model

Before we go into the details of how AWS secures its resources, we should talk about how security in the cloud is slightly different than security in your on-premises data centers. When you move computer systems and data to the cloud, security responsibilities become shared between you and your cloud service provider. In this case, AWS is responsible for securing the underlying infrastructure that supports the cloud, and you're responsible for anything you put on the cloud or connect to the cloud. This shared responsibility model can reduce your operational burden in many ways, and in some cases it may even improve your default security posture without additional action on your part. Figure 12.1 illustrates AWS responsibilities versus those of the customer. Essentially, AWS is responsible for security *of* the cloud, and customers are responsible for security *in* the cloud.

FIGURE 12.1   The shared responsibility model

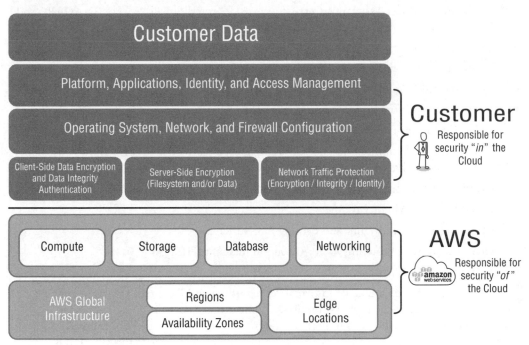

AWS Compliance Program

AWS compliance enables customers to understand the robust controls in place at AWS to maintain security and data protection in the cloud. As you build systems on top of AWS Cloud infrastructure, you share compliance responsibilities with AWS. By tying together governance-focused, audit-friendly service features with applicable compliance or audit standards, AWS compliance enablers build on traditional programs, helping you to establish and operate in an AWS security control environment. The IT infrastructure that AWS provides is designed and managed in alignment with security best practices and a variety of IT security standards, including (at the time of this writing):

- Service Organization Control (SOC) 1/Statement on Standards for Attestation Engagements (SSAE)16/International Standards for Assurance Engagements No. 3402 (ISAE) 3402 (formerly Statement on Auditing Standards [SAS] 70)
- SOC 2
- SOC 3

- Federal Information Security Management Act (FISMA), Department of Defense (DoD) Information Assurance Certification and Accreditation Process (DIACAP), and Federal Risk and Authorization Management Program (FedRAMP)
- DoD Cloud Computing Security Requirements Guide (SRG) Levels 2 and 4
- Payment Card Industry Data Security Standard (PCI DSS) Level 1
- International Organization for Standardization (ISO) 9001 and ISO 27001
- International Traffic in Arms Regulations (ITAR)
- Federal Information Processing Standard (FIPS) 140-2

In addition, the flexibility and control that the AWS platform provides allows customers to deploy solutions that meet several industry-specific standards, including:

- Criminal Justice Information Services (CJIS)
- Cloud Security Alliance (CSA)
- Family Educational Rights and Privacy Act (FERPA)
- Health Insurance Portability and Accountability Act (HIPAA)
- Motion Picture Association of America (MPAA)

AWS provides a wide range of information regarding its IT control environment to customers through whitepapers, reports, certifications, accreditations, and other third-party attestations. To aid in preparation for your AWS Certified Solutions Architect Associate exam, see Chapter 13, "AWS Risk and Compliance." More information is available in the "AWS Risk and Compliance" whitepaper available on the AWS website.

AWS Global Infrastructure Security

AWS operates the global cloud infrastructure that you use to provision a variety of basic computing resources such as processing and storage. The AWS global infrastructure includes the facilities, network, hardware, and operational software (for example, host operating system and virtualization software) that support the provisioning and use of these resources. The AWS global infrastructure is designed and managed according to security best practices as well as a variety of security compliance standards. As an AWS customer, you can be assured that you're building web architectures on top of some of the most secure computing infrastructure in the world.

Physical and Environmental Security

AWS data centers are state of the art, using innovative architectural and engineering approaches. Amazon has many years of experience in designing, constructing, and operating large-scale data centers. This experience has been applied to the AWS platform and infrastructure. AWS data centers are housed in nondescript facilities. Physical access is strictly controlled both at the perimeter and at building ingress points by professional security staff using video surveillance, intrusion detection systems, and other electronic means. Authorized staff must pass two-factor authentication a minimum of two times to access data center floors. All visitors and contractors are required to present identification and are signed in and continually escorted by authorized staff.

AWS only provides data center access and information to employees and contractors who have a legitimate business need for such privileges. When an employee no longer has a business need for these privileges, his or her access is immediately revoked, even if they continue to be an employee of Amazon or AWS. All physical access to data centers by AWS employees is logged and audited routinely.

Fire Detection and Suppression

AWS data centers have automatic fire detection and suppression equipment to reduce risk. The fire detection system uses smoke detection sensors in all data center environments, mechanical and electrical infrastructure spaces, chiller rooms and generator equipment rooms. These areas are protected by wet-pipe, double-interlocked pre-action, or gaseous sprinkler systems.

Power

AWS data center electrical power systems are designed to be fully redundant and maintainable without impact to operations, 24 hours a day, and 7 days a week. Uninterruptible Power Supply (UPS) units provide backup power in the event of an electrical failure for critical and essential loads in the facility. AWS data centers use generators to provide backup power for the entire facility.

Climate and Temperature

Climate control is required to maintain a constant operating temperature for servers and other hardware, which prevents overheating and reduces the possibility of service outages. AWS data centers are built to maintain atmospheric conditions at optimal levels. Personnel and systems monitor and control temperature and humidity at appropriate levels.

Management

AWS monitors electrical, mechanical, and life support systems and equipment so that any issues are immediately identified. AWS staff performs preventative maintenance to maintain the continued operability of equipment.

Storage Device Decommissioning

When a storage device has reached the end of its useful life, AWS procedures include a decommissioning process that is designed to prevent customer data from being exposed to unauthorized individuals.

Business Continuity Management

Amazon's infrastructure has a high level of availability and provides customers with the features to deploy a resilient IT architecture. AWS has designed its systems to tolerate system or hardware failures with minimal customer impact. Data center Business Continuity Management at AWS is under the direction of the Amazon Infrastructure Group.

Availability

Data centers are built in clusters in various global regions. All data centers are online and serving customers; no data center is "cold." In case of failure, automated processes move data traffic away from the affected area. Core applications are deployed in an N+1 configuration, so that in the event of a data center failure, there is sufficient capacity to enable traffic to be load-balanced to the remaining sites.

AWS provides its customers with the flexibility to place instances and store data within multiple geographic regions and also across multiple Availability Zones within each region. Each Availability Zone is designed as an independent failure zone. This means that Availability Zones are physically separated within a typical metropolitan region and are located in lower risk flood plains (specific flood zone categorization varies by region). In addition to having discrete UPS and on-site backup generation facilities, they are each fed via different grids from independent utilities to further reduce single points of failure. Availability Zones are all redundantly connected to multiple tier-1 transit providers. Figure 12.2 illustrates how AWS regions are comprised of Availability Zones.

FIGURE 12.2 Amazon Web Services regions

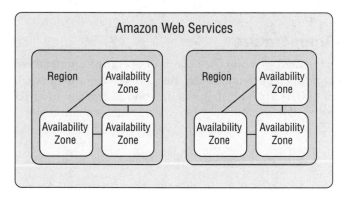

You should architect your AWS usage to take advantage of multiple regions and Availability Zones. Distributing applications across multiple Availability Zones provides the ability to remain resilient in the face of most failure modes, including natural disasters or system failures.

Incident Response

The Amazon Incident Management team employs industry-standard diagnostic procedures to drive resolution during business-impacting events. Staff operators provide $24 \times 7 \times 365$ coverage to detect incidents and to manage the impact and resolution.

Communication

AWS has implemented various methods of internal communication at a global level to help employees understand their individual roles and responsibilities and to communicate significant events in a timely manner. These methods include orientation and training programs for newly hired employees, regular management meetings for updates on business performance and other matters, and electronics means such as video conferencing, electronic mail messages, and the posting of information via the Amazon intranet.

AWS has also implemented various methods of external communication to support its customer base and the community. Mechanisms are in place to allow the customer support team to be notified of operational issues that impact the customer experience. A Service Health Dashboard is available and maintained by the customer support team to alert customers to any issues that may be of broad impact. The AWS Security Center is available to provide you with security and compliance details about AWS. Customers can also subscribe to AWS Support offerings that include direct communication with the customer support team and proactive alerts to any customer-impacting issues.

Network Security

The AWS network has been architected to permit you to select the level of security and resiliency appropriate for your workload. To enable you to build geographically dispersed, fault-tolerant web architectures with cloud resources, AWS has implemented a world-class network infrastructure that is carefully monitored and managed.

Secure Network Architecture

Network devices, including firewall and other boundary devices, are in place to monitor and control communications at the external boundary of the network and at key internal boundaries within the network. These boundary devices employ rule sets, *access control lists (ACLs)*, and configurations to enforce the flow of information to specific information system services.

ACLs, or traffic flow policies, are established on each managed interface, which manage and enforce the flow of traffic. ACL policies are approved by Amazon Information Security. These policies are automatically pushed to ensure these managed interfaces enforce the most up-to-date ACLs.

Secure Access Points

AWS has strategically placed a limited number of access points to the cloud to allow for a more comprehensive monitoring of inbound and outbound communications and network traffic. These customer access points are called Application Programming Interface (API) endpoints, and they permit secure HTTP access (HTTPS), which allows you to establish a secure communication session with your storage or compute instances within AWS. To support customers with Federal Information Processing Standard (FIPS) cryptographic requirements, the Secure Sockets Layer (SSL)-terminating load balancers in AWS GovCloud (US) are FIPS 140-2 compliant.

In addition, AWS has implemented network devices that are dedicated to managing interfacing communications with Internet Service Providers (ISPs). AWS employs a redundant connection to more than one communication service at each Internet-facing edge of the AWS network. These connections each have dedicated network devices.

Transmission Protection

You can connect to an AWS access point via HTTP or HTTPS using SSL, a cryptographic protocol that is designed to protect against eavesdropping, tampering, and message forgery. For customers who require additional layers of network security, AWS offers the Amazon Virtual Private Cloud (Amazon VPC) (as referenced in Chapter 4, "Amazon Virtual Private Cloud (Amazon VPC)," which provides a private subnet within the AWS Cloud and the ability to use an IPsec Virtual Private Network (VPN) device to provide an encrypted tunnel between the Amazon VPC and your data center.

Network Monitoring and Protection

The AWS network provides significant protection against traditional network security issues, and you can implement further protection. The following are a few examples:

Distributed Denial of Service (DDoS) Attacks   AWS API endpoints are hosted on a large, Internet-scale, world-class infrastructure that benefits from the same engineering expertise that has built Amazon into the world's largest online retailer. Proprietary DDoS mitigation techniques are used. Additionally, AWS networks are multi-homed across a number of providers to achieve Internet access diversity.

Man in the Middle (MITM) Attacks   All of the AWS APIs are available via SSL-protected endpoints that provide server authentication. Amazon Elastic Compute Cloud (Amazon EC2) AMIs automatically generate new Secure Shell (SSH) host certificates on first boot and log them to the instance's console. You can then use the secure APIs to call the console and access the host certificates before logging into the instance for the first time. AWS encourages you to use SSL for all of your interactions.

IP Spoofing   Amazon EC2 instances cannot send spoofed network traffic. The AWS-controlled, host-based firewall infrastructure will not permit an instance to send traffic with a source IP or Machine Access Control (MAC) address other than its own.

Port Scanning   Unauthorized port scans by Amazon EC2 customers are a violation of the AWS Acceptable Use Policy. Violations of the AWS Acceptable Use Policy are taken seriously, and every reported violation is investigated. Customers can report suspected abuse via the contacts available on the AWS website. When unauthorized port scanning is detected by AWS, it is stopped and blocked. Port scans of Amazon EC2 instances are generally ineffective because, by default, all inbound ports on Amazon EC2 instances are closed and are only opened by the customer. Strict management of security groups can further mitigate the threat of port scans. If you configure the security group to allow traffic from any source to a specific port, that specific port will be vulnerable to a port scan. In these cases, you must use appropriate security measures to protect listening services that may be essential to their application from being discovered by an unauthorized port scan. For example, a web server must clearly have port 80 (HTTP) open to the world, and the administrator of this server is responsible for the security of the HTTP server software, such as Apache. You may request permission to conduct vulnerability scans as required to meet your specific compliance requirements. These scans must be limited to your own instances and must not violate the AWS Acceptable Use Policy. Advanced approval for these types of scans can be initiated by submitting a request via the AWS website.

Packet Sniffing by Other Tenants   While you can place your interfaces into promiscuous mode, the hypervisor will not deliver any traffic to them that is not addressed to them. Even two virtual instances that are owned by the same customer located on the same physical host cannot listen to each other's traffic. While Amazon EC2 does provide ample protection against one customer inadvertently or maliciously attempting to view another customer's data, as a standard practice you should *encrypt* sensitive traffic.

It is not possible for a virtual instance running in promiscuous mode to receive or "sniff" traffic that is intended for a different virtual instance.

Attacks such as Address Resolution Protocol (ARP) cache poisoning do not work within Amazon EC2 and Amazon VPC.

AWS Account Security Features

AWS provides a variety of tools and features that you can use to keep your *AWS account* and resources safe from unauthorized use. This includes *credentials* for access control, HTTPS endpoints for encrypted data transmission, the creation of separate AWS Identity and Access Management (IAM) user accounts, and user activity logging for security monitoring. You can take advantage of all of these security tools no matter which AWS services you select.

AWS Credentials

To help ensure that only authorized users and processes access your AWS account and resources, AWS uses several types of credentials for *authentication*. These include passwords, cryptographic keys, digital signatures, and certificates. AWS also provides the option of requiring *Multi-Factor Authentication (MFA)* to log in to your AWS Account or *IAM user* accounts. Table 12.1 highlights the various AWS credentials and their uses.

TABLE 12.1   AWS Credentials

Credential Type	Use	Description
Passwords	AWS root account or IAM user account login to the AWS Management Console	A string of characters used to log in to your AWS account or IAM account. AWS passwords must be a minimum of 6 characters and may be up to 128 characters.
Multi-Factor Authentication (MFA)	AWS root account or IAM user account login to the AWS Management Console	A six-digit, single-use code that is required in addition to your password to log in to your AWS account or IAM user account.
Access Keys	Digitally-signed requests to AWS APIs (using the AWS Software Development Kit [SDK], Command Line Interface [CLI], or REST/Query APIs)	Includes an access key ID and a secret access key. You use access keys to sign programmatic requests digitally that you make to AWS.
Key Pairs	SSH login to Amazon EC2 instances Amazon CloudFront-signed URLs	A key pair is required to connect to an Amazon EC2 instance launched from a public AMI. The keys that Amazon EC2 uses are 1024-bit SSH-2 RSA keys. You can have a key pair generated automatically for you when you launch the instance, or you can upload your own.
X.509 Certificates	Digitally signed SOAP requests to AWS APIs SSL server certificates for HTTPS	X.509 certificates are only used to sign SOAP-based requests (currently used only with Amazon Simple Storage Service [Amazon S3]). You can have AWS create an X.509 certificate and private key that you can download, or you can upload your own certificate by using the Security Credentials page.

For security reasons, if your credentials have been lost or forgotten, you cannot recover them or re-download them. However, you can create new credentials and then disable or delete the old set of credentials. In fact, AWS recommends that you change (rotate) your *access keys* and certificates on a regular basis. To help you do this without potential impact to your application's availability, AWS supports multiple concurrent access keys and certificates. With this feature, you can rotate keys and certificates into and out of operation on a regular basis without any downtime to your application. This can help to mitigate risk from lost or compromised access keys or certificates.

The AWS IAM API enables you to rotate the access keys of your AWS account and also for IAM user accounts.

Passwords

Passwords are required to access your AWS Account, individual IAM user accounts, AWS Discussion Forums, and the AWS Support Center. You specify the password when you first create the account, and you can change it at any time by going to the Security Credentials page. AWS passwords can be up to 128 characters long and contain special characters, giving you the ability to create very strong passwords.

You can set a password policy for your IAM user accounts to ensure that strong passwords are used and that they are changed often. A password policy is a set of rules that define the type of password an IAM user can set.

AWS Multi-Factor Authentication (AWS MFA)

AWS MFA is an additional layer of security for accessing AWS Cloud services. When you enable this optional feature, you will need to provide a six-digit, single-use code in addition to your standard user name and password credentials before access is granted to your AWS account settings or AWS Cloud services and resources. You get this single-use code from an authentication device that you keep in your physical possession. This is MFA because more than one authentication factor is checked before access is granted: a password (something you know) and the precise code from your authentication device (something you have). You can enable MFA devices for your AWS account and for the users you have created under your AWS account with AWS IAM. In addition, you can add MFA protection for access across AWS accounts, for when you want to allow a user you've created under one AWS account to use an *IAM role* to access resources under another AWS account. You can require the user to use MFA before assuming the role as an additional layer of security.

AWS MFA supports the use of both hardware tokens and virtual MFA devices. Virtual MFA devices use the same protocols as the physical MFA devices, but can run on any mobile hardware device, including a smart phone. A virtual MFA device uses a software application that generates six-digit authentication codes that are compatible with the Time-Based One-Time Password (TOTP) standard, as described in RFC 6238. Most virtual MFA applications allow you to host more than one virtual MFA device, which makes them more convenient than hardware MFA devices. However, you should be aware that because a virtual MFA may be run on a less secure device such as a smart phone, a virtual MFA might not provide the same level of security as a hardware MFA device.

You can also enforce MFA authentication for AWS Cloud service APIs in order to provide an extra layer of protection over powerful or privileged actions such as terminating Amazon EC2 instances or reading sensitive data stored in Amazon S3. You do this by adding an MFA requirement to an IAM access policy. You can attach these access policies to IAM users, *IAM groups*, or resources that support ACLs like Amazon S3 buckets, Amazon Simple Queue Service (Amazon SQS) queues, and Amazon Simple Notification Service (Amazon SNS) topics.

Access Keys

Access keys are created by AWS IAM and delivered as a pair: the *Access Key ID (AKI)* and the *Secret Access Key (SAK)*. AWS requires that all API requests be signed by the SAK; that is, they must include a digital signature that AWS can use to verify the identity of the requestor. You calculate the digital signature using a cryptographic hash function. If you use any of the AWS SDKs to generate requests, the digital signature calculation is done for you.

Not only does the signing process help protect message integrity by preventing tampering with the request while it is in transit, but it also helps protect against potential replay attacks. A request must reach AWS within 15 minutes of the timestamp in the request. Otherwise, AWS denies the request.

The most recent version of the digital signature calculation process at the time of this writing is *Signature Version 4*, which calculates the signature using the *Hashed Message Authentication Mode (HMAC)*-Secure Hash Algorithm (SHA)-256 protocol. Version 4 provides an additional measure of protection over previous versions by requiring that you sign the message using a key that is derived from your SAK instead of using the SAK itself. In addition, you derive the signing key based on credential scope, which facilitates cryptographic isolation of the signing key.

> TIP
>
> Because access keys can be misused if they fall into the wrong hands, AWS encourages you to save them in a safe place and to not embed them in your code. For customers with large fleets of elastically scaling Amazon EC2 instances, the use of IAM roles can be a more secure and convenient way to manage the distribution of access keys.

IAM roles provide temporary credentials, which not only get automatically loaded to the target instance, but are also automatically rotated multiple times a day.

Amazon EC2 uses an Instance Profile as a container for an IAM role. When you create an IAM role using the AWS Management Console, the console creates an instance profile automatically and gives it the same name as the role to which it corresponds. If you use the AWS CLI, API, or an AWS SDK to create a role, you create the role and instance profile as separate actions, and you might give them different names. To launch an instance with an IAM role, you specify the name of its instance profile. When you launch an instance using the Amazon EC2 console, you can select a role to associate with the instance; however, the list that's displayed is actually a list of instance profile names.

Key pairs

Amazon EC2 supports RSA 2048 SSH keys for gaining first access to an Amazon EC2 instance. On a Linux instance, access is granted through showing possession of the SSH private key. On a Windows instance, access is granted by showing possession of the SSH private key in order to decrypt the administrator password. The public key is embedded in your instance, and you use the private key to sign in securely without a password. After you create your own AMIs, you can choose other mechanisms to log in to your new instances securely. You can have a *key pair* generated automatically for you when you launch the instance or you can upload your own. Save the private key in a safe place on your system and record the location where you saved it.

For Amazon CloudFront, you use key pairs to create signed URLs for private content, such as when you want to distribute restricted content that someone paid for. You create Amazon CloudFront key pairs by using the Security Credentials page. Amazon CloudFront key pairs can be created only by the root account and cannot be created by IAM users.

X.509 Certificates

X.509 certificates are used to sign SOAP-based requests. X.509 certificates contain a public key that is associated with a private key. When you create a request, you create a digital signature with your private key and then include that signature in the request, along with your certificate. AWS verifies that you're the sender by decrypting the signature with the public key that is in your certificate. AWS also verifies that the certificate that you sent matches the certificate that you uploaded to AWS.

For your AWS account, you can have AWS create an X.509 certificate and private key that you can download, or you can upload your own certificate by using the Security Credentials page. For IAM users, you must create the X.509 certificate (signing certificate) by using third-party software. In contrast to root account credentials, AWS cannot create an X.509 certificate for IAM users. After you create the certificate, you attach it to an IAM user by using IAM.

In addition to SOAP requests, X.509 certificates are used as SSL/*Transport Layer Security (TLS)* server certificates for customers who want to use HTTPS to encrypt their transmissions. To use them for HTTPS, you can use an open-source tool like OpenSSL to create a unique private key. You'll need the private key to create the Certificate Signing Request (CSR) that you submit to a Certificate Authority (CA) to obtain the server certificate. You'll then use the AWS CLI to upload the certificate, private key, and certificate chain to IAM.

You will also need an X.509 certificate to create a customized Linux AMI for Amazon EC2 instances. The certificate is only required to create an instance-backed AMI (as opposed to an Amazon Elastic Block Store [Amazon EBS]-backed AMI). You can have AWS create an X.509 certificate and private key that you can download, or you can upload your own certificate by using the Security Credentials page.

AWS CloudTrail

AWS CloudTrail is a web service that records API calls made on your account and delivers log files to your Amazon S3 bucket. AWS CloudTrail's benefit is visibility into account activity by recording API calls made on your account. AWS CloudTrail records the following information about each API call:

- The name of the API
- The identity of the caller
- The time of the API call
- The request parameters
- The response elements returned by the AWS Cloud service

This information helps you to track changes made to your AWS resources and to troubleshoot operational issues. AWS CloudTrail makes it easier to ensure compliance with internal policies and regulatory standards.

AWS CloudTrail supports log file integrity, which means you can prove to third parties (for example, auditors) that the log file sent by AWS CloudTrail has not been altered. Validated log files are invaluable in security and forensic investigations. This feature is built using industry standard algorithms: SHA-256 for hashing and SHA-256 with RSA for digital signing. This makes it computationally unfeasible to modify, delete, or forge AWS CloudTrail log files without detection.

AWS Cloud Service-Specific Security

Not only is security built into every layer of the AWS infrastructure, but also into each of the services available on that infrastructure. AWS Cloud services are architected to work efficiently and securely with all AWS networks and platforms. Each service provides additional security features to enable you to protect sensitive data and applications.

Compute Services

AWS provides a variety of cloud-based computing services that include a wide selection of compute instances that can scale up and down automatically to meet the needs of your application or enterprise.

Amazon Elastic Compute Cloud (Amazon EC2) Security

Amazon EC2 is a key component in Amazon's Infrastructure as a Service (IaaS), providing resizable computing capacity using server instances in AWS data centers. Amazon EC2 is designed to make web-scale computing easier by enabling you to obtain and configure capacity with minimal friction. You create and launch instances, which are collections of platform hardware and software.

Multiple Levels of Security   Security within Amazon EC2 is provided on multiple levels: the operating system (OS) of the host platform, the virtual instance OS or guest OS, a firewall, and signed API calls. Each of these items builds on the capabilities of the others.

The goal is to prevent data contained within Amazon EC2 from being intercepted by unauthorized systems or users and to make Amazon EC2 instances themselves as secure as possible without sacrificing the flexibility in configuration that customers demand.

The Hypervisor   Amazon EC2 currently uses a highly customized version of the Xen hypervisor, taking advantage of paravirtualization (in the case of Linux guests). Because paravirtualized guests rely on the hypervisor to provide support for operations that normally require privileged access, the guest OS has no elevated access to the CPU. The CPU provides four separate privilege modes: 0–3, called rings. Ring 0 is the most privileged and 3 the least. The host OS executes in Ring 0. However, instead of executing in Ring 0 as most OSs do, the guest OS runs in lesser-privileged Ring 1, and applications in the least privileged in Ring 3. This explicit virtualization of the physical resources leads to a clear separation between guest and hypervisor, resulting in additional security separation between the two.

Instance Isolation   Different instances running on the same physical machine are isolated from each other via the Xen hypervisor. Amazon is active in the Xen community, which provides AWS with awareness of the latest developments. In addition, the AWS firewall resides within the hypervisor layer, between the physical network interface and the instance's virtual interface. All packets must pass through this layer; thus, an instance's neighbors have no more access to that instance than any other host on the Internet and can be treated as if they are on separate physical hosts. The physical RAM is separated using similar mechanisms. Customer instances have no access to raw disk devices, but instead are presented with virtualized disks. The AWS proprietary disk virtualization layer automatically resets every block of storage used by the customer, so that one customer's data is never unintentionally exposed to another customer. In addition, memory allocated to guests is scrubbed (set to zero) by the hypervisor when it is unallocated to a guest. The memory is not returned to the pool of free memory available for new allocations until the memory scrubbing is completed. Figure 12.3 depicts instance isolation within Amazon EC2.

FIGURE 12.3   Amazon EC2 multiple layers of security

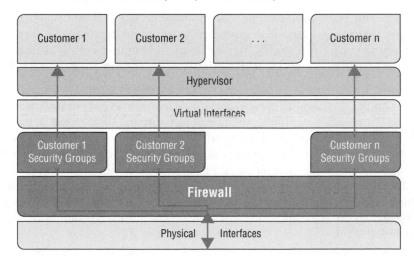

Host Operating System   Administrators with a business need to access the management plane are required to use MFA to gain access to purpose-built administration hosts. These administrative hosts are systems that are specifically designed, built, configured, and hardened to protect the management plane of the cloud. All such access is logged and audited. When an employee no longer has a business need to access the management plane, the privileges and access to these hosts and relevant systems can be revoked.

Guest Operating System   Virtual instances are completely controlled by you, the customer. You have full root access or administrative control over accounts, services, and applications. AWS does not have any access rights to your instances or the guest OS. AWS recommends a base set of security best practices to include disabling password-only access to your guests, and using some form of MFA to gain access to your instances (or at a minimum certificate-based SSH Version 2 access). Additionally, you should employ a privilege escalation mechanism with logging on a per-user basis. For example, if the guest OS is Linux, after hardening, your instance you should use certificate-based SSHv2 to access the virtual instance, disable remote root login, use command-line logging, and use sudo for privilege escalation. You should generate your own key pairs in order to guarantee that they are unique and not shared with other customers or with AWS. AWS also supports the use of the SSH network protocol to enable you to log in securely to your UNIX/Linux Amazon EC2 instances. Authentication for SSH used with AWS is via a public/private key pair to reduce the risk of unauthorized access to your instance. You can also connect remotely to your Windows instances using Remote Desktop Protocol (RDP) by using an RDP certificate generated for your instance. You also control the updating and patching of your guest OS, including security updates. Amazon-provided Windows and Linux-based AMIs are updated regularly with the latest patches, so if you do not need to preserve data or customizations on your running Amazon AMI instances, you can simply relaunch new instances with the latest updated AMI. In addition, updates are provided for the Amazon Linux AMI via the Amazon Linux yum repositories.

Firewall   Amazon EC2 provides a mandatory inbound firewall that is configured in a default deny-all mode; Amazon EC2 customers must explicitly open the ports needed to allow inbound traffic. The traffic may be restricted by protocol, by service port, and by source IP address (individual IP or Classless Inter-Domain Routing [CIDR] block).

The firewall can be configured in groups, permitting different classes of instances to have different rules. Consider, for example, the case of a traditional three-tiered web application. The group for the web servers would have port 80 (HTTP) and/or port 443 (HTTPS) open to the Internet. The group for the application servers would have port 8000 (application specific) accessible only to the web server group. The group for the database servers would have port 3306 (MySQL) open only to the application server group. All three groups would permit administrative access on port 22 (SSH), but only from the customer's corporate network. Highly secure applications can be deployed using this approach, which is also depicted in Figure 12.4.

FIGURE 12.4   Amazon EC2 security group firewall

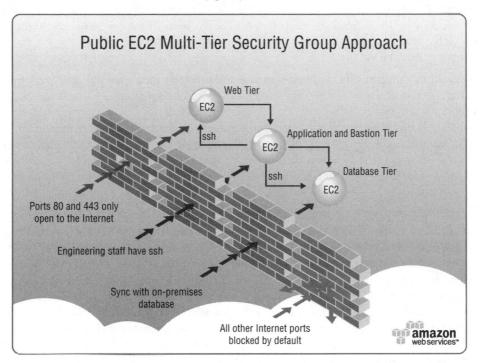

The level of security afforded by the firewall is a function of which ports you open and for what duration and purpose. Well-informed traffic management and security design are still required on a per-instance basis. AWS further encourages you to apply additional per-instance filters with host-based firewalls such as IPtables or the Windows Firewall and VPNs. This can restrict both inbound and outbound traffic.

The default state is to deny all incoming traffic, and you should carefully plan what you will open when building and securing your applications.

API Access   API calls to launch and terminate instances, change firewall parameters, and perform other functions are all signed by your Amazon Secret Access Key, which could be either the AWS account's Secret Access Key or the Secret Access key of a user created with AWS IAM. Without access to your Secret Access Key, Amazon EC2 API calls cannot be made on your behalf. API calls can also be encrypted with SSL to maintain confidentiality. AWS recommends always using SSL-protected API endpoints.

Amazon Elastic Block Storage (Amazon EBS) Security   *Amazon EBS* allows you to create storage volumes from 1 GB to 16 TB that can be mounted as devices by Amazon EC2 instances. Storage volumes behave like raw, unformatted block devices, with user-supplied device names and a block device interface. You can create a file system on top of Amazon

EBS volumes or use them in any other way you would use a block device (like a hard drive). Amazon EBS volume access is restricted to the AWS account that created the volume and to the users under the AWS account created with AWS IAM (if the user has been granted access to the EBS operations). All other AWS accounts and users are denied the permission to view or access the volume.

Data stored in Amazon EBS volumes is redundantly stored in multiple physical locations as part of normal operation of those services and at no additional charge. However, Amazon EBS replication is stored within the same Availability Zone, not across multiple zones; therefore, it is highly recommended that you conduct regular snapshots to Amazon S3 for long-term data durability. For customers who have architected complex transactional databases using Amazon EBS, it is recommended that backups to Amazon S3 be performed through the database management system so that distributed transactions and logs can be checkpointed. AWS does not automatically perform backups of data that are maintained on virtual disks attached to running instances on Amazon EC2.

You can make Amazon EBS volume snapshots publicly available to other AWS accounts to use as the basis for creating duplicate volumes. Sharing Amazon EBS volume snapshots does not provide other AWS accounts with the permission to alter or delete the original snapshot, as that right is explicitly reserved for the AWS account that created the volume. An Amazon EBS snapshot is a block-level view of an entire Amazon EBS volume. Note that data that is not visible through the filesystem on the volume, such as files that have been deleted, may be present in the Amazon EBS snapshot. If you want to create shared snapshots, you should do so carefully. If a volume has held sensitive data or has had files deleted from it, you should create a new Amazon EBS volume to share. The data to be contained in the shared snapshot should be copied to the new volume, and the snapshot created from the new volume.

Amazon EBS volumes are presented to you as raw unformatted *block devices* that have been wiped prior to being made available for use. Wiping occurs immediately before reuse so that you can be assured that the wipe process is completed. If you have procedures requiring that all data be wiped via a specific method, you have the ability to do so on Amazon EBS. You should conduct a specialized wipe procedure prior to deleting the volume for compliance with your established requirements.

Encryption of sensitive data is generally a good security practice, and AWS provides the ability to encrypt Amazon EBS volumes and their snapshots with Advanced Encryption Standard (AES)-256. The encryption occurs on the servers that host the Amazon EC2 instances, providing encryption of data as it moves between Amazon EC2 instances and Amazon EBS storage. In order to be able to do this efficiently and with low latency, the Amazon EBS encryption feature is only available on Amazon EC2's more powerful instance types.

Networking

AWS provides a range of networking services that enable you to create a logically isolated network that you define, establish a private network connection to the AWS Cloud, use a highly available and scalable Domain Name System (DNS) service, and deliver content to your end users with low latency at high data transfer speeds with a content delivery web service.

Elastic Load Balancing Security

Elastic Load Balancing is used to manage traffic on a fleet of Amazon EC2 instances, distributing traffic to instances across all Availability Zones within a region. Elastic Load Balancing has all of the advantages of an on-premises load balancer, plus several security benefits:

- Takes over the encryption and decryption work from the Amazon EC2 instances and manages it centrally on the load balancer.

- Offers clients a single point of contact, and can also serve as the first line of defense against attacks on your network.

- When used in an Amazon VPC, supports creation and management of security groups associated with your Elastic Load Balancing to provide additional networking and security options.

- Supports end-to-end traffic encryption using TLS (previously SSL) on those networks that use secure HTTP (HTTPS) connections. When TLS is used, the TLS server certificate used to terminate client connections can be managed centrally on the load balancer, instead of on every individual instance.

HTTPS/TLS uses a long-term secret key to generate a short-term session key to be used between the server and the browser to create the encrypted message. Elastic Load Balancing configures your load balancer with a pre-defined cipher set that is used for TLS negotiation when a connection is established between a client and your load balancer. The pre-defined cipher set provides compatibility with a broad range of clients and uses strong cryptographic algorithms. However, some customers may have requirements for allowing only specific ciphers and protocols (for example, Payment Card Industry Data Security Standard [PCI DSS], Sarbanes-Oxley Act [SOX]) from clients to ensure that standards are met. In these cases, Elastic Load Balancing provides options for selecting different configurations for TLS protocols and ciphers. You can choose to enable or disable the ciphers depending on your specific requirements.

To help ensure the use of newer and stronger cipher suites when establishing a secure connection, you can configure the load balancer to have the final say in the cipher suite selection during the client-server negotiation. When the Server Order Preference option is selected, the load balancer will select a cipher suite based on the server's prioritization of cipher suites instead of the client's. This gives you more control over the level of security that clients use to connect to your load balancer.

For even greater communication privacy, Elastic Load Balancing allows the use of Perfect Forward Secrecy, which uses session keys that are ephemeral and not stored anywhere. This prevents the decoding of captured data, even if the secret long-term key itself is compromised.

Elastic Load Balancing allows you to identify the originating IP address of a client connecting to your servers, whether you're using HTTPS or TCP load balancing. Typically, client connection information, such as IP address and port, is lost when requests are proxied through a load balancer. This is because the load balancer sends requests to the server on behalf of the client, making your load balancer appear as though it is the requesting client. Having the originating client IP address is useful if you need more information about visitors to your applications in order to gather connection statistics, analyze traffic logs, or manage whitelists of IP addresses.

Elastic Load Balancing access logs contain information about each HTTP and TCP request processed by your load balancer. This includes the IP address and port of the requesting client, the back-end IP address of the instance that processed the request, the size of the request and response, and the actual request line from the client (for example, GET http://www.example.com: 80/HTTP/1.1). All requests sent to the load balancer are logged, including requests that never make it to back-end instances.

Amazon Virtual Private Cloud (Amazon VPC) Security

Normally, each Amazon EC2 instance you launch is randomly assigned a public IP address in the Amazon EC2 address space. *Amazon VPC* enables you to create an isolated portion of the AWS Cloud and launch Amazon EC2 instances that have private (RFC 1918) addresses in the range of your choice (for example, 10.0.0.0/16). You can define subnets within your Amazon VPC, grouping similar kinds of instances based on IP address range and then set up routing and security to control the flow of traffic in and out of the instances and subnets.

Security features within Amazon VPC include security groups, *network ACLs*, routing tables, and external gateways. Each of these items is complementary to providing a secure, isolated network that can be extended through selective enabling of direct Internet access or private connectivity to another network. Amazon EC2 instances running within an Amazon VPC inherit all of the benefits described below related to the guest OS and protection against packet sniffing. Note, however, that you must create security groups specifically for your Amazon VPC; any Amazon EC2 security groups you have created will not work inside your Amazon VPC. In addition, Amazon VPC security groups have additional capabilities that Amazon EC2 security groups do not have, such as being able to change the security group after the instance is launched and being able to specify any protocol with a standard protocol number (as opposed to just TCP, User Datagram Protocol [UDP], or Internet Control Message Protocol [ICMP]).

Each Amazon VPC is a distinct, isolated network within the cloud; network traffic within each Amazon VPC is isolated from all other Amazon VPCs. At creation time, you select an IP address range for each Amazon VPC. You may create and attach an Internet gateway, virtual private gateway, or both to establish external connectivity, subject to the following controls.

API Access   Calls to create and delete Amazon VPCs; change routing, security group, and network ACL parameters; and perform other functions are all signed by your Amazon Secret Access Key, which could be either the AWS account's Secret Access Key or the Secret Access key of a user created with AWS IAM. Without access to your Secret Access Key, Amazon VPC API calls cannot be made on your behalf. In addition, API calls can be encrypted with SSL to maintain confidentiality. AWS recommends always using SSL-protected API endpoints. AWS IAM also enables a customer to further control what APIs a newly created user has permissions to call.

Subnets and Route Tables   You create one or more subnets within each Amazon VPC; each instance launched in the Amazon VPC is connected to one subnet. Traditional Layer 2 security attacks, including MAC spoofing and ARP spoofing, are blocked. Each subnet in an Amazon VPC is associated with a routing table, and all network traffic leaving the subnet is processed by the routing table to determine the destination.

Firewall (Security Groups)   Like Amazon EC2, Amazon VPC supports a complete firewall solution, enabling filtering on both ingress and egress traffic from an instance. The default group enables inbound communication from other members of the same group and outbound communication to any destination. Traffic can be restricted by any IP protocol, by service port, and source/destination IP address (individual IP or CIDR block). The firewall isn't controlled through the guest OS; rather, it can be modified only through the invocation of Amazon VPC APIs. AWS supports the ability to grant granular access to different administrative functions on the instances and the firewall, therefore enabling you to implement additional security through separation of duties. The level of security afforded by the firewall is a function of which ports you open and for what duration and purpose. Well-informed traffic management and security design are still required on a per-instance basis. AWS further encourages you to apply additional per-instance filters with host-based firewalls such as IPtables or the Windows Firewall. Figure 12.5 illustrates an Amazon VPC with two types of subnets—public and private—and two network paths with two different networks—a customer data center and the Internet.

FIGURE 12.5   Amazon VPC network architecture

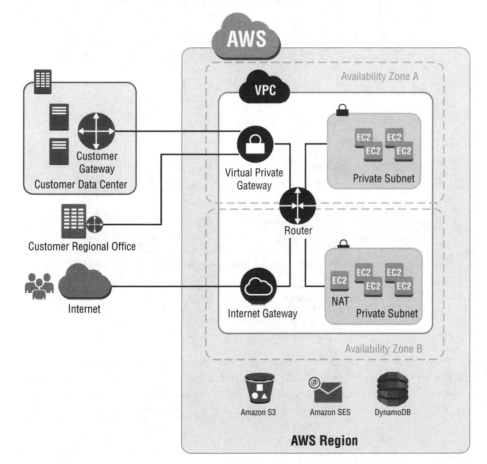

Network ACLs   To add a further layer of security within Amazon VPC, you can configure network ACLs. These are stateless traffic filters that apply to all traffic inbound or outbound from a subnet within Amazon VPC. These ACLs can contain ordered rules to allow or deny traffic based on IP protocol, by service port, and source/destination IP address.

Like security groups, network ACLs are managed through Amazon VPC APIs, adding an additional layer of protection and enabling additional security through separation of duties. Figure 12.6 depicts how the security controls above interrelate to enable flexible network topologies while providing complete control over network traffic flows.

FIGURE 12.6   Flexible network architectures

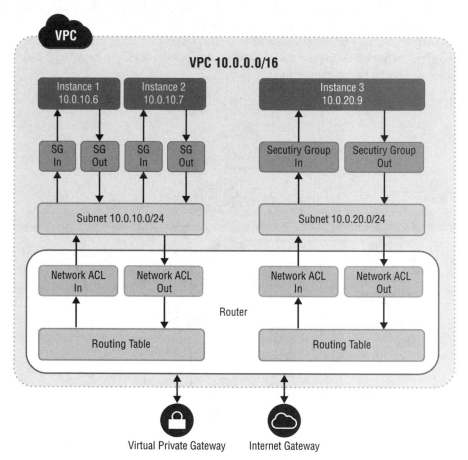

Virtual Private Gateway   Internet Gateway

Virtual Private Gateway   A virtual private gateway enables private connectivity between the Amazon VPC and another network. Network traffic within each virtual private gateway is isolated from network traffic within all other virtual private gateways. You can establish VPN connections to the virtual private gateway from gateway devices at your premises. Each connection is secured by a preshared key in conjunction with the IP address of the customer gateway device.

Internet Gateway   An Internet gateway may be attached to an Amazon VPC to enable direct connectivity to Amazon S3, other AWS services, and the Internet. Each instance desiring this access must either have an Elastic IP associated with it or route traffic through a Network Address Translation (NAT) instance. Additionally, network routes are configured to direct traffic to the Internet gateway (see Figure 12.6). AWS provides reference NAT AMIs that you can extend to perform network logging, deep packet inspection, application layer filtering, or other security controls.

This access can only be modified through the invocation of Amazon VPC APIs. AWS supports the ability to grant granular access to different administrative functions on the instances and the Internet gateway, enabling you to implement additional security through separation of duties.

Dedicated Instances   Within an Amazon VPC, you can launch Amazon EC2 instances that are physically isolated at the host hardware level (that is, they will run on single-tenant hardware). An Amazon VPC can be created with "dedicated" tenancy, so that all instances launched into the Amazon VPC will use this feature. Alternatively, an Amazon VPC may be created with "default" tenancy, but you can specify dedicated tenancy for particular instances launched into it.

Amazon CloudFront Security

Amazon CloudFront gives customers an easy way to distribute content to end users with low latency and high data transfer speeds. It delivers dynamic, static, and streaming content using a global network of edge locations. Requests for customers' objects are automatically routed to the nearest edge location, so content is delivered with the best possible performance. Amazon CloudFront is optimized to work with other AWS services like Amazon S3, Amazon EC2, Elastic Load Balancing, and Amazon Route 53. It also works seamlessly with any non-AWS origin server that stores the original, definitive versions of your files.

Amazon CloudFront requires that every request made to its control API is authenticated so only authorized users can create, modify, or delete their own Amazon CloudFront distributions. Requests are signed with an HMAC-SHA-1 signature calculated from the request and the user's private key. Additionally, the Amazon CloudFront control API is only accessible via SSL-enabled endpoints.

There is no guarantee of durability of data held in Amazon CloudFront edge locations. The service may sometimes remove objects from edge locations if those objects are not requested frequently. Durability is provided by Amazon S3, which works as the origin server for Amazon CloudFront by holding the original, definitive copies of objects delivered by Amazon CloudFront.

If you want control over who can download content from Amazon CloudFront, you can enable the service's private content feature. This feature has two components. The first controls how content is delivered from the Amazon CloudFront edge location to viewers on the

Internet. The second controls how the Amazon CloudFront edge locations access objects in Amazon S3. Amazon CloudFront also supports geo restriction, which restricts access to your content based on the geographic location of your viewers.

To control access to the original copies of your objects in Amazon S3, Amazon CloudFront allows you to create one or more Origin Access Identities and associate these with your distributions. When an Origin Access Identity is associated with an Amazon CloudFront distribution, the distribution will use that identity to retrieve objects from Amazon S3. You can then use Amazon S3's ACL feature, which limits access to that Origin Access Identity so the original copy of the object is not publicly readable.

To control who can download objects from Amazon CloudFront edge locations, the service uses a signed-URL verification system. To use this system, you first create a public-private key pair and upload the public key to your account via the AWS Management Console. You then configure your Amazon CloudFront distribution to indicate which accounts you would authorize to sign requests—you can indicate up to five AWS accounts that you trust to sign requests. As you receive requests, you will create policy documents indicating the conditions under which you want Amazon CloudFront to serve your content. These policy documents can specify the name of the object that is requested, the date and time of the request, and the source IP (or CIDR range) of the client making the request. You then calculate the SHA-1 hash of your policy document and sign this using your private key. Finally, you include both the encoded policy document and the signature as query string parameters when you reference your objects. When Amazon CloudFront receives a request, it will decode the signature using your public key. Amazon CloudFront will only serve requests that have a valid policy document and matching signature.

Note that private content is an optional feature that must be enabled when you set up your Amazon CloudFront distribution. Content delivered without this feature enabled will be publicly readable.

Amazon CloudFront provides the option to transfer content over an encrypted connection (HTTPS). By default, Amazon CloudFront will accept requests over both HTTP and HTTPS protocols. However, you can also configure Amazon CloudFront to require HTTPS for all requests or have Amazon CloudFront redirect HTTP requests to HTTPS. You can even configure Amazon CloudFront distributions to allow HTTP for some objects but require HTTPS for other objects.

Storage

AWS provides low-cost data storage with high durability and availability. AWS offers storage choices for backup, archiving, and disaster recovery, and also for block and object storage.

Amazon Simple Storage Service (Amazon S3) Security

Amazon S3 allows you to upload and retrieve data at any time, from anywhere on the web. Amazon S3 stores data as objects within buckets. An object can be any kind of file: a text file, a photo, a video, and more. When you add a file to Amazon S3, you have the option of including metadata with the file and setting permissions to control access to the file. For each bucket, you can control access to the bucket (who can create, delete, and list objects in the bucket), view access logs for the bucket and its objects, and choose the geographical region where Amazon S3 will store the bucket and its contents.

Data Access

Access to data stored in Amazon S3 is restricted by default; only bucket and object owners have access to the Amazon S3 resources they create. (Note that a bucket/object owner is the AWS account owner, not the user who created the bucket/object.) There are multiple ways to control access to buckets and objects:

IAM Policies   AWS IAM enables organizations with many employees to create and manage multiple users under a single AWS account. IAM policies are attached to the users, enabling centralized control of permissions for users under your AWS account to access buckets or objects. With IAM policies, you can only grant users within your own AWS account permission to access your Amazon S3 resources.

ACLs   Within Amazon S3, you can use ACLs to give read or write access on buckets or objects to groups of users. With ACLs, you can only grant other AWS accounts (not specific users) access to your Amazon S3 resources.

Bucket Policies   Bucket policies in Amazon S3 can be used to add or deny permissions across some or all of the objects within a single bucket. Policies can be attached to users, groups, or Amazon S3 buckets, enabling centralized management of permissions. With bucket policies, you can grant users within your AWS account or other AWS accounts access to your Amazon S3 resources.

Query String Authentication   You can use a query string to express a request entirely in a URL. In this case, you use query parameters to provide request information, including the authentication information. Because the request signature is part of the URL, this type of URL is often referred to as a *pre-signed URL*. You can use pre-signed URLs to embed clickable links, which can be valid for up to seven days, in HTML.

You can further restrict access to specific resources based on certain conditions. For example, you can restrict access based on request time (Date Condition), whether the request was sent using SSL (Boolean Conditions), a requester's IP address (IP Address Condition), or the requester's client application (String Conditions). To identify these conditions, you use policy keys.

Amazon S3 also gives developers the option to use query string authentication, which allows them to share Amazon S3 objects through URLs that are valid for a predefined period of time. Query string authentication is useful for giving HTTP for browser access to resources that would normally require authentication. The signature in the query string secures the request.

Data Transfer

For maximum security, you can securely upload/download data to Amazon S3 via the SSL-encrypted endpoints. The encrypted endpoints are accessible from both the Internet and from within Amazon EC2, so that data is transferred securely both within AWS and to and from sources outside of AWS.

Data Storage

Amazon S3 provides multiple options for protecting data at rest. For customers who prefer to manage their own encryption, they can use a client encryption library like the Amazon S3 Encryption Client to encrypt data before uploading to Amazon S3. Alternatively, you can use Amazon S3 *Server Side Encryption (SSE)* if you prefer to have Amazon S3 manage the encryption process for you. Data is encrypted with a key generated by AWS or with a key you supply, depending on your requirements. With Amazon S3 SSE, you can encrypt data on upload simply by adding an additional request header when writing the object. Decryption happens automatically when data is retrieved. Note that metadata, which you can include with your object, is not encrypted.

AWS recommends that customers not place sensitive information in Amazon S3 metadata.

Amazon S3 SSE uses one of the strongest block ciphers available: AES-256. With Amazon S3 SSE, every protected object is encrypted with a unique encryption key. This object key itself is then encrypted with a regularly rotated master key. Amazon S3 SSE provides additional security by storing the encrypted data and encryption keys in different hosts. Amazon S3 SSE also makes it possible for you to enforce encryption requirements. For example, you can create and apply bucket policies that require that only encrypted data can be uploaded to your buckets.

When an object is deleted from Amazon S3, removal of the mapping from the public name to the object starts immediately and is generally processed across the distributed system within several seconds. After the mapping is removed, there is no remote access to the deleted object. The underlying storage area is then reclaimed for use by the system.

Amazon S3 Standard is designed to provide 99.999999999 percent durability of objects over a given year. This durability level corresponds to an average annual expected loss of 0.000000001 percent of objects. For example, if you store 10,000 objects with Amazon S3, you can, on average, expect to incur a loss of a single object once every 10,000,000 years. In addition, Amazon S3 is designed to sustain the concurrent loss of data in two facilities.

Access Logs

An Amazon S3 bucket can be configured to log access to the bucket and objects within it. The access log contains details about each access request including request type, the requested resource, the requestor's IP, and the time and date of the request. When logging is enabled for a bucket, log records are periodically aggregated into log files and delivered to the specified Amazon S3 bucket.

Cross-Origin Resource Sharing (CORS)

AWS customers who use Amazon S3 to host static web pages or store objects used by other web pages can load content securely by configuring an Amazon S3 bucket to explicitly enable cross-origin requests. Modern browsers use the Same Origin policy to block JavaScript or HTML5 from allowing requests to load content from another site or domain as a way to help ensure that malicious content is not loaded from a less reputable source (such as during cross-site scripting attacks). With the *Cross-Origin Resource Sharing (CORS)* policy enabled, assets such as web fonts and images stored in an Amazon S3 bucket can be safely referenced by external web pages, style sheets, and HTML5 applications.

Amazon Glacier Security

Like Amazon S3, the *Amazon Glacier* service provides low-cost, secure, and durable storage. Where Amazon S3 is designed for rapid retrieval, however, Amazon Glacier is meant to be used as an archival service for data that is not accessed often and for which retrieval times of several hours are suitable.

Amazon Glacier stores files as archives within vaults. Archives can be any data such as a photo, video, or document, and can contain one or several files. You can store an unlimited number of archives in a single vault and can create up to 1,000 vaults per region. Each archive can contain up to 40 TB of data.

Data Transfer

For maximum security, you can securely upload/download data to Amazon Glacier via the SSL encrypted endpoints. The encrypted endpoints are accessible from both the Internet and from within Amazon EC2, so that data is transferred securely both within AWS and to and from sources outside of AWS.

Data Retrieval

Retrieving archives from Amazon Glacier requires the initiation of a retrieval job, which is generally completed in three to five hours. You can then access the data via HTTP GET requests. The data will remain available to you for 24 hours. You can retrieve an entire archive or several files from an archive. If you want to retrieve only a subset of an archive, you can use one retrieval request to specify the range of the archive that contains the files in which you are interested or you can initiate multiple retrieval requests, each with a range for one or more files.

You can also limit the number of vault inventory items retrieved by filtering on an archive creation date range or by setting a maximum items limit. Whichever method you choose, when you retrieve portions of your archive, you can use the supplied checksum to help ensure the integrity of the files provided that the range that is retrieved is aligned with the tree hash of the overall archive.

Data Storage

Amazon Glacier automatically encrypts the data using AES-256 and stores it durably in an immutable form. Amazon Glacier is designed to provide average annual durability of 99.999999999 percent for an archive. It stores each archive in multiple facilities and multiple devices. Unlike traditional systems, which can require laborious data verification and manual repair, Amazon Glacier performs regular, systematic data integrity checks and is built to be self-healing.

Data Access

Only your account can access your data in Amazon Glacier. To control access to your data in Amazon Glacier, you can use AWS IAM to specify which users within your account have rights to operations on a given vault.

AWS Storage Gateway Security

The *AWS Storage Gateway* service connects your on-premises software appliance with cloud-based storage to provide seamless and secure integration between your IT environment and AWS storage infrastructure. The service enables you to upload data securely to AWS scalable, reliable, and secure Amazon S3 storage service for cost-effective backup and rapid disaster recovery.

Data Transfer

Data is asynchronously transferred from your on-premises storage hardware to AWS over SSL.

Data Storage

The data is stored encrypted in Amazon S3 using AES 256, a symmetric key encryption standard using 256-bit encryption keys. The AWS Storage Gateway only uploads data that has changed, minimizing the amount of data sent over the Internet.

Database

AWS provides a number of database solutions for developers and businesses from managed relational and NoSQL database services, to in-memory caching as a service and petabyte-scale data warehouse service.

Amazon DynamoDB Security

Amazon DynamoDB is a managed NoSQL database service that provides fast and predictable performance with seamless scalability. Amazon DynamoDB enables you to offload the administrative burdens of operating and scaling distributed databases to AWS, so you don't have to worry about hardware provisioning, setup and configuration, replication, software patching, or cluster scaling.

You can create a database table that can store and retrieve any amount of data and serve any level of request traffic. Amazon DynamoDB automatically spreads the data and traffic for the table over a sufficient number of servers to handle the request capacity you specified and the amount of data stored, while maintaining consistent, fast performance. All data items are stored on Solid State Drives (SSDs) and are automatically replicated across multiple Availability Zones in a region to provide built-in high availability and data durability.

You can set up automatic backups using a special template in AWS Data Pipeline that was created just for copying Amazon DynamoDB tables. You can choose full or incremental backups to a table in the same region or a different region. You can use the copy for disaster recovery in the event that an error in your code damages the original table or to federate Amazon DynamoDB data across regions to support a multi-region application.

To control who can use the Amazon DynamoDB resources and API, you set up permissions in AWS IAM. In addition to controlling access at the resource-level with IAM, you can also control access at the database level—you can create database-level permissions that allow or deny access to items (rows) and attributes (columns) based on the needs of your application. These database-level permissions are called *fine-grained access controls*, and you create them using an IAM policy that specifies under what circumstances a user or application can access an Amazon DynamoDB table. The IAM policy can restrict access to individual items in a table, access to the attributes in those items, or both at the same time.

In addition to requiring database and user permissions, each request to the Amazon DynamoDB service must contain a valid HMAC-SHA-256 signature or the request is rejected. The AWS SDKs automatically sign your requests; however, if you want to write your own HTTP POST requests, you must provide the signature in the header of your request to Amazon DynamoDB. To calculate the signature, you must request temporary security credentials from the AWS Security Token Service. Use the temporary security credentials to sign your requests to Amazon DynamoDB. Amazon DynamoDB is accessible via SSL-encrypted endpoints, and the encrypted endpoints are accessible from both the Internet and from within Amazon EC2.

Amazon Relational Database Service (Amazon RDS) Security

Amazon Relational Database Service (Amazon RDS) allows you to quickly create a relational Database Instance (DB Instance) and flexibly scale the associated compute resources and storage capacity to meet application demand. Amazon RDS manages the database instance on your behalf by performing backups, handling failover, and maintaining the database software. As of the time of this writing, Amazon RDS is available for MySQL, Oracle, Microsoft SQL Server, MariaDB, Amazon Aurora, and PostgreSQL database engines.

Amazon RDS has multiple features that enhance reliability for critical production databases, including DB security groups, permissions, SSL connections, automated backups, DB snapshots, and multiple Availability Zone (Multi-AZ) deployments. DB Instances can also be deployed in an Amazon VPC for additional network isolation.

Access Control   When you first create a DB Instance within Amazon RDS, you will create a master user account, which is used only within the context of Amazon RDS to control access to your DB Instance(s). The master user account is a native database user account that allows you to log on to your DB Instance with all database privileges. You can specify the master user name and password you want associated with each DB Instance when you create the DB Instance. After you have created your DB Instance, you can connect to the database using the master user credentials. Subsequently, you can create additional user accounts so that you can restrict who can access your DB Instance.

You can control Amazon RDS DB Instance access via *DB security groups*, which are similar to Amazon EC2 security groups but not interchangeable. DB security groups act like a firewall controlling network access to your DB Instance. DB security groups default to deny all access mode, and customers must specifically authorize network ingress. There are two ways of doing this:

- Authorizing a network IP range
- Authorizing an existing Amazon EC2 security group

DB security groups only allow access to the database server port (all others are blocked) and can be updated without restarting the Amazon RDS DB Instance, which gives you seamless control of their database access.

Using AWS IAM, you can further control access to your Amazon RDS DB instances. AWS IAM enables you to control what Amazon RDS operations each individual AWS IAM user has permission to call.

Network Isolation   For additional network access control, you can run your DB Instances in an Amazon VPC. Amazon VPC enables you to isolate your DB Instances by specifying the IP range you want to use and connect to your existing IT infrastructure through industry-standard encrypted IPsec VPN. Running Amazon RDS in a VPC enables you to have a DB instance within a private subnet. You can also set up a virtual private gateway that extends your corporate network into your VPC, and allows access to the RDS DB instance in that VPC.

For Multi-AZ deployments, defining a subnet for all Availability Zones in a region, will allow Amazon RDS to create a new standby in another Availability Zone should the need arise. You can create DB subnet groups, which are collections of subnets that you may want to designate for your Amazon RDS DB Instances in an Amazon VPC. Each DB subnet group should have at least one subnet for every Availability Zone in a given region. In this case, when you create a DB Instance in an Amazon VPC, you select a DB subnet group; Amazon RDS then uses that DB subnet group and your preferred Availability Zone to select a subnet and an IP address within that subnet. Amazon RDS creates and associates an Elastic Network Interface to your DB Instance with that IP address.

DB Instances deployed within an Amazon VPC can be accessed from the Internet or from Amazon EC2 instances outside the Amazon VPC via VPN or bastion hosts that you can launch in your public subnet. To use a bastion host, you will need to set up a public subnet with an Amazon EC2 instance that acts as a SSH Bastion. This public subnet must have an Internet gateway and routing rules that allow traffic to be directed via the SSH host, which must then forward requests to the private IP address of your Amazon RDS DB Instance.

DB security groups can be used to help secure DB Instances within an Amazon VPC. In addition, network traffic entering and exiting each subnet can be allowed or denied via network ACLs. All network traffic entering or exiting your Amazon VPC via your IPsec VPN connection can be inspected by your on-premises security infrastructure, including network firewalls and intrusion detection systems.

Encryption   You can encrypt connections between your application and your DB Instance using SSL. For MySQL and SQL Server, Amazon RDS creates an SSL certificate and installs the certificate on the DB Instance when the instance is provisioned. For MySQL, you launch the MySQL client using the `--ssl_ca` parameter to reference the public key in order to encrypt connections. For SQL Server, download the public key and import the certificate into your Windows operating system. Oracle RDS uses Oracle native network encryption with a DB Instance. You simply add the native network encryption option to an option group and associate that option group with the DB Instance. After an encrypted connection is established, data transferred between the DB Instance and your application will be encrypted during transfer. You can also require your DB Instance to accept only encrypted connections.

Amazon RDS supports Transparent Data Encryption (TDE) for SQL Server (SQL Server Enterprise Edition) and Oracle (part of the Oracle Advanced Security option available in Oracle Enterprise Edition). The TDE feature automatically encrypts data before it is written to storage and automatically decrypts data when it is read from storage. If you require your MySQL data to be encrypted while at rest in the database, your application must manage the encryption and decryption of data.

Note that SSL support within Amazon RDS is for encrypting the connection between your application and your DB Instance; it should not be relied on for authenticating the DB Instance itself. While SSL offers security benefits, be aware that SSL encryption is a compute intensive operation and will increase the latency of your database connection.

Automated Backups and DB Snapshots   Amazon RDS provides two different methods for backing up and restoring your DB Instance(s): automated backups and Database Snapshots (DB Snapshots). Turned on by default, the automated backup feature of Amazon RDS enables point-in-time recovery for your DB Instance. Amazon RDS will back up your database and transaction logs and store both for a user-specified retention period. This allows you to restore your DB Instance to any second during your retention period, up to the last five minutes. Your automatic backup retention period can be configured to up to 35 days.

DB Snapshots are user-initiated backups of your DB Instance. These full database backups are stored by Amazon RDS until you explicitly delete them. You can copy DB snapshots of any size and move them between any of AWS public regions, or copy the same snapshot to multiple regions simultaneously. You can then create a new DB Instance from a DB Snapshot whenever you desire.

During the backup window, storage I/O may be suspended while your data is being backed up. This I/O suspension typically lasts a few minutes. This I/O suspension is avoided with Multi-AZ DB deployments, because the backup is taken from the standby.

DB Instance Replication   AWS Cloud computing resources are housed in highly available data center facilities in different regions of the world, and each region contains multiple distinct locations called Availability Zones. Each Availability Zone is engineered to be isolated from failures in other Availability Zones and provide inexpensive, low-latency network connectivity to other Availability Zones in the same region.

To architect for high availability of your Oracle, PostgreSQL, or MySQL databases, you can run your Amazon RDS DB Instance in several Availability Zones, an option called a *Multi-AZ deployment*. When you select this option, AWS automatically provisions and maintains a synchronous standby replica of your DB Instance in a different Availability Zone. The primary DB Instance is synchronously replicated across Availability Zones to the standby replica. In the event of DB Instance or Availability Zone failure, Amazon RDS will automatically failover to the standby so that database operations can resume quickly without administrative intervention.

For customers who use MySQL and need to scale beyond the capacity constraints of a single DB Instance for read-heavy database workloads, Amazon RDS provides a read replica option. After you create a read replica, database updates on the source DB Instance are replicated to the read replica using MySQL's native, asynchronous replication. You can create multiple read replicas for a given source DB instance and distribute your application's read traffic among them. Read replicas can be created with Multi-AZ deployments to gain read scaling benefits in addition to the enhanced database write availability and data durability provided by Multi-AZ deployments.

Automatic Software Patching   Amazon RDS will make sure that the relational database software powering your deployment stays up-to-date with the latest patches. When necessary, patches are applied during a maintenance window that you can control. You can think of the Amazon RDS maintenance window as an opportunity to control when DB Instance modifications (such as scaling DB Instance class) and software patching occur, in the event either are requested or required. If a maintenance event is scheduled for a given week, it will be initiated and completed at some point during the 30-minute maintenance window you identify.

The only maintenance events that require Amazon RDS to take your DB Instance offline are scale compute operations (which generally take only a few minutes from start to finish) or required software patching. Required patching is automatically scheduled only for patches that are related to security and durability. Such patching occurs infrequently (typically once every few months) and should seldom require more than a fraction of your maintenance window. If you do not specify a preferred weekly maintenance window when creating your DB Instance, a 30-minute default value is assigned. If you want to modify when maintenance is performed on your behalf, you can do so by modifying your DB Instance in the AWS Management Console or by using the ModifyDBInstance API. Each of your DB Instances can have different preferred maintenance windows, if you so choose.

Running your DB Instance in a Multi-AZ deployment can further reduce the impact of a maintenance event, as Amazon RDS will conduct maintenance via the following steps:

1. Perform maintenance on standby.
2. Promote standby to primary.
3. Perform maintenance on old primary, which becomes the new standby.

When an Amazon RDS DB Instance deletion API (DeleteDBInstance) is run, the DB Instance is marked for deletion. After the instance no longer indicates deleting status, it has been removed. At this point, the instance is no longer accessible, and unless a final snapshot copy was asked for, it cannot be restored and will not be listed by any of the tools or APIs.

Amazon Redshift Security

Amazon Redshift is a petabyte-scale SQL data warehouse service that runs on highly optimized and managed AWS compute and storage resources. The service has been architected not only to scale up or down rapidly, but also to improve query speeds significantly even on extremely large datasets. To increase performance, Amazon Redshift uses techniques such as columnar storage, data compression, and zone maps to reduce the amount of I/O needed to perform queries. It also has a Massively Parallel Processing (MPP) architecture, parallelizing and distributing SQL operations to take advantage of all available resources.

Cluster Access   By default, clusters that you create are closed to everyone. Amazon Redshift enables you to configure firewall rules (security groups) to control network access to your data warehouse cluster. You can also run Amazon Redshift inside an Amazon VPC to isolate your data warehouse cluster in your own virtual network and connect it to your existing IT infrastructure using industry-standard encrypted IPsec VPN.

The AWS account that creates the cluster has full access to the cluster. Within your AWS account, you can use AWS IAM to create user accounts and manage permissions for those accounts. By using IAM, you can grant different users permission to perform only the cluster operations that are necessary for their work. Like all databases, you must grant permission in Amazon Redshift at the database level in addition to granting access at the resource level. Database users are named user accounts that can connect to a database and are authenticated when they log in to Amazon Redshift. In Amazon Redshift, you grant database user permissions on a per-cluster basis instead of on a per-table basis. However, users can see data only in the table rows that were generated by their own activities; rows generated by other users are not visible to them.

The user who creates a database object is its owner. By default, only a super user or the owner of an object can query, modify, or grant permissions on the object. For users to use an object, you must grant the necessary permissions to the user or the group that contains the user. In addition, only the owner of an object can modify or delete it.

Data Backups   Amazon Redshift distributes your data across all compute nodes in a cluster. When you run a cluster with at least two compute nodes, data on each node will always be mirrored on disks on another node, reducing the risk of data loss. In addition, all data written to a node in your cluster is continuously backed up to Amazon S3 using snapshots. Amazon Redshift stores your snapshots for a user-defined period, which can be from 1 to 35 days. You can also take your own snapshots at any time; these snapshots leverage all existing system snapshots and are retained until you explicitly delete them.

Amazon Redshift continuously monitors the health of the cluster and automatically re-replicates data from failed drives and replaces nodes as necessary. All of this happens without any effort on your part, although you may see a slight performance degradation during the re-replication process.

You can use any system or user snapshot to restore your cluster using the AWS Management Console or the Amazon Redshift APIs. Your cluster is available as soon as the system metadata has been restored, and you can start running queries while user data is spooled down in the background.

Data Encryption   When creating a cluster, you can choose to encrypt it in order to provide additional protection for your data at rest. When you enable encryption in your cluster, Amazon Redshift stores all data in user-created tables in an encrypted format using hardware-accelerated AES-256 block encryption keys. This includes all data written to disk and any backups.

Amazon Redshift uses a four-tier, key-based architecture for encryption. These keys consist of data encryption keys, a database key, a cluster key, and a master key.

- Data encryption keys encrypt data blocks in the cluster. Each data block is assigned a randomly-generated AES256 key. These keys are encrypted by using the database key for the cluster.

- The database key encrypts data encryption keys in the cluster. The database key is a randomly-generated AES-256 key. It is stored on disk in a separate network from the Amazon Redshift cluster and encrypted by a master key. Amazon Redshift passes the database key across a secure channel and keeps it in memory in the cluster.

- The cluster key encrypts the database key for the Amazon Redshift cluster. You can use either AWS or a Hardware Security Module (HSM) to store the cluster key. HSMs provide direct control of key generation and management and make key management separate and distinct from the application and the database.

- The master key encrypts the cluster key if it is stored in AWS. The master key encrypts the cluster-key-encrypted database key if the cluster key is stored in an HSM.

You can have Amazon Redshift rotate the encryption keys for your encrypted clusters at any time. As part of the rotation process, keys are also updated for all of the cluster's automatic and manual snapshots. Note that enabling encryption in your cluster will impact performance, even though it is hardware accelerated.

Encryption also applies to backups. When you're restoring from an encrypted snapshot, the new cluster will be encrypted as well.

To encrypt your table load data files when you upload them to Amazon S3, you can use Amazon S3 server-side encryption. When you load the data from Amazon S3, the COPY command will decrypt the data as it loads the table.

Database Audit Logging   Amazon Redshift logs all SQL operations, including connection attempts, queries, and changes to your database. You can access these logs using SQL queries against system tables or choose to have them downloaded to a secure Amazon S3 bucket. You can then use these audit logs to monitor your cluster for security and troubleshooting purposes.

Automatic Software Patching   Amazon Redshift manages all the work of setting up, operating, and scaling your data warehouse, including provisioning capacity, monitoring the cluster, and applying patches and upgrades to the Amazon Redshift engine. Patches are applied only during specified maintenance windows.

SSL Connections   To protect your data in transit within the AWS Cloud, Amazon Redshift uses hardware-accelerated SSL to communicate with Amazon S3 or Amazon DynamoDB for COPY, UNLOAD, backup, and restore operations. You can encrypt the connection between your client and the cluster by specifying SSL in the parameter group associated with the cluster. To have your clients also authenticate the Amazon Redshift server, you can install the public key (.pem file) for the SSL certificate on your client and use the key to connect to your clusters.

Amazon Redshift offers the newer, stronger cipher suites that use the Elliptic Curve Diffie-Hellman Ephemeral (ECDHE) protocol. ECDHE allows SSL clients to provide Perfect Forward Secrecy between the client and the Amazon Redshift cluster. Perfect Forward Secrecy uses session keys that are ephemeral and not stored anywhere, which prevents the decoding of captured data by unauthorized third parties, even if the secret long-term key itself is compromised. You do not need to configure anything in Amazon Redshift to enable ECDHE; if you connect from an SQL client tool that uses ECDHE to encrypt communication between the client and server, Amazon Redshift will use the provided cipher list to make the appropriate connection.

Amazon ElastiCache Security

Amazon ElastiCache is a web service that makes it easy to set up, manage, and scale distributed in-memory cache environments in the cloud. The service improves the performance of web applications by allowing you to retrieve information from a fast, managed, in-memory caching system, instead of relying entirely on slower disk-based databases. It can be used to improve latency and throughput significantly for many read-heavy application workloads (such as social networking, gaming, media sharing, and Q and A portals) or compute-intensive workloads (such as a recommendation engine). Caching improves application performance by storing critical pieces of data in memory for low-latency access. Cached information may include the results of I/O-intensive database queries or the results of computationally-intensive calculations.

The Amazon ElastiCache service automates time-consuming management tasks for in-memory cache environments, such as patch management, failure detection, and recovery. It works in conjunction with other AWS Cloud services (such as Amazon EC2, Amazon CloudWatch, and Amazon SNS) to provide a secure, high-performance, and managed in-memory cache. For example, an application running in Amazon EC2 can securely access an Amazon ElastiCache cluster in the same region with very low latency.

Using the Amazon ElastiCache service, you create a *Cache Cluster*, which is a collection of one or more *Cache Nodes*, each running an instance of the Memcached service. A Cache Node is a fixed-size chunk of secure, network-attached RAM. Each Cache Node runs an instance of the Memcached service and has its own DNS name and port. Multiple types of Cache Nodes are supported, each with varying amounts of associated memory. A Cache Cluster can be set up with a specific number of Cache Nodes and a Cache Parameter Group that controls the properties for each Cache Node. All Cache Nodes within a Cache Cluster are designed to be of the same Node Type and have the same parameter and security group settings.

Data Access   Amazon ElastiCache allows you to control access to your Cache Clusters using *Cache Security Groups*. A Cache Security Group acts like a firewall, controlling network access to your Cache Cluster. By default, network access is turned off to your Cache Clusters. If you want your applications to access your Cache Cluster, you must explicitly enable access from hosts in specific Amazon EC2 security groups. After ingress rules are configured, the same rules apply to all Cache Clusters associated with that Cache Security Group.

To allow network access to your Cache Cluster, create a Cache Security Group and use the Authorize Cache Security Group Ingress API or CLI command to authorize the desired Amazon EC2 security group (which in turn specifies the Amazon EC2 instances allowed). IP-range based access control is currently not enabled for Cache Clusters. All clients to a Cache Cluster must be within the Amazon EC2 network, and authorized via Cache Security Groups.

Amazon ElastiCache for Redis provides backup and restore functionality, where you can create a snapshot of your entire Redis cluster as it exists at a specific point in time. You can schedule automatic, recurring daily snapshots, or you can create a manual snapshot at any time. For automatic snapshots, you specify a retention period; manual snapshots are retained until you delete them. The snapshots are stored in Amazon S3 with high durability, and can be used for warm starts, backups, and archiving.

Application Services

AWS offers a variety of managed services to use with your applications, including services that provide application streaming, queueing, push notification, email delivery, search, and transcoding.

Amazon Simple Queue Service (Amazon SQS) Security

Amazon SQS is a highly reliable, scalable message queuing service that enables asynchronous message-based communication between distributed components of an application. The components can be computers or Amazon EC2 instances or a combination of both. With Amazon SQS, you can send any number of messages to an Amazon SQS queue at any time from any component. The messages can be retrieved from the same component or a different one, right away or at a later time (within 14 days). Messages are highly durable; each message is persistently stored in highly available, highly reliable queues. Multiple processes can read/write from/to an Amazon SQS queue at the same time without interfering with each other.

Data Access   Amazon SQS access is granted based on an AWS account or a user created with AWS IAM. After it is authenticated, the AWS account has full access to all user operations. An IAM user, however, only has access to the operations and queues for which they have been granted access via policy. By default, access to each individual queue is restricted to the AWS account that created it. However, you can allow other access to a queue, using either an Amazon SQS-generated policy or a policy you write.

SQS & Encrypto

Encryption   Amazon SQS is accessible via SSL-encrypted endpoints. The encrypted endpoints are accessible from both the Internet and from within Amazon EC2. Data stored within Amazon SQS is not encrypted by AWS; however, the user can encrypt data before it is uploaded to Amazon SQS, provided that the application using the queue has a means to decrypt the message when it's retrieved. Encrypting messages before sending them to Amazon SQS helps protect against access to sensitive customer data by unauthorized persons, including AWS.

Amazon Simple Notification Service (Amazon SNS) Security

Amazon SNS is a web service that makes it easy to set up, operate, and send notifications from the cloud. It provides developers with a highly scalable, flexible, and cost-effective capability to publish messages from an application and immediately deliver them to subscribers or other applications. Amazon SNS provides a simple web services interface that can be used to create topics that customers want to notify applications (or people) about, subscribe clients to these topics, publish messages, and have these messages delivered over clients' protocol of choice (for example, HTTP/HTTPS, email).

Amazon SNS delivers notifications to clients using a push mechanism that eliminates the need to check or poll for new information and updates periodically. Amazon SNS can be leveraged to build highly reliable, event-driven workflows and messaging applications without the need for complex middleware and application management. The potential uses for Amazon SNS include monitoring applications, workflow systems, time-sensitive information updates, mobile applications, and many others.

Data Access   Amazon SNS provides access control mechanisms so that topics and messages are secured against unauthorized access. Topic owners can set policies for a topic that restricts who can publish or subscribe to a topic. Additionally, topic owners can encrypt transmission by specifying that the delivery mechanism must be HTTPS. Amazon SNS access is granted based on an AWS account or a user created with AWS IAM. After it is authenticated, the AWS account has full access to all user operations. An IAM user, however, only has access to the operations and topics for which they have been granted access via policy. By default, access to each individual topic is restricted to the AWS account that created it. However, you can allow other access to Amazon SNS, using either an Amazon SNS-generated policy or a policy you write.

Analytics Services

AWS provides cloud-based analytics services to help you process and analyze any volume of data, whether your need is for managed Hadoop clusters, real-time streaming data, petabyte scale data warehousing, or orchestration.

Amazon Elastic MapReduce (Amazon EMR) Security

Amazon Elastic MapReduce (Amazon EMR) is a managed web service you can use to run Hadoop clusters that process vast amounts of data by distributing the work and data among several servers. It uses an enhanced version of the Apache Hadoop framework running on the web-scale infrastructure of Amazon EC2 and Amazon S3. You simply upload your input data and a data processing application into Amazon S3. Amazon EMR then launches the number of Amazon EC2 instances you specify. The service begins the job flow execution while pulling the input data from Amazon S3 into the launched Amazon EC2 instances. After the job flow is finished, Amazon EMR transfers the output data to Amazon S3, where you can then retrieve it or use it as input in another job flow.

When launching job flows on your behalf, Amazon EMR sets up two Amazon EC2 security groups: one for the master nodes and another for the slaves. The master security group has a port open for communication with the service. It also has the SSH port open to allow you to SSH into the instances using the key specified at startup. The slaves start in a separate security group, which only allows interaction with the master instance. By default, both security groups are set up to not allow access from external sources, including Amazon EC2 instances belonging to other customers. Because these are security groups within your account, you can reconfigure them using the standard EC2 tools or dashboard. To protect customer input and output datasets, Amazon EMR transfers data to and from Amazon S3 using SSL.

Amazon EMR provides several ways to control access to the resources of your cluster. You can use AWS IAM to create user accounts and roles and configure permissions that control which AWS features those users and roles can access. When you launch a cluster, you can associate an Amazon EC2 key pair with the cluster, which you can then use when you connect to the cluster using SSH. You can also set permissions that allow users other than the default Hadoop user to submit jobs to your cluster.

By default, if an IAM user launches a cluster, that cluster is hidden from other IAM users on the AWS account. This filtering occurs on all Amazon EMR interfaces (the AWS Management Console, CLI, API, and SDKs) and helps prevent IAM users from accessing and inadvertently changing clusters created by other IAM users.

For an additional layer of protection, you can launch the Amazon EC2 instances of your Amazon EMR cluster into an Amazon VPC, which is like launching it into a private subnet. This allows you to control access to the entire subnet. You can also launch the cluster into an Amazon VPC and enable the cluster to access resources on your internal network using a VPN connection. You can encrypt the input data before you upload it to Amazon S3 using any common data encryption tool. If you do encrypt the data before it is uploaded, you then need to add a decryption step to the beginning of your job flow when Amazon EMR fetches the data from Amazon S3.

Amazon Kinesis Security

Amazon Kinesis is a managed service designed to handle real-time streaming of big data. It can accept any amount of data, from any number of sources, scaling up and down as needed. You can use Amazon Kinesis in situations that call for large-scale, real-time data ingestion and processing, such as server logs, social media, or market data feeds, and web clickstream data. Applications read and write data records to Amazon Kinesis in streams. You can create any number of Amazon Kinesis streams to capture, store, and transport data.

You can control logical access to Amazon Kinesis resources and management functions by creating users under your AWS account using AWS IAM, and controlling which Amazon Kinesis operations these users have permission to perform. To facilitate running your producer or consumer applications on an Amazon EC2 instance, you can configure that instance with an IAM role. That way, AWS credentials that reflect the permissions associated with the IAM role are made available to applications on the instance, which means you don't have to use your long-term AWS security credentials. Roles have the added benefit of providing temporary credentials that expire within a short timeframe, which adds an additional measure of protection.

The Amazon Kinesis API is only accessible via an SSL-encrypted endpoint (kinesis.us-east-1.amazonaws.com) to help ensure secure transmission of your data to AWS. You must connect to that endpoint to access Amazon Kinesis, but you can then use the API to direct Amazon Kinesis to create a stream in any AWS region.

Deployment and Management Services

AWS provides a variety of tools to help with the deployment and management of your applications. This includes services that allow you to create individual user accounts with credentials for access to AWS services. It also includes services for creating and updating stacks of AWS resources, deploying applications on those resources, and monitoring the health of those AWS resources. Other tools help you manage cryptographic keys using HSMs and log AWS API activity for security and compliance purposes.

AWS Identity and Access Management (IAM) Security

AWS IAM allows you to create multiple users and manage the permissions for each of these users within your AWS account. A user is an identity (within an AWS account) with unique security credentials that can be used to access AWS Cloud services. IAM eliminates the need to share passwords or keys and makes it easy to enable or disable a user's access as appropriate.

AWS IAM enables you to implement security best practices, such as least privilege, by granting unique credentials to every user within your AWS account and only granting permission to access the AWS Cloud services and resources required for the users to perform their jobs. IAM is secure by default; new users have no access to AWS until permissions are explicitly granted.

AWS IAM is also integrated with AWS Marketplace so that you can control who in your organization can subscribe to the software and services offered in AWS Marketplace. Because subscribing to certain software in AWS Marketplace launches an Amazon EC2 instance to run the software, this is an important access control feature. Using IAM to control access to AWS Marketplace also enables AWS account owners to have fine-grained control over usage and software costs.

AWS IAM enables you to minimize the use of your AWS account credentials. After you create IAM user accounts, all interactions with AWS Cloud services and resources should occur with IAM user security credentials.

Roles   An *IAM role* uses temporary security credentials to allow you to delegate access to users or services that normally don't have access to your AWS resources. A role is a set of permissions to access specific AWS resources, but these permissions are not tied to a specific IAM user or group. An authorized entity (for example, mobile user or Amazon EC2 instance) assumes a role and receives temporary security credentials for authenticating to the resources defined in the role. Temporary security credentials provide enhanced security due to their short lifespan (the default expiration is 12 hours) and the fact that they cannot be reused after they expire. This can be particularly useful in providing limited, controlled access in certain situations:

Federated (Non-AWS) User Access   *Federated users* are users (or applications) who do not have AWS accounts. With roles, you can give them access to your AWS resources for a limited amount of time. This is useful if you have non-AWS users that you can authenticate with an external service, such as Microsoft Active Directory, Lightweight Directory Access Protocol (LDAP), or Kerberos. The temporary AWS credentials used with the roles provide identity federation between AWS and your non-AWS users in your corporate identity and authorization system.

Security Assertion Markup Language (SAML) 2.0   If your organization supports SAML 2.0, you can create trust between your organization as an Identity Provider (IdP) and other organizations as service providers. In AWS, you can configure AWS as the service provider and use SAML to provide your users with federated Single-Sign On (SSO) to the AWS Management Console or to get federated access to call AWS APIs.

Roles are also useful if you create a mobile or web-based application that accesses AWS resources. AWS resources require security credentials for programmatic requests; however, you shouldn't embed long-term security credentials in your application because they are accessible to the application's users and can be difficult to rotate. Instead, you can let users sign in to your application using Login with Amazon, Facebook, or Google and then use their authentication information to assume a role and get temporary security credentials.

Cross-Account Access   For organizations that use multiple AWS accounts to manage their resources, you can set up roles to provide users who have permissions in one account to access resources under another account. For organizations that have personnel who only rarely need access to resources under another account, using roles helps to ensure that credentials are provided temporarily and only as needed.

Applications Running on EC2 Instances That Need to Access AWS Resources   If an application runs on an Amazon EC2 instance and needs to make requests for AWS resources, such as Amazon S3 buckets or a DynamoDB table, it must have security credentials. Using roles instead of creating individual IAM accounts for each application on each instance can save significant time for customers who manage a large number of instances or an elastically scaling fleet using AWS Auto Scaling.

The temporary credentials include a security token, an Access Key ID, and a Secret Access Key. To give a user access to certain resources, you distribute the temporary security credentials to the user to whom you are granting temporary access. When the user makes calls to your resources, the user passes in the token and Access Key ID and signs the request with the Secret Access Key. The token will not work with different access keys.

The use of temporary credentials provides additional protection for you because you don't have to manage or distribute long-term credentials to temporary users. In addition, the temporary credentials get automatically loaded to the target instance so you don't have to embed them somewhere unsafe like your code. Temporary credentials are automatically rotated or changed multiple times a day without any action on your part and are stored securely by default.

Mobile Services

AWS mobile services make it easier for you to build, ship, run, monitor, optimize, and scale cloud-powered applications for mobile devices. These services also help you authenticate users to your mobile application, synchronize data, and collect and analyze application usage.

Amazon Cognito Security

Amazon Cognito provides identity and sync services for mobile and web-based applications. It simplifies the task of authenticating users and storing, managing, and syncing their data across multiple devices, platforms, and applications. It provides temporary, limited-privilege credentials for both authenticated and unauthenticated users without having to manage any back-end infrastructure.

Amazon Cognito works with well-known identity providers like Google, Facebook, and Amazon to authenticate end users of your mobile and web applications. You can take advantage of the identification and authorization features provided by these services instead of having to build and maintain your own. Your application authenticates with one of these identity providers using the provider's SDK. After the end user is authenticated with the provider, an OAuth or OpenID Connect token returned from the provider is passed by your application to Amazon Cognito, which returns a new Amazon Cognito ID for the user and a set of temporary, limited-privilege AWS credentials.

To begin using Amazon Cognito, you create an identity pool through the Amazon Cognito console. The *identity pool* is a store of user identity information that is specific to your AWS account. During the creation of the identity pool, you will be asked to create a new IAM role or pick an existing one for your end users. An *IAM role* is a set of permissions to access specific AWS resources, but these permissions are not tied to a specific IAM user or group. An authorized entity (for example, mobile user, Amazon EC2 instance) assumes a role and receives temporary security credentials for authenticating to the AWS resources defined in the role. Temporary security credentials provide enhanced security due to their short lifespan (the default expiration is 12 hours) and the fact that they cannot be reused after they expire.

The role you select has an impact on which AWS Cloud services your end users will be able to access with the temporary credentials. By default, Amazon Cognito creates a new role with limited permissions; end users only have access to the Amazon Cognito Sync service and Amazon Mobile Analytics. If your application needs access to other AWS resources, such as Amazon S3 or Amazon DynamoDB, you can modify your roles directly from the IAM console.

With Amazon Cognito, there is no need to create individual AWS accounts or even IAM accounts for every one of your web/mobile application end users who will need to access your AWS resources. In conjunction with IAM roles, mobile users can securely access AWS resources and application features and even save data to the AWS Cloud without having to create an account or log in. If they choose to create an account or log in later, Amazon Cognito will merge data and identification information.

Because Amazon Cognito stores data locally and also in the service, your end users can continue to interact with their data even when they are offline. Their offline data may be stale, but they can immediately retrieve anything they put into the dataset whether or not they are online. The client SDK manages a local SQLite store so that the application can work even when it is not connected. The SQLite store functions as a cache and is the target of all read and write operations. Amazon Cognito's sync facility compares the local version of the data to the cloud version and pushes up or pulls down deltas as needed. Note that in order to sync data across devices, your identity pool must support authenticated identities. Unauthenticated identities are tied to the device, so unless an end user authenticates, no data can be synced across multiple devices.

With Amazon Cognito, your application communicates directly with a supported public identity provider (Amazon, Facebook, or Google) to authenticate users. Amazon Cognito does not receive or store user credentials, only the OAuth or OpenID Connect token received from the identity provider. After Amazon Cognito receives the token, it returns a new Amazon Cognito ID for the user and a set of temporary, limited-privilege AWS credentials. Each Amazon Cognito identity has access only to its own data in the sync store, and this data is encrypted when stored. In addition, all identity data is transmitted over HTTPS. The unique Amazon Cognito identifier on the device is stored in the appropriate secure location. For example on iOS, the Amazon Cognito identifier is stored in the iOS keychain. User data is cached in a local SQLite database within the application's sandbox; if you require additional security, you can encrypt this identity data in the local cache by implementing encryption in your application.

Applications

AWS applications are managed services that enable you to provide your users with secure, centralized storage and work areas in the cloud.

Amazon WorkSpaces Security

Amazon WorkSpaces is a managed desktop service that allows you to quickly provision cloud-based desktops for your users. Simply choose a Windows 7 bundle that best meets the needs of your users and the number of WorkSpaces that you want to launch. After the WorkSpaces are ready, users receive an email informing them where they can download the relevant client and log in to their WorkSpace. They can then access their cloud-based desktops from a variety of endpoint devices, including PCs, laptops, and mobile devices.

However, your organization's data is never sent to or stored on the end-user device because Amazon WorkSpaces uses PC-over-IP (PCoIP), which provides an interactive video stream without transmitting actual data. The PCoIP protocol compresses, encrypts, and encodes the users' desktop computing experience and transmits as pixels only across any standard IP network to end-user devices.

In order to access their WorkSpace, users must sign in using a set of unique credentials or their regular Active Directory credentials. When you integrate Amazon WorkSpaces with your corporate Active Directory, each WorkSpace joins your Active Directory domain and can be managed just like any other desktop in your organization. This means that you can use Active Directory Group Policies to manage your users WorkSpaces to specify configuration options that control the desktop. If you choose not to use Active Directory or other type of on-premises directory to manage your user WorkSpaces, you can create a private cloud directory within Amazon WorkSpaces that you can use for administration.

To provide an additional layer of security, you can also require the use of MFA upon sign-in in the form of a hardware or software token. Amazon WorkSpaces supports MFA using an on-premises Remote Authentication Dial In User Service (RADIUS) server or any security provider that supports RADIUS authentication. It currently supports the PAP, CHAP, MS-CHAP1, and MS-CHAP2 protocols, along with RADIUS proxies.

Each WorkSpace resides on its own Amazon EC2 instance within an Amazon VPC. You can create WorkSpaces in an Amazon VPC you already own or have the Amazon WorkSpaces service create one for you automatically using the Amazon WorkSpaces Quick Start option. When you use the Quick Start option, Amazon WorkSpaces not only creates the Amazon VPC, but it also performs several other provisioning and configuration tasks for you, such as creating an Internet Gateway for the Amazon VPC, setting up a directory within the Amazon VPC that is used to store user and WorkSpace information, creating a directory administrator account, creating the specified user accounts and adding them to the directory, and creating the Amazon WorkSpaces instances. Or the Amazon VPC can be connected to an on-premises network using a secure VPN connection to allow access to an existing on-premises Active Directory and other intranet resources. You can add a security group that you create in your Amazon VPC to all of the WorkSpaces that belong to your Active Directory. This allows you to control network access from Amazon WorkSpaces in your Amazon VPC to other resources in your Amazon VPC and on-premises network.

Persistent storage for Amazon WorkSpaces is provided by Amazon EBS and is automatically backed up twice a day to Amazon S3. If Amazon WorkSpaces Sync is enabled on a WorkSpace, the folder a user chooses to sync will be continuously backed up and stored in Amazon S3. You can also use Amazon WorkSpaces Sync on a Mac or PC to sync documents to or from your WorkSpace so that you can always have access to your data regardless of the desktop computer you are using.

Because it is a managed service, AWS takes care of several security and maintenance tasks like daily backups and patching. Updates are delivered automatically to your WorkSpaces during a weekly maintenance window. You can control how patching is configured for a user's WorkSpace. By default, Windows Update is turned on, but you have the ability to customize these settings or use an alternative patch management approach if you desire. For the underlying OS, Windows Update is enabled by default on Amazon

WorkSpaces and configured to install updates on a weekly basis. You can use an alternative patching approach or configure Windows Update to perform updates at a time of your choosing. You can use IAM to control who on your team can perform administrative functions like creating or deleting WorkSpaces or setting up user directories. You can also set up a WorkSpace for directory administration, install your favorite Active Directory administration tools, and create organizational units and Group Policies in order to apply Active Directory changes more easily for all of your Amazon WorkSpaces users.

Summary

In this chapter, you learned that the first priority at AWS is Cloud security. Security within AWS is based on a "defense in depth" model where no one, single element is used to secure systems on AWS. Rather, AWS uses a multitude of elements—each acting at different layers of a system—in total to secure the system. AWS is responsible for some layers of this model, and customers are responsible for others. AWS also offers security tools and features of services for customers to use at their discretion. Several of these concepts, tools, and features were discussed in this chapter.

Security Model

The shared responsibility model is the security model where AWS is responsible for the security of the underlying cloud infrastructure, and the customer is responsible for securing workloads deployed in AWS. Customers benefit from a data center and network architecture built to satisfy the requirements of AWS most security-sensitive customers. This means that customers get a resilient infrastructure, designed for high security, without the capital outlay and operational overhead of a traditional data center.

Account Level Security

AWS credentials help ensure that only authorized users and processes access your AWS account and resources. AWS uses several types of credentials for authentication. These include passwords, cryptographic keys, digital signatures, and certificates. AWS also provides the option of requiring MFA to log in to your AWS account or IAM user accounts.

Passwords are required to access your AWS account, individual IAM user accounts, AWS Discussion Forums, and the AWS Support Center. You specify the password when you first create the account, and you can change it at any time by going to the Security Credentials page.

AWS MFA is an additional layer of security for accessing AWS Cloud services. When you enable this optional feature, you will need to provide a six-digit, single-use code in addition to your standard user name and password credentials before access is granted to your AWS account settings or AWS Cloud services and resources. You get this single-use code from an authentication device that you keep in your physical possession. This is multi-factor because more than one authentication factor is checked before access is granted: a password (something you know) and the precise code from your authentication device (something you have). An MFA device uses a software application that generates six-digit authentication codes that are compatible with the TOTP standard, as described in RFC 6238.

Access Keys are created by AWS IAM and delivered as a pair: the Access Key ID (AKI) and the Secret Access Key (SAK). AWS requires that all API requests be signed by the SAK; that is, they must include a digital signature that AWS can use to verify the identity of the requestor. You calculate the digital signature using a cryptographic hash function. If you use any of the AWS SDKs to generate requests, the digital signature calculation is done for you. The most recent version of the digital signature calculation process at the time of this writing is Signature Version 4, which calculates the signature using the HMAC-SHA-256 protocol.

AWS CloudTrail is a web service that records API calls made on your account and delivers log files to your Amazon S3 bucket. AWS CloudTrail's benefit is visibility into account activity by recording API calls made on your account.

Service-Specific Security

In addition to the Shared Responsibility Model and Account Level security, AWS offers security features for each of the services it provides. These security features are outlined below by technology domain.

Compute

Amazon Elastic Compute Cloud (Amazon EC2)   Amazon EC2 supports RSA 2048 SSH-2 Key pairs for gaining first access to an Amazon EC2 instance. On a Linux instance, access is granted through showing possession of the SSH private key. On a Windows instance, access is granted by showing possession of the SSH private key in order to decrypt the administrator password.

Amazon Elastic Block Store (Amazon EBS)   Data stored in Amazon EBS volumes is redundantly stored in multiple physical locations within the same Availability Zone as part of normal operation of that service and at no additional charge. AWS provides the ability to encrypt Amazon EBS volumes and their snapshots with AES-256. The encryption occurs on the servers that host the Amazon EC2 instances, providing encryption of data as it moves between Amazon EC2 instances and Amazon EBS storage.

Networking

Elastic Load Balancing   Elastic Load Balancing configures your load balancer with a pre-defined cipher set that is used for TLS negotiation when a connection is established between a client and your load balancer. The pre-defined cipher set provides compatibility with a broad range of clients and uses strong cryptographic algorithms. Elastic Load Balancing allows you to identify the originating IP address of a client connecting to your servers, whether you're using HTTPS or TCP load balancing.

Amazon Virtual Private Cloud (Amazon VPC)   Amazon VPC enables you to create an isolated portion of the AWS Cloud and launch Amazon EC2 instances that have private (RFC 1918) addresses in the range of your choice. Security features within Amazon VPC include security groups, network ACLs, routing tables, and external gateways. Each of these items is complementary to providing a secure, isolated network that can be extended through selective enabling of direct Internet access or private connectivity to another network.

Amazon CloudFront   Amazon CloudFront gives customers an easy way to distribute content to end users with low latency and high data transfer speeds. It delivers dynamic, static, and streaming content using a global network of edge locations. To control access to the original copies of your objects in Amazon S3, Amazon CloudFront allows you to create one or more Origin Access Identities and associate these with your distributions. To control who can download objects from Amazon CloudFront edge locations, the service uses a signed-URL verification system.

Storage

Amazon Simple Storage Service (Amazon S3)   Amazon S3 allows you to upload and retrieve data at any time, from anywhere on the web. Access to data stored in Amazon S3 is restricted by default; only bucket and object owners have access to the Amazon S3 resources they create. You can securely upload and download data to Amazon S3 via the SSL-encrypted endpoints. Amazon S3 supports several methods to encrypt data at rest.

Amazon Glacier   Amazon Glacier service provides low-cost, secure, and durable storage. You can securely upload and download data to Amazon Glacier via the SSL-encrypted endpoints, and the service automatically encrypts the data using AES-256 and stores it durably in an immutable form.

AWS Storage Gateway   AWS Storage Gateway service connects your on-premises software appliance with cloud-based storage to provide seamless and secure integration between your IT environment and AWS storage infrastructure. Data is asynchronously transferred from your on-premises storage hardware to AWS over SSL and stored encrypted in Amazon S3 using AES-256.

Database

Amazon DynamoDB   Amazon DynamoDB is a managed NoSQL database service that provides fast and predictable performance with seamless scalability. You can control access at the database level by creating database-level permissions that allow or deny access to items (rows) and attributes (columns) based on the needs of your application.

Amazon Relational Database Service (RDS)   Amazon RDS allows you to quickly create a relational DB Instance and flexibly scale the associated compute resources and storage capacity to meet application demand. You can control Amazon RDS DB Instance access via DB security groups, which act like a firewall controlling network access to your DB Instance. Database security groups default to deny all access mode, and customers must specifically authorize network ingress. Amazon RDS is supported within an Amazon VPC, and for Multi-AZ deployments, defining a subnet for all Availability Zones in a region will allow Amazon RDS to create a new standby in another Availability Zone should the need arise. You can encrypt connections between your application and your DB Instance using SSL, and you can encrypt data at rest within Amazon RDS instances for all database engines.

Amazon Redshift   Amazon Redshift is a petabyte-scale SQL data warehouse service that runs on highly optimized and managed AWS compute and storage resources. The service enables you to configure firewall rules (security groups) to control network access to your data warehouse cluster. Database users are named user accounts that can connect to a database and are authenticated when they log in to Amazon Redshift. In Amazon Redshift, you grant database user permissions on a per-cluster basis instead of on a per-table basis. You may choose for Amazon Redshift to store all data in user-created tables in an encrypted format using hardware-accelerated AES-256 block encryption keys. This includes all data written to disk and also any backups. Amazon Redshift uses a four-tier, key-based architecture for encryption. These keys consist of data encryption keys, a database key, a cluster key, and a master key.

Amazon ElastiCache   Amazon ElastiCache is a web service that makes it easy to set up, manage, and scale distributed in-memory cache environments in the cloud. Amazon ElastiCache allows you to control access to your Cache Clusters using Cache Security Groups. A Cache Security Group acts like a firewall, controlling network access to your Cache Cluster.

Application Services

Amazon Simple Queue Service (SQS)   Amazon SQS is a highly reliable, scalable message queuing service that enables asynchronous message-based communication between distributed components of an application. Amazon SQS access is granted based on an AWS account or a user created with AWS IAM. Data stored within Amazon SQS is not encrypted by AWS; however, the user can encrypt data before it is uploaded to Amazon SQS, provided that the application using the queue has a means to decrypt the message when it's retrieved.

Amazon Simple Notification Service (SNS)   Amazon SNS is a web service that makes it easy to set up, operate, and send notifications from the cloud. It provides developers with a highly scalable, flexible, and cost-effective capability to publish messages from an application and immediately deliver them to subscribers or other applications. Amazon SNS allows topic owners to set policies for a topic that restrict who can publish or subscribe to a topic.

Analytics

Amazon Elastic MapReduce (Amazon EMR)   Amazon EMR is a managed web service you can use to run Hadoop clusters that process vast amounts of data by distributing the work and data among several servers. When launching job flows on your behalf, Amazon

EMR sets up two Amazon EC2 security groups: one for the master nodes and another for the slaves. You can launch the Amazon EC2 instances of your Amazon EMR cluster into an Amazon VPC, which is like launching it into a private subnet. You can encrypt the input data before you upload it to Amazon S3 using any common data encryption tool. If you do encrypt the data before it is uploaded, you then need to add a decryption step to the beginning of your job flow when Amazon EMR fetches the data from Amazon S3.

Amazon Kinesis   Amazon Kinesis is a managed service designed to handle real-time streaming of big data. You can control logical access to Amazon Kinesis resources and management functions by creating users under your AWS account using AWS IAM and controlling which Amazon Kinesis operations these users have permission to perform. The Amazon Kinesis API is only accessible via an SSL-encrypted endpoint to help ensure secure transmission of your data to AWS.

Deployment and Management

AWS Identity and Access Management (IAM)   AWS IAM allows you to create multiple users and manage the permissions for each of these users within your AWS account. A user is an identity (within an AWS account) with unique security credentials that can be used to access AWS Cloud services. IAM is secure by default; new users have no access to AWS until permissions are explicitly granted. A role is a set of permissions to access specific AWS resources, but these permissions are not tied to a specific IAM user or group.

Mobile Services

Amazon Cognito   Amazon Cognito provides identity and sync services for mobile and web-based applications. Your application authenticates with one of the well-known identity providers such as Google, Facebook, and Amazon using the provider's SDK. After the end user is authenticated with the provider, an OAuth or OpenID Connect token returned from the provider is passed by your application to Amazon Cognito, which returns a new Amazon Cognito ID for the user and a set of temporary, limited-privilege AWS credentials.

Applications

Amazon Workspaces   Amazon WorkSpaces is a managed desktop service that allows you to quickly provision cloud-based desktops for your users. Amazon WorkSpaces uses PCoIP, which provides an interactive video stream without transmitting actual data. The PCoIP protocol compresses, encrypts, and encodes the user's desktop computing experience and transmits as pixels only across any standard IP network to end-user devices. In order to access their WorkSpace, users must sign in using a set of unique credentials or their regular Active Directory credentials. You can also require the use of MFA upon sign-in in the form of a hardware or software token. Amazon WorkSpaces supports MFA using an on-premises RADIUS server or any security provider that supports RADIUS authentication. It currently supports the PAP, CHAP, MS-CHAP1, and MS-CHAP2 protocols, along with RADIUS proxies.

Exam Essentials

Understand the shared responsibility model.   AWS is responsible for securing the underlying infrastructure that supports the cloud, and you're responsible for anything you put on the cloud or connect to the cloud.

Understand regions and Availability Zones.   Each region is completely independent. Each region is designed to be completely isolated from the other regions. This achieves the greatest possible fault tolerance and stability. Regions are a collection of Availability Zones. Each Availability Zone is isolated, but the Availability Zones in a region are connected through low-latency links.

Understand High-Availability System Design within AWS.   You should architect your AWS usage to take advantage of multiple regions and Availability Zones. Distributing applications across multiple Availability Zones provides the ability to remain resilient in the face of most failure modes, including natural disasters or system failures.

Understand the network security of AWS.   Network devices, including firewall and other boundary devices, are in place to monitor and control communications at the external boundary of the network and at key internal boundaries within the network. These boundary devices employ rule sets, ACLs, and configurations to enforce the flow of information to specific information system services.

AWS has strategically placed a limited number of access points to the cloud to allow for a more comprehensive monitoring of inbound and outbound communications and network traffic. These customer access points are called API endpoints, and they allow HTTPS access, which allows you to establish a secure communication session with your storage or compute instances within AWS.

Amazon EC2 instances cannot send spoofed network traffic. The AWS-controlled, host-based firewall infrastructure will not permit an instance to send traffic with a source IP or MAC address other than its own.

Unauthorized port scans by Amazon EC2 customers are a violation of the AWS Acceptable Use Policy. Violations of the AWS Acceptable Use Policy are taken seriously, and every reported violation is investigated.

It is not possible for an Amazon EC2 instance running in promiscuous mode to receive or "sniff" traffic that is intended for a different virtual instance.

Understand the use of credentials on AWS.   AWS employs several credentials in order to positively identify a person or authorize an API call to the platform. Credentials include:

- Passwords
- AWS root account or IAM user account login to the AWS Management Console
- Multi-Factor Authentication (MFA)
- AWS root account or IAM user account login to the AWS Management Console

- Access Keys
- Digitally signed requests to AWS APIs (using the AWS SDK, CLI, or REST/Query APIs)

Understand the proper use of access keys.   Because access keys can be misused if they fall into the wrong hands, AWS encourages you to save them in a safe place and not to embed them in your code. For customers with large fleets of elastically-scaling Amazon EC2 instances, the use of IAM roles can be a more secure and convenient way to manage the distribution of access keys.

Understand the value of AWS CloudTrail.   AWS CloudTrail is a web service that records API calls made on your account and delivers log files to your Amazon S3 bucket. AWS CloudTrail's benefit is visibility into account activity by recording API calls made on your account.

Understand the security features of Amazon EC2.   Amazon EC2 uses public-key cryptography to encrypt and decrypt login information. Public-key cryptography uses a public key to encrypt a piece of data, such as a password, and then the recipient uses the private key to decrypt the data. The public and private keys are known as a key pair.

To log in to your instance, you must create a key pair, specify the name of the key pair when you launch the instance, and provide the private key when you connect to the instance. Linux instances have no password, and you use a key pair to log in using SSH. With Windows instances, you use a key pair to obtain the administrator password and then log in using RDP.

A security group acts as a virtual firewall that controls the traffic for one or more instances. When you launch an instance, you associate one or more security groups with the instance. You add rules to each security group that allow traffic to or from its associated instances. You can modify the rules for a security group at any time; the new rules are automatically applied to all instances that are associated with the security group.

Understand AWS use of encryption of data in transit.   All service endpoints support encryption of data in transit via HTTPS.

Know which services offer encryption of data at rest as a feature.   The following services offer a feature to encrypt data at rest:

- Amazon S3
- Amazon EBS
- Amazon Glacier
- AWS Storage Gateway
- Amazon RDS
- Amazon Redshift
- Amazon WorkSpaces

Exercises

The best way to become familiar with the security features of AWS is to do the exercises for each chapter and inspect the security features offered by the service. Take a look at this list of AWS Cloud services covered in different chapters and their security features:

Chapter 6, AWS IAM

- Exercise 6.1: Create an IAM Group
- Exercise 6.2: Create a Customized Sign-In Link and Password Policy
- Exercise 6.3: Create an IAM User
- Exercise 6.4: Create and Use an IAM Role
- Exercise 6.5: Rotate Keys
- Exercise 6.6: Set Up MFA
- Exercise 6.7: Resolve Conflicting Permissions

Chapter 3, Amazon EC2

- Exercise 3.1: Launch and Connect to a Linux Instance
- Exercise 3.2: Launch a Windows Instance with Bootstrapping

Chapter 3, Amazon EBS

- Exercise 3.8: Launch an Encrypted Volume

Chapter 2, Amazon S3

- Exercise 2.1: Create an Amazon Simple Storage Service (Amazon S3) Bucket
- Exercise 2.2: Upload, Make Public, Rename, and Delete Objects in Your Bucket

Chapter 4, Amazon VPC

- Exercise 4.1: Create a Custom Amazon VPC
- Exercise 4.2: Create Two Subnets for Your Custom Amazon VPC
- Exercise 4.3: Connect Your Amazon VPC to the Internet and Establish Routing
- Exercise 4.4: Launch an Amazon EC2 Instance and Test the Connection to the Internet.

Chapter 7, Amazon RDS

- Exercise 7.1: Create a MySQL Amazon RDS Instance
- Exercise 7.2: Simulate a Failover from One AZ to Another

Review Questions

1. Which is an operational process performed by AWS for data security?

   A. Advanced Encryption Standard (AES)-256 encryption of data stored on any shared storage device

   B. Decommissioning of storage devices using industry-standard practices

   C. Background virus scans of Amazon Elastic Block Store (Amazon EBS) volumes and Amazon EBS snapshots

   D. Replication of data across multiple AWS regions

   E. Secure wiping of Amazon EBS data when an Amazon EBS volume is unmounted

2. You have launched a Windows Amazon Elastic Compute Cloud (Amazon EC2) instance and specified an Amazon EC2 key pair for the instance at launch. Which of the following accurately describes how to log in to the instance?

   A. Use the Amazon EC2 key pair to securely connect to the instance via Secure Shell (SSH).

   B. Use your AWS Identity and Access Management (IAM) user X.509 certificate to log in to the instance.

   C. Use the Amazon EC2 key pair to decrypt the administrator password and then securely connect to the instance via Remote Desktop Protocol (RDP) as the administrator.

   D. A key pair is not needed. Securely connect to the instance via RDP.

3. A Database security group controls network access to a database instance that is inside a Virtual Private Cloud (VPC) and by default allows access from?

   A. Access from any IP address for the standard ports that the database uses is provided by default.

   B. Access from any IP address for any port is provided by default in the DB security group.

   C. No access is provided by default, and any access must be explicitly added with a rule to the DB security group.

   D. Access for the database connection string is provided by default in the DB security group.

4. Which encryption algorithm is used by Amazon Simple Storage Service (Amazon S3) to encrypt data at rest with Service-Side Encryption (SSE)?

   A. Advanced Encryption Standard (AES)-256

   B. RSA 1024

   C. RSA 2048

   D. AES-128

5. How many access keys may an AWS Identity and Access Management (IAM) user have active at one time?

   A. 0

   B. 1

    C. 2

    D. 3

6. Which of the following is the name of the security model employed by AWS with its customers?

    A. The shared secret model

    B. The shared responsibility model

    C. The shared secret key model

    D. The secret key responsibility model

7. Which of the following describes the scheme used by an Amazon Redshift cluster leveraging AWS Key Management Service (AWS KMS) to encrypt data-at-rest?

    A. Amazon Redshift uses a one-tier, key-based architecture for encryption.

    B. Amazon Redshift uses a two-tier, key-based architecture for encryption.

    C. Amazon Redshift uses a three-tier, key-based architecture for encryption.

    D. Amazon Redshift uses a four-tier, key-based architecture for encryption.

8. Which of the following Elastic Load Balancing options ensure that the load balancer determines which cipher is used for a Secure Sockets Layer (SSL) connection?

    A. Client Server Cipher Suite

    B. Server Cipher Only

    C. First Server Cipher

    D. Server Order Preference

9. Which technology does Amazon WorkSpaces use to provide data security?

    A. Secure Sockets Layer (SSL)/Transport Layer Security (TLS)

    B. Advanced Encryption Standard (AES)-256

    C. PC-over-IP (PCoIP)

    D. AES-128

10. As a Solutions Architect, how should you architect systems on AWS?

    A. You should architect for least cost.

    B. You should architect your AWS usage to take advantage of Amazon Simple Storage Service's (Amazon S3) durability.

    C. You should architect your AWS usage to take advantage of multiple regions and Availability Zones.

    D. You should architect with Amazon Elastic Compute Cloud (Amazon EC2) Auto Scaling to ensure capacity is available when needed.

11. Which security scheme is used by the AWS Multi-Factor Authentication (AWS MFA) token?

    A. Time-Based One-Time Password (TOTP)

    B. Perfect Forward Secrecy (PFC)

    C. Ephemeral Diffie Hellman (EDH)

    D. Split-Key Encryption (SKE)

12. DynamoDB tables may contain sensitive data that needs to be protected. Which of the following is a way for you to protect DynamoDB table content? (Choose 2 answers)

    A. DynamoDB encrypts all data server-side by default so nothing is required.

    B. DynamoDB can store data encrypted with a client-side encryption library solution before storing the data in DynamoDB.

    C. DynamoDB obfuscates all data stored so encryption is not required.

    D. DynamoDB can be used with the AWS Key Management Service to encrypt the data before storing the data in DynamoDB.

    E. DynamoDB should not be used to store sensitive information requiring protection.

13. You have launched an Amazon Linux Elastic Compute Cloud (Amazon EC2) instance into EC2-Classic, and the instance has successfully passed the System Status Check and Instance Status Check. You attempt to securely connect to the instance via Secure Shell (SSH) and receive the response, "WARNING: UNPROTECTED PRIVATE KEY FILE," after which the login fails. Which of the following is the cause of the failed login?

    A. You are using the wrong private key.

    B. The permissions for the private key are too insecure for the key to be trusted.

    C. A security group rule is blocking the connection.

    D. A security group rule has not been associated with the private key.

14. Which of the following public identity providers are supported by Amazon Cognito Identity?

    A. Amazon

    B. Google

    C. Facebook

    D. All of the above

15. Which feature of AWS is designed to permit calls to the platform from an Amazon Elastic Compute Cloud (Amazon EC2) instance without needing access keys placed on the instance?

    A. AWS Identity and Access Management (IAM) instance profile

    B. IAM groups

    C. IAM roles

    D. Amazon EC2 key pairs

16. Which of the following Amazon Virtual Private Cloud (Amazon VPC) elements acts as a stateless firewall?

    A. Security group

    B. Network Access Control List (ACL)

    C. Network Address Translation (NAT) instance

    D. An Amazon VPC cndpoint

17. Which of the following is the most recent version of the AWS digital signature calculation process?

    A. Signature Version 1

    B. Signature Version 2

    C. Signature Version 3

    D. Signature Version 4

18. Which of the following is the name of the feature within Amazon Virtual Private Cloud (Amazon VPC) that allows you to launch Amazon Elastic Compute Cloud (Amazon EC2) instances on hardware dedicated to a single customer?

    A. Amazon VPC-based tenancy

    B. Dedicated tenancy

    C. Default tenancy

    D. Host-based tenancy

19. Which of the following describes how Amazon Elastic MapReduce (Amazon EMR) protects access to the cluster?

    A. The master node and the slave nodes are launched into an Amazon Virtual Private Cloud (Amazon VPC).

    B. The master node supports a Virtual Private Network (VPN) connection from the key specified at cluster launch.

    C. The master node is launched into a security group that allows Secure Shell (SSH) and service access, while the slave nodes are launched into a separate security group that only permits communication with the master node.

    D. The master node and slave nodes are launched into a security group that allows SSH and service access.

20. To help prevent data loss due to the failure of any single hardware component, Amazon Elastic Block Storage (Amazon EBS) automatically replicates EBS volume data to which of the following?

    A. Amazon EBS replicates EBS volume data within the same Availability Zone in a region.

    B. Amazon EBS replicates EBS volume data across other Availability Zones within the same region.

    C. Amazon EBS replicates EBS volume data across Availability Zones in the same region and in Availability Zones in one other region.

    D. Amazon EBS replicates EBS volume data across Availability Zones in the same region and in Availability Zones in every other region.

AWS Risk and Compliance

THE AWS CERTIFIED SOLUTIONS ARCHITECT ASSOCIATE EXAM OBJECTIVES COVERED IN THIS CHAPTER MAY INCLUDE, BUT ARE NOT LIMITED TO, THE FOLLOWING:

Domain 2.0: Implementation/Deployment

✓ **2.1 Identify the appropriate techniques and methods using Amazon EC2, Amazon Simple Storage Service (Amazon S3), AWS Elastic Beanstalk, AWS CloudFormation, AWS OpsWorks, Amazon Virtual Private Cloud (Amazon VPC), and AWS Identity and Access Management (IAM) to code and implement a cloud solution.**

Content may include the following:

- Configure services to support compliance requirements in the cloud

Domain 3.0: Data Security

✓ **3.1 Recognize and implement secure practices for optimum cloud deployment and maintenance.**

Content may include the following:

- Shared security responsibility model
- Security Architecture with AWS
- AWS platform compliance
- AWS security attributes
- Design patterns

Introduction

AWS and its customers share control over the IT environment, so both parties have responsibility for managing that environment. AWS part in this shared responsibility includes providing its services on a highly secure and controlled platform and providing a wide array of security features customers can use.

The customer is responsible for configuring their IT environment in a secure and controlled manner for their purposes. While customers don't communicate their use and configurations to AWS, AWS does communicate with customers regarding its security and control environment, as relevant. AWS disseminates this information using three primary mechanisms. First, AWS works diligently to obtain industry certifications and independent third-party attestations. Second, AWS openly publishes information about its security and control practices in whitepapers and website content. Finally, AWS provides certificates, reports, and other documentation directly to its customers under Non-Disclosure Agreements (NDAs) as required.

Overview of Compliance in AWS

When customers move their production workloads to the AWS Cloud, both parties become responsible for managing the IT environment. The customers are responsible for setting up their environment in a secure and controlled manner. The customers also need to maintain adequate governance over their entire IT control environment. This section describes the AWS shared responsibility model and gives advice for how to establish strong compliance.

Shared Responsibility Model

As mentioned in Chapter 12, "Security on AWS," as customers migrate their IT environments to AWS, they create a model of shared responsibility between themselves and AWS. This shared responsibility model can help lessen a customer's IT operational burden, as it is AWS responsibility to manage the components from the host operating system and virtualization layer down to the physical security of the data centers in which these services operate. The customer is responsible for the components from the guest operating system upward (including updates, security patches, and antivirus software). The customer is also responsible for any other application software, as well as the configuration of security groups, Virtual Private Clouds (VPCs), and so on.

While AWS manages the security of the cloud, security in the cloud is the responsibility of the customer. Customers retain control of what security they choose to implement to protect their own content, platform, applications, systems, and networks, no differently than they would for applications in an on-site data center. Figure 13.1 illustrates the demarcation between customer and AWS responsibilities.

FIGURE 13.1 Shared responsibility model

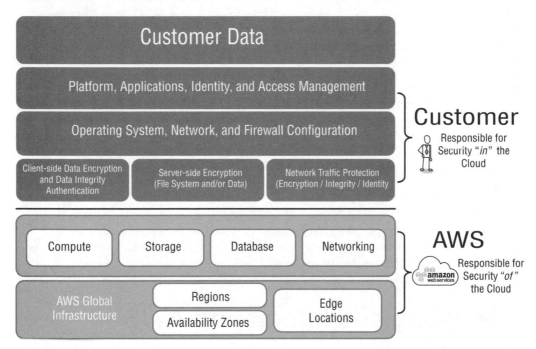

Customers need to be aware of any applicable laws and regulations with which they have to comply, and then they must consider whether the services that they consume on AWS are compliant with these laws. In some cases, it may be necessary to enhance an existing platform on AWS with additional security measures (such as deploying a web application firewall, Intrusion Detection System [IDS], or Intrusion Prevention System [IPS], or using some form of encryption for data at rest).

This customer/AWS shared responsibility model is not just limited to security considerations, but it also extends to IT controls. For example, the management, operation, and verification of IT controls are shared between AWS and the customer. Before moving to the AWS Cloud, customers were responsible for managing all of the IT controls in their environments. AWS manages the controls for the physical infrastructure, thereby taking the undifferentiated heavy lifting from customers, allowing them to focus on managing the relevant IT controls. Because every customer is deployed differently in AWS, customers can shift management of certain IT controls to AWS. This change in management of IT controls results in a new, distributed control environment. Customers can then use the AWS control and compliance documentation available to them to perform their control evaluation and verification procedures as required.

Strong Compliance Governance

It is still the customers' responsibility to maintain adequate governance over the entire IT control environment, regardless of how their IT is deployed (whether it is on-premises, on the cloud, or part of a hybrid environment). By deploying to the AWS Cloud, customers have options to apply different types of controls and various verification methods.

To achieve strong compliance and governance, customers may want to follow this basic methodology:

1. Take a holistic approach. Review the information available from AWS together with all other information to understand as much of the IT environment as they can. After this is complete, document all compliance requirements.

2. Design and implement control objectives to meet the organization's compliance requirements.

3. Identify and document controls owned by all third parties.

4. Verify that all control objectives are met and all key controls are designed and operating effectively.

By using this basic methodology, customers can gain a better understanding of their control environment. Ultimately, this will streamline the process and help separate any verification activities that need to be performed.

Evaluating and Integrating AWS Controls

AWS provides customers with a wide range of information regarding its IT control environment through whitepapers, reports, certifications, and other third-party attestations. This documentation assists customers in understanding the controls in place relevant to the AWS Cloud services they use and how those controls have been validated. This information also assists customers in their efforts to account for and validate that controls in their extended IT environment are operating effectively.

Traditionally, the design and operating effectiveness of controls and control objectives are validated by internal and/or external auditors via process walkthroughs and evidence evaluation. Direct observation and verification, by the customer or customer's external auditor, is generally performed to validate controls. In the case where service providers such as AWS are used, companies request and evaluate third-party attestations and certifications in order to gain reasonable assurance of the design and operating effectiveness of controls and control objectives. As a result, although a customer's key controls may be managed by AWS, the control environment can still be a unified framework in which all controls are accounted for and are verified as operating effectively. AWS third-party attestations and certifications not only provide a higher level of validation of the control environment, but may also relieve customers of the requirement to perform certain validation work themselves.

AWS IT Control Information

AWS provides IT control information to customers in the following two ways.

Specific Control Definition

AWS customers can identify key controls managed by AWS. Key controls are critical to the customer's control environment and require an external attestation of the operating effectiveness of these key controls in order to meet compliance requirements (for example, an annual financial audit). For this purpose, AWS publishes a wide range of specific IT controls in its *Service Organization Controls 1 (SOC 1)* Type II report. The SOC 1 Type II report, formerly the *Statement on Auditing Standards (SAS) No. 70*, is a widely recognized auditing standard developed by the American Institute of Certified Public Accountants (AICPA). The SOC 1 audit is an in-depth audit of both the design and operating effectiveness of AWS defined control objectives and control activities (which include control objectives and control activities over the part of the infrastructure that AWS manages). "Type II" refers to the fact that each of the controls described in the report are not only evaluated for adequacy of design, but are also tested for operating effectiveness by the external auditor. Because of the independence and competence of AWS external auditor, controls identified in the report should provide customers with a high level of confidence in AWS control environment.

AWS controls can be considered effectively designed and operating for many compliance purposes, including Sarbanes-Oxley (SOX) Section 404 financial statement audits. Leveraging SOC 1 Type II reports is also generally permitted by other external certifying bodies. For example, *International Organization for Standardization (ISO) 27001* auditors may request a SOC 1 Type II report in order to complete their evaluations for customers.

General Control Standard Compliance

If an AWS customer requires a broad set of control objectives to be met, evaluation of AWS industry certifications may be performed. With the *ISO 27001* certification, AWS complies with a broad, comprehensive security standard and follows best practices in maintaining a secure environment. With the *Payment Card Industry (PCI) Data Security Standard (DSS)* certification, AWS complies with a set of controls important to companies that handle credit card information. AWS compliance with *Federal Information Security Management Act (FISMA)* standards means that AWS complies with a wide range of specific controls required by U.S. government agencies. AWS compliance with these general standards provides customers with in-depth information on the comprehensive nature of the controls and security processes in place in the AWS Cloud.

AWS Global Regions

The AWS Cloud infrastructure is built around regions and *Availability Zones*. A region is a physical location in the world where we have multiple Availability Zones. Availability Zones consist of one or more discrete data centers, each with redundant power, networking, and connectivity, housed in separate facilities. These Availability Zones offer customers the ability to operate production applications and databases that are more highly available, fault tolerant, and scalable than would be possible using a single data center.

As of this writing, the AWS Cloud operates 33 Availability Zones within 12 geographic regions around the world. The 12 regions are US East (Northern Virginia), US West (Oregon), US West (Northern California), AWS GovCloud (US) (Oregon), EU (Frankfurt), EU (Ireland), Asia Pacific (Singapore), Asia Pacific (Tokyo), Asia Pacific (Sydney), Asia Pacific (Seoul), China (Beijing), and South America (Sao Paulo).

AWS Risk and Compliance Program

AWS Risk and Compliance is designed to build on traditional programs and help customers establish and operate in an AWS security control environment. AWS provides detailed information about its risk and compliance program to enable customers to incorporate AWS controls into their governance frameworks. This information can assist customers in documenting complete control and governance frameworks in which AWS is included as an important part.

The three core areas of the risk and compliance program—risk management, control environment, and information security—are described next.

Risk Management

AWS has developed a strategic business plan that includes risk identification and the implementation of controls to mitigate or manage risks. An AWS management team reevaluates the business risk plan at least twice a year. As a part of this process, management team members are required to identify risks within their specific areas of responsibility and implement controls designed to address and perhaps even eliminate those risks.

The AWS control environment is subject to additional internal and external risk assessments. The AWS compliance and security teams have established an information security framework and policies based on the Control Objectives for Information and Related

Technology (COBIT) framework, and they have effectively integrated the *ISO 27001* certifiable framework based on ISO 27002 controls, AICPA Trust Services Principles, PCI DSS v3.1, and the *National Institute of Standards and Technology (NIST)*Publication 800–53, Revision 3, Recommended Security Controls for Federal Information Systems. AWS maintains the security policy and provides security training to its employees. Additionally, AWS performs regular application security reviews to assess the confidentiality, integrity, and availability of data, and conformance to the information security policy.

The AWS security team regularly scans any public-facing endpoint IP addresses for vulnerabilities. It is important to understand that these scans do not include customer instances. AWS security notifies the appropriate parties to remediate any identified vulnerabilities. In addition, independent security firms regularly perform external vulnerability threat assessments. Findings and recommendations resulting from these assessments are categorized and delivered to AWS leadership. These scans are done in a manner for the health and viability of the underlying AWS infrastructure and are not meant to replace the customer's own vulnerability scans that are required to meet their specific compliance requirements.

As mentioned in Chapter 12, customers can request permission to conduct their own vulnerability scans on their own environments. These vulnerability scans must not violate the AWS acceptable use policy, and they must be requested in advance of the scan.

Control Environment

AWS manages a comprehensive control environment that consists of policies, processes, and control activities. This control environment is in place for the secure delivery of AWS service offerings. The collective control environment includes people, processes, and technology necessary to establish and maintain an environment that supports the operating effectiveness of AWS control framework. AWS has integrated applicable, cloud-specific controls identified by leading cloud computing industry bodies into the AWS control framework. AWS continues to monitor these industry groups for ideas on which leading practices can be implemented to better assist customers with managing their control environments.

The control environment at AWS begins at the highest level of the company. Executive and senior leadership play important roles in establishing the company's tone and core values. Every employee is provided with the company's code of business conduct and ethics and completes periodic training. Compliance audits are performed so that employees understand and follow the established policies.

The AWS organizational structure provides a framework for planning, executing, and controlling business operations. The organizational structure assigns roles and responsibilities to provide for adequate staffing, efficiency of operations, and the segregation of duties. Management has also established authority and appropriate lines of reporting for key personnel. Included as part of the company's hiring verification processes are education, previous employment, and, in some cases, background checks as permitted by law for employees commensurate with the employee's position and level of access to AWS facilities. The company follows a structured onboarding process to familiarize new employees with Amazon tools, processes, systems, policies, and procedures.

Information Security

AWS uses a formal information security program that is designed to protect the confidentiality, integrity, and availability of customers' systems and data. AWS publishes several security whitepapers that are available on the main AWS website. These whitepapers are recommended reading prior to taking the AWS Solutions Architect Associate exam.

AWS Reports, Certifications, and Third-Party Attestations

AWS engages with external certifying bodies and independent auditors to provide customers with considerable information regarding the policies, processes, and controls established and operated by AWS. A high-level description of the various AWS reports, certifications, and attestations is provided here.

- *Criminal Justice Information Services (CJIS)*—AWS complies with the Federal Bureau of Investigation's (FBI) CJIS standard. AWS signs CJIS security agreements with AWS customers, which include allowing or performing any required employee background checks according to the CJIS security policy.

- *Cloud Security Alliance (CSA)*—In 2011, the CSA launched the Security, Trust, & Assurance Registry (STAR), an initiative to encourage transparency of security practices within cloud providers. CSA STAR is a free, publicly accessible registry that documents the security controls provided by various cloud computing offerings, thereby helping users assess the security of cloud providers they currently use or with whom they are considering contracting. AWS is a CSA STAR registrant and has completed the CSA Consensus Assessments Initiative Questionnaire (CAIQ).

- *Cyber Essentials Plus*—Cyber Essentials Plus is a UK government-backed, industry-supported certification schema introduced in the UK to help organizations demonstrate operational security against common cyber-attacks. It demonstrates the baseline controls that AWS implements to mitigate the risk from common Internet-based threats within the context of the UK government's "10 Steps to Cyber Security." It is backed by industry, including the Federation of Small Businesses, the Confederation of British Industry, and a number of insurance organizations that offer incentives for businesses holding this certification.

- *Department of Defense (DoD) Cloud Security Model (SRG)*—The DoD SRG provides a formalized assessment and authorization process for Cloud Service Providers (CSPs) to gain a DoD provisional authorization, which can subsequently be leveraged by DoD customers. A provisional authorization under the SRG provides a reusable certification that attests to AWS compliance with DoD standards, reducing the time necessary for a DoD mission owner to assess and authorize one of their systems for operation on AWS.

As of this writing, AWS holds provisional authorizations at Levels 2 (all AWS US-based regions) and 4 (AWS GovCloud [US]) of the SRG.

- *Federal Risk and Authorization Management Program (FedRAMP)*—AWS is a FedRAMP-compliant CSP. AWS has completed the testing performed by a FedRAMP-accredited third-party assessment organization (3PAO) and has been granted two Agency Authority to Operate (ATOs) by the U.S. Department of Health and Human Services (HHS) after demonstrating compliance with FedRAMP requirements at the moderate impact level.

- *Family Educational Rights and Privacy Act (FERPA)*—FERPA (20 U.S.C. § 1232g; 34 CFR Part 99) is a federal law that protects the privacy of student education records. The law applies to all schools that receive funds under an applicable program of the U.S. Department of Education. FERPA gives parents certain rights with respect to their children's education records. These rights transfer to the student when he or she reaches the age of 18 or attends a school beyond the high school level. Students to whom the rights have transferred are "eligible students." AWS enables covered entities and their business associates subject to FERPA to leverage the secure AWS environment to process, maintain, and store protected education information.

- *Federal Information Processing Standard (FIPS) 140–2*—FIPS Publication 140–2 is a US government security standard that specifies the security requirements for cryptographic modules protecting sensitive information. To support customers with FIPS 140–2 requirements, Secure Sockets Layer (SSL) terminations in AWS GovCloud (US) operate using FIPS 140–2-validated hardware. AWS works with AWS GovCloud (US) customers to provide the information they need to help manage compliance when using the AWS GovCloud (US) environment.

- *FISMA and DoD Information Assurance Certification and Accreditation Process (DIACAP)*—AWS enables U.S. government agencies to achieve and sustain compliance with FISMA. The AWS infrastructure has been evaluated by independent assessors for a variety of government systems as part of their system owners' approval process. Numerous federal civilian and DoD organizations have successfully achieved security authorizations for systems hosted on AWS in accordance with the Risk Management Framework (RMF) process defined in NIST 800–37 and DIACAP.

- *Health Insurance Portability and Accountability Act (HIPAA)*—AWS enables covered entities and their business associates subject to HIPAA to leverage the secure AWS environment to process, maintain, and store protected health information. AWS signs business associate agreements with such customers.

- *Information Security Registered Assessors Program (IRAP)*—IRAP enables Australian government customers to validate that appropriate controls are in place and determine the appropriate responsibility model for addressing the needs of the Australian Signals Directorate (ASD) Information Security Manual (ISM). AWS has completed an independent assessment that has determined that all applicable ISM controls are in place relating to the processing, storage, and transmission of Unclassified Dissemination Limiting Marker (DLM) workloads for the Asia Pacific (Sydney) region.

- *ISO 9001*—AWS has achieved ISO 9001 certification. AWS ISO 9001 certification directly supports customers who develop, migrate, and operate their quality-controlled IT systems in the AWS Cloud. Customers can leverage AWS compliance reports as evidence for their own ISO 9001 programs and industry-specific quality programs, such as Good Laboratory, Clinical, or Manufacturing Practices (GxP) in life sciences, ISO 13485 in medical devices, AS9100 in aerospace, and ISO Technical Specification (ISO/TS) 16949 in the automotive industry. AWS customers who don't have quality system requirements can still benefit from the additional assurance and transparency that an ISO 9001 certification provides.

- *ISO 27001*—AWS has achieved ISO 27001 certification of the Information Security Management System (ISMS) covering AWS infrastructure, data centers, and services that are detailed in the AWS Risk and Compliance whitepaper, available on the AWS website.

- *ISO 27017*—ISO 27017 is the newest code of practice released by ISO. It provides implementation guidance on information security controls that specifically relate to cloud services. AWS has achieved ISO 27017 certification of the ISMS covering AWS infrastructure, data centers, and services that are detailed in the AWS Risk and Compliance whitepaper, available on the AWS website.

- *ISO 27018*—This is the first international code of practice that focuses on protection of personal data in the cloud. It is based on ISO information security standard 27002, and it provides implementation guidance on ISO 27002 controls applicable to public cloud-related Personally Identifiable Information (PII). It also provides a set of controls and associated guidance intended to address public cloud PII protection requirements not addressed by the existing ISO 27002 control set. AWS has achieved ISO 27018 certification of the AWS ISMS covering AWS infrastructure, data centers, and services that are detailed in the AWS Risk and Compliance whitepaper, available on the AWS website.

- *U.S. International Traffic in Arms Regulations (ITAR)*—The AWS GovCloud (US) region supports ITAR compliance. As a part of managing a comprehensive ITAR compliance program, companies subject to ITAR export regulations must control unintended exports by restricting access to protected data to U.S. persons and restricting physical location of that data to the U.S. AWS GovCloud (US) provides an environment physically located in the United States where access by AWS personnel is limited to U.S. persons, thereby allowing qualified companies to transmit, process, and store protected articles and data subject to ITAR restrictions. The AWS GovCloud (US) environment has been audited by an independent third party to validate that the proper controls are in place to support customer export compliance programs for this requirement.

- *Motion Picture Association of America (MPAA)*—MPAA has established a set of best practices for securely storing, processing, and delivering protected media and content. Media companies use these best practices as a way to assess risk and security of their content and infrastructure. AWS has demonstrated alignment with the MPAA best practices, and the AWS infrastructure is compliant with all applicable MPAA infrastructure controls. While MPAA does not offer a certification, media industry customers can use the AWS MPAA documentation to augment their risk assessment and evaluation of MPAA-type content on AWS.

- *Multi-Tier Cloud Security (MTCS) Tier 3 Certification*—MTCS is an operational Singapore security management standard (SPRING SS 584:2013) based on the ISO 27001/02 ISMS standards.

- *NIST*—In June 2015, NIST released guideline 800–171, Final Guidelines for Protecting Sensitive Government Information Held by Contractors. This guidance is applicable to the protection of Controlled Unclassified Information (CUI) on non-federal systems. AWS is already compliant with these guidelines, and customers can effectively comply with NIST 800–171 immediately. NIST 800–171 outlines a subset of the NIST 800–53 requirements, a guideline under which AWS has already been audited under the FedRAMP program. The FedRAMP moderate security control baseline is more rigorous than the recommended requirements established in NIST 800–171, and it includes a significant number of security controls above and beyond those required of FISMA moderate systems that protect CUI data.

- *PCI DSS Level 1*—AWS is Level 1-compliant under PCI DSS. Customers can run applications on the AWS PCI-compliant technology infrastructure for storing, processing, and transmitting credit card information in the cloud. In February 2013, the PCI Security Standards Council released the PCI DSS cloud computing guidelines. These guidelines provide customers who are managing a cardholder data environment with considerations for maintaining PCI DSS controls in the cloud. AWS has incorporated the PCI DSS cloud computing guidelines into the AWS PCI compliance package for customers.

- *SOC 1/International Standards for Assurance Engagements No. 3402 (ISAE 3402)*— AWS publishes a SOC 1, Type II report. The audit for this report is conducted in accordance with AICPA: AT 801 (formerly Statement on Standards for Attestation Engagements No. 16 [SSAE 16]) and ISAE 3402). This dual-standard report is intended to meet a broad range of financial auditing requirements for U.S. and international auditing bodies. The SOC 1 report audit attests that AWS control objectives are appropriately designed and that the individual controls defined to safeguard customer data are operating effectively. This report is the replacement of the SAS 70, Type II audit report.

- *SOC 2*—In addition to the SOC 1 report, AWS publishes a SOC 2, Type II report. Similar to SOC 1 in the evaluation of controls, the SOC 2 report is an attestation report that expands the evaluation of controls to the criteria set forth by AICPA trust services principles. These principles define leading practice controls relevant to security, availability, processing integrity, confidentiality, and privacy applicable to service organizations such as AWS. The AWS SOC 2 is an evaluation of the design and operating effectiveness of AWS controls that meet the criteria for the security and availability principles set forth in the AICPA trust services principles criteria. The report provides additional transparency into AWS security and availability based on a predefined industry standard of leading practices and further demonstrates AWS commitment to protecting customer data. The SOC 2 report scope covers the same services covered in the SOC 1 report.

- *SOC 3*—AWS publishes a SOC 3 report. The SOC 3 report is a publicly available summary of the AWS SOC 2 report. The report includes the external auditor's opinion of the operation of controls (based on the AICPA security trust principles included in the SOC 2 report), the assertion from AWS management regarding the effectiveness of controls, and an overview of AWS infrastructure and services. The AWS SOC 3 report includes all AWS data centers worldwide that support in-scope services. This is a great resource for customers to validate that AWS has obtained external auditor assurance without going through the process of requesting a SOC 2 report. The SOC 3 report covers the same services covered in the SOC 1 report.

Summary

AWS communicates with customers regarding its security and control environment through the following mechanisms:

- Obtaining industry certifications and independent third-party attestations
- Publishing information about security and AWS control practices via the website, whitepapers, and blogs
- Directly providing customers with certificates, reports, and other documentation (under NDA in some cases)

The shared responsibility model is not just limited to security considerations; it also extends to IT controls. The management, operation, and verification of IT controls are shared between AWS and the customer. AWS manages these controls where it relates to the physical infrastructure, and the customer manages these controls for the guest operating systems and upward (depending on the service).

It is the customer's responsibility to maintain adequate governance over the entire IT control environment, regardless of how their IT is deployed (on-premises, cloud, or hybrid). By deploying to the AWS Cloud, customers have different options for applying different types of controls and various verification methods that align with their business requirements.

The control environment for AWS contains a large volume of information. This information is provided to customers through whitepapers, reports, certifications, and other third-party attestations. AWS provides IT control information to customers in two ways: specific control definition and general control standard compliance.

AWS provides documentation about its risk and compliance program. This documentation can enable customers to include AWS controls in their governance frameworks. The three core areas of the risk and compliance program are risk management, control environment, and information security.

AWS has achieved a number of internationally recognized certifications and accreditations that demonstrate AWS compliance with third-party assurance frameworks, including:

- FedRAMP
- FIPS 140–2
- FISMA and DIACAP
- HIPAA
- ISO 9001
- ISO 27001
- ITAR
- PCI DSS Level 1
- SOC 1/ISAE 3402
- SOC 2
- SOC 3

AWS is constantly listening to customers and examining other certifications for the future.

Exam Essentials

Understand the shared responsibility model.   The shared responsibility model is not just limited to security considerations; it also extends to IT controls. For example, the management, operation, and verification of IT controls are shared between AWS and the customer. AWS manages these controls where it relates to physical infrastructure.

Remember that IT governance is the customer's responsibility.   It is the customer's responsibility to maintain adequate governance over the entire IT control environment, regardless of how its IT is deployed (on-premises, cloud, or hybrid).

Understand how AWS provides control information.   AWS provides IT control information to customers in two ways: via specific control definition and through a more general control standard compliance.

Remember that AWS is very proactive about risk management.   AWS takes risk management very seriously, so it has developed a business plan to identify any risks and to implement controls to mitigate or manage those risks. An AWS management team reevaluates the business risk plan at least twice a year. As a part of this process, management team members are required to identify risks within their specific areas of responsibility and then implement controls designed to address and perhaps even eliminate those risks.

Remember that the control environment is not just about technology.   The AWS control environment consists of policies, processes, and control activities. This control environment includes people, processes, and technology.

Remember the key reports, certifications, and third-party attestations.   The key reports, certifications, and third-party attestations include, but are not limited to, the following:

- FedRAMP
- FIPS 140–2
- FISMA and DIACAP
- HIPAA
- ISO 9001
- ISO 27001
- ITAR
- PCI DSS Level 1
- SOC 1/ISAE 3402
- SOC 2
- SOC 3

Review Questions

1. AWS communicates with customers regarding its security and control environment through a variety of different mechanisms. Which of the following are valid mechanisms? (Choose 3 answers)

   A. Obtaining industry certifications and independent third-party attestations

   B. Publishing information about security and AWS control practices via the website, whitepapers, and blogs

   C. Directly providing customers with certificates, reports, and other documentation (under NDA in some cases)

   D. Allowing customers' auditors direct access to AWS data centers, infrastructure, and senior staff

2. Which of the following statements is true when it comes to the AWS shared responsibility model?

   A. The shared responsibility model is limited to security considerations only; it does not extend to IT controls.

   B. The shared responsibility model is only applicable for customers who want to be compliant with SOC 1 Type II.

   C. The shared responsibility model is not just limited to security considerations; it also extends to IT controls.

   D. The shared responsibility model is only applicable for customers who want to be compliant with ISO 27001.

3. AWS provides IT control information to customers in which of the following ways?

   A. By using specific control definitions or through general control standard compliance

   B. By using specific control definitions or through SAS 70

   C. By using general control standard compliance and by complying with ISO 27001

   D. By complying with ISO 27001 and SOC 1 Type II

4. Which of the following is a valid report, certification, or third-party attestation for AWS? (Choose 3 answers)

   A. SOC 1

   B. PCI DSS Level 1

   C. SOC 4

   D. ISO 27001

5. Which of the following statements is true?

   A. IT governance is still the customer's responsibility, despite deploying their IT estate onto the AWS platform.

   B. The AWS platform is PCI DSS-compliant to Level 1. Customers can deploy their web applications to this platform, and they will be PCI DSS-compliant automatically.

    C. The shared responsibility model applies to IT security only; it does not relate to governance.

    D. AWS doesn't take risk management very seriously, and it's up to the customer to mitigate risks to the AWS infrastructure.

6. Which of the following statements is true when it comes to the risk and compliance advantages of the AWS environment?

    A. Workloads must be moved entirely into the AWS Cloud in order to be compliant with various certifications and third-party attestations.

    B. The critical components of a workload must be moved entirely into the AWS Cloud in order to be compliant with various certifications and third-party attestations, but the non-critical components do not.

    C. The non-critical components of a workload must be moved entirely into the AWS Cloud in order to be compliant with various certifications and third-party attestations, but the critical components do not.

    D. Few, many, or all components of a workload can be moved to the AWS Cloud, but it is the customer's responsibility to ensure that their entire workload remains compliant with various certifications and third-party attestations.

7. Which of the following statements best describes an Availability Zone?

    A. Each Availability Zone consists of a single discrete data center with redundant power and networking/connectivity.

    B. Each Availability Zone consists of multiple discrete data centers with redundant power and networking/connectivity.

    C. Each Availability Zone consists of multiple discrete regions, each with a single data center with redundant power and networking/connectivity.

    D. Each Availability Zone consists of multiple discrete data centers with shared power and redundant networking/connectivity.

8. With regard to vulnerability scans and threat assessments of the AWS platform, which of the following statements are true? (Choose 2 answers)

    A. AWS regularly performs scans of public-facing endpoint IP addresses for vulnerabilities.

    B. Scans performed by AWS include customer instances.

    C. AWS security notifies the appropriate parties to remediate any identified vulnerabilities.

    D. Customers can perform their own scans at any time without advance notice.

9. Which of the following best describes the risk and compliance communication responsibilities of customers to AWS?

    A. AWS and customers both communicate their security and control environment information to each other at all times.

    B. AWS publishes information about the AWS security and control practices online, and directly to customers under NDA. Customers do not need to communicate their use and configurations to AWS.

    C. Customers communicate their use and configurations to AWS at all times. AWS does not communicate AWS security and control practices to customers for security reasons.

    D. Both customers and AWS keep their security and control practices entirely confidential and do not share them in order to ensure the greatest security for all parties.

10. When it comes to risk management, which of the following is true?

    A. AWS does not develop a strategic business plan; risk management and mitigation is entirely the responsibility of the customer.

    B. AWS has developed a strategic business plan to identify any risks and implemented controls to mitigate or manage those risks. Customers do not need to develop and maintain their own risk management plans.

    C. AWS has developed a strategic business plan to identify any risks and has implemented controls to mitigate or manage those risks. Customers should also develop and maintain their own risk management plans to ensure they are compliant with any relevant controls and certifications.

    D. Neither AWS nor the customer needs to worry about risk management, so no plan is needed from either party.

11. The AWS control environment is in place for the secure delivery of AWS Cloud service offerings. Which of the following does the collective control environment NOT explicitly include?

    A. People

    B. Energy

    C. Technology

    D. Processes

12. Who is responsible for the configuration of security groups in an AWS environment?

    A. The customer and AWS are both jointly responsible for ensuring that security groups are correctly and securely configured.

    B. AWS is responsible for ensuring that all security groups are correctly and securely configured. Customers do not need to worry about security group configuration.

    C. Neither AWS nor the customer is responsible for the configuration of security groups; security groups are intelligently and automatically configured using traffic heuristics.

    D. AWS provides the security group functionality as a service, but the customer is responsible for correctly and securely configuring their own security groups.

13. Which of the following is NOT a recommended approach for customers trying to achieve strong compliance and governance over an entire IT control environment?

    A. Take a holistic approach: Review information available from AWS together with all other information, and document all compliance requirements.

    B. Verify that all control objectives are met and all key controls are designed and operating effectively.

    C. Implement generic control objectives that are not specifically designed to meet their organization's compliance requirements.

    D. Identify and document controls owned by all third parties.

Architecture Best Practices

THE AWS CERTIFIED SOLUTIONS ARCHITECT ASSOCIATE EXAM OBJECTIVES COVERED IN THIS CHAPTER MAY INCLUDE, BUT ARE NOT LIMITED TO, THE FOLLOWING:

Domain 1.0: Designing highly available, cost-efficient, fault-tolerant, and scalable systems

✓ **1.1 Identify and recognize cloud architecture considerations, such as fundamental components and effective designs.**

Content may include the following:

- How to design cloud services
- Planning and design
- Familiarity with:
    - Best practices for AWS architecture
    - Hybrid IT architectures (e.g., AWS Direct Connect, AWS Storage Gateway, Amazon Virtual Private Cloud [Amazon VPC], AWS Directory Service)
    - Elasticity and scalability (e.g., Auto Scaling, Amazon Simple Queue Service [Amazon SQS], Elastic Load Balancing, Amazon CloudFront)

Introduction

For several years, software architects have created and implemented patterns and best practices to build highly scalable applications. Whether migrating existing applications to the cloud or building new applications on the cloud, these concepts are even more important because of ever-growing datasets, unpredictable traffic patterns, and the demand for faster response times.

Migrating applications to AWS, even without significant changes, provides organizations with the benefits of a secured and cost-efficient infrastructure. To make the most of the elasticity and agility possible with cloud computing, however, Solutions Architects need to evolve their architectures to take full advantage of AWS capabilities.

For new applications, AWS customers have been discovering cloud-specific IT architecture patterns that drive even more efficiency and scalability for their solutions. Those new architectures can support anything from real-time analytics of Internet-scale data to applications with unpredictable traffic from thousands of connected *Internet of Things (IoT)* or mobile devices. This leaves endless possibilities for applications architected using AWS best practices.

This chapter highlights the tenets of architecture best practices to consider whether you are migrating existing applications to AWS or designing new applications for the cloud. These tenets include:

- Design for failure and nothing will fail.
- Implement elasticity.
- Leverage different storage options.
- Build security in every layer.
- Think parallel.
- Loose coupling sets you free.
- Don't fear constraints.

Understanding the services covered in this book in the context of these practices is key to succeeding on the exam.

Design for Failure and Nothing Fails

The first architecture best practice for AWS is the fundamental principle of designing for failure.

> *Everything fails, all the time*
>
> —Werner Vogels, CTO, AWS

Typically, production systems come with defined or implicit requirements in terms of uptime. A system is *highly available* when it can withstand the failure of an individual or multiple components. If you design architectures around the assumption that any component will eventually fail, systems won't fail when an individual component does. As an example, one goal when designing for failure would be to ensure an application survives when the underlying physical hardware for one of the servers fails.

Let's take a look at the simple web application illustrated in Figure 14.1. This application has some fundamental design issues for protecting against component failures. To start, there is no redundancy or failover, which results in single points of failure.

FIGURE 14.1   Simple web application architecture

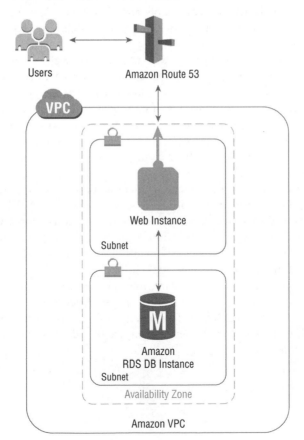

- If the single web server fails, the system fails.
- If the single database fails, the system fails.
- If the Availability Zone (AZ) fails, the system fails.

Bottom line, there are too many eggs in one basket.

Now let's walk through transforming this simple application into a more resilient architecture. To begin, we are going to address the single points of failure in the current architecture. Single points of failure can be removed by introducing *redundancy*, which is having multiple resources for the same task. Redundancy can be implemented in either standby or active mode.

In standby redundancy when a resource fails, functionality is recovered on a secondary resource using a process called *failover*. The failover will typically require some time before it is completed, and during that period the resource remains unavailable. The secondary resource can either be launched automatically only when needed (to reduce cost), or it can be already running idle (to accelerate failover and minimize disruption). Standby redundancy is often used for stateful components such as relational databases.

In active redundancy, requests are distributed to multiple redundant compute resources, and when one of them fails, the rest can simply absorb a larger share of the workload. Compared to standby redundancy, it can achieve better utilization and affect a smaller population when there is a failure.

To address the redundancy issues, we will add another web instance and add a standby instance for Amazon Relational Database Service (Amazon RDS) to provide high availability and automatic failover. The key is that we are going to add the new resources in another AZ. An AZ consists of one or more discrete data centers. AZs within a region provide inexpensive, low-latency network connectivity to other AZs in the same region. This allows our application to replicate data across data centers in a synchronous manner so that failover can be automated and be transparent for the users.

Additionally, we are going to implement active redundancy by swapping out the Elastic IP Address (EIP) on our web instance with an Elastic Load Balancer (ELB). The ELB allows inbound requests to be distributed between the web instances. Not only will the ELB help with distributing load between multiple instances, it will also stop sending traffic to the affected web node if an instance fails its health checks. Figure 14.2 shows the updated architecture with redundancy for the web application.

This *Multi-AZ* architecture helps to ensure that the application is isolated from failures in a single Availability Zone. In fact, many of the higher level services on AWS are inherently designed according to the Multi-AZ principle. For example, Amazon Simple Storage Service (Amazon S3) and Amazon DynamoDB ensure that data is redundantly stored across multiple facilities.

FIGURE 14.2   Updated web application architecture with redundancy

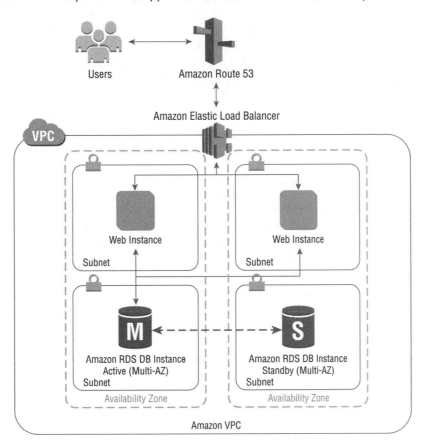

 One rule of thumb to keep in mind when designing architectures in the cloud is to be a pessimist; that is, assume things will fail. In other words, always design, implement, and deploy for automated recovery from failure.

Implement Elasticity

Elasticity is the ability of a system to grow to handle increased load, whether gradually over time or in response to a sudden change in business needs. To achieve elasticity, it is important that the system be built on a scalable architecture. Such architectures can support growth in users, traffic, or data size with no drop in performance. These architectures should provide scale in a linear manner, where adding extra resources results in at least a proportional increase in ability to serve additional system load. The growth in resources should introduce economies of scale, and cost should follow the same dimension that generates business value out of that system. While cloud computing provides virtually unlimited on-demand capacity, system architectures need to be able to take advantage of those resources seamlessly. There are generally two ways to scale an IT architecture: vertically and horizontally.

Scaling Vertically

Vertical scaling takes place through an increase in the specifications of an individual resource (for example, upgrading a server with a larger hard drive, more memory, or a faster CPU). On Amazon Elastic Compute Cloud (Amazon EC2), this can easily be achieved by stopping an instance and resizing it to an instance type that has more RAM, CPU, I/O, or networking capabilities. Vertical scaling will eventually hit a limit, and it is not always a cost-efficient or highly available approach. Even so, it is very easy to implement and can be sufficient for many use cases, especially in the short term.

Scaling Horizontally

Horizontal scaling takes place through an increase in the number of resources (for example, adding more hard drives to a storage array or adding more servers to support an application). This is a great way to build Internet-scale applications that leverage the elasticity of cloud computing. Not all architectures are designed to distribute their workload to multiple resources, and it is important to understand system characteristics that can affect a system's ability to scale horizontally. One key characteristic is the impact of stateless and stateful architectures.

Stateless Applications

When users or services interact with an application, they will often perform a series of interactions that form a session. A *stateless application* needs no knowledge of the previous interactions and stores no session information. A stateless application can scale horizontally, because any request can be serviced by any of the available system compute resources. Because no session data needs to be shared between system resources, compute resources can be added as needed. When excess capacity is no longer required, any individual resource can be safely terminated. Those resources do not need to be aware of the presence of their peers; all that is required is a way to distribute the workload to them.

Let's assume that the web application we used in the previous section is a stateless application with unpredictable demand. In order for our web instances to meet the peaks and valleys associated with our demand profile, we need to scale elastically. A great way to introduce elasticity and horizontal scaling is by leveraging Auto Scaling for web instances. An Auto Scaling group can automatically add Amazon EC2 instances to an application in response to heavy traffic and remove them when traffic slows. Figure 14.3 shows our web application architecture after the introduction of an Auto Scaling group.

FIGURE 14.3   Updated web application architecture with auto scaling

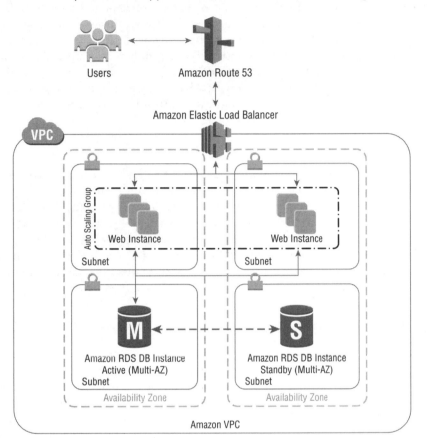

Stateless Components

In practice, most applications need to maintain some kind of state information. For example, web applications need to track whether a user is signed in, or else they might present personalized content based on previous actions. You can still make a portion of these architectures stateless by not storing state information locally on a horizontally-scaling resource, as those resources can appear and disappear as the system scales up and down.

For example, web applications can use HTTP cookies to store information about a session at the client's browser (such as items in the shopping cart). The browser passes that information back to the server at each subsequent request so that the application does not need to store it. However, there are two drawbacks with this approach. First, the content of the HTTP cookies can be tampered with at the client side, so you should always treat them as untrusted data that needs to be validated. Second, HTTP cookies are transmitted with every request, which means that you should keep their size to a minimum to avoid unnecessary latency.

Consider only storing a unique session identifier in a HTTP cookie and storing more detailed user session information server-side. Most programming platforms provide a native session management mechanism that works this way; however, these management mechanisms often store the session information locally by default. This would result in a stateful architecture. A common solution to this problem is to store user session information in a database. Amazon DynamoDB is a great choice due to its scalability, high availability, and durability characteristics. For many platforms, there are open source, drop-in replacement libraries that allow you to store native sessions in Amazon DynamoDB.

Stateful Components

Inevitably, there will be layers of your architecture that you won't turn into stateless components. First, by definition, databases are stateful. In addition, many legacy applications were designed to run on a single server by relying on local compute resources. Other use cases might require client devices to maintain a connection to a specific server for prolonged periods of time. For example, real-time multiplayer gaming must offer multiple players a consistent view of the game world with very low latency. This is much simpler to achieve in a non-distributed implementation where participants are connected to the same server.

Deployment Automation

Whether you are deploying a new environment for testing or increasing capacity of an existing system to cope with extra load, you will not want to set up new resources manually with their configuration and code. It is important that you make this an automated and repeatable process that avoids long lead times and is not prone to human error. Automating the deployment process and streamlining the configuration and build process is key to implementing elasticity. This will ensure that the system can scale without any human intervention.

Automate Your Infrastructure

One of the most important benefits of using a cloud environment is the ability to use the cloud's Application Program Interfaces (APIs) to automate your deployment process. It is recommended that you take the time to create an automated deployment process early on during the migration process and not wait until the end. Creating an automated and repeatable deployment process will help reduce errors and facilitate an efficient and scalable update process.

Bootstrap Your Instances

When you launch an AWS resource like an Amazon EC2 instance, you start with a default configuration. You can then execute automated bootstrapping actions as described in

Chapter 3, "Amazon Elastic Compute Cloud (Amazon EC2) and Amazon Elastic Block Store (Amazon EBS)." Let your instances ask a question at boot: "Who am I and what is my role?" Every instance should have a role to play in the environment (such as database server, application server, or slave server in the case of a web application). Roles may be applied during launch and can instruct the AMI on the steps to take after it has booted. On boot, an instance should grab the necessary resources (for example, code, scripts, or configuration) based on the role and "attach" itself to a cluster to serve its function.

Benefits of bootstrapping your instances include:

- Recreate environments (for example, development, staging, production) with few clicks and minimal effort.

- Maintain more control over your abstract, cloud-based resources.

- Reduce human-induced deployment errors.

- Create a self-healing and self-discoverable environment that is more resilient to hardware failure.

Designing intelligent elastic cloud architectures, where infrastructure runs only when you need it, is an art. As a Solutions Architect, elasticity should be one of the fundamental design requirements when defining your architectures. Here are some questions to keep in mind when designing cloud architectures:

- What components or layers in my application architecture can become elastic?

- What will it take to make that component elastic?

- What will be the impact of implementing elasticity to my overall system architecture?

Leverage Different Storage Options

AWS offers a broad range of storage choices for backup, archiving, and disaster recovery, as well as block, file, and object storage to suit a plethora of use cases. For example, services like Amazon Elastic Block Storage (Amazon EBS), Amazon S3, Amazon RDS, and Amazon CloudFront provide a wide range of choices to meet different storage needs. It is important from a cost, performance, and functional aspect to leverage different storage options available in AWS for different types of datasets.

One Size Does Not Fit All

Your workload and use case should dictate what storage option to leverage in AWS. No one storage option is suitable for all situations. Table 14.1 provides a list of some storage scenarios and which AWS storage option you should consider to meet the identified need. This table is not meant to be an all-encompassing capture of scenarios, but an example guide.

TABLE 14.1 Storage Scenarios and AWS Storage Options

Sample Scenario	Storage Option
Your web application needs large-scale storage capacity and performance. *-or-* You need cloud storage with high data durability to support backup and active archives for disaster recovery.	Amazon S3
You require cloud storage for data archiving and long-term backup.	Amazon Glacier
You require a content delivery network to deliver entire websites, including dynamic, static, streaming, and interactive content using a global network of edge locations.	Amazon CloudFront
You require a fast and flexible NoSQL database with a flexible data model and reliable performance.	Amazon DynamoDB
You need reliable block storage to run mission-critical applications such as Oracle, SAP, Microsoft Exchange, and Microsoft SharePoint.	Amazon EBS
You need a highly available, scalable, and secure MySQL database without the time-consuming administrative tasks.	Amazon RDS
You need a fast, powerful, fully-managed, petabyte-scale data warehouse to support business analytics of your e-commerce application.	Amazon Redshift
You need a Redis cluster to store session information for your web application.	Amazon ElastiCache
You need a common file system for your application that is shared between more than one Amazon EC2 instance.	Amazon Elastic File System (Amazon EFS)

Let's return to our sample web application architecture and show how different storage options can be leveraged to optimize cost and architecture. We can start by moving any static assets from our web instances to Amazon S3, and then serve those objects via Amazon CloudFront. These static assets would include all of the images, videos, CSS, JavaScript, and any other heavy static content that is currently delivered via the web instances. By serving these files via an Amazon S3 origin with global caching and distribution via Amazon CloudFront, the load will be reduced on the web instances and allow the web tier footprint to be reduced. Figure 14.4 shows the updated architecture for our sample web application.

FIGURE 14.4   Updated web application architecture with Amazon S3 and Amazon CloudFront

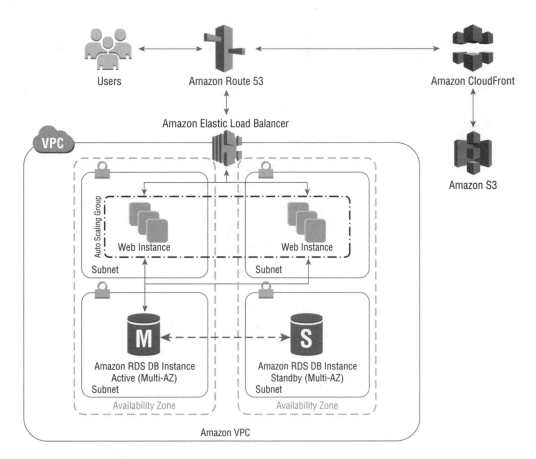

To further optimize our storage options, the session information for our sample web application can be moved to Amazon DynamoDB or even to Amazon ElastiCache. For our scenario, we will use Amazon DynamoDB to store the session information because the AWS Software Development Kits (SDK) provide connectors for many popular web development frameworks that make storing session information in Amazon DynamoDB easy. By removing session state from our web tier, the web instances do not lose session information when horizontal scaling from Auto Scaling happens. Additionally, we will leverage Amazon ElastiCache to store common database query results, thereby taking the load off of our database tier. Figure 14.5 shows the addition of Amazon ElastiCache and Amazon DynamoDB to our web application architecture.

FIGURE 14.5   Updated web application architecture with Amazon ElastiCache and Amazon DynamoDB

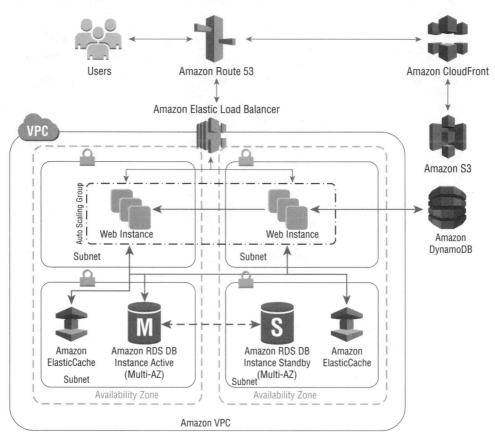

As a Solutions Architect, you will ultimately come to a point where you need to decide and define what your storage requirements are for the data that you need to store on AWS. There are a variety of options to choose from depending on your needs, each with different attributes ranging from database storage, block storage, highly available object-based storage, and even cold archival storage. Ultimately, your workload requirements will dictate which storage option makes sense for your use case.

Build Security in Every Layer

With traditional IT, infrastructure security auditing would often be a periodic and manual process. The AWS Cloud instead provides governance capabilities that enable continuous monitoring of configuration changes to your IT resources. Because AWS assets are programmable resources, your security policy can be formalized and embedded with the design of your infrastructure. With the ability to spin up temporary environments, security testing can now become part of your continuous delivery pipeline. Solutions Architects can leverage a plethora of native AWS security and *encryption* features that can help achieve higher levels of data protection and compliance at every layer of cloud architectures.

Best Practice

Inventory your data, prioritize it by value, and apply the appropriate level of encryption for the data in transit and at rest.

Most of the security tools and techniques with which you might already be familiar in a traditional IT infrastructure can be used in the cloud. At the same time, AWS allows you to improve your security in a variety of ways. AWS is a platform that allows you to formalize the design of security controls in the platform itself. It simplifies system use for administrators and those running IT and makes your environment much easier to audit in a continuous manner.

Use AWS Features for Defense in Depth

AWS provides a wealth of features that help Solutions Architects build *defense in depth*. Starting at the network level, you can build an Amazon Virtual Private Cloud (Amazon VPC) topology that isolates parts of the infrastructure through the use of subnets, security groups, and routing controls. Services like AWS Web Application Firewall (AWS WAF) can help protect your web applications from SQL injection and other vulnerabilities in your application code. For access control, you can use AWS Identity and Access Management (IAM) to define a granular set of policies and assign them to users, groups, and AWS resources. Finally, the AWS platform offers a breadth of options for protecting data with encryption, whether the data is in transit or at rest.

 Understanding the security features offered by AWS is important for the exam, and it is covered in detail in Chapter 12, "Security on AWS."

Offload Security Responsibility to AWS

AWS operates under a shared responsibility model, where AWS is responsible for the security of the underlying cloud infrastructure, and you are responsible for securing the workloads you deploy on AWS. This way, you can reduce the scope of your responsibility and focus on your core competencies through the use of AWS managed services. For example, when you use managed services such as Amazon RDS, Amazon ElastiCache, Amazon CloudSearch, and others, security patches become the responsibility of AWS. This not only reduces operational overhead for your team, but it could also reduce your exposure to vulnerabilities.

Reduce Privileged Access

Another common source of security risk is the use of service accounts. In a traditional environment, service accounts would often be assigned long-term credentials stored in a configuration file. On AWS, you can instead use IAM roles to grant permissions to applications running on Amazon EC2 instances through the use of temporary security tokens. Those credentials are automatically distributed and rotated. For mobile applications, the use of Amazon Cognito allows client devices to get controlled access to AWS resources via temporary tokens. For AWS Management Console users, you can similarly provide federated access through temporary tokens instead of creating IAM users in your AWS account. In that way, an employee who leaves your organization and is removed from your organization's identity directory will also lose access to your AWS account.

Best Practice

Follow the standard security practice of granting least privilege—that is, granting only the permissions required to perform a task—to IAM users, groups, roles, and policies.

Security as Code

Traditional security frameworks, regulations, and organizational policies define security requirements related to things such as firewall rules, network access controls, internal/external subnets, and operating system hardening. You can implement these in an AWS environment as well, but you now have the opportunity to capture them all in a script that defines a "Golden Environment." This means that you can create an AWS CloudFormation script that captures and reliably deploys your security policies. Security best practices can now be reused among multiple projects and become part of your continuous integration pipeline. You can perform security testing as part of your release cycle and automatically discover application gaps and drift from your security policies.

Additionally, for greater control and security, AWS CloudFormation templates can be imported as "products" into AWS Service Catalog. This enables centralized management of resources to support consistent governance, security, and compliance requirements while enabling users to deploy quickly only the approved IT services they need. You apply IAM permissions to control who can view and modify your products, and you define constraints to restrict the ways that specific AWS resources can be deployed for a product.

Real-Time Auditing

Testing and auditing your environment is key to moving fast while staying safe. Traditional approaches that involve periodic (and often manual or sample-based) checks are not sufficient, especially in agile environments where change is constant. On AWS, you can implement continuous monitoring and automation of controls to minimize exposure to security risks. Services like AWS Config Rules, Amazon Inspector, and AWS Trusted Advisor continually monitor for compliance or vulnerabilities giving you a clear overview of which IT resources are or are not in compliance. With AWS Config Rules, you will also know if some component was out of compliance even for a brief period of time, making both point-in-time and period-in-time audits very effective. You can implement extensive logging for your applications using Amazon CloudWatch Logs and for the actual AWS API calls by enabling AWS CloudTrail. AWS CloudTrail is a web service that records API calls to supported AWS Cloud services in your AWS account and creates a log file. AWS CloudTrail logs are stored in an immutable manner to an Amazon S3 bucket of your choice. These logs can then be automatically processed either to notify or even take action on your behalf, protecting your organization from non-compliance. You can use AWS Lambda, Amazon Elastic MapReduce (Amazon EMR), Amazon Elasticsearch Service, or third-party tools from the AWS Marketplace to scan logs to detect things like unused permissions, overuse of privileged accounts, usage of keys, anomalous logins, policy violations, and system abuse.

While AWS provides an excellent service management layer around infrastructure or platform services, organizations are still responsible for protecting the confidentiality, integrity, and availability of their data in the cloud. AWS provides a range of security services and architectural concepts that organizations can use to manage security of their assets and data in the cloud.

Think Parallel

The cloud makes *parallelization* effortless. Whether it is requesting data from the cloud, storing data to the cloud, or processing data in the cloud, as a Solutions Architect you need to internalize the concept of parallelization when designing architectures in the cloud. It is advisable not only to implement parallelization wherever possible, but also to automate it because the cloud allows you to create a repeatable process very easily.

When it comes to accessing (retrieving and storing) data, the cloud is designed to handle massively parallel operations. In order to achieve maximum performance and throughput, you should leverage request parallelization. Multi-threading your requests by using multiple concurrent threads will store or fetch the data faster than requesting it sequentially. Hence, a general best practice for developing cloud applications is to design the processes for leveraging multi-threading.

When it comes to processing or executing requests in the cloud, it becomes even more important to leverage parallelization. A general best practice, in the case of a web application, is to distribute the incoming requests across multiple asynchronous web servers using a load balancer. In the case of a batch processing application, you can leverage a master node with multiple slave worker nodes that processes tasks in parallel (as in distributed processing frameworks like Hadoop).

The beauty of the cloud shines when you combine elasticity and parallelization. Your cloud application can bring up a cluster of compute instances that are provisioned within minutes with just a few API calls, perform a job by executing tasks in parallel, store the results, and then terminate all of the instances.

Loose Coupling Sets You Free

As application complexity increases, a desirable characteristic of an IT system is that it can be broken in to smaller, *loosely coupled* components. This means that IT systems should be designed in a way that reduces interdependencies, so that a change or a failure in one component does not cascade to other components.

Best Practice

Design system architectures with independent components that are "black boxes." The more loosely system components are coupled, the larger they scale.

A way to reduce interdependencies in a system is to allow the various components to interact with each other only through specific, technology-agnostic interfaces (such as RESTful APIs). In this way, the technical implementation details are hidden so that teams can modify the underlying implementation without affecting other components. As long as those interfaces maintain backward compatibility, the different components that an overall system is comprised of remain decoupled.

Amazon API Gateway provides a way to expose well-defined interfaces. Amazon API Gateway is a fully managed service that makes it easy for developers to create, publish, maintain, monitor, and secure APIs at any scale. It handles all of the tasks involved in accepting and processing up to hundreds of thousands of concurrent API calls, including traffic management, authorization and access control, monitoring, and API version management.

Asynchronous integration is a common pattern for implementing loose coupling between services. This model is suitable for any interaction that does not need an immediate response and where an acknowledgement that a request has been registered will suffice. It involves one component that generates events and another that consumes them. The two components do not integrate through direct point-to-point interaction, but usually through an intermediate durable storage layer, such as an Amazon Simple Queue Service (Amazon SQS) queue or a streaming data platform like Amazon Kinesis. Figure 14.6 shows the logical flow for tight and loosely coupled architectures.

FIGURE 14.6   Tight and loose coupling

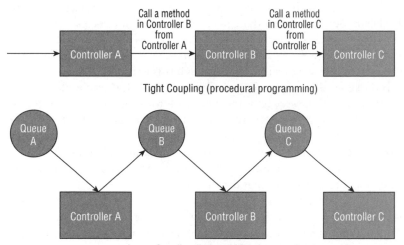

Tight Coupling (procedural programming)

Loose Coupling (independent phases using queues)

Leveraging asynchronous integration decouples the two components and introduces additional resiliency. For example, if a process that is reading messages from the queue fails, messages can still be added to the queue to be processed when the system recovers. It also allows you to protect a less scalable back-end service from front-end spikes and find the right tradeoff between cost and processing lag. For example, you can decide that you don't need to scale your database to accommodate for an occasional peak of write queries if you eventually process those queries asynchronously with some delay. Finally, by moving slow operations off of interactive request paths, you can also improve the end-user experience.

Design Scenario

Sample Loosely Coupled Architecture

A company provides transcoding services for amateur producers to format their short films to a variety of video formats. The service provides end users with an easy-to-use website to submit videos for transcoding. The videos are stored in Amazon S3, and a message ("the request message") is placed in an Amazon SQS queue ("the incoming queue") with a pointer to the video and to the target video format in the message. The transcoding engine, running on a set of Amazon EC2 instances, reads the request message from the incoming queue, retrieves the video from Amazon S3 using the pointer, and transcodes the video into the target format. The converted video is put back into Amazon S3 and another message ("the response message") is placed in another Amazon SQS queue ("the outgoing queue") with a pointer to the converted video. At the same time, metadata about the video (such as format, date created, and length) can be indexed into Amazon DynamoDB for easy querying. During this whole workflow, a dedicated Amazon EC2 instance can constantly monitor the incoming queue and, based on the number of messages in the incoming queue, can dynamically adjust the number of transcoding Amazon EC2 instances to meet customers' response time requirements.

Applications that are deployed as a set of smaller services will depend on the ability of those services to interact with each other. Because each of those services could be running across multiple compute resources, there needs to be a way for each service to be addressed. For example, in a traditional infrastructure, if your front-end web service needed to connect with your back-end web service, you could hardcode the IP address of the compute resource where this service was running. Although this approach can still work on cloud computing, if those services are meant to be loosely coupled, they should be able to be consumed without prior knowledge of their network topology details. Apart from hiding complexity, this also allows infrastructure details to change at any time. In order to achieve this agility, you will need some way of implementing service discovery. Service discovery manages how processes and services in an environment can find and talk to one another. It involves a directory of services, registering services in that directory, and then being able to look up and connect to services in that directory.

Loose coupling is a crucial element if you want to take advantage of the elasticity of cloud computing, where new resources can be launched or terminated at any point in time. By architecting system components without tight dependencies on each other, applications are positioned to take full advantage of the cloud's scale.

Don't Fear Constraints

When organizations decide to move applications to the cloud and try to map their existing system specifications to those available in the cloud, they notice that the cloud might not have the exact specification of the resource that they have on premises. For example, observations may include "Cloud does not provide X amount of RAM in a server" or "My database needs to have more IOPS than what I can get in a single instance."

You should understand that the cloud provides abstract resources that become powerful when you combine them with the on-demand provisioning model. You should not be afraid and constrained when using cloud resources because even if you might not get an exact replica of your on-premises hardware in the cloud environment, you have the ability to get more of those resources in the cloud to compensate.

When you push up against a constraint, think about what it's telling you about a possible underlying architectural issue. For example, if AWS does not have an Amazon RDS instance type with enough RAM, consider whether you have inadvertently trapped yourself in a scale-up paradigm. Consider changing the underlying technology and using a scalable distributed cache like Amazon ElastiCache or sharding your data across multiple servers. If it is a read-heavy application, you can distribute the read load across a fleet of synchronized slaves.

Organizations are challenged with developing, managing, and operating applications at scale with a wide variety of underlying technology components. With traditional IT infrastructure, companies would have to build and operate all of those components. While these components may not map directly into a cloud environment, AWS offers a broad set of complementary services that help organizations overcome these constraints and to support agility and lower IT costs.

On AWS, there is a set of managed services that provides building blocks for developers to leverage for powering their applications. These managed services include databases, machine learning, analytics, queuing, search, email, notifications, and more. For example, with Amazon SQS, you can offload the administrative burden of operating and scaling a highly available messaging cluster while paying a low price for only what you use. The same applies to Amazon S3, where you can store as much data as required and access it when needed without having to think about capacity, hard disk configurations, replication, and other hardware-based considerations.

There are many other examples of managed services on AWS, such as Amazon CloudFront for content delivery, Elastic Load Balancing for load balancing, Amazon DynamoDB for NoSQL databases, Amazon CloudSearch for search workloads, Amazon Elastic Transcoder for video encoding, Amazon Simple Email Service (Amazon SES) for sending and receiving emails, and more.

Architectures that do not leverage the breadth of AWS Cloud services (for example, they use only Amazon EC2) might be self-constraining the ability to make the most of cloud computing. This oversight often leads to missing key opportunities to increase developer productivity and operational efficiency. When organizations combine on-demand provisioning, managed services, and the inherent flexibility of the cloud, they realize that apparent constraints can actually be broken down in ways that will actually improve the scalability and overall performance of their systems.

Summary

Typically, production systems come with defined or implicit requirements in terms of uptime. A system is highly available when it can withstand the failure of an individual or multiple components. If you design architectures around the assumption that any component will eventually fail, systems won't fail when an individual component does.

Traditional infrastructure generally necessitates predicting the amount of computing resources your application will use over a period of several years. If you underestimate, your applications will not have the horsepower to handle unexpected traffic, potentially resulting in customer dissatisfaction. If you overestimate, you're wasting money with superfluous resources. The on-demand and elastic nature of the cloud enables the infrastructure to be closely aligned with the actual demand, thereby increasing overall utilization and reducing cost. While cloud computing provides virtually unlimited on-demand capacity, system architectures need to be able to take advantage of those resources seamlessly. There are generally two ways to scale an IT architecture: vertically and horizontally.

The AWS Cloud provides governance capabilities that enable continuous monitoring of configuration changes to your IT resources. Because AWS assets are programmable resources, your security policy can be formalized and embedded with the design of your infrastructure. With the ability to spin up temporary environments, security testing can now become part of your continuous delivery pipeline. Solutions Architects can leverage a plethora of native AWS security and encryption features that can help achieve higher levels of data protection and compliance at every layer of cloud architectures.

Because AWS makes parallelization effortless, Solutions Architects need to internalize the concept of parallelization when designing architectures in the cloud. It is advisable not only to implement parallelization wherever possible, but also to automate it because the cloud allows you to create a repeatable process very easily.

As application complexity increases, a desirable characteristic of an IT system is that it can be broken into smaller, loosely coupled components. Solutions Architects should design systems in a way that reduces interdependencies, so that a change or a failure in one component does not cascade to other components.

When organizations try to map their existing system specifications to those available in the cloud, they notice that the cloud might not have the exact specification of the resource that they have on-premises. Organizations should not be afraid and feel constrained when using cloud resources. Even if you might not get an exact replica of your hardware in the cloud environment, you have the ability to get more of those resources in the cloud to compensate.

By focusing on concepts and best practices—like designing for failure, decoupling the application components, understanding and implementing elasticity, combining it with parallelization, and integrating security in every aspect of the application architecture— Solutions Architects can understand the design considerations necessary for building highly scalable cloud applications.

As each use case is unique, Solutions Architects need to remain diligent in evaluating how best practices and patterns can be applied to each implementation. The topic of cloud computing architectures is broad and continuously evolving.

Exam Essentials

Understand highly available architectures.   A system is highly available when it can withstand the failure of an individual or multiple components. If you design architectures around the assumption that any component will eventually fail, systems won't fail when an individual component does.

Understand redundancy.   Redundancy can be implemented in either standby or active mode. When a resource fails in standby redundancy, functionality is recovered on a secondary resource using a process called failover. The failover will typically require some time before it is completed, and during that period the resource remains unavailable. In active redundancy, requests are distributed to multiple redundant compute resources, and when one of them fails, the rest can simply absorb a larger share of the workload. Compared to standby redundancy, active redundancy can achieve better utilization and affect a smaller population when there is a failure.

Understand elasticity.   Elastic architectures can support growth in users, traffic, or data size with no drop in performance. It is important to build elastic systems on top of a scalable architecture. These architectures should scale in a linear manner, where adding extra resources results in at least a proportional increase in ability to serve additional system load. The growth in resources should introduce economies of scale, and cost should follow the same dimension that generates business value out of that system. There are generally two ways to scale an IT architecture: vertically and horizontally.

Understand vertical scaling.   Scaling vertically takes place through an increase in the specifications of an individual resource (for example, upgrading a server with a larger hard drive or a faster CPU). This way of scaling can eventually hit a limit, and it is not always a cost efficient or highly available approach.

Understand horizontal scaling.   Scaling horizontally takes place through an increase in the number of resources. This is a great way to build Internet-scale applications that leverage the elasticity of cloud computing. It is important to understand the impact of stateless and stateful architectures before implementing horizontal scaling.

Understand stateless applications.   A stateless application needs no knowledge of the previous interactions and stores no session information. A stateless application can scale horizontally because any request can be serviced by any of the available system compute resources.

Understand loose coupling.   As application complexity increases, a desirable characteristic of an IT system is that it can be broken into smaller, loosely coupled components. This means that IT systems should be designed as "black boxes" to reduce interdependencies so that a change or a failure in one component does not cascade to other components. The more loosely system components are coupled, the larger they scale.

Understand the different storage options in AWS.   AWS offers a broad range of storage choices for backup, archiving, and disaster recovery, as well as block, file, and object storage to suit a plethora of use cases. It is important from a cost, performance, and functional aspect to leverage different storage options available in AWS for different types of datasets.

Exercises

In this section, you will implement a resilient application leveraging some of the best practices outlined in this chapter. You will build the architecture depicted in Figure 14.7 in the following series of exercises.

FIGURE 14.7 Sample web application for chapter exercises

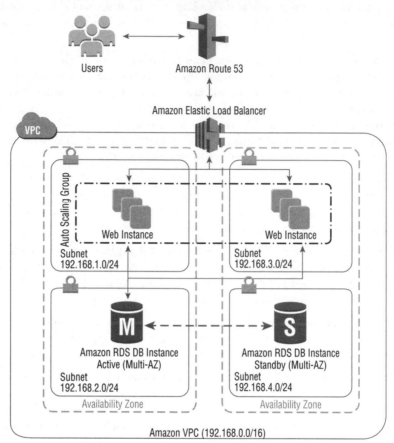

For assistance in completing the following exercises, reference the following user guides:

- **Amazon VPC**—http://docs.aws.amazon.com/AmazonVPC/latest/UserGuide/
  GetStarted.html

- **Amazon EC2 (Linux)**—http://docs.aws.amazon.com/AWSEC2/latest/UserGuide/
  concepts.html

- **Amazon RDS (MySQL)**—http://docs.aws.amazon.com/AmazonRDS/latest/
  UserGuide/CHAP_GettingStarted.CreatingConnecting.MySQL.html

EXERCISE 14.1

Create a Custom Amazon VPC

1. Log in to the AWS Management Console.

2. Navigate to the Amazon VPC console.

3. Create an Amazon VPC with a Classless Inter-Domain Routing (CIDR) block equal to
   192.168.0.0/16, a name tag of **Ch 14–VPC**, and default tenancy.

EXERCISE 14.2

Create an Internet Gateway for Your Custom Amazon VPC

1. Log in to the AWS Management Console.

2. Navigate to the Amazon VPC console.

3. Create an Internet gateway with a name tag of **Ch 14-IGW.**

4. Attach the Ch 14-IGW Internet gateway to the Amazon VPC from Exercise 14.1.

EXERCISE 14.3

Update the Main Route Table for Your Custom Amazon VPC

1. Log in to the AWS Management Console.

2. Navigate to Amazon VPC console.

3. Locate the main route table for the Amazon VPC from Exercise 14.1.

4. Update the route table name tag to a value of **Ch 14—Main Route Table**.

5. Update the route table routes by adding a destination of 0.0.0.0/0 with a target of the Internet gateway from Exercise 14.2.

EXERCISE 14.4

Create Public Subnets for Your Custom Amazon VPC

1. Log in to the AWS Management Console.

2. Navigate to the Amazon VPC console.

3. Create a subnet with a CIDR block equal to 192.168.1.0/24 and a name tag of **Ch 14—Public Subnet 1**. Create the subnet in the Amazon VPC from Exercise 14.1, and specify an Availability Zone for the subnet (for example, US-East-1a).

4. Create a subnet with a CIDR block equal to 192.168.3.0/24 and a name tag of **Ch 14—Public Subnet 2**. Create the subnet in the Amazon VPC from Exercise 14.1, and specify an Availability Zone for the subnet that is different from the one previously specified (for example, US-East-1b).

EXERCISE 14.5

Create a NAT Gateway for Your Custom Amazon VPC

1. Log in to the AWS Management Console.

2. Navigate to the Amazon VPC console.

3. Create a Network Address Translation (NAT) gateway in the Amazon VPC from Exercise 14.1 within the **Ch 14—Public Subnet 1** subnet from Exercise 14.4.

Create a Private Route Table for Your Custom Amazon VPC

1. Log in to the AWS Management Console.

2. Navigate to the Amazon VPC console.

3. Create a route table for the Amazon VPC from Exercise 14.1 with a name tag of **Ch 14–Private Route Table**.

4. Update the route table routes by adding a destination of 0.0.0.0/0 with a target of the NAT gateway from Exercise 14.5.

Create Private Subnets for Your Custom Amazon VPC

1. Log in to the AWS Management Console.

2. Navigate to the Amazon VPC console.

3. Create a subnet with a CIDR block equal to 192.168.2.0/24 and a name tag of **Ch 14–Private Subnet 1**. Create the subnet in the Amazon VPC from Exercise 14.1, and specify the same Availability Zone for the subnet that was used in Exercise 14.4 for the **Ch 14–Public Subnet 1** (for example, US-East-1a).

4. Update the route table for the created subnet to the **Ch 14–Private Route Table** from Exercise 14.6.

5. Create a subnet with a CIDR block equal to 192.168.4.0/24 and a name tag of **Ch 14–Private Subnet 2**. Create the subnet in the Amazon VPC from Exercise 14.1, and specify the same Availability Zone for the subnet that was used in Exercise 14.4 for the **Ch 14–Public Subnet 2** (for example, US-East-1b).

6. Update the route table for the created subnet to the **Ch 14–Private Route Table** from Exercise 14.6.

Create Security Groups for Each Application Tier

1. Log in to the AWS Management Console.

2. Navigate to the Amazon VPC console.

3. Create an Amazon VPC security group for the ELB with a name tag and group tab of **Ch14-ELB-SG** and a description of **Load balancer security group for Ch 14**

exercises. Create the security group in the Amazon VPC from Exercise 14.1 with an inbound rule of Type HTTP, a protocol of TCP, a port range of 80, and a source of 0.0.0.0/0.

4. Create an Amazon VPC security group for the web servers with a name tag and group tab of **Ch14-WebServer-SG** and a description of **Web server security group for Ch 14 exercises**. Create the security group in the Amazon VPC from Exercise 14.1 with an inbound rule of Type HTTP, a protocol of TCP, a port range of 80, and a source of the **Ch14-ELB-SG** security group. You may want to add another inbound rule of Type SSH, a protocol of TCP, a port range of 22, and a source of your IP address to provide secure access to manage the servers.

5. Create an Amazon VPC security group for the Amazon RDS MySQL database with a name tag and group tab of **Ch14-DB-SG** and a description of **Database security group for Ch 14 exercises**. Create the security group in the Amazon VPC from Exercise 14.1 with an inbound rule of Type MYSQL/Aurora, a protocol of TCP, a port range of 3306, and a source of the **Ch14-WebServer-SG** security group.

EXERCISE 14.9

Create a MySQL Multi-AZ Amazon RDS Instance

1. Log in to the AWS Management Console.

2. Navigate to the Amazon RDS console.

3. Create a DB subnet group with a name of **Ch14-SubnetGroup** and a description of **Subnet group for Ch 14 exercises**. Create the DB subnet group in the Amazon VPC from Exercise 14.1 with the private subnets from Exercise 14.7.

4. Launch a MySQL Amazon RDS instance with the following characteristics:

    DB Instance Class: db.t2.small

    Multi-AZ Deployment: yes

    Allocated Storage: no less than 5GB

    DB Instance Identifier: ch14db

    Master User Name: your choice

    Master Password: your choice

    VPC: the Amazon VPC from Exercise 14.1

    DB Security Group: Ch14-SubnetGroup

    Publicly Accessible: No

    VPC Security Group: Ch14-DB-SG

    Database Name: appdb

    Database Port: 3306

EXERCISE 14.10

Create an Elastic Load Balancer (ELB)

1. Log in to the AWS Management Console.

2. Navigate to the Amazon EC2 console.

3. Create an ELB with a load balancer name of **Ch14-WebServer-ELB**. Create the ELB in the Amazon VPC from Exercise 14.1 with a listener configuration of the following:

Load Balancer Protocol: HTTP

Load Balancer Port: 80

Instance Protocol: HTTP

Instance Port: 80

4. Add the public subnets created in Exercise 14.4.

5. Assign the existing security group of **Ch14-ELB-SG** created in Exercise 14.8.

6. Configure the health check with a ping protocol of HTTP, a ping port of 80, and a ping path of /index.html.

7. Add a tag with a key of **Name** and value of **Ch14-WebServer-ELB**.

8. Update the ELB port configuration to enable load-balancer generated cookie stickiness with an expiration period of 30 seconds.

EXERCISE 14.11

Create a Web Server Auto Scaling Group

1. Log in to the AWS Management Console.

2. Navigate to the Amazon EC2 console.

3. Create a launch configuration for the web server Auto Scaling group with the following characteristics:

AMI: latest Amazon Linux AMI

Instance Type: t2.small

Name: Ch14-WebServer-LC

User data:

```
#!/bin/bash
yum update -y
```

```
yum install -y php
yum install -y php-mysql
yum install -y mysql
yum install -y httpd
echo "<html><body><h1>powered by AWS</h1></body></html>" >
/var/www/html/index.html
service httpd start
```

Security Group: Ch14-WebServer-SG

Key Pair: existing or new key pair for your account

4. Create an Auto Scaling group for the web servers from the launch configuration
    Ch14-WebServer-LC with a group name of **Ch14-WebServer-AG**. Create the Auto
    Scaling group in the Amazon VPC from Exercise 14.1 with the public subnets created
    in Exercise 14.4 and a group size of 2.

5. Associate the load balancer **Ch14-WebServer-ELB** created in Exercise 14.10 to the
    Auto Scaling group.

6. Add a name tag with a key of **Name** and value of **Ch14-WebServer-AG** to the Auto
    Scaling group.

 You will need your own domain name to complete this section, and you
should be aware that Amazon Route 53 is not eligible for AWS Free Tier.
Hosting a zone on Amazon Route 53 will cost approximately $0.50 per
month per hosted zone, and additional charges will be levied depending on
what routing policy you choose. For more information on Amazon Route
53 pricing, refer to http://aws.amazon.com/route53/pricing/.

EXERCISE 14.12

Create a Route 53 Hosted Zone

1. Log in to the AWS Management Console.

2. Navigate to the Amazon Route 53 console and create a hosted zone.

3. Enter your domain name and create your new zone file.

4. In the new zone file, you will see the Start of Authority (SOA) record and name
    servers. You will need to log in to your domain registrar's website and update the
    name servers with your AWS name servers.

EXERCISE 14.12 *(continued)*

 If the registrar has a method to change the Time To Live (TTL) settings for their name servers, it is recommended that you reset the settings to 900 seconds. This limits the time during which client requests will try to resolve domain names using obsolete name servers. You will need to wait for the duration of the previous TTL for resolvers and clients to stop caching the DNS records with their previous values.

5. After you update your name servers with your domain registrars, Amazon Route 53 will be configured to serve DNS requests for your domain.

EXERCISE 14.13

Create an Alias A Record

1. Log in to the AWS Management Console.

2. Navigate to the Amazon Route 53 console.

3. Select your Route 53 hosted zone created in Exercise 14.12. Create a record set with a name of **www** and a type of **A–IPv4 Address**.

4. Create an alias with an alias target of the ELB **Ch14-WebServer-ELB** created in Exercise 14.10 and leave your routing policy as simple.

EXERCISE 14.14

Test Your Configuration

1. Log in to the AWS Management Console.

2. Navigate to the Amazon EC2 console.

3. Verify that the ELB created in Exercise 14.11 has **2 of 2 instances in service**.

4. In a web browser, navigate to the web farm (www.example.com) using the Hosted Zone A record created in Exercise 14.13. You should see the **powered by AWS** on the web page.

Review Questions

1. When designing a loosely coupled system, which AWS services provide an intermediate durable storage layer between components? (Choose 2 answers)

    A.   Amazon CloudFront

    B.   Amazon Kinesis

    C.   Amazon Route 53

    D.   AWS CloudFormation

    E.   Amazon Simple Queue Service (Amazon SQS)

2. Which of the following options will help increase the availability of a web server farm? (Choose 2 answers)

    A.   Use Amazon CloudFront to deliver content to the end users with low latency and high data transfer speeds.

    B.   Launch the web server instances across multiple Availability Zones.

    C.   Leverage Auto Scaling to recover from failed instances.

    D.   Deploy the instances in an Amazon Virtual Private Cloud (Amazon VPC).

    E.   Add more CPU and RAM to each instance.

3. Which of the following AWS Cloud services are designed according to the Multi-AZ principle? (Choose 2 answers)

    A.   Amazon DynamoDB

    B.   Amazon ElastiCache

    C.   Elastic Load Balancing

    D.   Amazon Virtual Private Cloud (Amazon VPC)

    E.   Amazon Simple Storage Service (Amazon S3)

4. Your e-commerce site was designed to be stateless and currently runs on a fleet of Amazon Elastic Compute Cloud (Amazon EC2) instances. In an effort to control cost and increase availability, you have a requirement to scale the fleet based on CPU and network utilization to match the demand curve for your site. What services do you need to meet this requirement? (Choose 2 answers)

    A.   Amazon CloudWatch

    B.   Amazon DynamoDB

    C.   Elastic Load Balancing

    D.   Auto Scaling

    E.   Amazon Simple Storage Service (Amazon S3)

5. Your compliance department has mandated a new requirement that all data on Amazon Elastic Block Storage (Amazon EBS) volumes must be encrypted. Which of the following steps would you follow for your existing Amazon EBS volumes to comply with the new requirement? (Choose 3 answers)

   A. Move the existing Amazon EBS volume into an Amazon Virtual Private Cloud (Amazon VPC).

   B. Create a new Amazon EBS volume with encryption enabled.

   C. Modify the existing Amazon EBS volume properties to enable encryption.

   D. Attach an Amazon EBS volume with encryption enabled to the instance that hosts the data, then migrate the data to the encryption-enabled Amazon EBS volume.

   E. Copy the data from the unencrypted Amazon EBS volume to the Amazon EBS volume with encryption enabled.

6. When building a Distributed Denial of Service (DDoS)-resilient architecture, how does Amazon Virtual Private Cloud (Amazon VPC) help minimize the attack surface area? (Choose 3 answers)

   A. Reduces the number of necessary Internet entry points

   B. Combines end user traffic with management traffic

   C. Obfuscates necessary Internet entry points to the level that untrusted end users cannot access them

   D. Adds non-critical Internet entry points to the architecture

   E. Scales the network to absorb DDoS attacks

7. Your e-commerce application provides daily and *ad hoc* reporting to various business units on customer purchases. This is resulting in an extremely high level of read traffic to your MySQL Amazon Relational Database Service (Amazon RDS) instance. What can you do to scale up read traffic without impacting your database's performance?

   A. Increase the allocated storage for the Amazon RDS instance.

   B. Modify the Amazon RDS instance to be a Multi-AZ deployment.

   C. Create a read replica for an Amazon RDS instance.

   D. Change the Amazon RDS instance DB engine version.

8. Your website is hosted on a fleet of web servers that are load balanced across multiple Availability Zones using an Elastic Load Balancer (ELB). What type of record set in Amazon Route 53 can be used to point myawesomeapp.com to your website?

   A. Type A Alias resource record set

   B. MX record set

   C. TXT record set

   D. CNAME record set

9. You need a secure way to distribute your AWS credentials to an application running on Amazon Elastic Compute Cloud (Amazon EC2) instances in order to access supplementary AWS Cloud services. What approach provides your application access to use short-term credentials for signing requests while protecting those credentials from other users?

   A. Add your credentials to the `UserData` parameter of each Amazon EC2 instance.

   B. Use a configuration file to store your access and secret keys on the Amazon EC2 instances.

   C. Specify your access and secret keys directly in your application.

   D. Provision the Amazon EC2 instances with an instance profile that has the appropriate privileges.

10. You are running a suite of microservices on AWS Lambda that provide the business logic and access to data stored in Amazon DynamoDB for your task management system. You need to create well-defined RESTful Application Program Interfaces (APIs) for these microservices that will scale with traffic to support a new mobile application. What AWS Cloud service can you use to create the necessary RESTful APIs?

   A. Amazon Kinesis

   B. Amazon API Gateway

   C. Amazon Cognito

   D. Amazon Elastic Compute Cloud (Amazon EC2) Container Registry

11. Your WordPress website is hosted on a fleet of Amazon Elastic Compute Cloud (Amazon EC2) instances that leverage Auto Scaling to provide high availability. To ensure that the content of the WordPress site is sustained through scale up and scale down events, you need a common file system that is shared between more than one Amazon EC2 instance. Which AWS Cloud service can meet this requirement?

   A. Amazon CloudFront

   B. Amazon ElastiCache

   C. Amazon Elastic File System (Amazon EFS)

   D. Amazon Elastic Beanstalk

12. You are changing your application to move session state information off the individual Amazon Elastic Compute Cloud (Amazon EC2) instances to take advantage of the elasticity and cost benefits provided by Auto Scaling. Which of the following AWS Cloud services is best suited as an alternative for storing session state information?

   A. Amazon DynamoDB

   B. Amazon Redshift

   C. Amazon Storage Gateway

   D. Amazon Kinesis

13. A media sharing application is producing a very high volume of data in a very short period of time. Your back-end services are unable to manage the large volume of transactions. What option provides a way to manage the flow of transactions to your back-end services?

    A. Store the inbound transactions in an Amazon Relational Database Service (Amazon RDS) instance so that your back-end services can retrieve them as time permits.

    B. Use an Amazon Simple Queue Service (Amazon SQS) queue to buffer the inbound transactions.

    C. Use an Amazon Simple Notification Service (Amazon SNS) topic to buffer the inbound transactions.

    D. Store the inbound transactions in an Amazon Elastic MapReduce (Amazon EMR) cluster so that your back-end services can retrieve them as time permits.

14. Which of the following are best practices for managing AWS Identity and Access Management (IAM) user access keys? (Choose 3 answers)

    A. Embed access keys directly into application code.

    B. Use different access keys for different applications.

    C. Rotate access keys periodically.

    D. Keep unused access keys for an indefinite period of time.

    E. Configure Multi-Factor Authentication (MFA) for your most sensitive operations.

15. You need to implement a service to scan Application Program Interface (API) calls and related events' history to your AWS account. This service will detect things like unused permissions, overuse of privileged accounts, and anomalous logins. Which of the following AWS Cloud services can be leveraged to implement this service? (Choose 3 answers)

    A. AWS CloudTrail

    B. Amazon Simple Storage Service (Amazon S3)

    C. Amazon Route 53

    D. Auto Scaling

    E. AWS Lambda

16. Government regulations require that your company maintain all correspondence for a period of seven years for compliance reasons. What is the best storage mechanism to keep this data secure in a cost-effective manner?

    A. Amazon S3

    B. Amazon Glacier

    C. Amazon EBS

    D. Amazon EFS

17. Your company provides media content via the Internet to customers through a paid subscription model. You leverage Amazon CloudFront to distribute content to your customers with low latency. What approach can you use to serve this private content securely to your paid subscribers?

    A. Provide signed Amazon CloudFront URLs to authenticated users to access the paid content.

    B. Use HTTPS requests to ensure that your objects are encrypted when Amazon Cloud-Front serves them to viewers.

    C. Configure Amazon CloudFront to compress the media files automatically for paid subscribers.

    D. Use the Amazon CloudFront geo restriction feature to restrict access to all of the paid subscription media at the country level.

18. Your company provides transcoding services for amateur producers to format their short films to a variety of video formats. Which service provides the best option for storing the videos?

    A. Amazon Glacier

    B. Amazon Simple Storage Service (Amazon S3)

    C. Amazon Relational Database Service (Amazon RDS)

    D. AWS Storage Gateway

19. A week before Cyber Monday last year, your corporate data center experienced a failed air conditioning unit that caused flooding into the server racks. The resulting outage cost your company significant revenue. Your CIO mandated a move to the cloud, but he is still concerned about catastrophic failures in a data center. What can you do to alleviate his concerns?

    A. Distribute the architecture across multiple Availability Zones.

    B. Use an Amazon Virtual Private Cloud (Amazon VPC) with subnets.

    C. Launch the compute for the processing services in a placement group.

    D. Purchase Reserved Instances for the processing services instances.

20. Your Amazon Virtual Private Cloud (Amazon VPC) includes multiple private subnets. The instances in these private subnets must access third-party payment Application Program Interfaces (APIs) over the Internet. Which option will provide highly available Internet access to the instances in the private subnets?

    A. Create an AWS Storage Gateway in each Availability Zone and configure your routing to ensure that resources use the AWS Storage Gateway in the same Availability Zone.

    B. Create a customer gateway in each Availability Zone and configure your routing to ensure that resources use the customer gateway in the same Availability Zone.

    C. Create a Network Address Translation (NAT) gateway in each Availability Zone and configure your routing to ensure that resources use the NAT gateway in the same Availability Zone.

    D. Create a NAT gateway in one Availability Zone and configure your routing to ensure that resources use that NAT gateway in all the Availability Zones.

Appendix
A

Answers to Review Questions

Chapter 1: Introduction to AWS

1. D. A region is a named set of AWS resources in the same geographical area. A region comprises at least two Availability Zones. Endpoint, Collection, and Fleet do not describe a physical location around the world where AWS clusters data centers.

2. A. An Availability Zone is a distinct location within a region that is insulated from failures in other Availability Zones and provides inexpensive, low-latency network connectivity to other Availability Zones in the same region. Replication areas, geographic districts, and compute centers are not terms used to describe AWS data center locations.

3. B. A hybrid deployment is a way to connect infrastructure and applications between cloud-based resources and existing resources that are not located in the cloud. An all-in deployment refers to an environment that exclusively runs in the cloud. An on-premises deployment refers to an environment that runs exclusively in an organization's data center.

4. C. Amazon CloudWatch is a monitoring service for AWS Cloud resources and the applications organizations run on AWS. It allows organizations to collect and track metrics, collect and monitor log files, and set alarms. AWS IAM, Amazon SNS, and AWS CloudFormation do not provide visibility into resource utilization, application performance, and the operational health of your AWS resources.

5. B. Amazon DynamoDB is a fully managed, fast, and flexible NoSQL database service for all applications that need consistent, single-digit millisecond latency at any scale. Amazon SQS, Amazon ElastiCache, and Amazon RDS do not provide a NoSQL database service. Amazon SQS is a managed message queuing service. Amazon ElastiCache is a service that provides in-memory cache in the cloud. Finally, Amazon RDS provides managed relational databases.

6. A. Auto Scaling helps maintain application availability and allows organizations to scale Amazon Elastic Compute Cloud (Amazon EC2) capacity up or down automatically according to conditions defined for the particular workload. Not only can it be used to help ensure that the desired number of Amazon EC2 instances are running, but it also allows resources to scale in and out to match the demands of dynamic workloads. Amazon Glacier, Amazon SNS, and Amazon VPC do not provide services to scale compute capacity automatically.

7. D. Amazon CloudFront is a web service that provides a CDN to speed up distribution of your static and dynamic web content—for example, .html, .css, .php, image, and media files—to end users. Amazon CloudFront delivers content through a worldwide network of edge locations. Amazon EC2, Amazon Route 53, and AWS Storage Gateway do not provide CDN services that are required to meet the needs for the photo sharing service.

8. A. Amazon EBS provides persistent block-level storage volumes for use with Amazon EC2 instances on the AWS Cloud. Amazon DynamoDB, Amazon Glacier, and AWS CloudFormation do not provide persistent block-level storage for Amazon EC2 instances. Amazon DynamoDB provides managed NoSQL databases. Amazon Glacier provides low-cost archival storage. AWS CloudFormation gives developers and systems administrators an easy way to create and manage a collection of related AWS resources.

9. C. Amazon VPC lets organizations provision a logically isolated section of the AWS Cloud where they can launch AWS resources in a virtual network that they define. Amazon SWF, Amazon Route 53, and AWS CloudFormation do not provide a virtual network. Amazon SWF helps developers build, run, and scale background jobs that have parallel or sequential steps. Amazon Route 53 provides a highly available and scalable cloud Domain Name System (DNS) web service. Amazon CloudFormation gives developers and systems administrators an easy way to create and manage a collection of related AWS resources.

10. B. Amazon SQS is a fast, reliable, scalable, fully managed message queuing service that allows organizations to decouple the components of a cloud application. With Amazon SQS, organizations can transmit any volume of data, at any level of throughput, without losing messages or requiring other services to be always available. AWS CloudTrail records AWS API calls, and Amazon Redshift is a data warehouse, neither of which would be useful as an architecture component for decoupling components. Amazon SNS provides a messaging bus complement to Amazon SQS; however, it doesn't provide the decoupling of components necessary for this scenario.

Chapter 2: Amazon Simple Storage Service (Amazon S3) and Amazon Glacier Storage

1. D, E. Objects are stored in buckets, and objects contain both data and metadata.

2. B, D. Amazon S3 cannot be mounted to an Amazon EC2 instance like a file system and should not serve as primary database storage.

3. A, B, D. C and E are incorrect—objects are private by default, and storage in a bucket does not need to be pre-allocated.

4. B, C, E. Static website hosting does not restrict data access, and neither does an Amazon S3 lifecycle policy.

5. C, E. Versioning protects data against inadvertent or intentional deletion by storing all versions of the object, and MFA Delete requires a one-time code from a Multi-Factor Authentication (MFA) device to delete objects. Cross-region replication and migration to the Amazon Glacier storage class do not protect against deletion. Vault locks are a feature of Amazon Glacier, not a feature of Amazon S3.

6. C. Migrating the data to Amazon S3 Standard-IA after 30 days using a lifecycle policy is correct. Amazon S3 RRS should only be used for easily replicated data, not critical data. Migration to Amazon Glacier might minimize storage costs if retrievals are infrequent, but documents would not be available in minutes when needed.

7. B. Data is automatically replicated within a region. Replication to other regions and versioning are optional. Amazon S3 data is not backed up to tape.

8. C. In a URL, the bucket name precedes the string "s3.amazonaws.com/," and the object key is everything after that. There is no folder structure in Amazon S3.

9. C. Amazon S3 server access logs store a record of what requestor accessed the objects in your bucket, including the requesting IP address.

10. B, C. Cross-region replication can help lower latency and satisfy compliance requirements on distance. Amazon S3 is designed for eleven nines durability for objects in a single region, so a second region does not significantly increase durability. Cross-region replication does not protect against accidental deletion.

11. C. If data must be encrypted before being sent to Amazon S3, client-side encryption must be used.

12. B. Amazon S3 scales automatically, but for request rates over 100 GETS per second, it helps to make sure there is some randomness in the key space. Replication and logging will not affect performance or scalability. Using sequential key names could have a negative effect on performance or scalability.

13. A, D. You must enable versioning before you can enable cross-region replication, and Amazon S3 must have IAM permissions to perform the replication. Lifecycle rules migrate data from one storage class to another, not from one bucket to another. Static website hosting is not a prerequisite for replication.

14. B. Amazon S3 is the most cost effective storage on AWS, and lifecycle policies are a simple and effective feature to address the business requirements.

15. B, C, E. Amazon S3 bucket policies cannot specify a company name or a country or origin, but they can specify request IP range, AWS account, and a prefix for objects that can be accessed.

16. B, C. Amazon S3 provides read-after-write consistency for PUTs to new objects (new key), but eventual consistency for GETs and DELETEs of existing objects (existing key).

17. A, B, D. A, B, and D are required, and normally you also set a friendly CNAME to the bucket URL. Amazon S3 does not support FTP transfers, and HTTP does not need to be enabled.

18. B. Pre-signed URLs allow you to grant time-limited permission to download objects from an Amazon Simple Storage Service (Amazon S3) bucket. Static web hosting generally requires world-read access to all content. AWS IAM policies do not know who the authenticated users of the web app are. Logging can help track content loss, but not prevent it.

19. A, C. Amazon Glacier is optimized for long-term archival storage and is not suited to data that needs immediate access or short-lived data that is erased within 90 days.

20. C, D, E. Amazon Glacier stores data in archives, which are contained in vaults. Archives are identified by system-created archive IDs, not key names.

Chapter 3: Amazon Elastic Compute Cloud (Amazon EC2) and Amazon Elastic Block Store (Amazon EBS)

1. C. Reserved Instances provide cost savings when you can commit to running instances full time, such as to handle the base traffic. On-Demand Instances provide the flexibility to handle traffic spikes, such as on the last day of the month.

2. B. Spot Instances are a very cost-effective way to address temporary compute needs that are not urgent and are tolerant of interruption. That's exactly the workload described here. Reserved Instances are inappropriate for temporary workloads. On-Demand Instances are good for temporary workloads, but don't offer the cost savings of Spot Instances. Adding more queues is a non-responsive answer as it would not address the problem.

3. C, D. The Amazon EC2 instance ID will be assigned by AWS as part of the launch process. The administrator password is assigned by AWS and encrypted via the public key. The instance type defines the virtual hardware and the AMI defines the initial software state. You must specify both upon launch.

4. A, C. You can change the instance type only within the same instance type family, or you can change the Availability Zone. You cannot change the operating system nor the instance type family.

5. D. When there are multiple security groups associated with an instance, all the rules are aggregated.

6. A, B, E. These are the benefits of enhanced networking.

7. A, B, D. The other answers have nothing to do with networking.

8. C. Dedicated Instances will not share hosts with other accounts.

9. B, C. Instance stores are low-durability, high-IOPS storage that is included for free with the hourly cost of an instance.

10. A, C. There are no tapes in the AWS infrastructure. Amazon EBS volumes persist when the instance is stopped. The data is automatically replicated within an Availability Zone. Amazon EBS volumes can be encrypted upon creation and used by an instance in the same manner as if they were not encrypted.

11. B. There is no delay in processing when commencing a snapshot.

12. B. The volume is created immediately but the data is loaded lazily. This means that the volume can be accessed upon creation, and if the data being requested has not yet been restored, it will be restored upon first request.

13. A, C. B and D are incorrect because an instance store will not be durable and a magnetic volume offers an average of 100 IOPS. Amazon EBS-optimized instances reserve network bandwidth on the instance for IO, and Provisioned IOPS SSD volumes provide the highest consistent IOPS.

14. D. Bootstrapping runs the provided script, so anything you can accomplish in a script you can accomplish during bootstrapping.

15. C. The public half of the key pair is stored on the instance, and the private half can then be used to connect via SSH.

16. B, C. These are the possible outputs of VM Import/Export.

17. B, D. Neither the Windows machine name nor the Amazon EC2 instance ID can be resolved into an IP address to access the instance.

18. A. None of the other options will have any effect on the ability to connect.

19. C. A short period of heavy traffic is exactly the use case for the bursting nature of general-purpose SSD volumes—the rest of the day is more than enough time to build up enough IOPS credits to handle the nightly task. Instance stores are not durable, magnetic volumes cannot provide enough IOPS, and to set up a Provisioned IOPS SSD volume to handle the peak would mean spending money for more IOPS than you need.

20. B. There is a very small hourly charge for allocated elastic IP addresses that are not associated with an instance.

Chapter 4: Amazon Virtual Private Cloud (Amazon VPC)

1. C. The minimum size subnet that you can have in an Amazon VPC is /28.

2. C. You need two public subnets (one for each Availability Zone) and two private subnets (one for each Availability Zone). Therefore, you need four subnets.

3. A. Network ACLs are associated to a VPC subnet to control traffic flow.

4. A. The maximum size subnet that you can have in a VPC is /16.

5. D. By creating a route out to the Internet using an IGW, you have made this subnet public.

6. A. When you create an Amazon VPC, a route table is created by default. You must manually create subnets and an IGW.

7. C. When you provision an Amazon VPC, all subnets can communicate with each other by default.

8. A. You may only have one IGW for each Amazon VPC.

9. B. Security groups are stateful, whereas network ACLs are stateless.

10. C. You should disable source/destination checks on the NAT.

11. B, E. In the EC2-Classic network, the EIP will be disassociated with the instance; in the EC2-VPC network, the EIP remains associated with the instance. Regardless of the underlying network, a stop/start of an Amazon EBS-backed Amazon EC2 instance always changes the host computer.

12. D. Six VPC Peering connections are needed for each of the four VPCs to send traffic to the other.

13. B. A DHCP option set allows customers to define DNS servers for DNS name resolution, establish domain names for instances within an Amazon VPC, define NTP servers, and define the NetBIOS name servers.

14. D. A CGW is the customer side of a VPN connection, and an IGW connects a network to the Internet. A VPG is the Amazon side of a VPN connection.

15. A. The default limit for the number of Amazon VPCs that a customer may have in a region is 5.

16. B. Network ACL rules can deny traffic.

17. D. IPsec is the security protocol supported by Amazon VPC.

18. D. An Amazon VPC endpoint enables you to create a private connection between your Amazon VPC and another AWS service without requiring access over the Internet or through a NAT device, VPN connection, or AWS Direct Connect.

19. A, C. The CIDR block is specified upon creation and cannot be changed. An Amazon VPC is associated with exactly one region which must be specified upon creation. You can add a subnet to an Amazon VPC any time after it has been created, provided its address range falls within the Amazon VPC CIDR block and does not overlap with the address range of any existing CIDR block. You can set up peering relationships between Amazon VPCs after they have been created.

20. B. Attaching an ENI associated with a different subnet to an instance can make the instance dual-homed.

Chapter 5: Elastic Load Balancing, Amazon CloudWatch, and Auto Scaling

1. A, D. An Auto Scaling group must have a minimum size and a launch configuration defined in order to be created. Health checks and a desired capacity are optional.

2. B. The load balancer maintains two separate connections: one connection with the client and one connection with the Amazon EC2 instance.

3. D. Amazon CloudWatch metric data is kept for 2 weeks.

4. A. Only the launch configuration name, AMI, and instance type are needed to create an Auto Scaling launch configuration. Identifying a key pair, security group, and a block device mapping are optional elements for an Auto Scaling launch configuration.

5. B. You can use the Amazon CloudWatch Logs Agent installer on existing Amazon EC2 instances to install and configure the CloudWatch Logs Agent.

6. C. You configure your load balancer to accept incoming traffic by specifying one or more listeners.

7. D. The default Amazon EC2 instance limit for all regions is 20.

8. A. An SSL certificate must specify the name of the website in either the subject name or listed as a value in the SAN extension of the certificate in order for connecting clients to not receive a warning.

9. C. When Amazon EC2 instances fail the requisite number of consecutive health checks, the load balancer stops sending traffic to the Amazon EC2 instance.

10. D. Amazon CloudWatch metrics provide hypervisor visible metrics.

11. C. Auto Scaling is designed to scale out based on an event like increased traffic while being cost effective when not needed.

12. B. Auto Scaling will provide high availability across three Availability Zones with three Amazon EC2 instances in each and keep capacity above the required minimum capacity, even in the event of an entire Availability Zone becoming unavailable.

13. B, E, F. Auto Scaling responds to changing conditions by adding or terminating instances, launches instances from an AMI specified in the launch configuration associated with the Auto Scaling group, and enforces a minimum number of instances in the min-size parameter of the Auto Scaling group.

14. D. A, B, and C are all true statements about launch configurations being loosely coupled and referenced by the Auto Scaling group instead of being part of the Auto Scaling group.

15. A, C. An Auto Scaling group may use On-Demand and Spot Instances. An Auto Scaling group may not use already stopped instances, instances running someplace other than AWS, and already running instances not started by the Auto Scaling group itself.

16. A, F. Amazon CloudWatch has two plans: basic, which is free, and detailed, which has an additional cost. There is no ad hoc plan for Amazon CloudWatch.

17. A, C, D. An Elastic Load Balancing health check may be a ping, a connection attempt, or a page that is checked.

18. B, C. When connection draining is enabled, the load balancer will stop sending requests to a deregistered or unhealthy instance and attempt to complete in-flight requests until a connection draining timeout period is reached, which is 300 seconds by default.

19. B, E, F. Elastic Load Balancing supports Internet-facing, internal, and HTTPS load balancers.

20. B, D, E. Auto Scaling supports maintaining the current size of an Auto Scaling group using four plans: maintain current levels, manual scaling, scheduled scaling, and dynamic scaling.

Chapter 6: AWS Identity and Access Management (IAM)

1. B, C. Programmatic access is authenticated with an access key, not with user names/passwords. IAM roles provide a temporary security token to an application using an SDK.

2. A, C. IAM policies are independent of region, so no region is specified in the policy. IAM policies are about authorization for an already-authenticated principal, so no password is needed.

3. A, B, C, E. Locking down your root user and all accounts to which the administrator had access is the key here. Deleting all IAM accounts is not necessary, and it would cause great disruption to your operations. Amazon EC2 roles use temporary security tokens, so relaunching Amazon EC2 instances is not necessary.

4. B, D. IAM controls access to AWS resources only. Installing ASP.NET will require Windows operating system authorization, and querying an Oracle database will require Oracle authorization.

5. A, C. Amazon DynamoDB global secondary indexes are a performance feature of Amazon DynamoDB; Consolidated Billing is an accounting feature allowing all bills to roll up under a single account. While both are very valuable features, neither is a security feature.

6. B, C. Amazon EC2 roles must still be assigned a policy. Integration with Active Directory involves integration between Active Directory and IAM via SAML.

7. A, D. Amazon EC2 roles provide a temporary token to applications running on the instance; federation maps policies to identities from other sources via temporary tokens.

8. A, C, D. Neither B nor E are features supported by IAM.

9. B, C. Access requires an appropriate policy associated with a principal. Response A is merely a policy with no principal, and response D is not a principal as IAM groups do not have user names and passwords. Response B is the best solution; response C will also work but it is much harder to manage.

10. C. An IAM policy is a JSON document.

Chapter 7: Databases and AWS

1. B. Amazon RDS is best suited for traditional OLTP transactions. Amazon Redshift, on the other hand, is designed for OLAP workloads. Amazon Glacier is designed for cold archival storage.

2. D. Amazon DynamoDB is best suited for non-relational databases. Amazon RDS and Amazon Redshift are both structured relational databases.

3. C. In this scenario, the best idea is to use read replicas to scale out the database and thus maximize read performance. When using Multi-AZ, the secondary database is not accessible and all reads and writes must go to the primary or any read replicas.

4. A. Amazon Redshift is best suited for traditional OLAP transactions. While Amazon RDS can also be used for OLAP, Amazon Redshift is purpose-built as an OLAP data warehouse.

5. B. DB Snapshots can be used to restore a complete copy of the database at a specific point in time. Individual tables cannot be extracted from a snapshot.

6. A. All Amazon RDS database engines support Multi-AZ deployment.

7. B. Read replicas are supported by MySQL, MariaDB, PostgreSQL, and Aurora.

8. A. You can force a failover from one Availability Zone to another by rebooting the primary instance in the AWS Management Console. This is often how people test a failover in the real world. There is no need to create a support case.

9. D. Monitor the environment while Amazon RDS attempts to recover automatically. AWS will update the DB endpoint to point to the secondary instance automatically.

10. A. Amazon RDS supports Microsoft SQL Server Enterprise edition and the license is available only under the BYOL model.

11. B. General Purpose (SSD) volumes are generally the right choice for databases that have bursts of activity.

12. B. NoSQL databases like Amazon DynamoDB excel at scaling to hundreds of thousands of requests with key/value access to user profile and session.

13. A, C, D. DB snapshots allow you to back up and recover your data, while read replicas and a Multi-AZ deployment allow you to replicate your data and reduce the time to failover.

14. C, D. Amazon RDS allows for the creation of one or more read-replicas for many engines that can be used to handle reads. Another common pattern is to create a cache using Memcached and Amazon ElastiCache to store frequently used queries. The secondary slave DB Instance is not accessible and cannot be used to offload queries.

15. A, B, C. Protecting your database requires a multilayered approach that secures the infrastructure, the network, and the database itself. Amazon RDS is a managed service and direct access to the OS is not available.

16. A, B, C. Vertically scaling up is one of the simpler options that can give you additional processing power without making any architectural changes. Read replicas require some application changes but let you scale processing power horizontally. Finally, busy databases are often I/O- bound, so upgrading storage to General Purpose (SSD) or Provisioned IOPS (SSD) can often allow for additional request processing.

17. C. Query is the most efficient operation to find a single item in a large table.

18. A. Using the Username as a partition key will evenly spread your users across the partitions. Messages are often filtered down by time range, so Timestamp makes sense as a sort key.

19. B, D. You can only have a single local secondary index, and it must be created at the same time the table is created. You can create many global secondary indexes after the table has been created.

20. B, C. Amazon Redshift is an Online Analytical Processing (OLAP) data warehouse designed for analytics, Extract, Transform, Load (ETL), and high-speed querying. It is not well suited for running transactional applications that require high volumes of small inserts or updates.

Chapter 8: SQS, SWF, and SNS

1. D. Amazon DynamoDB is not a supported Amazon SNS protocol.

2. A. When you create a new Amazon SNS topic, an Amazon ARN is created automatically.

3. A, C, D. Publishers, subscribers, and topics are the correct answers. You have subscribers to an Amazon SNS topic, not readers.

4. A. The default time for an Amazon SQS visibility timeout is 30 seconds.

5. D. The maximum time for an Amazon SQS visibility timeout is 12 hours.

6. B, D. The valid properties of an SQS message are Message ID and Body. Each message receives a system-assigned Message ID that Amazon SQS returns to you in the SendMessage response. The Message Body is composed of name/value pairs and the unstructured, uninterpreted content.

7. B. Use a single domain with multiple workflows. Workflows within separate domains cannot interact.

8. A, B, C. In Amazon SWF, actors can be activity workers, workflow starters, or deciders.

9. B. Amazon SWF would best serve your purpose in this scenario because it helps developers build, run, and scale background jobs that have parallel or sequential steps. You can think of Amazon SWF as a fully-managed state tracker and task coordinator in the Cloud.

10. D. Amazon SQS does not guarantee in what order your messages will be delivered.

11. A. Multiple queues can subscribe to an Amazon SNS topic, which can enable parallel asynchronous processing.

12. D. Long polling allows your application to poll the queue, and, if nothing is there, Amazon Elastic Compute Cloud (Amazon EC2) waits for an amount of time you specify (between 1 and 20 seconds). If a message arrives in that time, it is delivered to your application as soon as possible. If a message does not arrive in that time, you need to execute the ReceiveMessage function again.

13. B. The maximum time for an Amazon SQS long polling timeout is 20 seconds.

14. D. The longest configurable message retention period for Amazon SQS is 14 days.

15. B. The default message retention period that can be set in Amazon SQS is four days.

16. D. With Amazon SNS, you send individual or multiple messages to large numbers of recipients using publisher and subscriber client types.

17. B. The decider schedules the activity tasks and provides input data to the activity workers. The decider also processes events that arrive while the workflow is in progress and closes the workflow when the objective has been completed.

18. C. Topic names should typically be available for reuse approximately 30–60 seconds after the previous topic with the same name has been deleted. The exact time will depend on the number of subscriptions active on the topic; topics with a few subscribers will be available instantly for reuse, while topics with larger subscriber lists may take longer.

19. C. The main difference between Amazon SQS policies and IAM policies is that an Amazon SQS policy enables you to grant a different AWS account permission to your Amazon SQS queues, but an IAM policy does not.

20. C. No. After a message has been successfully published to a topic, it cannot be recalled.

Chapter 9: Domain Name System (DNS) and Amazon Route 53

1. C. An AAAA record is used to route traffic to an IPv6 address, whereas an A record is used to route traffic to an IPv4 address.

2. B. Domain names are registered with a domain registrar, which then registers the name to InterNIC.

3. C. You should route your traffic based on where your end users are located. The best routing policy to achieve this is geolocation routing.

4. D. A PTR record is used to resolve an IP address to a domain name, and it is commonly referred to as "reverse DNS."

5. B. You want your users to have the fastest network access possible. To do this, you would use latency-based routing. Geolocation routing would not achieve this as well as latency-based routing, which is specifically geared toward measuring the latency and thus would direct you to the AWS region in which you would have the lowest latency.

6. C. You would use Mail eXchange (MX) records to define which inbound destination mail server should be used.

7. B. SPF records are used to verify authorized senders of mail from your domain.

8.　B.　Weighted routing would best achieve this objective because it allows you to specify which percentage of traffic is directed to each endpoint.

9.　D.　The start of a zone is defined by the SOA; therefore, all zones must have an SOA record by default.

10.　D.　Failover-based routing would best achieve this objective.

11.　B.　The CNAME record maps a name to another name. It should be used only when there are no other records on that name.

12.　C.　Amazon Route 53 performs three main functions: domain registration, DNS service, and health checking.

13.　A.　A TXT record is used to store arbitrary and unformatted text with a host.

14.　C.　The resource record sets contained in a hosted zone must share the same suffix.

15.　B.　DNS uses port number 53 to serve requests.

16.　D.　DNS primarily uses UDP to serve requests.

17.　A.　The TCP protocol is used by DNS server when the response data size exceeds 512 bytes or for tasks such as zone transfers.

18.　B.　Using Amazon Route 53, you can create two types of hosted zones: public hosted zones and private hosted zones.

19.　D.　Amazon Route 53 can route queries to a variety of AWS resources such as an Amazon CloudFront distribution, an Elastic Load Balancing load balancer, an Amazon EC2 instance, a website hosted in an Amazon S3 bucket, and an Amazon Relational Database (Amazon RDS).

20.　D.　You must first transfer the existing domain registration from another registrar to Amazon Route 53 to configure it as your DNS service.

Chapter 10: Amazon ElastiCache

1.　A, B, C.　Many types of objects are good candidates to cache because they have the potential to be accessed by numerous users repeatedly. Even the balance of a bank account could be cached for short periods of time if the back-end database query is slow to respond.

2.　B, C.　Amazon ElastiCache supports Memcached and Redis cache engines. MySQL is not a cache engine, and Couchbase is not supported.

3.　C.　The default limit is 20 nodes per cluster.

4.　A.　Redis clusters can only contain a single node; however, you can group multiple clusters together into a replication group.

5.   B, C. Amazon ElastiCache is Application Programming Interface (API)-compatible with existing Memcached clients and does not require the application to be recompiled or linked against the libraries. Amazon ElastiCache manages the deployment of the Amazon Elasti-Cache binaries.

6.   B, C. Amazon ElastiCache with the Redis engine allows for both manual and automatic snapshots. Memcached does not have a backup function.

7.   B, C, D. Limit access at the network level using security groups or network ACLs, and limit infrastructure changes using IAM.

8.   C. Amazon ElastiCache with Redis provides native functions that simplify the development of leaderboards. With Memcached, it is more difficult to sort and rank large datasets. Amazon Redshift and Amazon S3 are not designed for high volumes of small reads and writes, typical of a mobile game.

9.   A. When the clients are configured to use AutoDiscovery, they can discover new cache nodes as they are added or removed. AutoDiscovery must be configured on each client and is not active server side. Updating the configuration file each time will be very difficult to manage. Using an Elastic Load Balancer is not recommended for this scenario.

10. A, B. Amazon ElastiCache supports both Memcached and Redis. You can run self-managed installations of Membase and Couchbase using Amazon Elastic Compute Cloud (Amazon EC2).

Chapter 11: Additional Key Services

1.   B, C, E. Amazon CloudFront can use an Amazon S3 bucket or any HTTP server, whether or not it is running in Amazon EC2. A Route 53 Hosted Zone is a set of DNS resource records, while an Auto Scaling Group launches or terminates Amazon EC2 instances automatically. Neither can be specified as an origin server for a distribution.

2.   A, C. The site in A is "popular" and supports "users around the world," key indicators that CloudFront is appropriate. Similarly, the site in C is "heavily used," and requires private content, which is supported by Amazon CloudFront. Both B and D are corporate use cases where the requests come from a single geographic location or appear to come from one (because of the VPN). These use cases will generally not see benefit from Amazon CloudFront.

3.   C, E. Using multiple origins and setting multiple cache behaviors allow you to serve static and dynamic content from the same distribution. Origin Access Identifiers and signed URLs support serving private content from Amazon CloudFront, while multiple edge locations are simply how Amazon CloudFront serves any content.

4.   B. Amazon CloudFront OAI is a special identity that can be used to restrict access to an Amazon S3 bucket only to an Amazon CloudFront distribution. Signed URLs, signed cookies, and IAM bucket policies can help to protect content served through Amazon CloudFront, but OAIs are the simplest way to ensure that only Amazon CloudFront has access to a bucket.

5. C. AWS Storage Gateway allows you to access data in Amazon S3 locally, with the Gateway-Cached volume configuration allowing you to expand a relatively small amount of local storage into Amazon S3.

6. B. Simple AD is a Microsoft Active Directory-compatible directory that is powered by Samba 4. Simple AD supports commonly used Active Directory features such as user accounts, group memberships, domain-joining Amazon Elastic Compute Cloud (Amazon EC2) instances running Linux and Microsoft Windows, Kerberos-based Single Sign-On (SSO), and group policies.

7. C. AWS KMS CMKs are the fundamental resources that AWS KMS manages. CMKs can never leave AWS KMS unencrypted, but data keys can.

8. D. AWS KMS uses envelope encryption to protect data. AWS KMS creates a data key, encrypts it under a Customer Master Key (CMK), and returns plaintext and encrypted versions of the data key to you. You use the plaintext key to encrypt data and store the encrypted key alongside the encrypted data. You can retrieve a plaintext data key only if you have the encrypted data key and you have permission to use the corresponding master key.

9. A. AWS CloudTrail records important information about each API call, including the name of the API, the identity of the caller, the time of the API call, the request parameters, and the response elements returned by the AWS Cloud service.

10. B, C. Encryption context is a set of key/value pairs that you can pass to AWS KMS when you call the Encrypt, Decrypt, ReEncrypt, GenerateDataKey, and GenerateDataKey-WithoutPlaintext APIs. Although the encryption context is not included in the ciphertext, it is cryptographically bound to the ciphertext during encryption and must be passed again when you call the Decrypt (or ReEncrypt) API. Invalid ciphertext for decryption is plaintext that has been encrypted in a different AWS account or ciphertext that has been altered since it was originally encrypted.

11. B. Because the Internet connection is full, the best solution will be based on using AWS Import/Export to ship the data. The most appropriate storage location for data that must be stored, but is very rarely accessed, is Amazon Glacier.

12. C. Because the job is run monthly, a persistent cluster will incur unnecessary compute costs during the rest of the month. Amazon Kinesis is not appropriate because the company is running analytics as a batch job and not on a stream. A single large instance does not scale out to accommodate the large compute needs.

13. D. The Amazon Kinesis services enable you to work with large data streams. Within the Amazon Kinesis family of services, Amazon Kinesis Firehose saves streams to AWS storage services, while Amazon Kinesis Streams provide the ability to process the data in the stream.

14. C. Amazon Data Pipeline allows you to run regular Extract, Transform, Load (ETL) jobs on Amazon and on-premises data sources. The best storage for large data is Amazon S3, and Amazon Redshift is a large-scale data warehouse service.

15. B. Amazon Kinesis Firehose allows you to ingest massive streams of data and store the data on Amazon S3 (as well as Amazon Redshift and Amazon Elasticsearch).

16. C. AWS OpsWorks uses Chef recipes to start new app server instances, configure application server software, and deploy applications. Organizations can leverage Chef recipes to automate operations like software configurations, package installations, database setups, server scaling, and code deployment.

17. A. With AWS CloudFormation, you can reuse your template to set up your resources consistently and repeatedly. Just describe your resources once and then provision the same resources over and over in multiple stacks.

18. B. AWS Trusted Advisor inspects your AWS environment and makes recommendations when opportunities exist to save money, improve system availability and performance, or help close security gaps. AWS Trusted Advisor draws upon best practices learned from the aggregated operational history of serving hundreds of thousands of AWS customers.

19. A. AWS Config is a fully managed service that provides you with an AWS resource inventory, configuration history, and configuration change notifications to enable security and governance. With AWS Config, you can discover existing and deleted AWS resources, determine your overall compliance against rules, and dive into configuration details of a resource at any point in time. These capabilities enable compliance auditing.

20. D. AWS Elastic Beanstalk is the fastest and simplest way to get an application up and running on AWS. Developers can simply upload their application code, and the service automatically handles all the details such as resource provisioning, load balancing, Auto Scaling, and monitoring.

Chapter 12: Security on AWS

1. B. All decommissioned magnetic storage devices are degaussed and physically destroyed in accordance with industry-standard practices.

2. C. The administrator password is encrypted with the public key of the key pair, and you provide the private key to decrypt the password. Then log in to the instance as the administrator with the decrypted password.

3. C. By default, network access is turned off to a DB Instance. You can specify rules in a security group that allows access from an IP address range, port, or Amazon Elastic Compute Cloud (Amazon EC2) security group.

4. A. Amazon S3 SSE uses one of the strongest block ciphers available, 256-bit AES.

5. C. IAM permits users to have no more than two active access keys at one time.

6. B. The shared responsibility model is the name of the model employed by AWS with its customers.

7. D. When you choose AWS KMS for key management with Amazon Redshift, there is a four-tier hierarchy of encryption keys. These keys are the master key, a cluster key, a database key, and data encryption keys.

8. D. Elastic Load Balancing supports the Server Order Preference option for negotiating connections between a client and a load balancer. During the SSL connection negotiation process, the client and the load balancer present a list of ciphers and protocols that they each support, in order of preference. By default, the first cipher on the client's list that matches any one of the load balancer's ciphers is selected for the SSL connection. If the load balancer is configured to support Server Order Preference, then the load balancer selects the first cipher in its list that is in the client's list of ciphers. This ensures that the load balancer determines which cipher is used for SSL connection. If you do not enable Server Order Preference, the order of ciphers presented by the client is used to negotiate connections between the client and the load balancer.

9. C. Amazon WorkSpaces uses PCoIP, which provides an interactive video stream without transmitting actual data.

10. C. Distributing applications across multiple Availability Zones provides the ability to remain resilient in the face of most failure modes, including natural disasters or system failures.

11. A. A virtual MFA device uses a software application that generates six-digit authentication codes that are compatible with the TOTP standard, as described in RFC 6238.

12. B, D. Amazon DynamoDB does not have a server-side feature to encrypt items within a table. You need to use a solution outside of DynamoDB such as a client-side library to encrypt items before storing them, or a key management service like AWS Key Management Service to manage keys that are used to encrypt items before storing them in DynamoDB.

13. B. If your private key can be read or written to by anyone but you, then SSH ignores your key.

14. D. Amazon Cognito Identity supports public identity providers—Amazon, Facebook, and Google—as well as unauthenticated identities.

15. A. An instance profile is a container for an IAM role that you can use to pass role information to an Amazon EC2 instance when the instance starts.

16. B. A network ACL is an optional layer of security for your Amazon VPC that acts as a firewall for controlling traffic in and out of one or more subnets. You might set up network ACLs with rules similar to your security groups in order to add an additional layer of security to your Amazon VPC.

17. D. The Signature Version 4 signing process describes how to add authentication information to AWS requests. For security, most requests to AWS must be signed with an access key (Access Key ID [AKI] and Secret Access Key [SAK]). If you use the AWS Command Line Interface (AWS CLI) or one of the AWS Software Development Kits (SDKs), those tools automatically sign requests for you based on credentials that you specify when you configure the tools. However, if you make direct HTTP or HTTPS calls to AWS, you must sign the requests yourself.

18. B. Dedicated instances are physically isolated at the host hardware level from your instances that aren't dedicated instances and from instances that belong to other AWS accounts.

19. C. Amazon EMR starts your instances in two Amazon Elastic Compute Cloud (Amazon EC2) security groups, one for the master and another for the slaves. The master security group has a port open for communication with the service. It also has the SSH port open to allow you to securely connect to the instances via SSH using the key specified at startup. The slaves start in a separate security group, which only allows interaction with the master instance. By default, both security groups are set up to prevent access from external sources, including Amazon EC2 instances belonging to other customers. Because these are security groups in your account, you can reconfigure them using the standard Amazon EC2 tools or dashboard.

20. A. When you create an Amazon EBS volume in an Availability Zone, it is automatically replicated within that Availability Zone to prevent data loss due to failure of any single hardware component. An EBS Snapshot creates a copy of an EBS volume to Amazon S3 so that copies of the volume can reside in different Availability Zones within a region.

Chapter 13: AWS Risk and Compliance

1. A, B, C. Answers A through C describe valid mechanisms that AWS uses to communicate with customers regarding its security and control environment. AWS does not allow customers' auditors direct access to AWS data centers, infrastructure, or staff.

2. C. The shared responsibility model can include IT controls, and it is not just limited to security considerations. Therefore, answer C is correct.

3. A. AWS provides IT control information to customers through either specific control definitions or general control standard compliance.

4. A, B, D. There is no such thing as a SOC 4 report, therefore answer C is incorrect.

5. A. IT governance is still the customer's responsibility.

6. D. Any number of components of a workload can be moved into AWS, but it is the customer's responsibility to ensure that the entire workload remains compliant with various certifications and third-party attestations.

7. B. An Availability Zone consists of multiple discrete data centers, each with their own redundant power and networking/connectivity, therefore answer B is correct.

8. A, C. AWS regularly scans public-facing, non-customer endpoint IP addresses and notifies appropriate parties. AWS does not scan customer instances, and customers must request the ability to perform their own scans in advance, therefore answers A and C are correct.

9. B. AWS publishes information publicly online and directly to customers under NDA, but customers are not required to share their use and configuration information with AWS, therefore answer B is correct.

10. C. AWS has developed a strategic business plan, and customers should also develop and maintain their own risk management plans, therefore answer C is correct.

11. B. The collective control environment includes people, processes, and technology necessary to establish and maintain an environment that supports the operating effectiveness of AWS control framework. Energy is not a discretely identified part of the control environment, therefore B is the correct answer.

12. D. Customers are responsible for ensuring all of their security group configurations are appropriate for their own applications, therefore answer D is correct.

13. C. Customers should ensure that they implement control objectives that are designed to meet their organization's own unique compliance requirements, therefore answer C is correct.

Chapter 14: Architecture Best Practices

1. B, E. Amazon Kinesis is a platform for streaming data on AWS, offering powerful services to make it easy to load and analyze streaming data. Amazon SQS is a fast, reliable, scalable, and fully managed message queuing service. Amazon SQS makes it simple and cost-effective to decouple the components of a cloud application.

2. B, C. Launching instances across multiple Availability Zones helps ensure the application is isolated from failures in a single Availability Zone, allowing the application to achieve higher availability. Whether you are running one Amazon EC2 instance or thousands, you can use Auto Scaling to detect impaired Amazon EC2 instances and unhealthy applications and replace the instances without your intervention. This ensures that your application is getting the compute capacity that you expect, thereby maintaining your availability.

3. A, E. Amazon DynamoDB runs across AWS proven, high-availability data centers. The service replicates data across three facilities in an AWS region to provide fault tolerance in the event of a server failure or Availability Zone outage. Amazon S3 provides durable infrastructure to store important data and is designed for durability of 99.999999999% of objects. Your data is redundantly stored across multiple facilities and multiple devices in each facility. While Elastic Load Balancing and Amazon ElastiCache can be deployed across multiple Availability Zones, you must explicitly take such steps when creating them.

4. A, D. Auto Scaling enables you to follow the demand curve for your applications closely, reducing the need to provision Amazon EC2 capacity manually in advance. For example, you can set a condition to add new Amazon EC2 instances in increments to the Auto Scaling group when the average CPU and network utilization of your Amazon EC2 fleet monitored in Amazon CloudWatch is high; similarly, you can set a condition to remove instances in the same increments when CPU and network utilization are low.

5. B, D, E. There is no direct way to encrypt an existing unencrypted volume. However, you can migrate data between encrypted and unencrypted volumes.

6. A, C, D. The attack surface is composed of the different Internet entry points that allow access to your application. The strategy to minimize the attack surface area is to (a) reduce the number of necessary Internet entry points, (b) eliminate non-critical Internet entry points, (c) separate end user traffic from management traffic, (d) obfuscate necessary Internet entry points to the level that untrusted end users cannot access them, and (e) decouple Internet entry points to minimize the effects of attacks. This strategy can be accomplished with Amazon VPC.

7. C. Amazon RDS read replicas provide enhanced performance and durability for Amazon RDS instances. This replication feature makes it easy to scale out elastically beyond the capacity constraints of a single Amazon RDS instance for read-heavy database workloads. You can create one or more replicas of a given source Amazon RDS instance and serve high-volume application read traffic from multiple copies of your data, thereby increasing aggregate read throughput.

8. A. An alias resource record set can point to an ELB. You cannot create a CNAME record at the top node of a Domain Name Service (DNS) namespace, also known as the zone apex, as the case in this example. Alias resource record sets can save you time because Amazon Route 53 automatically recognizes changes in the resource record sets to which the alias resource record set refers.

9. D. An instance profile is a container for an AWS Identity and Access Management (IAM) role that you can use to pass role information to an Amazon EC2 instance when the instance starts. The IAM role should have a policy attached that only allows access to the AWS Cloud services necessary to perform its function.

10. B. Amazon API Gateway is a fully managed service that makes it easy for developers to publish, maintain, monitor, and secure APIs at any scale. You can create an API that acts as a "front door" for applications to access data, business logic, or functionality from your code running on AWS Lambda. Amazon API Gateway handles all of the tasks involved in accepting and processing up to hundreds of thousands of concurrent API calls, including traffic management, authorization and access control, monitoring, and API version management.

11. C. Amazon EFS is a file storage service for Amazon EC2 instances. Multiple Amazon EC2 instances can access an Amazon EFS file system at the same time, providing a common data source for the content of the WordPress site running on more than one instance.

12. A. Amazon DynamoDB is a NoSQL database store that is a great choice as an alternative due to its scalability, high-availability, and durability characteristics. Many platforms provide open-source, drop-in replacement libraries that allow you to store native sessions in Amazon DynamoDB. Amazon DynamoDB is a great candidate for a session storage solution in a share-nothing, distributed architecture.

13. B. Amazon SQS is a fast, reliable, scalable, and fully managed message queuing service. Amazon SQS should be used to decouple the large volume of inbound transactions, allowing the back-end services to manage the level of throughput without losing messages.

14. B, C, E. You should protect AWS user access keys like you would your credit card numbers or any other sensitive secret. Use different access keys for different applications so that you can isolate the permissions and revoke the access keys for individual applications if an access key is exposed. Remember to change access keys on a regular basis. For increased security, it is recommended to configure MFA for any sensitive operations. Remember to remove any IAM users that are no longer needed so that the user's access to your resources is removed. Always avoid having to embed access keys in an application.

15. A, B, E. You can enable AWS CloudTrail in your AWS account to get logs of API calls and related events' history in your account. AWS CloudTrail records all of the API access events as objects in an Amazon S3 bucket that you specify at the time you enable AWS CloudTrail. You can take advantage of Amazon S3's bucket notification feature by directing Amazon S3 to publish object-created events to AWS Lambda. Whenever AWS CloudTrail writes logs to your Amazon S3 bucket, Amazon S3 can then invoke your AWS Lambda function by passing the Amazon S3 object-created event as a parameter. The AWS Lambda function code can read the log object and process the access records logged by AWS CloudTrail.

16. B. Amazon Glacier enables businesses and organizations to retain data for months, years, or decades, easily and cost effectively. With Amazon Glacier, customers can retain more of their data for future analysis or reference, and they can focus on their business instead of operating and maintaining their storage infrastructure. Customers can also use Amazon Glacier Vault Lock to meet regulatory and compliance archiving requirements.

17. A. Many companies that distribute content via the Internet want to restrict access to documents, business data, media streams, or content that is intended for selected users, such as users who have paid a fee. To serve this private content securely using Amazon CloudFront, you can require that users access your private content by using special Amazon CloudFront-signed URLs or signed cookies.

18. B. Amazon S3 provides highly durable and available storage for a variety of content. Amazon S3 can be used as a big data object store for all of the videos. Amazon S3's low cost combined with its design for durability of 99.999999999% and for up to 99.99% availability make it a great storage choice for transcoding services.

19. A. An Availability Zone consists of one or more physical data centers. Availability zones within a region provide inexpensive, low-latency network connectivity to other zones in the same region. This allows you to distribute your application across data centers. In the event of a catastrophic failure in a data center, the application will continue to handle requests.

20. C. You can use a NAT gateway to enable instances in a private subnet to connect to the Internet or other AWS services, but prevent the Internet from initiating a connection with those instances. If you have resources in multiple Availability Zones and they share one NAT gateway, resources in the other Availability Zones lose Internet access in the event that the NAT gateway's Availability Zone is down. To create an Availability Zone-independent architecture, create a NAT gateway in each Availability Zone and configure your routing to ensure that resources use the NAT gateway in the same Availability Zone.

Index

Index

T

Comprehensive Online Learning Environment

Register on Sybex.com to gain access to the comprehensive online interactive learning environment and test bank to help you study for your AWS Certified Solutions Architect - Associate exam.

The online test bank includes:

- **Assessment Test** to help you focus your study to specific objectives
- **Chapter Tests** to reinforce what you've learned
- **Practice Exams** to test your knowledge of the material
- **Digital Flashcards** to reinforce your learning and provide last-minute test prep before the exam
- **Searchable Glossary** to define the key terms you'll need to know for the exam

Go to http://www.wiley.com/go/sybextestprep **to register and gain access to this comprehensive study tool package.**